D1130940

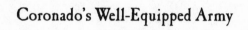

Coronado's Well-Equipped Army

# CORONADO'S
# Well-Equipped
# Army

## THE
## SPANISH
## INVASION
## OF THE
## AMERICAN
## SOUTHWEST

# John M. Hutchins

WESTHOLME
Yardley

Frontis: An early twentieth-century illustration of Coronado's forces attacking the Zuni "Cibola" Pueblo of Hawikuh on July 7, 1540. Note the Pueblo dwellers pumelling the Spanish with stones and what may be an injured Coronado in the shadow of the walls being pulled to safety by two of his men. See Chapter 11. (*Author*)

Westholme Publishing, LLC
904 Edgewood Road
Yardley, Pennsylvania 19067
Visit our Web site at www.westholmepublishing.com

First Printing November 2014
10 9 8 7 6 5 4 3 2 1
ISBN: 978-1-59416-208-4
Also available as an eBook.

Printed in the United States of America

# CONTENTS

# Introduction

*A Fresh Look at Coronado's Expedition*

In recent years, there has been a renewed interest in the conquest by Spain of the New World. Undoubtedly, new studies were called for, since North American scholars in the first half of the twentieth century— partly to implement a "good neighbor policy" by improving relations with Central and South America—emphasized the heroic blood-and-thunder aspects of Spain (as well as the more subtle sacrifices of Roman Catholic martyrs).[1]

This past and traditional historical literature therefore often emphasized the conquistadors as great—although flawed—men who overcame immense challenges to tame a wilderness and to subjugate indigenous peoples. The 1540–1542 expedition of Francisco Vasquez de Coronado certainly has been subjected to this boosterism. Also carefully studied were the clerics and priests of this age of religious contention, and how the New World was brought into the Christian era and within the folds of Western civilization.

Specifically relating to the United States, a nation whose basic institutions are anything but Spanish, there nonetheless was much interest in exposing the non-northern European roots of much early discovery and settlement. This was seen as educating Americans to take pride in their local regions and resulted in pageants and festivals glorifying such tainted worthies as Ponce de Leon, Hernando De Soto, and Francisco Vasquez de Coronado.[2]

This conscious program and overall positive perspective has changed. The new scholarship definitely has not been a focused effort to improve international relations or to build national pride in the United States (as contrasted with ethnic pride within the United States). The new emphasis, using many more primary materials in foreign archives, has focused on previously neglected aspects of the one-hundred-year period (circa 1500–1600) that transformed North, Central, and South America, shook Europe to its foundations, and certainly affected the rest of the world.

These newer studies, taking the little pictures and blowing them up to big pictures, often have emphasized the now-forgotten people of the sixteenth century: the natives, the women, the Africans, the servants, the slaves, and even the bankers, the entrepreneurs, and the lawyers. Much good work in new research and scholarship has occurred, but much needless (and inaccurate) denigration of traditional viewpoints has been a by-product.

Especially with the new histories about the importance of local, indigenous, and ordinary people in epochal events—which seemingly must rebut the proofs of the primacy of great men (and more-occasional great women) and the obvious impact of Western civilization—there is a disinclination to accept anything smacking of "Eurocentricity." For example, in a recent chapter about the Indian allies of the Spanish, the authors ask one of the right questions about sixteenth-century warfare in the Americas: "What was customary in Europe at the time?" The question is then dismissed, pretty much out of hand, as being generally irrelevant in the New World.[3]

The customs and the institutions of Europe obviously did matter much in the subjugation of the Western Hemisphere. Nonmute evidence of this proposition is provided by those in the Americas who speak Spanish (as well as Portuguese, English, and French). Further evidence is provided by counting the residents of the Western Hemisphere who have long-dead ancestors and who still are Roman Catholic (or Anglican/Episcopal or British Calvinist or Dutch Reformed).

However, this emphasis on the European impact should not be equated with an unthinking paean to everything the foreign intruders introduced or accomplished. Like those revisionists who have emphasized the native viewpoint over the pro-Spanish perspective of Herbert Eugene Bolton, this effort certainly is not of the Boltonian school.[4] Herein, as will become evident, the Spaniards (and other Europeans) under Coronado will be praised for their positive conduct or attributes and will be equally and appropriately damned (historically) for any evil or incompetence, particularly those actions or characteristics directly affecting true military success.

In any event, one problem with discussing these historical events of times long gone by is the relative paucity of sources, even given the renaissance within the ranks of those current scholars who continue to dig and translate much newly discovered material. However, much of this newly discovered information, even if physically collected and collated, is scattered and fragmentary in topic and scope. This situation is one which, instead of being used to flesh out the previously accepted general or more complete narratives, more often encourages side-trip extrapolations to make those small pictures into the big pictures.

But the continued discovery, translation, and publication of these documents, from estate settlements and court cases to receipts and bills of lading, still have not changed the fact that many of the most important documents (such as official reports of expeditions) have not survived.[5] This relative scarcity of lengthy and complete primary sources certainly is so with the Coronado Expedition, a situation in which the official chronicler's product (if it ever was written) has been lost. However, rather than being distraught about how few seminal sources there are, one should be grateful that there is so much, especially the wonderful narrative of Coronado Expedition member Pedro de Castaneda.

Nonetheless, all of the contemporary or near-contemporary sources, including Castaneda, are riddled with contradictions and omissions. As for much of the recent material translated by such indefatigable researchers as Dr. Richard Flint and Dr. Shirley Cushing Flint,[6] many of these documents are fragments of often self-serving quasi-judicial testimony and must be used advisedly.[7]

Of course, there are ways to add material information even to relevant primary sources. The mining and translating of the old documents in the dusty archives already has been recognized. In addition, significant finds in archaeology finally are rearing their heads regarding the Coronado Expedition, as will be noted in several of the following chapters. But there are other historical sources that can shed accurate light on the more hidden (or ignored) aspects of the endeavor.

As will be demonstrated, the expedition was a military operation. It was a campaign, or, in the parlance of the time, an "enterprise."[8] Knowing this important militant fact about a colonial period, historians of the early twentieth century often employed the theory of institutional history and engrafted known European paradigms into the context of the New World.[9] This exercise, used with discretion, still has validity, especially since, "Sixteenth century [military] theory and practice were more interdependent than might at first be realised."[10] Indeed, placing some emphasis on what ordnance and equipment likely was used—as is done here regarding both sides—certainly is a form of institutional analysis that makes a lot of sense.[11]

But this institutional application can be taken a step further—and it is a step that reins in the tendency to apply unrealistic organizational models to the real world (especially when that real world is the New World of the sixteenth century). Nonacademic historians (meaning those who have either practical experiences or who have educational backgrounds required for non-academic employment), especially in the case of omissions regarding military endeavors, often will resort to what British Lieutenant Colonel A. H. Burne called his "theory of 'inherent military probability'—that is to say, what would a sensible commander of troops do in a given situation?"[12]

While hardly foolproof, such a methodology has much appeal when it comes to filling in gaps regarding warlike undertakings in the distant past. As Burne wrote, when reliable records of battles "are distressingly meagre" and when "one has discounted the exaggerations . . . , the distortions due to misconception, the errors due to lack of maps, and sometimes even deliberate fabrication," then, "To complete the picture many gaps have to be filled in." Burne's methodology, coming from an educated and career combat officer, was necessarily egocentric. "My method here is to start with what appear to be undisputed facts, then to place myself in the shoes of each commander in turn, and to ask myself in each case what I would have done. This I call working on Inherent Military Probability."[13]

The methodology employed in this volume, incorporated by an attorney and retired staff-branch field officer of nonbattle military experience, is not so egocentric. Yet the process should be doubly helpful in filling gaps because the question—rather than "what would I do?"—is further refined to seek how a sensible sixteenth-century commander, with available sixteenth-century knowledge and resources, would react to a given sixteenth-century problem.

Therefore, although there will be occasions when the supplemental information will not be limited to the sixteenth century but will be derived from military principles or experiences seemingly applicable to any age (especially when the facts seem on point), the Burne method of Inherent Military Probability becomes, as applied, Historical Military

Probability—less controlled by the "school solution" of modern military theory and more determined by the then-relevant knowledge, morale, technology, and geographical and communication limitations. Of course, since sixteenth-century military knowledge pretty much included everything since the beginning of organized warfare up to that time, on some occasions the analysis will be akin to stating the obvious.[14] But all too often in the past, the obvious has been overlooked in examining the Coronado Expedition.

For the historian, this placement of the events surrounding this armed incursion into the context of standard Spanish military practice of the era—occasionally supported by a still-all-too-scant archaeological record—will shed additional light on those happenings and can be used (with appropriate caution) to fill in the many factual gaps evident from careful readings of the limited contemporary documents.

Also, this detailed analysis should be particularly useful for students of military science since many of the previous examinations of the expedition have been by persons unfamiliar with military ordnance, military routine, military terminology, and military history. These shortcomings, by otherwise perfectly qualified historians and archaeologists, occasionally have caused misinterpretations.[15]

In addition, the speculation in this study about additional military equipment and personal paraphernalia, items not specifically included in the known narratives, should serve archaeologists. When they plan future digs or schedule "archaeological road shows" (archaeologist-sponsored events inviting the public to bring in previously discovered curiosities), the tentative discussions herein might aid in identifying new metal objects of European origin for which archaeologists should be on the lookout in their searches.

On the other hand, this study will note or merely summarize many details available in previous narrations of the expedition, including much on the internal government of Spain's major dependency in the New World and much relating to the anthropology of the peoples encountered. Many otherwise important personages will be given only cursory acknowledgment in this military examination. This volume also will not overly concern itself with some other very important aspects of the expedition, including coming up with a guaranteed route of the travels of Coronado and his companions. That specific mystery, which has seen more-qualified persons wrestle with it for at least 150 years (and which is being aided by recent-but-very-occasional archaeological finds), generally is not important to the military discussions herein. Additionally, this examination will not tackle many of the specific dates of events—trying to figure when Julian (Old Style) dates are meant and when Gregorian (New Style) dates are implied in original or translated documents. The season of the year often suffices when the questions of military actions arise.[16]

Finally, a word must be said regarding translations. Like architects, scholars seemingly must come up with new designs based on the same foundations. Such imaginative leeway is encouraged because the source documents are often fragmentary and sometimes use technical language that is five hundred years old. Recently one scholar, in discussing an important expedition document, argued that "a series of inaccuracies and misinterpretations continue to obscure the information provided by the manuscript and compromise its historical, anthropological, and linguistic utility."[17] In his viewpoint, these inaccuracies and misinterpretations included both old and recent attempts at translation. Thus, no matter what anybody says, a bit of subjectivity—if not temporal and political bias—always is involved in interpretation of the original Spanish.[18]

As for the present effort, the author, both to avoid intruding too much on single sources and to ensure a wide familiarity with many sources, will use a variety of translations, both old and new. However, Frederick W. Hodge's "The Narrative of the Expedition of Coronado, by Pedro De Castaneda," in *Original Narratives of Early American History: Spanish Explorers in the Southern United States, 1528–1543* (New York: Charles Scribner's Sons, 1907), will be heavily relied upon as a primary translated source. Hodge, as editor, used the early translation of this most important document by George Parker Winship,[19] "Barring a few corrections, most of which were communicated" to Hodge by Winship.[20] Some consider the seminal Winship translation too flowery, perhaps bordering on inaccuracy.[21] Nonetheless, the Hodge edition of Castaneda will be used herein almost exclusively, but differences with more recent translations or editions will be quoted and noted when important to the discussion. Similarly, as to other documents, the author also often will turn first to the translations of George Parker Winship, as well as those of George Hammond, Agapito Rey, and Arthur S. Aiton—associates of the now largely passé Herbert Bolton—before going to more recent attempts. Of course, for many documents, only the amazing Flints have done the monumental job of translation. May that productive couple long continue to collaborate.[22]

With such groundbreaking help, the job of every subsequent historian, even the amateur, remains to explain the past; it is not to critique the present or to influence the future. Hopefully, herein, an honest explanation of an important military endeavor has been produced.[23]

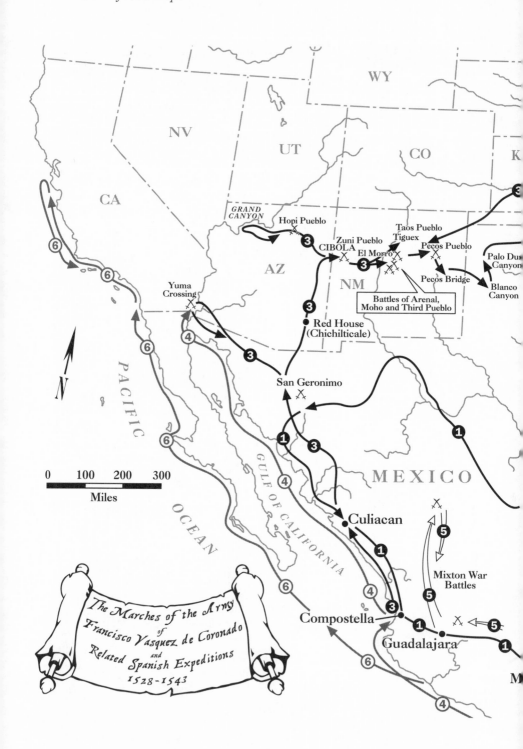

WY

NV

UT

CO

K

CA

GRAND CANYON

Hopi Pueblo

Taos Pueblo
Tiguex

Zuni Pueblo
CIBOLA

El Morro

Pecos Pueblo

Palo Du
Canyon

AZ

NM

Pecos Bridge

Blanco
Canyon

Yuma
Crossing

Red House
(Chichilticale)

Battles of Arenal,
Moho and Third Pueblo

N

San Geronimo

PACIFIC

0   100   200   300
Miles

GULF OF CALIFORNIA

MEXICO

OCEAN

Culiacan

Mixton War
Battles

The Marches of the Army
of
Francisco Vasquez de Coronado
and
Related Spanish Expeditions
1528-1543

Compostella

Guadalajara

M

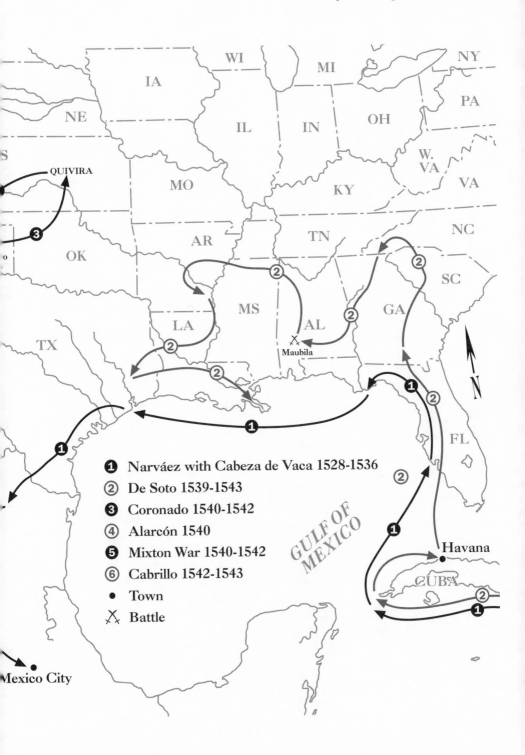

WI
MI
NY
IA
PA
NE
IL
IN
OH
W. VA
VA
QUIVIRA
MO
KY
NC
S
AR
TN
SC
OK
❸
o
MS
GA
LA
AL
TX
Maubila
N
FL

❶ Narváez with Cabeza de Vaca 1528-1536
② De Soto 1539-1543
❸ Coronado 1540-1542
④ Alarcón 1540
❺ Mixton War 1540-1542
⑥ Cabrillo 1542-1543
• Town
✗ Battle

GULF OF MEXICO

Havana

CUBA

Mexico City

# ONE

# The Military Revolution of the Sixteenth Century

I n the closing years of the fifteenth century, Europe went through one of its periodic desires to reach out to the world—a world both vaguely known and totally unknown—and discover what was on the other side of the waters. For its part, Portugal had been inching its way east around the African continent and toward the Indian subcontinent for years. As for that other Iberian nation, Spain, it, not coincidentally, had just celebrated the end of the Moorish Muslim occupation by granting a trading franchise to an obscure Italian mariner named Christopher Columbus (who sailed west). He ended up discovering (in European eyes) a new hemisphere, occupied with a couple of major empires—likewise totally ignorant of the Eastern Hemisphere—and a vast number of small pagan tribes and communities. As the extent of these discoveries became known, the geographers, mapmakers, and entrepreneurs quickly realized that a revolution of knowledge and trading possibilities had occurred.

These discoveries, which entailed lengthy voyages on the open sea, also encouraged revolutions in ship design and seamanship. "The early 16th century was a time of maritime innovation," and for the Spaniards, the wars with the Turks and the need to transport golden and silver loot from the New World brought about the development of the famous Spanish galleon.[1]

In addition, major changes were going on in Europe, many of them also related to the new concerns of the mapmakers. This was a Europe occupied by numerous relatively petty kingdoms and a couple of major political powerhouses like France and the so-called Holy Roman Empire of the Hapsburgs (to be renamed the Holy Roman Empire of the German Nation in 1512), all of which were Christian communities under siege from the East after the bloody Muslim conquest of Constantinople in 1453. Of course, there was that other major secular Christian power—also claiming to be holy—the Roman Catholic Church. All of these European players found the sixteenth century to be revolutionary and unsettling in so many ways.

However, it was the printing press—the invention and implementation of which caused perhaps the greatest revolution of the sixteenth century, that of information—that started a world-changing religious revolution in Europe called the Reformation. This Reformation revolution upset many apple carts from Tudor Britain to the Mediterranean. It caused momentous events that shook the Vatican of numerous pontiffs and the Holy Roman Empire of Maximilian I and his heir, Charles V, and would incite wars within France and throughout northern Europe, as well as other violence elsewhere.

For its part, the Holy Roman Empire, not always on the side of the secular Vatican in Rome but always outwardly supporting its conservative religious pronouncements, got into the Counter-Reformation picture early on. In 1521, Charles V issued the Edict of Worms, in which he declared that Martin Luther was "not a man, but a devil under the form of a man, and clothed in the dress of a priest," bringing "the human race to hell and damnation," and he and his followers were deserving of the announced punishment of "death and forfeiture of all their goods."[2] Several years later, after the capture and sack of Rome and the Vatican by soldiers belonging to Emperor Charles V caused political ramifications that frustrated a divorce for Henry VIII, England in effect joined the rising tide against Roman religious authority.[3]

But Germany's Luther and England's Henry VIII were not the only serious challengers to the Vatican and its claimed monopoly over the souls of men and women. From France arose a French lawyer and theologian, John Calvin. While hardly a true democrat, his deeply held leveling faith was, if anything, even more of a direct threat to the power of Rome and the Holy Roman Empire. Calvin not only went after the pope and his bishops, who held themselves up as representing the

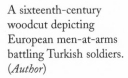

A sixteenth-century woodcut depicting European men-at-arms battling Turkish soldiers. (*Author*)

church "and therefore cannot err," but he counseled waiting for "the strong hand of the Lord, which doubtless will appear in its own good time, and show itself armed, both to rescue the poor from affliction, and also take vengeance on the despisers, who are now exulting so securely."[4] With such a sentiment, expressed in 1536 to the king of France, it was little wonder that Calvin was seen as a supporter of the German revolts that constituted the Peasant Wars.[5] Later in the century, both Elizabeth I's English Protestants and Germany's Lutherans were reluctant to form defensive alliances with Dutch Calvinists against Spain and Rome, since these radical iconoclasts seemed to threaten the hierarchies of both church and state even in Protestant countries.[6]

In addition to these internal divisions and disorders—all of which fueled military development, since Charles V believed military force against the Protestants would ultimately prevail, just as it had against a recalcitrant pro-French pope[7]—Christendom faced those external threats to its existence. The Ottoman Empire of the Turks "haunted the imagination of sixteenth-century Europeans. . . . [B]ut the threat it posed to Europe's eastern and southern frontiers was real."[8] After subjugating Egypt in 1516–1517, the Turks, under Suleiman the Magnificent, redoubled their efforts against Europe, crushing the Hungarians in the Battle of Mohacs in 1526.[9]

By 1529, the Turks were threatening Vienna, later to become the permanent capital of the Holy Roman Empire under the Hapsburgs. Even Martin Luther desired to put aside differences with Rome in order to fight the Turks, not as a holy crusade, but because they were invading Europe in a "war [that] is nothing else than outrage and robbery."[10] Of course, Rome, which had failed to help a Constantinople that was not Roman Catholic, was not willing to concede that Lutheran heretics were qualified to be allies against the infidel Ottomans, especially under a European (rather than papal) banner.[11] But Charles V did force the German Protestant princes to contribute money to the cause, and the Muslim invaders faltered before Vienna and withdrew, only to try again in 1532. While this follow-up effort also failed—the logistical demands on the huge Ottoman armies of invasion being too much—Transylvania was occupied by the invaders in 1540.[12]

Meanwhile, a Turkish threat was also advancing across the waters of the Mediterranean, as the Ottomans consolidated their holdings in North Africa, seized the island of Rhodes, and raided Italy. The army of Charles V was able to counter and delay these advances, however, with an intervention and seizure of Tunis in 1535. This counterstroke largely was funded from the wealth arriving from Francisco Pizarro's conquest of Peru.[13]

If nothing else, this constant military pressure on Charles V and his worldly domain distracted him from seriously trying to stamp out Protestantism within Germany and the Low Countries, at least until 1544.[14] But the Vatican—which had become, since the virtual destruction of its secular fiefdom in 1527, more prone to issuing proclamations than to raising its own armies—could fight such a two-front war on paper more easily than Charles could on the battlefield.

Thus, to face both the perceived internal and real external threats, the Roman Catholics of Europe did not just rely on military rearmament. Church militancy could be legalistic as well. The so-called Holy Inquisition first appeared in Spain in 1478, while the Spanish were in the process of finally expelling their Moorish invaders.[15] As for northern Europe, the Vatican introduced the Inquisition there just after Charles V provided muscle with his Edict of Worms. In 1523, the first victims of such a tribunal were two heretical Augustine monks accused of Lutheranism, burned alive at the stake in Brussels. Erasmus, still loyal to a Rome that considered him less than a model churchman, commented that "two had been burned at Brussels, and . . . the city now began strenuously to favor Lutheranism."[16]

Nonetheless, even with such a hot start, these ecclesiastical tribunals were in their mere dangerous infancy early in the sixteenth century. The Inquisition, especially that of Spain, would only gain in power during the next one hundred years. Certainly, in 1540, the worst of the inglorious days were in the not-too-distant future.

An early seventeenth-century engraving depicting Spanish, Italians, and Germans under Charles V sacking Rome in 1527, while Pope Clement VII attempts to escape. (*Author*)

Although primary motivators, religion and faith were not alone in encouraging or contesting revolutionary leanings during the era. Politics and other worldly thoughts occasioned conflict and violence. "The sixteenth century was an excessively war-prone period in European history," one historian wrote, "with no shortage of young men ready to risk their lives for the expectation of profits from the risky business of war."[17] As demonstrated in 1527 by the capture of Rome by an army of Catholics and Lutherans, Roman Catholic solidarity could not overcome nationalism, ambitious rulers, and greed. And, in 1536, the France of the Most Christian Francis I concluded a treaty with the Muslim Mediterranean pirate Barbarossa that targeted Charles V and the Vatican.[18]

Even before the turmoil of the Reformation, and even discounting regular warfare, life in Europe's Holy Roman Empire in the early six- teenth century was not that secure. With the almost constant threat of peasant uprisings due to heavy-handed treatment, "it is worth repeating the point that a very high level of crime with violence was the normal state of affairs. In its turn, this made swift, arbitrary, royal prerogative justice very desirable to all who had any property to protect. That applied to the serf peasants themselves." [19] Thus, violence—not debate—often was the norm, fitting all occasions.

As for the warfare of the era, behavior of the contestants ranged from chivalric to the barbaric. During the Spanish Reconquista in the closing days of the fifteenth century, when Ferdinand and Isabella reclaimed Spain from the Moors, the Christians sometimes beheaded prisoners, while the Muslims sometime paid bounties on scalps.[20] Later, as demonstrated by the brutal massacres and pillaging resulting from the capture of Rome by that mixed army of Spaniards, Germans, and Italians, putative Christians could be just as cruel to their own kind.

Thus, when it came to military matters, especially in the manner of waging war, the times were not idyllic. This would apply doubly to any conflicts in the New World, for, like flogging, war tended to make good men bad and bad men worse, especially when close religious, political, and administrative oversight (or effective opposition) was lacking.

However, while there obviously was a religious revolution in Europe (epitomized for Catholics by Martin Luther) and the beginnings of a political revolution (largely pushed along by the theology of John Calvin), even more revolutions were being forced onto the stage. Not surprisingly, with all the turmoil, there was a so-called "military revolution" regarding the "art of war" during the sixteenth century.[21] Certainly, the period saw a realignment of military thought and practice throughout Europe:

> Occasionally there was still a good old-fashioned charge with lance and sword, but even then, such a force was expected to fit into the general battle plan and each man to subordinate his impetuosity to the interest of achieving maximum shock as a compact group. War had become more professional, more impersonal: it had become a study, a science, and though drum and fife, armor and horse trappings, pavilions and banners still gave an army a picturesque appearance, and though the highest commands were still allotted to birth rather than experience, and though inefficiency and peculation dogged every step between recruitment and battlefield, the wars of the Renaissance reflect the period's interest in statistics, learning, and method rather than its famed "individualism."[22]

Whether or not it was a true revolution, the military events of the century were part of the revolutionary era. The times were coupled with significant improvements in weaponry—especially with gunpowder firearms[23]—and with vast changes in battlefield tactics. If nothing else, as later caricatured by Cervantes, the age of knighthood and the era of chivalry seemed to be dying on the vine. "By the 16th century, the changes wrought on the battlefield meant that the notion of chivalry of the 13th century . . . had all but disappeared. . . . By the end of the 16th century the knight . . . had become a thing of the past. His social dominance had been subsumed within the gentry of courtiers, functionaries and landowners, his traditional battlefield role had disappeared beneath a forest of pikes and cloud of gun-smoke."[24] But this sea change in military affairs—just as political revolutions do—took most of the years of the applicable century to succeed.

As late as 1494, despite the victories of the pikemen of Switzerland over Hapsburg Austria, "Europe as a whole still regarded the elaborately equipped mounted warrior, the descendant of the mailed knight of the Middle Ages, as the most important instrument of battle."[25] In addition, the potential of gunpowder-powered missiles was not recognized yet as being as effective as the quarrels or bolts of crossbows—and crossbows seemingly had been eclipsed by the English longbow in the signal French defeats in the Hundred Years War.[26]

However, during the course of the sixteenth century, warfare changed as armies adapted to the tactics of the Swiss pikemen and as gunpowder firepower became a more accepted method of killing one's fellow men. For example, following their particularly humiliating defeat at Pavia in 1525, the French began to neglect the training of pikemen and to replace crossbows with arquebuses (or harquebuses)—to such an extent that the French were encumbered with more firearms than they could use.[27]

As part and parcel of these changes, Spain, under the military guidance of one known by his contemporaries as "the Great Captain"— Gonsalvo de Cordova—started its own revolution in the conduct of war even before the fifteenth century was over. Under Cordova, the Spanish infantry gained in importance. Half of the footmen were pikemen, one-sixth had firearms (arquebuses or muskets), and the remaining third carried swords and daggers, in addition to defensive shields (targets or bucklers).[28] Cordova, although a commander representing the new technologies, also had a reputation for being chivalrous in the extreme: full of integrity and generous to vanquished foes.[29] This fact only added to Spain's growing military reputation, although his idealistic conduct eventually would be left in the dust, a victim of Spanish ambition.

In the event, in the wars in Italy, during the first three decades of the sixteenth century, the Spaniards got plenty of wartime experience and learned to deal with Swiss or German pikemen by hacking into the center of their formations with swords and bucklers.[30] In addition, the disciplined Spanish infantry generally showed its battlefield superiority over the French, including the French mounted men. Europe (having previously seen a similar situation with English longbowmen) was forced to sit up and take notice of this shift of power toward the pedestrian, whether pikeman, crossbowman, or arquebusier.[31]

"This does not mean that the footsoldier was ever held in higher esteem than his more specialized fellow-combatants," wrote F. L. Taylor.[32] The haughty horsemen still were considered superior. In addition, the new-fangled firearms were not without their critics. "Would to heaven that this accursed engine had never been invented," recalled Blaise de Monluc, a French veteran of the wars in Italy, about the arquebus. Otherwise, there would not have been "so many valiant men . . . slain for the most part by the most pitiful fellows and the greatest cowards; poltroons that had not dared to look those men in the face at hand, which at distance they laid dead with their confounded bullets."[33] Emphasizing this displeasure, an Italian commander during the late 1400s was known for "plucking out the eyes and cutting off the hands of arquebusiers captured in battle because he deemed it disgraceful that noble men-at-arms should be shot from distance by low-born infantrymen."[34]

As for cavalry, one of those more specialized combatant arms, the growth of the predominance of infantry and the increasing percentage of firearms among the ranks reduced the medieval standing of the mounted man-at-arms, at least relatively.[35] Also, as the English longbowman had discovered, the horses often were more vulnerable than the armor-plated knights; to dismount a rider was to put him, through death or capture, out of action.[36]

However, this did not mean that cavalry, including the heavy men-at-arms, became irrelevant on the battlefield. When they were supported by the infantry and artillery, the men-at-arms remained "the shock troops par excellence and were used on all occasions when the maximum impetus was needed in an assault."[37] Also, armored men-at-arms, being protected by quality armor, sometimes were dismounted and used to lead the way when a breach was being forced in a fortress's walls.[38]

In addition, for the individual men-at-arms of the sixteenth century, the knightly ideal was not quite dead. Young men of the nobility still had dreams of going forth and tilting with enemies to gain military glory. For example, in 1558, Pierre de Bourdeille left France and went off to the last of the fighting in Italy, "bearing," as he said, "a matchlock arquebuse, a fine powder-horn from Milan, and mounted on a hackney worth a hundred crowns, followed by six or seven gentlemen, soldiers themselves, well-set up, armed and mounted the same, but on good stout nags."[39]

Regarding the Spanish cavalry of the early part of the sixteenth century, its reputation was behind that of other European nations, even the Germans. The Spanish men-at-arms had what was considered, at least in Europe, inferior arms and armor. "Their helmets and shields were often of leather; their lances were so light as to be negligible against the French and Italians; their discipline, moreover, . . . was not equal to supplementing the defect of their arms."[40] Even with these perceived shortcomings, the Spanish did not indicate any interest in bolstering their plate-armored cavalry; in 1494, Spain was the first European power to institute light horsemen as a separate force, independent of the heavy men-at-arms. These light horsemen eventually replaced their light lances with arquebuses.[41]

Then there were the heavier guns. The early sixteenth century also saw a veritable revolution in the case of artillery. While siege guns and bombards had existed for some time, field guns mounted on wheeled carriages began to be produced. Although the barrels of some heavy cannon had to be transported separately in wagons, other guns were pulled by horses.[42] By the end of the fifteenth century, gun limbers had been sufficiently developed to be seen drawing artillery to the battlefield or the siege lines.[43] As for the early ammunition for these guns, it included cannonballs either of stone or iron.[44]

However, the artillery of the sixteenth century, although a vast improvement over that seen in the previous century, certainly had limitations. Blaise de Monluc noted of the enemy guns firing on a 1544 battlefield in Italy, "'Tis that which terrifies the most of anything and [that] oftentimes begets more fear than it does harm."[45]

Monluc knew of what he spoke, for the French were considered the leaders when it came to the early sixteenth-century artillery.[46] The Spanish were not known to be particularly gifted in this battlefield arm: during the Reconquista of their nation in the late fifteenth century, Holy Roman Emperor Maximilian lent his support by sending Burgundian artillerymen from the Low Countries.[47] Throughout the sixteenth century, the Spanish in Europe typically fell short when it came to having enough guns and sufficient transport. In addition, it was not until late in the century that the Spaniards began to develop their own expertise in gunnery.[48]

However, as in the case regarding sixteenth-century descriptions about hand firearms, the nomenclature that has traveled through the centuries does not prove what sort of a gun is meant in old documents. It was not until 1551 that the French officially came up with a uniform classification of artillery pieces. As set out by the French, only the heaviest of these bronze pieces were called cannon. Then the guns descended in weight to great culverins, bastard culverins, small culverins, falcons, and falconets. The petit falconet typically had a barrel weighing just over 400 pounds and a ball weighing about a pound, fitting into a two-inch bore.[49]

While much of contemporary Europe considered Spain a brutal and crude bully—especially after its exploits in the New World seemed to provide it with the financial wherewithal to dream of being the only European superpower—this nation and its citizens on the Iberian Peninsula were entitled to as much grudging respect as emotional fear. When it came to the military advances of the sixteenth century, according to F. L. Taylor (a historian who saw active service in the First World War), "mobility, with its corollary, adaptability, was the special virtue of the Spaniard. He cultivated speed not only in his practice of the art of war but also in his treatment of its problems." Unlike other, more hidebound nationalities, "the Spaniard remained an adventurer in military matters."[50]

But this adventurous attitude was backed up with on-the-job experience and observations. The early sixteenth-century warfare in Italy, according to Taylor, demonstrated to the Spanish "that in war no system is infallible and no difficulty insoluble," and the Spanish military used the experiences in Italy "to experiment, to improve, and, in a word, to win."[51] The Spaniards, according to another military historian, showed the flexibility of modern commandos in meeting and overcoming unusual situations, especially in the New World.[52]

In addition to obtaining practical real-life experience, Spanish military education included book learning, especially after having seen in Italy a "Renaissance [that] favored the study of the military arts, ballistics, and fortification, as [in] . . . all areas of knowledge."[53] As early as 1474–1475, a knight from Castile, serving the Duke of Burgundy in northern Europe, was able to advise his employer about the use and design of siege machines, having read "Vegetius and other venerable writers who were . . . authoritive for the art of war."[54] One expert on military matters emphasized that the Spaniards, during this era, made, "Everything connected with the profession of arms . . . the subject of close study and a matter for improvement."[55] Of course, the sixteenth century being a period of religious fervor, especially for the Spanish, many students of warfare looked to the Bible for proven military lessons in tactics and training.[56]

In addition, a wide dispersal of European military knowledge was enhanced by the fact that the early sixteenth century, immediately after the first of the Italian Wars, saw the publication of military manuals on both the practical side and the theoretical side of the art of war.[57] For example, Niccolo Machiavelli first published his *Art of War* in Italian in 1521, to be followed by editions in Latin, Spanish, French, and English.[58] Also, classical military treatises, such as the works of Vegitius and Aelian, were being republished.[59] Certainly Spaniards interested in military affairs partook of this type of literature, although specific evidence of such books reaching the Americas during the sixteenth century apparently is limited to the occasional mention of a biography of Julius Caesar or an unspecified book on military tactics.[60]

In any event, without judging whether it was for the best, the Spaniards, among the other Europeans eventually crowding into the Western Hemisphere, imported a lot of their military baggage along with their emotional baggage. While it is evident that there was a fair amount of adaptation to local conditions and sometimes innovative responses to the abilities (or weaknesses) of Europe's New World opponents, many of the solutions developed in conflicts in Europe were applied in the Americas.

Indeed, a fair military appraisal of the Coronado Expedition in particular will demonstrate this moderate adaptation rather than radical reinvention. In the occasional areas in which there is no direct evidence, recourse to known European habits—while it may not always provide answers—will be helpful in asking the right questions about sixteenth-century military operations in the American Southwest. In addition, recourse to examples of "typical" military behavior, both contemporary to Coronado and to other eras, ancient and modern, also will provide clues to what happened during this military invasion of 1540–1542. Finally, the still-limited archaeological record of the expedition will be consulted to better understand what happened during this intrusion (invariably called an *entrada* by the Spaniards) into the northern wilderness.

During the first half of the sixteenth century, the religious and military revolutions occurring in the Old World rushed headlong into the New World. This, in turn, caused a revolution for the native peoples of the Western Hemisphere that turned their unsuspecting world upside down.

# TWO

# The Early Conquistador Era

During much of the fifteenth century, intrepid sailors from Portugal were gradually creeping along the coastline of Africa, working their way to India with its spices and exotic produce. It would not be until 1499 that Vasco da Gama finally reached Goa, India, and was able to return. This was an event that laid the foundation for the Portuguese securing their trading empire to the east.[1]

Meanwhile, Spain, under the united crowns of Castile and Aragon, was conducting its homegrown crusade—the Reconquista—conquering their resident invaders, the Moors. In 1492, the Islamic kingdom of Granada fell, cementing the beginnings of a geographically united Spain in an Iberian Peninsula shared with Portugal.[2] And, dynastic families being what they were, Spain soon would become an integral part of the Hapsburg Empire.

Whether coincidental or providential, things only got better for Spain in the seminal year of 1492. When Christopher Columbus sailed under the Spanish flag into the Western Hemisphere that autumn, he unknowingly catapulted Spain into the Age of Discovery, seemingly challenging Portuguese efforts to gain a trade monopoly over the subcontinent of India.[3] But this challenge was an end run around Portuguese rights of discovery, avoiding a head-on collision by sailing west to the Indies.

Under pressure from Spain and Portugal to protect their rights and to avoid conflict between these Most Catholic nations (a designation awarded by the Vatican to countries not tolerating dissenting beliefs), Pope Alexander VI (of the notorious Borgia family) issued a papal bull in 1493 that presumed to divide the world—a world that was very much unknown in a geographic sense—between the two nations of the Iberian Peninsula. While these lines basically gave the Western Hemisphere to Spain as its sphere of influence and reserved the Eastern Hemisphere to Portugal, there was a later modification so that Portugal could exploit its 1500 discovery of Brazil, the result of a fortuitous landfall on this continental bulge into the Atlantic.[4]

During this era of growing nationalism and religious diversity within Christian Europe, many outside of Iberia thought the papal bull was just that. The rest of Europe, especially the seafaring nations, saw these artificial demarcation lines across the Earth—dividing the spoils of the globe into two monopolies, one for Catholic Spain and one for Catholic Portugal—as presumptuously arrogant on the part of Rome.

Of course (as both nationalistic leaders and religious reformers such as Calvin and Luther would assert), it did not help the argument in favor of the papal division that the Vatican was hardly an unbiased and disinterested judge of such matters. First, not only was the Vatican an active player in wide-ranging European military and political affairs, but the elections of the many pontiffs during the century were influenced by the crassest ins and outs of certain ambitious Italian families.[5] Second, the Italian city of Rome also then had a reputation—certainly based on fact—for "orgies, poisoned pontiffs, homicidal cardinals and nuns working as prostitutes on the streets of the holy city."[6] The attempted papal division of the globe, since it went against the obvious national interests of England, France, and the Netherlands, probably exacerbated the religious split of Europe into Catholic and Protestant.[7]

Even a cynical Spain did not consider the legal terms of division as carved in stone, for the edict was not seen in Madrid as a grant of limitation. Spain, although legalistically citing the papal bull whenever convenient, believed that the world was a Spanish oyster due to its own efforts, certainly not beholden to the pope.[8] The around-the-world voyage of Magellan (a Portuguese in Spanish service who died before he got home) in 1519–1521 only reinforced this Spanish view.[9]

The rest of maritime Europe, while rejecting the papal bull, recognized the longer-standing principle of possession by right of prior discovery, parochially defining discovery in a Eurocentric perspective. But even this principle still gave the initial advantage to Spain in the Western Hemisphere, for its early efforts in discovery dwarfed those of such countries as England and France, especially in the southern latitudes.

These early *entradas* of Spain—the exploration (and conquest) of lands inhabited by native peoples—inexorably moved west across the Caribbean into Central America and southwest into South America. While native opposition on the Caribbean islands had been pathetically sporadic, once the Spaniards gained toeholds on the continents, that changed. For example, not only was the Aztec Empire a military monster, the capital of Tenochtitlan (later redeveloped as Mexico City ) had a population of two hundred thousand when first seen by impressed Europeans.[10]

For the native residents, this Spanish intrusion into the Western Hemisphere caused more than a revolution—it "brought cataclysmic transformations unequalled in historical times.... Everywhere, the suppression of native cultures was brutal and, to a remarkable degree, complete. . . . [The Spanish] threw down idols, destroyed temples, and worked tirelessly to erase the memory of ancient beliefs."[11]

While the considerable talents of Spanish mariners should not be ignored, the tumultuous era saw the transfer of crusading Spaniards— conquistadors—from their battlefield victories in Iberia and Italy to new challenges in the New World. According to historian H. H. Bancroft, writing in the 1880s:

> The conqueror of that period was of different material from the soldier of the present day. He was not a mere machine; he was a great dealer in destiny. He would willingly adventure his life. If he lost, it was well; if he won, it was better. A hundred did lose where one gained, and this each might have known to be the risk had he taken the trouble to make a computation. His life was but one continuous game of hazard; but, if successful, he expected wealth and glory as a just reward.[12]

This initial and greatest age of the conquistadors, the high-adventure era of Cortes and the Pizarros, started with Juan Ponce de Leon's first visit to the mainland of Florida in 1513 and lasted until 1543, by which time the Spanish had at least a general notion of North America.[13] With Ponce de Leon's expedition, it also was precedentially established that while Spain was not responsible for paying for the expeditions, the royal treasurer almost always was entitled to collect one-fifth of the wealth found.[14]

During this initial era, a lot of almost-incidental exploration took place. As Hernando Cortes noted—in following up rumors of new rich provinces northward and toward the Pacific after his destruction of the Aztec Empire—when such exploration occurred, it was "because by learning the truth about this and whatever else there is on said coast, God our Lord and their Majesties will be greatly served."[15]

As previously indicated, it only added to the military luster of Spain that many of these years of conquest and exploration in the Americas encompassed, in the Old World, a "general war by land and sea that prevailed from 1536 to 1547 [that] was the final test of the relative strength of the [Holy Roman] Emperor and the Sultan [of Turkey]."[16] In other words, the Spanish adventurers in the New World carried on their military campaigns while there was a full-blown major war front in Eastern Europe and around the Mediterranean Sea. (Similarly during this era, the Portuguese exploiting and defending their trading outposts in India had to fight the Muslims in Africa, from Morocco to Abyssinia.)

Of course, in the New World, the standards for success for these Spanish warriors were established by the golden conquests of Aztec Mexico and the Peru of the Incas. Those two treasure troves, grabbed by the Spaniards under Cortes and Francisco Pizarro respectively, set the bar mighty high.

But with gold, particularly stolen or looted gold, there never was enough to go around, especially when royal coffers were entitled to a fifth off the top. Even when successful, but especially when not successful, these Spanish conquistadors often caught a permanent case of gold fever, for the number of Spaniards (and Portuguese) who went on repeat expeditions is significant. For example, Ponce de Leon and Hernando de Soto reentered the field to increase their fortunes, Panfilo de Narvaez sought a second chance to gain an initial fortune, and Pedro de Alvarado repeated several times seemingly just for the fun of fighting. This lust for golden adventure held for lesser known men as well. Juan Rodriguez Cabrillo was a crossbowman with Cortes in Mexico, was with Alvarado in Guatemala, and died in 1543 leading an expedition in Upper California.[17] This repeat business only added to the professional nature of the conquistadors when it came to soldiering.[18] But were these military skills all the result of on-the-job learning in the New World, or was there more to it?

Obviously, depending upon the geography and the opposition, European battlefield tactics sometimes did not work. The Spanish phalanx of massed pikemen and arquebusiers, a combat unit known as the *tercio*, could not be successful against an enemy who, utilizing classic guerrilla tactics, clashed at an opportune moment and then simply melted away to fight another day.[19]

Furthermore, the Europeans found that their technologies did not always make up for the shortcomings of their regular modes of warfare. The modern inventions were no more perfect in the bush than they were in set-piece warfare. Even the primitive weaponry of the natives could be effective under the right circumstances. Regarding a battle with Indian archers, a survivor of the Narvaez Expedition that penetrated inland from Florida in 1528 wrote, "Some of our men were wounded in this conflict, for whom the good armor they wore did not avail."[20]

Of course, as every schoolchild used to know, and as scholars who have completely rejected institutional history still believe, the European interlopers to the New World supposedly found conditions to be radically different when it came to the practice of warfare. It was not only the English at Jamestown who presumably were "mystified by the Indians' irregular tactics."[21] All the white invaders—whether Spanish, French, English, or Dutch—would be confronted with the type of warfare that frustrated even the battle-savvy Northmen under Leif Ericson (by then Christians, but still Vikings), who first attempted to settle on the North American continent.

Therefore, many of these noninstitutional historians have argued, it was not until the European colonists reinvented themselves by adopting the guerrilla warfare of the native peoples that they, with their superior numbers and resources, were able to prevail. These scholars often reduce those superior resources to the introduction of gunpowder and firepower, with perhaps a sprinkling of disciplined organization thrown into the mix.

Clearly, in seeking out these new worlds to conquer in the Western Hemisphere, the Renaissance Europeans, including the Spanish, chose adaptation rather than reinvention, for reinvention would have been counterproductive and against instinct. Indeed, some of the earliest military men exported to the New World, whether Spanish or not, learned their trade while fighting on the European continent or in other theaters. Cortes's chief of artillery in the invasion of Mexico, for example, was one Mesa, a military engineer who was a veteran of the Italian Wars.[22] In Peru, there was a conquistador officer named Rodrigo de

Orgonez who had been an ensign in Italy and a participant when Rome and the Vatican were sacked by the Spanish and other Imperialists. There young Orgonez had learned "to steel the heart against any too ready sensibility to human suffering."[23]

In addition, while it is not something that those committed to vague diversity notions wish to admit, the European methods, without addressing questions of moral or ethical superiority, developed a technical expertise superior to that in other civilizations. "Whatever the extent of their individual talents," wrote historian David Ralston, "Europeans have shown themselves able to think and act more effectively as members of a group than those of any other civilization. The preeminence of the Europeans in this regard seems to be founded on their capacity to conceive of and execute any large-scale endeavor. . . . These operations are entrusted to persons who make the proper performance of them their paramount interest."[24]

While these methods and organizational standards would, by necessity, have to be adjusted to changed environments, that does not mean that basic European institutions, including those relating to the art of war, would be tossed out. Supporting this view is the fact that other nations outside of Europe (admittedly those whose civilizations were either more ancient or "more advanced" than most of those found in the Americas) eventually adopted European military institutions. "Members of the ruling elite in lands around the periphery of Europe could not help but be progressively more aware of the effectiveness of European military techniques and institutions, either as they experienced it in direct confrontation or as they observed the discomfiture of others," noted Ralston.[25]

In other words, other societies recognized the truth: the European art of warfare, with its technology and discipline, generally was militarily superior.[26] Thus it was that when the Portuguese introduced the arquebus into Japan in 1542, many of the Japanese lords quickly adopted it as a weapon and, typical for that nation, improved it.[27] In addition, even European-designed fortifications soon were scattered worldwide, including in the New World.[28]

Of course, this worldwide dissemination of military expertise and knowledge was aided by the fact that so many young European men were bent on leaving home and risking their lives as soldiers, especially against infidels and pagans who might be wealthy. This applied to the Spaniards in the Americas as much as it did to Spaniards and

Hapsburgs on European battlefields. "Cortes exploited their daring during his campaigns against the Aztec Empire no less than Charles [V] in his campaigns against Tunis and Algiers."[29]

The Spaniards found plenty of opportunity early on to employ their visions of the art of war in the Americas. In fact, their first major confrontation probably convinced the Spaniards that the European way of war was the way to go. When Cortes decided to conquer the Aztecs, "The Mexican army, whether Aztec proper or from one of the surrounding principalities, was one of the very few instances in the New World where Europeans encountered members of a formal, organized military establishment, rather than tribal warriors."[30] As one of the Spanish conquistadors recalled of seeing the highly advanced military opposition, "They have their military system, for they have captains general and also captains of four hundred and two hundred men. Each company has its standard-bearer with the insignia on a staff tied to his back."[31]

This so-called Anonymous Conquistador, noting that the Aztecs even used a type of feathery uniform for each company, added, "It is one of the most beautiful sights in the world to see them in their battle array because they keep formation wonderfully and are very handsome."[32] It probably was only a lack of Spanish infantrymen that kept Cortes from employing the massed effect of the tercio (phalanx of pikemen), in addition to his using his horsemen to great advantage. Even without enough men to form a tercio, the Spaniards, with their arquebusiers, their pikemen, and their swordsmen, did use some tactics against the Aztecs that they learned fighting against the Swiss.[33]

However, with the exception of the empire of the Incas—a South American regime that crumbled, at least initially, more readily than did the military powerhouse of the Aztecs—the rest of Spain's New World opponents were lesser militarily than Mexico in a number of ways. Nonetheless, these continued expansions of the Spaniard into other domains were military conquests over the native peoples. They also were undertakings that would share similarities to the later Coronado and De Soto Expeditions occurring during the tail end of this early conquistador period.[34] Thus, in addition to the warfare against the Aztecs and the campaigns in Peru, the other earlier contests and their analogous military lessons can be instructive in determining Spanish military protocol by the time of the expeditions of Coronado and De Soto.

In addition, it would be naïve to think that such men as De Soto and Coronado lived in a vacuum when it came to military matters. They would have discussed with interest previous military ventures, whether in the Old or the New Worlds. As related by Blaise de Monluc, a French professional soldier of the sixteenth century, it was wise to consider the opinions of others on military matters. Study and attention (as well as Bismarckian detachment) were required if one wished to arrive at any degree of perfection in the practice of arms. "A man must seek not only all occasions of presenting himself at all encounters and battles, but must moreover be curious to hear and careful to retain the opinions and arguments of experienced men concerning the faults and oversights committed by commanders, and the loss or advantages to the one side and the other ensuing thereupon; for it is good to learn to be wise and to become a good master at another man's expense."[35]

Therefore, in particular, not only is it likely that Coronado and his officers would tend to react as other Spanish leaders in applying standard operating procedure for the times, they also would consider how specific analogous events were handled previously. In other words, they would try to apply the military lessons found in textbooks (including classic Roman literature) and the practical solutions learned on other fields.

And those other fields of instruction were not limited to battlefields in the New World. Spaniards were numbered among the Holy Roman Empire force that attacked Rome in 1527 and were part of the massive imperial army that invaded Tunis in 1535. Also, these other fields were not limited to battlefields involving only the Spanish or their imperial comrades. While the Spanish were battling it out with the natives in the Western Hemisphere (in addition to fighting other Christian Europeans in Italy, and Muslims around the Mediterranean), their cousins and competitors, the Portuguese, also were seeking new worlds to conquer, from Brazil to India. These frontier Portuguese conflicts also provide some lessons in sixteenth-century warfare and buttress the belief that the European way of war was exported—and sometimes those Portuguese scenarios bore obvious resemblance to those being played out by Spain in the Americas.

This similarity existed because Portugal, like Spain, was fighting the Ottoman threat on the Mediterranean rim and fighting colonial conflicts during the very period of the early Spanish conquistador activity. In fact, during the travails of Coronado in the American Southwest (and De Soto in the American Southeast and Francisco Orellana down the Amazon), Portugal was militarily aiding a third world Christian country. This story began in 1520, when the Portuguese reached out to Abyssinia (or Ethiopia) by sending an ambassador to that desolate but devout nation, then hard pressed by Somali Muslim rebels supplied by the Ottomans.

The Portuguese, when they arrived on the scene, found the Ethiopians to be abysmally armed when it came to resisting the forces of the Crescent. "Their arms are assegais, few swords, a few coats of mail . . . [said to be] not . . . good mail," wrote Father Francisco Alvares, a Catholic priest who was with the embassy mission. "There are many bows and arrows . . .; there are very few helmets and casques [cheaper helmets]. . . . There are plenty of strong bucklers; there are no bombards [medieval mortars], except two *bercos* [early breech-loading swivel guns] which we brought them. At our departure [returning to Portugal] there were fourteen muskets at Court, which were bought from the Turks who came there to trade." However, their African allies were willing to fight, for Alvares wrote that the Ethiopian emperor, called Prester John, "ordered men to be taught to shoot."[36] Thus the Portuguese, like the Spanish, recognized that European methods of warfare also ought to be applicable halfway around the world.

Soon thereafter, the Portuguese, in a move that was refreshing in a sixteenth-century Christian world that placed differences above similarities, dispatched troops (along with artillery and firearms) to assist their darker brethren. None other than a son of Vasco da Gama led the expeditionary force of about four hundred men. In 1542, Cristovao da Gama and his musketeers helped the Ethiopians defeat a Muslim army. However, shortly thereafter, da Gama himself was captured, tortured, and beheaded. Nonetheless, in 1543, da Gama's stubborn men regrouped and finally defeated the overconfident Somalis, saving Ethiopian Christianity.[37] These heroic Portuguese efforts also provide clues as to the conduct of the Spanish expedition of Francisco Vasquez de Coronado into the American Southwest during the same decade, especially when one remembers both Portuguese and Spanish soldiers occasionally served in each other's forces.

But, as noted, 1543 marked the end of the great age of the conquistadors, whether Spanish or Portuguese. One military revolution would be replaced by another, just as hegemonies wax and wane and balances of power shift. The military and geopolitical ascendency of the nations on the Iberian Peninsula—herein recognized, not necessarily extolled—could not last forever. Spain eventually would be humbled on land, after eighty years of brutal warfare, by the rebellious Dutch Protestants. The Spaniards, sailing their vast armada in 1588, also would be decisively beaten on the sea by the English and the awful weather in their channel. As for the Portuguese, they would meet their Waterloo (called Alcazar) in 1578 in the desert of Morocco and then would go through a humiliating era as a virtual appendage of Spain.

Nonetheless, before those sea changes occurred, both the Spaniards and the Portuguese would be the two world empires. It was, in the words of Harvard historian Francis H. Rogers, the Age of Latin Arrogance.[38] And that arrogance was backed up by military and naval might.

Obviously, while still in their era of military ascendency, neither Spain nor Portugal would see any reason not to favor their tried and tested military doctrines. For the Spanish, this would mean their battles in the Americas would in some respects resemble their victories against foes in Europe and North Africa. Their expeditions, including that of Coronado, also would be Spanish military endeavors, subject to the more-or-less regular rules of the Spanish road.

# THREE

# Penetrating Western
# North America

F ollowing the conquest of the Aztec Empire by Hernando Cortes
and his Indian allies, the Spanish kept at it, expanding their initial
gains and moving beyond the limits of the Aztec nation. This first
European administrative region of southern North America, called
Mexico by the Aztecs, was more or less rechristened New Spain by the
interlopers.[1] While eventually Mexico would encompass its modern-
day area, during the sixteenth century it consisted of only the more cen-
trally located lands surrounding what became the Spanish capital of
Mexico City.

Although the Spanish associates of Cortes at first pushed south
through Yucatan toward Honduras and Guatemala, other Spaniards
based in Cuba left Mexico alone and made more attempts on Florida—
a peninsula (and name) to which the Spanish also attached distant lands
to the north and the northwest. Eventually, as other exploring conquistadors headed north out of Mexico, there was a vague sense that they
might also intrude into the immense lands of Florida from the west.

The most ambitious expedition in the Northern Hemisphere during
the early years was led by Panfilo de Narvaez, who, on the orders of the
governor of Cuba, attempted to capture Cortes and take over the conquest of Mexico. For his trouble, Narvaez lost his expedition and one of
his eyes when Cortes stole a march on him, departing Mexico City with

much of his army to launch a surprise attack on the latecomers.[2] Narvaez got a second chance at gold and glory and, after obtaining a commission from Charles V, landed in April 1528, near present-day Tampa Bay with four hundred Spaniards and eighty horses.[3]

Despite its size, the Narvaez Expedition was an unmitigated disaster. Realizing that hugging the coast would not succeed in this region of unpredictable and severe weather, Narvaez threw caution to the wind, electing to head into the interior with 260 infantrymen and 40 cavalrymen. Encountering native resistance, the Spaniards heard vague reports of gold in faraway "Apalachen." However, once reaching that area in what might be present-day Georgia, the Spaniards found no gold, little food, and an increasingly hostile native population. The dispirited conquistadors resolved to retreat back to the coast.[4]

Fighting natives all the way, Narvaez and his men reached the shore. Their ships—manned by Spanish mariners who, like Narvaez, had made incorrect geographic assumptions about the coastline and the river systems—were not there.[5] Improvising as best they could, the Spaniards built some ramshackle craft and launched themselves into the Gulf of Mexico in late November 1528. They had no better luck on the open sea than they did on land. The boat carrying Narvaez disappeared, and he never was heard from again. The boat carrying Alvar Nunez Cabeza de Vaca, the treasurer of the expedition, was driven onto the coast of Texas, perhaps near Galveston.[6]

Joined by the survivors of another boat, the destitute Spaniards numbered eighty. By spring, after some had resorted to cannibalism, only fifteen remained. Eventually, only Vaca and three companions—fellow Spaniards Andres Dorantes and a Captain Castillo-Maldonaldo, and an African (Moorish) slave belonging to Dorantes named Esteban (Stephen)—managed to scratch out an existence among the various Indians they met. They also slowly migrated to the west, starting out their travels as slaves but gaining a reputation as healers—early Christian faith healers. Vaca undoubtedly was the leader of these miserable survivors, being known among the Indians as a premier medicine man and holy man.[7] In fact, because he is supposed to have traveled through south and far west Texas, he has been officially recognized as the first known surgeon in that state's history.[8]

Meanwhile, New Spain in Mexico was evolving from a conquered principality under Cortes to an administrative part of the growing Spanish Empire. An ambitious conquistador, Nuno Beltran de

A nineteenth century print depicting a boat containing members of the Narvaez Expedition, including Alvar Nunez Cabeza de Vaca, being driven onto the coast of Texas during a storm in the Gulf of Mexico in late 1528. (*Author*)

Guzman, arrived in the Indies from Spain in 1525. He initially was appointed governor of a coastal province north of Vera Cruz, an area detached from the Mexico that had originally been given to Cortes. On paper, Guzman looked capable, for he was soon fluent in Nahuatl, the native tongue of the Aztecs. Then, in 1528, Guzman was made a member of the government of New Spain, where he and his compatriots evidenced so much proof of venality that they eventually were replaced.[9]

But Guzman was a hard man to keep down. When he was on the rise, he had acquired an Indian slave who told stories of having seen, as a boy, "seven very large towns which had streets of silver workers." These cities, which also had gold, were forty days to the north, across the wilderness.[10] Having this extra incentive to keep one step ahead of the authorities, Guzman and his friends left Mexico City and organized a full-fledged expedition to the little known area northwest of Mexico, a vast area that later included such Mexican states as Colima, Jalisco, Sinaloa, Durango, Queretaro, San Luis Potosi, and part of Zacatecas.[11] According to his erstwhile cohort, Garcia del Pilar, who later testified in Mexico City against his former leader, Guzman and his force, "Indians as well as Spaniards," left Mexico City right before Christmas 1529.[12]

Starting with a core Spanish force of "both horsemen and musketeers and crossbowmen," Guzman headed for the Pacific coast.[13] However—and this was a bad sign for the Indians—Guzman reputedly hated Franciscans, so only "three secular priests as chaplains and no friars were with his forces."[14] Putting the Indian stories together with European folklore, Guzman's motivation was to find the mysterious seven cities said to have been founded by seven Portuguese bishops who had fled west after the invasion of the Moors into the Iberian Peninsula.[15]

In any event, once starting his far-ranging conquests, Guzman demonstrated irrationally brutal behavior, requisitioning local Spaniards and Indian allies and then imprisoning them or killing them when they did not meet his often unexpressed expectations. Many of the Indian allies were put in chains and forced to carry baggage.[16] Guzman's attempts to find new lands and treasure included terror and torture. According to Pilar, when some of the Indians ran away, Guzman hanged fifty others; when his Spaniards threatened mutiny, Guzman hanged one of them as an example.[17]

In gathering additional Indian porters, whom he treated as slaves, Guzman called on the help of one Diego de Alcaraz as a slave catcher.[18] The Spaniards, according to Pilar, began to talk about Guzman and his methods: "Everything is now done by trickery and deceit." However, even the trickery and deceit had a hard edge, for when one group of Indians greeted Guzman in peace, Guzman had his warrior Indian allies kill "more than two thousand people," testified Pilar.[19] Guzman had one chief in Jalisco burned at the stake. Hundreds of the local Indians of Aztatlan, seeing how things were, participated in mass suicide by hanging themselves from trees.[20]

As Guzman marched up the Pacific coast to where he would soon found the town of Culiacan, he and his army met considerable resistance. Near the site of Culiacan, Guzman won a battle. "We routed them," recalled Pilar, "and it was God's will that although these Indians use poison they did not wound any Spaniards."[21] Meanwhile, Guzman had underlings spread out and explore the countryside, even to the north of where Culiacan would be. According to Pilar, Captain Lope de Samaniego "set out with twenty horsemen and explored for forty leagues up the coast but never found any settlement; nor did the forty foot soldiers who went north over the mountains, though they walked a hundred leagues there and back."[22]

On one hard march Guzman led, "The Spaniards ate nothing but meat, and the Indians ate whatever greens they could find, therefore many of the Indians died." Finally, after losing about thirty horses, Guzman's force returned to the coast, "where all the rest of the Indians died that we had taken with us from these parts," recalled Pilar, testifying in Mexico City. Shortly thereafter, Guzman founded the town of

Culiacan and basically gave the authority to any Spaniards who settled there to enslave the local Indians.[23]

Although he had done nothing beneficial for the new region except to found a few towns, and had established a legacy of turmoil, treachery, and war, Guzman sent letters to Emperor Charles V that inflated his actions into a fair conquest of new lands. Consequently, by 1531, Guzman was appointed the first governor of the fresh province of New Galicia. Cortes, who claimed an interest in the new region, was ordered to let Guzman be.[24] Nonetheless, the jealous Cortes thereafter sponsored further explorations up the Pacific coast, into the waters of what would become Upper and Lower California.[25]

But murder will out, and eventually the royal court heard about Guzman's considerable misdeeds and sent out a new governor for New Galicia, Diego Perez de la Torre, who arrived at Mexico City in 1536. Guzman soon was arrested and thrown into jail. Two years later, he was permitted to travel to Spain to appeal his unwinnable case. In 1544, Guzman died in well-deserved poverty and obscurity.[26]

Historians, almost without exception, consider Guzman to have been one of the most vicious and vile of the conquistadors—quite a ranking in such rough company.[27] According to historian Arthur Aiton, who gave Guzman more than a fair shake, "He had been cruel, rapacious, and self-seeking, but worse than that, had failed to discover new stores of ready-made wealth, and this failure extinguished any hope of hiding his short-comings."[28] But if he did not extend Spain's glory, Guzman at least extended its knowledge of the northern frontier of Mexico.

The replacement of Guzman was part of increasing efforts on the part of Spain to reform and regulate its holdings in the New World. While Charles V was preparing for the expedition to Tunis in 1535, he revamped the government of New Spain by appointing Antonio de Mendoza viceroy of the colony. Although this put a lot of power into the hands of one man—who turned out to be a capable man—the appointment was accompanied with specific instructions as to how the viceroy was to exercise those powers within the administration of New Spain and how he was to provide for the defense of the colony. Further instructions, very important to the story of the Coronado Expedition, detailed how Mendoza was to attempt to cooperate with Roman Catholic officials in setting up churches and expanding the faith, and they detailed how the natives were to be better treated. Thus, enslavement of the Indians, for example, was to be more closely monitored.[29]

The sack of Guzman as governor of New Galicia in 1536 was not the only notable event affecting the northwestern lands of the Spanish Empire in Mexico that year. Also in 1536, a little before Guzman was removed from office, the long-lost Cabeza de Vaca and his three comrades reached the outskirts of Spanish occupation on the northern frontier.

Slowly working their way west, Vaca and his fellows, Dorantes, Castillo-Maldonaldo, and Esteban, reached a hospitable Indian village in what would become Mexico's Sonora Valley. The Spaniards called the village Corozones (hearts) because the natives feasted the visitors on the dressed hearts of deer.[30]

Finally, upon reaching the Sinaloa River, the four reluctant explorers, along with the Indians who had accompanied them on their later travels as mystics and medicine men, met up with some very surprised Spaniards. These Spaniards, as it turned out, were slave catchers under the leadership of Diego de Alcaraz. While Alcaraz initially was accommodating to his countrymen and to Esteban, he rounded up their Indian followers to be sold as slaves—an ironic situation that the redeemed Spanish captives (Vaca, Dorantes, and Castillo-Maldonaldo) vigorously opposed and thus caused Alcaraz to become less helpful to them.[31]

Vaca and his comrades were taken to the nearest Spanish town, Culiacan, there to be met by the alcalde (a mayoral-judicial officer), Melchior Diaz. Diaz apologized for the actions of Alcaraz (but apparently was unable or unwilling to take steps to rescue the seized Indians) and allowed the party to proceed to Mexico City the next day.[32] The four reached Compostela and were entertained by none other than Nuno Beltran de Guzman, who was still clinging to the governorship of New Galicia. Not long afterward, the rescued wayfarers arrived at Mexico City, where Vaca, a nobleman, became the guest of a very inquisitive Viceroy Mendoza.[33]

Obviously, Cabeza de Vaca and his companions had important intelligence about previously unknown lands, information the viceroy initially heard when he met with the returnees.[34] As for the rest of the world, Vaca's relation eventually was published as a book in 1542. However, there was an earlier written product, for a lengthy letter of their travels and travails was produced before the four survivors separated, and it essentially covered the material as it ultimately was published. In addition, Mendoza had them prepare a map of their remarkable journey.[35] Therefore, considerable information of the interior of North

America was available to Mendoza before it was available to other Spaniards.

It is true that Vaca's relation did not directly hold out the promise of another Mexico or Peru. There was hearsay information that some of the Indians encountered told of "others who were very rich," located "farther on."[36] The Spaniards also, when near the end of their journey, saw a country with "clear traces of gold and lead, iron, copper, and other metals," but the people there "regard[ed] silver and gold with indifference, nor can they conceive of any use for them."[37] Thus, there was no substantiated tale of seven wealthy cities; there was only geologic information, and such technical mineral data did not interest those Spaniards of the first era of the conquistadors.

A nineteenth century illustration of Cabeza de Vaca, Esteban, and other survivors of the ill-fated Narvaez Expedition reaching a hospitable Indian village. (*Author*)

Certainly, the rumors that Vaca had heard about rich people "farther on" inspired the expedition of Hernando de Soto, which was to land in Florida and to begin looking for rich provinces to the north and west. De Soto, while still in Spain preparing for his venture, met with Vaca upon his long-delayed return to his homeland.[38]

Even the great conqueror Hernando Cortes tried to get back into the game after hearing of the reports of Vaca. He attempted an end run around the opposition of Mendoza to Cortes's participation in what could be called the Seven Cities Project by directly approaching Mendoza's associate Francisco Vasquez de Coronado. That attempt came to naught, with Mendoza putting Cortes and Coronado in their respective subservient places.[39]

This excitement encouraging the cupidity of conquistadors and would-be conquistadors at least was to be expected. Beliefs in such golden legends as the gilded man of El Dorado and the Seven Cities— typical of oral tradition in that the tale bearers and listeners wanted the stories to be true regardless of logic and common sense—were not, of course, the only such geographic and political fantasies. In fact, during this early period of the printing press, imaginative adventure novels, pretending to be based on lost manuscripts of Marco Polo, were popular among the literate public, including the Spanish.[40]

In addition, the popular stories sometimes served deeper religious yearnings that went beyond mere greed. From medieval times, the Christians of Europe had passed on the story of Presbyter Johannes (Prester John), a powerful Christian monarch of the Far East who eventually was identified with the struggling Christian kingdom of Abyssinia (Ethiopia). Indeed, the legend of Prester John provided another incentive for the persistent courage of the Portuguese in working their ships around Africa's Cape of Good Hope and continuing on to the true Orient.[41] And, as encouragement to such tales, even on the uninviting east coast of Africa, the Portuguese heading toward India had found and looted prosperous Muslim trading towns full of gold, silver, and silk.[42]

The first-person stories of Cabeza de Vaca and his companions at least provided some accurate firsthand data regarding what lay beyond the coast of the land the Spanish called Florida and what lay beyond the limits of New Spain and New Galicia. Some information, in particular, was in the nature of military intelligence about the peoples to the north, and this obviously was made known to Mendoza.

For example, according to Vaca, "They are all warlike, and have as much strategy for protecting themselves against enemies as they could have were they reared in Italy in continual feuds." Vaca warned that if their territory were threatened by an enemy, the Indians would hide in a ditch during the night and, "If the enemy comes to assault the houses, they who are in the ditch make a sally; and from their trenches do much injury without those who are outside seeing or being able to find them."

Therefore, Vaca warned that the Indians were "the most watchful in danger of any people I ever saw." In addition to recognizing their powers of endurance, Vaca said, "I believe these people see and hear better, and have keener sense than any other in the world."[43]

When actually fighting, the natives would bend low and change their locations while shooting the arrows. "So effectual is their maneuvering that they can receive very little injury from crossbow or arquebus." Indeed, the Indians scoffed at these European arms, according to Vaca.[44] (Such information as this eventually would inspire the Spanish to attempt to counter the natives' ability to dodge single projectiles by loading their firearms with multiple balls or with shotgun-like bits of metal.)[45]

But even being hit and wounded did not stop these Indian berserkers. "Oftentimes the body of an Indian is traversed by the arrow," noted

Vaca, "yet unless the entrails or the heart be struck, he does not die but recovers from the wound."[46]

On the other hand, Vaca gave the impression that the chances of a Spaniard being wounded with an Indian arrow—and fatally—were good. The Narvaez Expedition had been decimated by native archers in the American South. Making them sound like English longbowmen, Vaca said these Indians "are all archers. . . . The bows they use are as thick as the arm, of eleven or twelve palms in length, which they will discharge at two hundred paces with so great precision that they miss nothing."[47] As for the Indian archers of the American Southwest, Vaca warned that they had available "poison from a certain tree the size of the apple. For effect, no more is necessary than to pluck the fruit and moisten the arrow with it."[48]

The Spaniards sat up and took military notice about these (and other) poisoned arrows, for during the Reconquista they had faced Moorish enemies who employed such deadly missiles.[49] Indeed, so impressed were the Spaniards with this New World poison that, much like in the cases of the potato and maize, there is evidence the Spanish took advantage of this technology "of a potent poison," which, when "[a]pplied to an arrowhead, . . . caused instant death with the merest pricking of the skin." The knowledge was taken home to Europe for possible use during this age of constant warfare, political assassination, and religious murder.[50] Thus, although poisoned arrows were not considered legitimate in European warfare,[51] sometimes the rule was proved by the exceptions.

In addition to providing helpful geographic, ethnological, and technical information, the relation of Cabeza de Vaca provided a salutary lesson in leadership—or the lack of it. Although the Narvaez endeavor was seemingly a well-provided-for voyage, "The expedition," in the words of a Cabeza de Vaca scholar, "had unraveled with frightening speed."[52] Obviously there were morals to be learned on how not to conduct such a reconnaissance in force.

Mendoza, especially since he was inclined to invest in a voyage of discovery and conquest with his own funds, made a reasonable attempt to verify the obvious hearsay provided by Vaca and his associates. The attempt was in conformance with Mendoza's commission from the emperor to cooperate with church authorities. Mendoza tasked a French member of the Franciscan Order, Friar Marcos de Niza (Mark of Nice), to walk north with Esteban. He was the only member of the

Vaca party—still unfairly enslaved—willing to assist the viceroy to scout out the country.[53] The two would be accompanied by as many of the Indian friends of Vaca as could be located and freed from Alcaraz's slaving.[54]

Although a churchman, de Niza basically was commissioned by the viceroy to make a reconnaissance for the secular authorities, a situation not unlike what sometimes occurred in Europe.[55] In this case, Mendoza provided detailed instructions to the cleric regarding his mission. In addition to trying to patch up relations with the natives around Culiacan, de Niza was ordered to "find a way to go on and penetrate the land in the interior . . . [taking] along Esteban de Dorantes as guide." Mendoza made it clear de Niza was to command the independent Esteban, not the other way around.[56]

As for the details regarding this geographic penetration, the friar, being as careful as he could be, was to observe and count the Indians they met and make note of the climate, geography, and fertility of the lands entered.[57] He was "always to learn if there is any information about the seacoast, both of the North and South seas, for it may be that the land narrows and that a sea inlet reaches the interior of the land." In addition to sending back Indian runners with occasional reports of his progress, the friar was told to erect wooden crosses (with letters buried beneath) at navigable points along the coast or along rivers, so that if Mendoza sent ships, "they will be advised to look for this sign."[58]

De Niza also was to scout out likely areas suitable for large settlements and for a monastery. Finally, "Although the whole land belongs to the Emperor, our lord," the friar was instructed to take specific possession of it for the emperor in the name of the viceroy, erecting any appropriate markers.[59]

Meanwhile, Perez de la Torre, the governor of New Galicia who had replaced Guzman, was killed when battling rebelling natives. In late summer 1538, the viceroy appointed his twenty-eight-year-old protégé, Francisco Vasquez de Coronado, as governor. Among other duties, Coronado was tasked with ending the Indian troubles and providing support for the reconnaissance mission of Friar Marcos and Esteban.[60]

Friar Marcos, along with a Friar Onorato, Esteban, and some of the Indians rescued from the clutches of Alcaraz and his minions, headed north into the unknown in March 1539.[61] Supposedly, as Pedro de Castaneda later heard it, de Niza and the Moor soon had a falling out, for the cleric disapproved of Esteban's taking advantage of the Indian women he was offered by the men of the villages as they traveled. In addition, de Niza was jealous of the influence the African had with the natives, for they had seen him pass by before with the itinerant and nonthreatening crew of Vaca.[62]

It was soon decided that Esteban would go on ahead with some Indian retainers while the friars followed behind with theirs. The objective of both parties was a land that now had a name: Cibola.[63] Apparently after the separation, and unknown to Esteban, Friar Onorato had to drop out of the mission because of illness.[64]

As he headed north, Esteban picked up the pace, but he continued to send back larger and larger crosses to Friar Marcos.

A fanciful nineteenth-century American print of the mendacious Friar Marcos de Niza. (*Author*)

These prearranged messages indicated that the lands he was passing through, or merely hearing about, were better and better. In addition to crosses, Esteban sent back an Indian who said he had been to Cibola, which was the first of the seven cities Esteban would reach.[65]

As Friar Marcos later reported it, this Indian described the cities as all being ruled by one man. The cities had large houses constructed of stone with lime, and the houses varied in height from one story to four stories. There were household decorations of turquoise. Perhaps more importantly, there were provinces beyond Cibola that were "much more important than these seven cities."[66] When de Niza met other Indians on the trail, their tales of the seven cities basically tallied with what the friar already had heard.[67] Once, when de Niza was skeptical about the height of the houses, his informants made a picture of a ladder to show how the natives ascended to the apartments.[68]

The crosses Esteban sent back were not the only Christian symbols constructed during this reconnaissance. De Niza also erected a couple of crosses and claimed the land for the emperor.[69]

Friar Marcos could not catch up with Esteban and his growing Indian entourage. Part of de Niza's problem with overtaking Esteban was that the friar supposedly was performing the other duties that had been assigned. For example, he indicated that he took a side jaunt to the west at about thirty-five degrees latitude, where he "saw clearly" that the coastline turned to the west. This discovery (which has since been discounted as an impossible journey in the time allowed), according to de Niza, "brought me no less joy than the good information of the country."[70]

Although Friar Marcos continued to plod along northward, crossing much desolate countryside and questioning many more locals about Cibola, he was destined never to catch up with his African advance man.

According to Castaneda, when Esteban finally reached Cibola (the land of the Zuni) with the Indians who were carrying his baggage and with "some beautiful women whom the Indians who followed him . . . have given him," those Zuni Indians suspiciously "lodged him in a little hut they had outside their village, and the older men and the governors of the pueblo heard his story and took steps to find out the reason he had come to that country."[71] Their reaction to Esteban's personal *entrada* amounted to both a rejection of Esteban's efforts to proselytize the Cibolans and to an early—if crude—case of racial profiling. But their reaction also exhibited a keen appreciation of what lay in store for them if they did not attempt to discourage such visitations on behalf of a foreign nation.

As Castaneda heard and reported the story years later:

> For three days they made inquiries about him and held council. The account which the negro gave them of two white men following him, sent by a great lord, who knew about the things in the sky, and how these were coming to instruct them in divine matters, made them think that he must be a spy or a guide from some nations who wished to come and conquer them, because it seemed to them unreasonable to say that the people were white in the country from which he came and that he was sent by them, he being black. Besides these other reasons, they thought it was hard of him to ask them for turquoises and women, and so they decided to kill him. They did this, but they did not kill any of those who went with him, although they kept some young fellows and let the others . . . return freely to their own country.[72]

When those of Esteban's followers who were able to retreated back south, they met up with Friar Marcos and gave him garbled accounts of what had transpired. They said the Cibolans first were hostile to Esteban because they associated some of the medicine man paraphernalia he had acquired while with Cabeza de Vaca with a tribe hostile to the Cibolans.[73] From another of that company of scared retainers, the son of a chief, de Niza heard that one morning, after this Indian left the hut wherein they were confined to get a drink of water, he "shortly afterward saw Esteban fleeing and people from the city pursuing him, and they killed some of those who came with him."[74] From others, the friar learned that Esteban was never seen again and presumably had been killed with arrows.[75] The frightened Indians also claimed that the Cibolans had killed three hundred of the people who followed Esteban to Cibola.[76]

Those who had fled Cibola were so distraught that it was only with much difficulty that the friar supposedly was able to convince two of the chiefs to escort him back to within eyesight of Cibola, which he later reported was "situated in a plain, at the base of a round hill." He also said the "pueblo has a fine appearance, the best I have seen in these regions. The houses are as they had been described to me by the Indians, all of stone, with terraces and flat roofs. . . . The city is larger than the city of Mexico."[77]

From his distant vantage point, Friar Marcos—as a good Franciscan—renamed the province "the new kingdom of St. Francis" and erected a cross to claim the land in the name of Don Antonio de Mendoza. He turned homeward "with much more fear than food."[78]

When de Niza finally got back to Mexico City, by August 1539, he wrote up his report for the viceroy. He certified that he wrote "only of what I saw and was told, of the countries I have traversed, and those of which I have been informed."[79] While this language left a legal loophole big enough for a mounted Spanish man-at-arms to ride through with ease, the friar later would be branded as a bald-faced liar by the European members of the Coronado Expedition.

As for the lamented Esteban and his legacy, he certainly garnered a fair share of contemporary blame from de Niza for the disastrous outcome of this Franciscan reconnaissance to Cibola. Considering the later questionable standing of the friar for veracity, this reputation may be unwarranted. There is at least a reasonable chance that the claims made against Esteban were motivated (or at least exaggerated) by envy and that Esteban (living up to his namesake, Saint Stephen) deserves to be remembered as the first Christian martyr of New Mexico, even if he suffered from some of the same vices as did some of the many sixteenth-century popes. But such a matter likely will only be resolved in the end times when the sea shall give up its dead.

As for a historical evaluation of Esteban's legacy, it is tempting to overemphasize his role during these politically correct times. One enthusiastic scholar has assessed "his place in history . . . as [being] as important as Viceroy Mendoza, Coronado, or [later explorer] Antonio de Esperjo."[80] Another writer called him an "African explorer, who ranks as one of the most extraordinary men in the history of the European discovery of America."[81] Based on the one-sided historical record, Esteban certainly added to the diversity and color of the players in the Coronado saga; he apparently was a Christian who, according to de Niza, descended into paganism and lechery to further his ambitions and carnal desires, and he died for his sins.

But Esteban *was* important. If he had not sent back those crosses— implicitly glowing reports—Friar Marcos likely would not have become overenthused about what he had not seen. While those exaggerated conclusions in turn inspired an immediate expedition that may have eventually occurred anyway, if Esteban had not been killed by the Zuni, the expedition might not have been such an overtly military endeavor— an actual invasion into lands to which the Spanish were not invited. Finally, if the Zuni had not had blood on their hands—if not on their consciences—the first encounter between the Spaniards and the natives at Cibola might not have been the initial warfare between races in what was to become the Southwestern United States.[82] Thus, while Esteban was not a primary mover, he certainly was no bit player.

The Zunis had their own view of Esteban's killing, believing them- selves the victims of threatened aggression. Their oral tradition thus corroborates much of the historical record. Their side about the killing of "the Black Mexican at Kia-ki-me" was that it happened during the days "when smoke hung over the house-tops and the ladder-rounds [rungs] were still unbroken."[83] The black Mexican arrived with "many Indians of Sono-li [Sonora], as they call it now, who carried war feath- ers and long bows and cane arrows like the Apaches, who were enemies of our ancients." The Zuni ancients, being "bad tempered and quick to anger," started a fight with "sling-stones and arrows and war clubs." The Sinaloa (New Galicia) Indians fled from Cibola, back to the "land of Everlasting Summer," but they left behind "one of the Black Mexicans," dead. Upon calmer reflection, the Zuni in those olden times thought that "these people, being angered, will come again."[84]

It seemingly was only later, after Coronado arrived, that the Zuni began to detail transgressions of Esteban that equaled or surpassed those charges made by de Niza. But even these assertions were hearsay and not events suffered by the Zuni. According to Coronado, "the

Indians say that they killed him here because the Indians of Chichilticale said that he was a bad man, and not like the Christians who never kill women, and he killed them, and because he assaulted their women, whom the Indians love better than themselves."[85] These supposed incidents were not even related by de Niza, who seemingly would have loved to tell them. They also were not related to Coronado when he marched through Chichilticale.

Regarding Friar Marcos's reputation for being disingenuous, some historians have come to his defense. One of the earliest Coronado experts, George Parker Winship, concluded, "Friar Marcos undoubtedly never willfully told an untruth about the country of Cibola, even in a barber's chair."[86] More recently, William Hartmann opined that the friar, in his reporting, "may have been biased by a greater interest in souls than in geographical or ethnological documentation," but he seems to have made "an earnest attempt to recount his journey."[87] Another defense of de Niza—non-faith-based although from a fellow Franciscan—noted that his being "not a Spaniard, but a son of the French Franciscan province of Aquitaine," undoubtedly meant, "His command of Spanish was none too perfect."[88]

These defenses, however, fall well short of making Friar Marcos a pillar of veracity and really do not satisfactorily answer why he obviously made up information for the viceroy, becoming one of "the [Baron] Munchausens of America," according to one of the best Coronado historians.[89] But there is a logical scenario that would account for the misinformation and de Niza's inability to explain it away. Winship, while noting it was unproven, wrote that Cortes accused de Niza of committing plagiarism by incorporating into his report information Cortes had told the friar about the coastal lands to the west.[90] In any event, even if not due to a character flaw but to some deeper psychological reason, de Niza was the source of much significant misinformation, especially when his scouting was on behalf of the secular authorities and men's lives (rather than their souls) would be the medium of exchange. Like Esteban, de Niza was another important player without whom history would have been somewhat different.[91]

Although Viceroy Mendoza then had no reason to disbelieve the hearsay related by the members of Vaca's group, seemingly verified by Friar Marcos, he again proved himself to be a cautious man. In November 1539, Mendoza ordered the frontier-wise Melchior Diaz north with fifteen mounted Spaniards and Indian allies. As it turned out, they ended going a total of fifteen hundred miles, round trip, pen-

etrating into the area of southern Arizona.[92] But this additional reconnaissance would be too late, for assumptions now were proving irresistible, and events were moving irresistibly. There was going to be a
full-fledged military expedition north to Cibola—and it was much
more an armed invasion than a voyage of discovery and exploration.

# FOUR

# Finding a General and
# Recruiting the Expedition

By late 1539, Viceroy Mendoza was intent on finding out what lay to the far north of Mexico, based upon the information provided by Cabeza de Vaca and seemingly verified by Friar Marcos de Niza. Mendoza well knew that others were interested in the project. Hernando De Soto, the governor of Cuba, was bent on heading into the interior of the vague region known to the grasping Spaniards as Florida, and Cortes was in Spain, lobbying to lead the next exploration north.[1] In fact, by spring 1539, De Soto already was sailing from Cuba to Florida with his army.[2] Although Mendoza sat astride the shortcut to Cibola and its seven cities, time was of the essence.

Therefore, after de Niza returned, Mendoza authorized an impressive expedition to run down the rumors, especially the optimistic hearsay provided by the religious reconnaissance of the good friar. This official attempt, naturally, was in the hope that these most extravagant rumors were true. Therefore, the operation would have to be prepared to meet and, if necessary, overcome the desired sophisticated Kingdom of Cibola.

Obviously, an expedition of this size and scope would need serious financing, for it would have to move as a self-sustaining unit most of the time. As an English professional soldier of the sixteenth century wrote, in order for an expedition to avoid starvation and to prevent looting the countryside traversed, "upon any long march and enterprise intended, with all foresight and providence [a leader must seek] to provide plenty of victual and all other things necessary for the sustenance of all their soldiers, even to the meanest and least of account, as also of great store and plenty of powder and shot, with some overplus of weapons of divers sorts for all accidents and employments, with all other things requisite."[3]

Consequently, in sixteenth-century Europe, "The provision of funds was the core problem of military organisation."[4] For example, the imperial army approaching Rome in 1527 was motivated as much by want and lack of funds as by military strategy. Also, Pope Paul III, in 1538, agreed to divert money raised from indulgences for the building of Saint Peter's in Rome to Charles V for the raising of a war fleet to fight the Ottomans.[5] This universal condition for military adventures likewise was true in the Americas. And where there was a need for money, bankers, investors, and money brokers became involved.

While the earliest conquistador efforts, including that of Cortes in Mexico, had seen the volunteers initially attracted by the promise of a soldierly salary, that had changed. "[N]ow that investors had woken up to the fantastic profits to be gained from the New World, it became the practice to form military companies, groups of men each in charge of his own equipment and weapons, who received no salary but a previously stipulated share of the spoils."[6] Among the investors hoping for a share of these anticipated profits from Cibola was a citizen of New Spain named Guido de Lavezariis, an immigrant of either Basque or Genoese extraction. Beginning in 1539, acting as a banker, he purchased warlike necessities for men-at-arms intending to go on the expedition, as well as for lending money to those selected as captains and men-at-arms.[7] Obviously, there were investors in addition to Lavezariis willing to gamble money on other men's lives.

Of course, by the time of Coronado's endeavor, the usual carrot held out to the actual European participants risking their lives was the hope of being granted an *encomienda*—a sort of feudal plantation by which the holder would become a member of the landed aristocracy, the leisure class to be found in the hacienda, permitting all the heavy lifting to be done by indentured or enslaved Indians.[8] Unfortunately, as all too often occurs with human institutions, "the system soon degenerated into one of shameful oppression, the defenceless condition of the natives inciting the adventurers to increased exactions and brutality."[9]

A nineteenth-century reproduction of a sixteenth-century woodcut showing bankers counting money. Funding with hard currency was critical to supplying and recruiting an expedition. (*Author*)

While the Coronado Expedition happened during the earliest round of conquistador endeavors, and despite it not being officially financed, it was more organized than those preceding it and was subject to more direct government oversight. "The Coronado expedition," wrote Elizabeth A. H. John, "marked a new style in Spanish conquest, under government control from the beginning and held accountable for the well-being of Indians whose lives it would touch."[10]

Partly because the force was not a professional army paid out of royal coffers, some accommodating American historians have tried to recast the march of Francisco Vasquez de Coronado as a pacific endeavor. Herbert Bolton characterized the expedition, at least from the perspective of Viceroy Mendoza, "as a missionary as well as business enterprise."[11]

For his part, professional politician Stewart Udall, another dedicated student of the expedition, conveniently minimized the traditionally accepted motives of gold, glory, and God and recast the individual conquistadors into the mold of solid Anglo-American pioneers. "Their feats reflected the hopes and ambitions of men who, on another level, were involved in a search for themselves," Udall poetically waxed. "Unprecedented opportunities for independent action—for Spaniards trapped in feudal social arrangements to improve their lot or even achieve fame—brought a flowering of individualism in the New World."[12] Udall also reduced the well-known story of Spanish subjugation and enslavement of entire Indian peoples, often without Vatican or official Roman Catholic and royal permission, into the mere Black Legend, unworthy of credence.[13]

Most recently, an eminently qualified Coronado scholar—either unfamiliar with the vast number and composition of army-camp followers in days gone by or wishing to give greater emphasis to the non-combat members of the expedition—wrote, "Like any other *quasi-military* [my italics] force of the day, the Coronado expedition included wives, children, and other companions."[14] There was nothing "quasi-military" about the expedition. It was commanded by a captain general, had the equivalent of two batteries of artillery, and was destined to participate in a couple of pitched battles, at least three major sieges, and innumerable bloody skirmishes—all without complaint by its soldier members (who were not averse to complaining about other matters).[15]

For all of this modern ruminating, the expedition was a military one, with military objectives—and, being clearly uninvited, it was an invasion of lands claimed and occupied by others. Nonetheless, if those objectives could be obtained peacefully, with the obvious threat of force backing up native submission, so much the better. But there is a reason the conquistadors are called conquistadors.[16] For all the criticism of modern historians regarding the colonial efforts of all the European powers, the methodology of Spain in the New World was vastly different from the goals and tactics of the French, the British, the Dutch, and the Swedish. While the efforts of all the major European players ended in deadly conflict with indigenous peoples, the Spanish, from the first (at least after the failed trading expeditions of Columbus to the "Indies"), never anticipated anything other than incorporation of the Americas into their national and religious empire. Their military methodology in building this empire was little different from those employed from Alexander the Great to Napoleon to more recent conquerors.[17] Not only were Spanish efforts reminiscent of the medieval crusades into the Holy Land, the Spanish efforts in the Americas were only smaller-scale models of the sixteenth-century endeavors against their European neighbors, from the Italian Wars to the Spanish Armada.

Consistent with this attitude of conquest and incorporation, there was no question that it was to be a military operation at the time. According to participant Pedro de Castaneda, Mendoza, after Friar Marcos's return, began "collecting an armed force and [started] . . . bringing together people to go and conquer them."[18] Similarly, a Spanish historian of the sixteenth century wrote that this expedition included "a quantity of arms, and munitions in abundance for a good and well equipped army. It was organized, embellished, and provi-

sioned, all in readiness for war."[19] Thus, taking function into account, it does not matter
that the sixteenth-century conquistadors did
not happen to call themselves soldiers; they
might have been rather more like mercenary
soldiers, but they were soldiers.[20]

Even today, conquest would seem a logical and necessary methodology for the sixteenth-century intrusion. After all, a diplomatic representative of Spain had been
slaughtered in a seemingly pacific attempt
to establish peaceful relations and a quiet
subjugation. A holy man of the Roman
Catholic Church even had been forced to
flee south for his life.

A sixteenth-century man-at-
arms depicted by Albrecht
Dürer. It provides a good
idea of how Coronado's
men-at-arms may have
appeared. Note the spurs,
horseshoes, stirrup, and
other details. (*Author*)

When he was appointed viceroy,
Mendoza was "given the power to assume
or delegate the supreme military office of
captain general."[21] Although the viceroy
initially thought about leading the *entrada*
himself, he soon settled on appointing his
young protégé Francisco Vasquez de
Coronado, the governor of New Galicia, as
captain general.[22] In the sixteenth century, such a rank—a captain general, or a general over a number of captains—was an important command level and sufficiently high to lead a crusade against infidels.[23]

In his instructions to his new captain general upon his appointment,
Mendoza made it clear that Coronado had the power to appoint and
dismiss his captains and to impose civil and criminal jurisdiction over
the Spaniards and the natives. Mendoza specifically commissioned
Coronado to find new lands, including the "provinces of Acus and
Cibola, and the seven cities and the kingdoms and provinces of Matata
and Totonteac." Making the job seem like that of an occupier,
Coronado could enforce his position of captain general over these people and punish "those who may be rebellious or disobedient." During
his "discovery and pacification" of these lands, Coronado was to protect
and defend the natives of the land, "bring its natives to the knowledge
of our holy Catholic faith," and bring the land within the authority of
the royal crown.[24]

Francisco Vasquez de Coronado, whom historian Herbert Bolton would dub a "Knight of Pueblos and Plains," was a younger son of a minor noble of Salamanca, Spain, and he and another brother, both having an elder brother and therefore not in line to inherit the family holdings, immigrated to the New World to make their fortunes. Francisco was fortunate to hitch his wagon to a star named Antonio de Mendoza, the new viceroy of New Spain. The young Coronado also was fortunate to marry well, to an heiress of New Spain who was reported to have a blood connection (illegitimate) with the late King Ferdinand of Spain. Coronado was a man on the rise, and at twenty-eight he was appointed governor of the frontier province of New Galicia.[25]

Bolton would wax eloquent about this golden boy; although no portrait of Francisco exists, his younger brother Juan was painted (apparently from life) as being a blond. Bolton pronounced him full of "dash and nerve" and "brave and soldierly."[26] Even after his expedition, which found no new rich province, Coronado had his sixteenth-century admirers. Fifty years after his expedition, a Spanish historian said Francisco Vasquez de Coronado, already "governor of the new kingdom of New Galicia," was "a gentleman who had the essential gifts and merits, well qualified for such duties."[27]

Coronado's Spanish hometown of Salamanca was known for its university. However, while the university made the town a seat of learning, it did not necessarily make it a location for anything approaching liberalism in the Iberian Peninsula. In 1492, the university fell under royal jurisdiction, a situation that guaranteed monetary support but hardly promised independent thinking. In addition, even in the first years of the sixteenth century, the university still considered itself a subsidiary of the Vatican. Therefore, although not actually running the institution, Rome greatly influenced the policies of the school.[28] Thus, while Coronado gave evidence of being an educated and moderately enlightened Spaniard, he hardly was the stereotypical Renaissance man of the era.[29]

But Coronado probably was a typical Spanish gentleman, steeped in the romantic notions of the era, and would attempt to live up to those standards. He easily could have read the mid-fourteenth-century book on nobility and chivalry written by Spanish mercenary soldier Diego de Valera. In this volume, Valera praised nobles who justified their rightful position through the validation of courageous warfare.[30] Coronado also might have been aware of the tribute Venetian Pietro Aretino wrote for his famous Condottieri friend Giovanni delle Bande Nere after he was killed in battle in 1526. Aretino said:

> He valued brave men more than he did riches and indeed only desired the latter to keep the valiant, who served him, from going hungry. There was nothing about his men's lodging or their conduct in action that he did not know about, for in battle he fought side by side with privates in the ranks. . . . [T]he very clothes he wore proved he was himself a fighting man. They were worn and shabby and they had armor stains upon the legs, and arms, and chest. . . . But what more than anything else won the hearts of his followers was that he said "Follow me!" instead of "Go ahead of me!" in time of peril.[31]

The captain general was not the only man of quality with romantic notions willing to head north. Members of the lesser nobility, hidalgos, rushed to join the expedition. In fact, as Castaneda later claimed, the recruits contained a great many men of status (if not distinction), with an extremely high percentage of dons, hidalgos, and the gentlemen called caballeros.[32] This is not amazing, for—unlike Englishmen (who had more options)—Spanish gentlemen thought "that soldiering was the only secular profession that befitted a gentleman."[33]

As with the mustering of medieval and Renaissance armies, there is evidence that a number of the recruits for Coronado came forward in groups or were otherwise associated with others in the expedition. These small units of men-at-arms seemingly followed a gentleman who operated like a feudal lord in collecting his retainers, or like a condottieri captain recruiting a company of mercenary soldiers.[34] In this, these volunteers for the Coronado Expedition merely mimicked a common practice of recruitment found in Spain.[35] In a couple of cases, fathers brought their sons to serve alongside them.[36]

While it is a disputed issue—and harkens to the theories of Frederick Jackson Turner about the American frontier functioning as a pressure-cooker release valve for the nation—the expedition seemingly provided an outlet for those who were unable to make a go in an upper-class colonial society that already was full of dissolute young men. In truth, Spain and its dominions were overrun with these gentlemen knights, for the king made a good business of selling these titles in the Kingdom of Castile. Since being a member of the nobility provided an exemption from taxes in Spain, there apparently was no shortage of applicant buyers.[37] Naturally, many of these unemployed gentlemen with aspirations ended up in the colonies, where they provided a source of trouble.[38] According to the Spanish historian Mota Padilla, Viceroy Mendoza took advantage of "the many noblemen who were in Mexico, who like cork on the water bobbed up and down without having anything to do or knowing what to busy themselves with, all depending upon the viceroy to do them favors and being maintained at the tables of the citizens of Mexico."[39] Indeed, some of the recruits for the army had recently been in jail.[40]

Nonetheless, the Spaniards who made up the leadership of such conquistador expeditions, especially the hidalgos, "brought with them from Castile the ambitions, the prejudices, the habits and the values that they had acquired at home." They were professional soldiers but were as legalistic as pettifogging lawyers, "always drawing up documents, even in the most improbable places and situations, to determine the exact right and duties of each member of an expedition."[41] Thus, "These men were dedicated fighters—tough, determined, contemptuous of danger, arrogant and touchy, extravagant and impossible."[42] In a nutshell, being the commander of such egotistical men was a situational disaster waiting to happen—although they would be just what was needed when the trouble hit the fan.

As for the officers under Coronado, with so many gentlemen available there were plenty of potential appointees for these captainships to be appointed by Mendoza. Pedro de Tovar was named ensign-general, a position comparable to the general's aide. The frontier-wise Lope de Samaniego was named army-master or master of the camp, a sort of adjutant and second in command whose duty was to control the line of march, choose campsites, and regulate order within the camp.[43] Diego Gutierres was appointed commander of cavalry. Pablo de Melgosa de Burgos was the commanding captain of infantry, and Hernando de Alvarado was in charge of the artillery to accompany the expedition. Other captains included Tristan de Arellano, Pedro de Guevara, Garcia Lopez de Cardenas, Rodrigo Maldonado, Diego Lopez, Francisco de Barrionuevo, Juan de Saldivar, Francisco de Ovando, Juan Gallego, and Melchior Diaz.[44]

Of course, even those gentlemen who were not named captains or company commanders, were, in effect, considered officers within the unit rank structure. For example, Pedro de Sotomayor was named official "chronicler for the army."[45] A young Alonso Alvarez served as Coronado's page and standard bearer for the expedition.[46] Alvarez pre-

A nineteenth-century copy of an earlier German woodcut depicting suppliers accounting and preparing provisions. (*Author*)

sumably had a fine physique; such a flag-carrying ensign had to be capable of carrying a standard and wielding a sword in the other hand at the same time.[47]

As was typical of most conquistador forces (as opposed to the few professional armies in Europe), this was not a paid army. In a way, this would be seen to be an improvement, for armies during the Italian Wars were notorious for mutinying when their promised pay was not forthcoming from impoverished or dishonest employers.[48] Surely acting as a great incentive for sticking with the endeavor, the European volunteers with Coronado were to pay their own way and hope for a big bonanza. However, reflecting the impecunious condition of many of these gentlemen soldiers, Viceroy Mendoza, from his collected military chest, advanced "some aid . . . to the most needy soldiers."[49] While these advances or loans probably were meant to be used to obtain mounts and equipage and were not to be wasted in dissipation, such advance pay was risky. In the sixteenth century (and other centuries), soldiers had a reputation for not knowing how to wisely handle cash; "they would spend it idly."[50]

In sixteenth-century Mexico, this spendthrift tendency was especially well known, and it was hoped that "pay and enlistment bonus[es] given the recruits should be spent for practical things, such as arms, clothes and horses, and other things necessary for a successful conquest." Such members of an expedition were to purchase similar items, so that "the men will not be jealous of one another on account of their personal appearance or military equipment." In addition, officers were to make sure that the recruits not spend their advances "on trappings, gambling, and illicit things."[51]

And there was a respectable number of those recruits. Fortunately for historians, a muster roll exists for the Coronado Expedition.[52] That list tallies "two hundred and thirty odd horsemen" and sixty-two infantrymen.[53] As to the horsemen, who would be the men-at-arms, they each personally possessed anywhere from one horse each to several or more. Coronado had a string of twenty-two or twenty-three horses.[54]

Also fortunate for those historians who want to argue about the number of those not-quite-angels mustering on the point of a pin, the roll is but a partial listing of participants and equipment, itself acknowledging that it does not include "those who have gone in advance in company with the religious [personnel] and those waiting in Mexico who are going on this expedition and journey."[55] Thus, not only were some members of the European contingent not listed, it is also possible that some of those listed did not long accompany the expedition. Sixteenth-century muster rolls must be cautiously used, for the numbers listed soon may have shrunk due to sickness and desertion.[56]

For his part, Castaneda recalled "more than 300 Spaniards" in the European contingent.[57] Richard Flint and Shirley Cushing Flint, those close students of the endeavor who are making efforts to document every member of the expedition, counted at least sixty-seven men-at-arms not listed in the roll.[58] Especially when one considers the various side excursions and express or dispatch riders showing up during the two-and-a-half years of the expedition, over 350 fighting men of European extraction were involved in the invasions of Cibola, Tiguex, Quivira, and other lands.

Discounting for some exaggeration to please high officials for whom he apparently was writing, Pedro de Castaneda remembered that Viceroy Mendoza believed the expedition to be "a noble company."[59] As for Castaneda's own opinion, he thought "that they had on this expedition the most brilliant company ever collected in the Indies to go in search of new lands."[60]

However, in hindsight, Castaneda thought that the choice for captain general was unfortunate in that the commander had not, metaphorically, burned his ships (as Cortes actually did when he resolved to conquer Aztec Mexico or die in the attempt), for Coronado had left behind "estates and a pretty wife."[61] In other words, unlike many in the expedition, he had a home to go back to.[62]

But where were the original homes of most of the European contingent? Based on the known names, almost all of which are Spanish (or

Hispanicized), it would appear that all the Europeans making up the core of Coronado's force were Spanish (or Portuguese) in nationality. This is too broad a conclusion regarding ethnicity. European armies during the late fifteenth and early sixteenth centuries tended to have at least an international sprinkling in the ranks, if not among the officers. Indeed, they sometimes were so diverse as to be recognized as "Noah's Ark" armies.[63]

For example, during the Reconquista in the late 1400s, the foreign mercenaries in Spain included Sicilian troops, English archers, Swiss infantry, and Burgundian artillerymen.[64] During the Italian Wars, at the Battle of Ravenna in 1512, the Spanish forces had Italians, Sicilians, Greeks, Africans, and others.[65] In 1519, when the crowns of Spain and the Holy Roman Empire were united under Charles V, Spanish forces would be even more likely to contain Italians and Germans.[66]

One individual example of this international aspect of Spanish forces in the Americas was Girolamo Benzoni, an Italian who fought with conquistadors against the Indians of Nicaragua. Benzoni hardly found the Spaniards to be brothers-in-arms, for he described them as "so vainglorious that they never cease praising themselves," and he was offended that they would "boast that one Spaniard is worth four Germans, three Frenchmen, or two Italians."[67] Also, many Spaniards, in numbering their own army, would tend to count only their countrymen, including allied Italians and Germans as an afterthought.[68] This proud obnoxiousness certainly was little different from what Spain practiced in Europe, where its soldiery was taught to have a national arrogance and sense of superiority not far removed from that of Germans during the Second World War.[69]

Nonetheless, although individual Spaniards might not support the "band-of-brothers" soldierly ideal encompassing outlanders, Coronado's force undoubtedly contained representatives of other European nations. According to Herbert Bolton, among those identifiable:

> [T]here were five Portuguese, two Italians, one Frenchman, one Scotchman, and one German. . . . The Scot was "Tomas Blaque," obviously Blake or Black, who left in Mexico his wife Francisca de Rivera, widow of one of the earliest Spanish settlers there. . . . Juan Fioz, a German born in Worms, was bugler of the expedition, and was present "at all the major actions." . . . There were several other persons with non-Spanish names who may or may not have been of non-Spanish birth.[70]

Even as the wars of the sixteenth century became more religious in nature, the international aspect of the contending forces, although certainly lessened in relative and raw numbers, remained a constant. Germans and Irishmen in particular served under the Spanish colors.[71] Even Protestants sometimes joined Catholic armies to fight the Turks—if not other Protestants.[72] Indeed, sometimes the professional soldiers of the era had little or no affinity for faith. "They can show God no reason and no good conscience for their gadding about," complained a dour Martin Luther, "but have only a foolhardy desire or eagerness for war or for the leading of a free, wild life."[73]

Nonetheless, for simplicity's sake herein, the European members of Coronado's army usually will be referred to as Spaniards—who usually served as "only the nucleus" of a Spanish force in the Old World, "to which [they] gave the example of bravery, endurance, and especially arrogance."[74] That shorthand designation of "Spaniards" likely will irritate only the Portuguese, but their individual Iberian contributions with Coronado and elsewhere often will be noted.

Similar to the multinational nature of the Europeans with the captain general, there also were a variety of vocations and avocations represented, for not all of the command were haughty men-at-arms, unskilled at anything but fighting.[75] As noted, when speaking merely of soldiery, there also were footmen and artillerymen. But many of these fighters also had technical specialties required of such an army. In addition, there were other expedition members who were not considered fighting men.

At least one surgeon was attached to the command, although Castaneda later would describe him after a battle as being "unskillful."[76] The presence of this surgeon would not have been exceptional; demonstrating the rising military reputation of Spain as the sixteenth century advanced, there were field hospitals in that nation's armies in Europe at least by 1484.[77] During the sixteenth century (especially after the Coronado and De Soto Expeditions) the Spanish recognized that "[w]hen going on expeditions one should carry medicinal remedies to cure the diseases and wounds that usually occur in time of war, and especially an antidote against the poisonous plant."[78] Most likely—and this is relevant when considering the transport of the column—an army surgeon, like a ship's surgeon, would require "a massive wooden ironbound chest to contain . . . [a] long list of items."[79]

Regarding chaplains, during this Catholic-crusading era there probably seldom was an occasion to worry about the absence of clerics from any Spanish military endeavor. Charles V, in 1526, mandated that priests should be part of every conquistador effort in the New World— although they were intended to act more as missionaries than as chaplains.[80] Of course, chaplains could run the gamut from dedicated saintliness to outright wickedness. Also, in keeping with the times, the common folk of Europe often thought that most friars and monks, like lawyers, were worthless parasites.[81]

In Europe, where the chaplaincy standards often were wretched, there were occasionally priests with the Spanish army whose regular sinning broke half the Ten Commandments with enthusiastic gusto.[82] The more typical chaplains at least wrote letters home for those soldiers who were illiterate, but sometimes would not compose a soldier's will unless a bequest to the scrivener priest was included.[83]

As for Coronado and his force, he had a plethora of papal representatives, and none of them are recalled for being venal. Although these clerics really were tasked by their church to be missionaries to the Indians, the priests could not but help to serve as ex-officio chaplains as well. But in their enthusiasm to be with the vanguard, they sometimes apparently tended to neglect the soldiery in the main army.

As for historically specifying these Roman Catholic worthies, there is considerable confusion about all their names and identities and some confusion as to their numbers. If there were six clergymen, all six were Franciscans, meaning they all were likely footmen, for their order forbade them from riding on such a march.[84]

First, of course, according to Pedro de Castaneda, there was Friar Marcos de Niza. In addition, there was Friar Juan de Padilla, "a regular brother of the lesser order,"[85] and Friar Luis Descalona, a lay brother.[86] There also was Friar Juan de la Cruz and Friar Antonio Victoria.[87] Friar Padilla was a former soldier or "fighting man in his youth,"[88] and his influence over the rough-hewn soldiery was thereby obviously enhanced. There seemingly was at least one other cleric or elder with the expedition: Andres del Campos, a native of Portugal (apparently a layman).[89] However, the more-or-less official Franciscan history says that the five religious companions accompanying their leader, Marcos de Niza, were Father Juan de Padilla, Brother Luis de Ubeda, Father Antonio de Castilblanco, Father Juan de la Cruz (like Niza a Frenchman), and Brother Daniel (an Italian laybrother).[90] When coming up with a truthful list of clerics, there is much room for scholars and readers to choose as they might.

Probably at least one member of the expedition, another educated gentleman, was skilled in alchemy. An alchemist could not change a base metal into gold, but, as a sixteenth-century chemist, he would be expected to know the difference between gold and iron pyrite, between gold and copper, and between silver and lead. Coronado, in a letter to Mendoza, indicated that he had present "those who know about minerals."[91]

In addition, as will be shown, at least one or two of the expedition were skilled enough to be considered military engineers. Usually this attribute amounted to skill in pioneering abilities and siege knowledge gained during previous military service, rather than to formal education, although familiarity with the Roman classics could have been considered the equivalent to classwork.

Many of the soldiers and accompanying Indian allies obviously did double duty when it came to some other required specialties. At least one expedition member would have been a gunsmith whose job, in addition to fixing arquebuses, would be "to keep [the artillery] in condition."[92] Blacksmiths, farriers, and carpenters undoubtedly were represented among the soldiery (as well as among the Indian allies). Smiths would "make, repair, and provide all necessary iron articles for the army that may be out of order or worn out."[93] Farriers would be needed "to cure and shoe the horses and mules belonging to the army."[94] As for carpenters, they could "build boats for crossing rivers, lakes, and gulfs that often hinder and prevent explorations."[95]

Regarding the extraordinary stamina of many of the individual Spanish conquistadors, including those with Coronado, there was an inner strength that morale (or lack thereof) could affect but not completely override. As conceded by a Scottish scholar who saw plenty of death and heroism during the Second World War:

> Most Spaniards of the sixteenth century had the good fortune to "know" that allegiance to their faith and scrupulous regard for the Church's daily program of worship gave them the certainty of a life after death that was (as certainly) denied to heretics. From this state of mind they drew some—by no means all—of the strength that enabled them, few though they were, to overturn the Indies. . . . They, the soldiers of the Spanish conquests, may well have been superior as fighting men to any who were before them and to any who have followed after; and whatever we may say or pretend . . . we are unlikely to have again . . . men of such steely spirit, such invincible confidence in destiny.[96]

As for the personal, secular lives of the soldiers while on campaign, whether men-at-arms or footmen, they almost certainly followed the custom of soldiers before and since, becoming members of small squads but teaming up with one or two others in particular for the duration. These comrades, mates, buddies, bunkies, pals, or chums would mess together, share guard duty, and generally look out for each other.[97] It was later recalled that "some hidalgos of the army were baking bread themselves because they did not have anyone to bake it for them."[98]

When the expedition finally was assembled, to be reviewed by Viceroy Mendoza, it included a formidable assemblage of European men. According to one Spanish historian of New Spain, Coronado's force had "two hundred and seventy mounted men with lances, swords, and other hand weapons, some with coats of mail and sallets with visors, both of iron and of raw cowhide, and the horses with bardings of native blankets; and seventy infantrymen, both musketeers and harquesbusiers, and others with swords and bucklers."[99]

Of course, even this eighteenth-century Spanish estimate of the sixteenth century was too conservative. As noted above, it has been documented that there were many more Spaniards in the expedition than the total in the muster roll. Other historians before Flint and Cushing Flint also have presumed the numbers were greater than even Castaneda recalled. Arthur Aiton, however, went too far (at least with the infantry), estimating that there were "three hundred mailed horsemen, armed with lances and mounted on picked steeds from the viceroy's ranches, accompanied by two hundred foot-soldiers."[100]

Although according to a fresh look at the original handwritten muster roll of the expedition, the Spaniards obviously were placed into particular companies under certain captains,[101] even this organizational makeup likely would be replaced with expedient reorganizations under commanders picked for particular assignments. On the other hand, most of the military organizational specialties (to use the modern term) of the Europeans are discernible from their individual weaponry, as will be seen in detail.

# FIVE

# Arquebuses, Crossbows, Falconets, and Other Implements of War

Having authorized the European fighting personnel, Viceroy Mendoza and Captain General Coronado had to see to the outfitting of the expedition. This logistical portion of the endeavor supposedly would be simplified by the theory that this was to be a combined operation, with Coronado's force marching north along the west coast of Mexico and being resupplied and revictualed by ships hugging the shore. These were to be sent out by Mendoza. "After the whole force had left Mexico," recounted Pedro de Castaneda, "he ordered Don Pedro de Alarcon to set sail with two ships that were . . . on the South Sea [Pacific] coast . . . to take the baggage which the soldiers were unable to carry."[1]

Nonetheless, even if this plan had been successful and not been frustrated by incorrect geographical assumptions, Coronado's army would be on its own at least initially. Food for anticipated needs had to be carried. But, just as important for a military operation, weaponry had to be transported so as to be readily accessible for defensive or offensive action.

While much already has been written about the weapons carried on the expedition, much more information, both direct and circumstantial, is available. In the many areas in which there is no direct evidence regarding particular equipage (or the personnel handling that specific paraphernalia), recourse can be made to known European technologies and habits. While mildly speculative, this additional discussion should assist archaeologists regarding future discoveries along the suspected Coronado trail. Such reasoned speculation may not provide all the answers, but it will help at least in asking the right questions.

Many of the details that are known about the expedition's weaponry show that the assembled force was based on the then-current European model, although there certainly were supply limitations and differences among the individual members of the expedition and their possessions. There also were modifications of the European standards to fit perceived local conditions in this part of the Americas.

But the conclusion that the Spanish contingent, the real mailed fist of the expedition, was predominant in appearance as well as in combat effectiveness has come under revisionist or politically correct attack, coupled with a fair-minded attempt to give the native peoples of Mexico a fair shake. Consequently, one of the premier Coronado scholars has written, based on the original muster roll of the expedition:

> The expeditionaries, however, carried relatively few items of European arms and armor: dozens of swords, 19 crossbows, 21 arquebuses, a dozen steel helmets, and assorted pieces of body armor. Only a few of the wealthiest participants had anything like a full suit of metal armor. . . . [I]ts war gear was dominated by articles of indigenous make: quilted cotton armor, obsidian-edged weapons such as *macanas* (double-edged swords) and lances, and circular, feather-decorated shields. . . . [T]he expedition had a decidedly Mexican Indian appearance. More than 90 percent of the European members of the expedition carried indigenous arms and armor. The corresponding European goods were in short supply.[2]

This colorful viewpoint, in addition to undercounting some of the known European items, involves a partial misinterpretation of the data. It equates the terms in the muster roll "arms of the country" and "armor of the country," terms employed by the Spanish, to "native arms and armor," that is, copies of arms shouldered by and armor worn by indigenous natives.[3] Relying on sixteenth-century Spanish military nomenclature, "of the country" actually just meant that the items were not "of Castile"—not Spanish made.[4] In the case of armor, the term "of the country" indicated it was not Spanish-made plate armor.[5] Thus, presumably, even the finely made German armor worn by the Spanish soldiers in 1547 when they suppressed the Protestant prince of Saxony was "of the country."[6]

This parochial outlook regarding equipment was analogous to the official attitude regarding enlistments into strictly Spanish units in Europe. To be accepted one had to be a native of Aragon or Castile; it was not enough to be of dual Spanish parentage but born in Italy.[7]

Thus, arms of the country meant locally produced weaponry, presumably of European style, which would amount at least to the bare minimum requirement for the proper outfitting of the local militia: most likely swords and bucklers and light lances or javelins for the horsemen, and pikes, swords, and bucklers for the infantry.[8] As for "armor of the country," that was more equivalent to what the native warriors wore, but only to an extent. The Spaniards had started to adopt quilted cotton corselets rather than thick canvas jackets even prior to invading central Mexico. These quilted corselets were quite effective protection against arrows. They were especially effective when chain mail (more accurately just called mail) was worn under the corselet,[9] a method obviously used by many of Coronado's men-at-arms.

However, even these protective items would not have given Coronado's Spaniards (probably marching in the vanguard) "a decidedly Mexican Indian appearance." European soldiery had long worn brigandines or jacks for light armor—vests that had a quilted look, although stuffed with bits of metal instead of cotton—and this style certainly continued to 1540.[10] Indeed, the soldiers of Aragon of the fifteenth century wore excellently made quilted brigandine jackets.[11]

Therefore, the Spanish contingent, even any members young enough to be native born to the New World, essentially was a European military force, especially regarding its arms and partially regarding its armor. At most, the group had a decidedly frontier appearance. The Spanish adventurers, in their quest to see the elephant (if not find gold), would have attempted to portray their European roots every bit as much as red-coated Britons overseas[12] if for no other reason than to instill intimidation and fear in their enemies.[13] "The Spaniards of the days of Pizarro and Cortes, like their [English] contemporaries, . . . courted war as a mistress, and strove to meet her in their bravest array," wrote a Spanish arms and armor expert. They "devoted attention . . . to their armour and the temper of their weapons. . . . The Castilian loved the glint of shimmering steel and the ring of a true forged blade."[14] Therefore, no self-respecting Spaniard with Coronado would have departed New Galicia with a wooden sword (even with imbedded obsidian chips), nor would he be permitted to join the expedition so inadequately armed.[15]

An early seventeenth-century print showing Spaniards fighting Spaniards in Peru in the 1540s. (*Author*)

Finally, further buttressing the fact that Coronado's Spaniards were fully equipped for combat even against a sixteenth-century foe, there was the realistic possibility that the entrada authorized by Viceroy Mendoza would come up against the more numerous—but without significant Indian allies—rival expedition of De Soto. Such a potential confrontation, of which both Mendoza and Coronado were aware, as evidenced in the viceroy's instructions to his captain general, meant there could be a violent collision on the European model with the clash of Spanish arms.[16] Such occasions between rival conquistadors did happen in the New World.

Nonetheless, much about the war materiel carried by Coronado's force, especially the metallic protective gear, is more obscure and ill defined than it is to be considered lacking in attendance. Very few pieces of ordnance and armor can be excluded as improbable. As students of the conquistadors have concluded, "To what extent the Conquistadors employed protective armor depended on the campaign and the finances available."[17] Based on these criteria, Coronado's expedition was at least reasonably blessed with steel accoutrements, limited more by the anticipated field of operations than by any lack of initial funding and dearth of preparation.

The muster roll lists a majority of the men-at-arms and the footmen and their personal equipment brought to service.[18] But it is a partial roll. Therefore, as to both personnel and equipment, this document is only a starting point. Other military equipment was issued from general stores and magazines to supplement property personally owned.[19]

The presence of this additional, state-owned issue should not be surprising. In Spanish America, pieces of equipment (such as pikes) were issued as needed for particular military operations.[20] In addition, while not as generous as the British later would be with their North American colonists, the Spanish crown, especially starting in the late 1530s, began providing more weaponry and armor for the local militias, although certainly in a niggardly fashion.[21]

In the case of the Coronado Expedition, the viceroy himself apparently provided or lent some weapons and accoutrements from his personal stock or provincial arsenal, for the captain general later asserted that Mendoza gave to some of the Spaniards "arms, horses, and money and to others lances and arms of the country."[22] Indeed, when the administration of Mendoza was subject to review only a few years later, Coronado testified that the viceroy then had a very well-stocked arsenal of "army stores of his own containing many corselets, armors, breastplates, cross-bows, harquebuses, shields, spears, lances, much ammunition, and other types of weapons."[23] While apparently most of these items were collected to fight the Mixton War after the departure of the expedition,[24] obviously the viceroy already had some sort of established ordnance depot in Mexico City. When appointed viceroy, he specifically was tasked with reporting on what artillery and munitions were needed for defense of the colony and was to make sure that every resident Spaniard possessed arms.[25]

As for the truly armored headpieces of Coronado's men (both cavalry and infantry), according to the muster roll there were up to fifty, including one for the captain general. Some of the pieces of "head armor" theoretically could have been mere steel or iron skullcaps to wear under soft hats, although this type of protection in the sixteenth century was more popular among German and Swiss infantry.[26] In any event, well over forty of the cavalry had European-style helmets (or pieces of head armor), some of them casques. Several of the men-at-arms had only "native" head protection or headpieces "of the country."[27] Only two of the infantrymen had metal helmets (both casques).[28] Steel or iron headpieces, while an encumbrance during a sun-baked march or in a sweltering jungle, were especially handy when the Spaniards assaulted native fortresses and had to endure a shower of stones and other missiles from above.[29]

Presumably most of these metal headpieces listed in the roll were open, as opposed to close helmets (enclosing and protecting the entire head), although there probably was at least one helmet that belonged with a full suit of armor that may have been a close helmet.[30] For those who were not officers or veteran soldiers, the metal headgear likely were catch-as-catch-can, perhaps handed down from father to son. Therefore, there probably were some old-fashioned *chapels de fer,* or kettle hats (steel pots, not unlike British and American helmets of the First World War); more advanced *cabassets,* which had a curious pear-stem projection on top; and perhaps even the iconic morions or morion-cabassets, the combed morion eventually becoming the dress helmet of the modern Vatican Guard.[31] The morion was so identified with the Spanish during the Dutch wars of the late sixteenth century that they all, apparently of whatever variation and wherever produced, came to be called Spanish morions.[32]

As for Coronado's helmet (and there is a good chance he carried more than one in his baggage), it was, according to his own words, "gilded and glittering," like his armor.[33] The helmet has been portrayed as being either a morion or, more likely, a burgonet—an elegant, open-faced helmet with a center comb.[34] As will be noted, it also could have a decorative plume.

There was that cheaper version of a burgonet, the casque, which, although it could be elegantly decorated, often was poor protection.[35] In addition to the two infantrymen, four of the men-at-arms with Coronado wore casques. Of course, depending on the status or luck of the wearer, any of the steel helmets might have been beautifully engraved.

There is much controversy among historians and antiquarians regarding the helmets likely worn by some of Coronado's troops. "The comb-morion helmet . . . is often mistakenly depicted as the typical headpiece of the early Spanish conquerors, but actually represents a form dating to the late 16th century," wrote Florida historian Walter Karcheski regarding a museum display in 1990.[36] "Hollywood notwithstanding, the classic morion . . . evolved too late to have been used by the early Conquistadors," he added confidently.[37]

Despite this criticism of popular conceptions, a couple of recognized European arms experts have defended the antiquity of the classic morion. "The generally received idea that the comb grew progressively taller in the course of the 16th century is well and truly contradicted by [known] examples. . . . The varying height of the crown of the helmet cannot be used as an indication of date either," wrote the respected Funckens of Belgium.[38] Other experts have found comb morions to date as early as 1530 to 1540.[39] In addition, there are some contemporaneous references to morions. In late 1533, an Inca noble fighting against the Spanish armed himself with European arms and armor, including "a morion upon his head."[40]

Morions, whether combed or not, often had attached cheek pieces, although few have survived the years.[41] The helmet also might have plume holders on the rear crown.[42]

Nonetheless, when artists such as N. C. Wyeth and Frederic Remington have portrayed Coronado and his men-at-arms in high-combed morions, that probably was just artistic license. While Coronado's conquistadors would have been in armor when marching toward battle, the more-open helmets like the morion were favored by arquebusiers and crossbowmen, who needed a wide range of vision, not by mounted men who wanted to shield against the anticipated missiles of arquebusiers and crossbowmen.[43] Regular men-at-arms of this era probably more often wore a *sallet*.[44] Sallets could have visors or be completely open-faced.[45]

Seemingly curious is the fact that a couple of the mounted men possessed, according to some translations, a "chin piece" but no helmet.[46] Although this sounds like close helmet visors without the helmet, such an interpretation is mistaken. While the Western Hemisphere's archaeological record apparently is barren regarding this so far, it is certain that what is meant is a *buffe*, a *volante* piece, or a falling beavor—sometimes spelled bevor or beaver.[47] As noted by Walter Karcheski, the Spanish in the Americas called such protection a *barbera*.[48] These beavors were parts of armor, used with open helmets, that were neck pieces that protected the throat and rose up to protect the face, including the chin and mouth.[49] Even without a helmet, such a face guard, strapped on behind the neck or attached to a breastplate, could be critical protection for a mounted man towering over a pedestrian Indian armed with a bow or a spear. Indeed, in such a tactical situation a chin piece by itself probably would be better protection than an open helmet without a beavor.

Left, a morion with
cheek pieces from the
sixteenth century at the
Museo de América,
Madrid. (*Luis García*)
Right, a Spanish falling
bevor with gorget, c.
1500. (*Art Institute of
Chicago*)

While it seems that other contemporaneous Spanish expeditions do
not specifically mention the presence of such chin pieces or beavors,
this might be because the Coronado Expedition took to heart the words
of Cabeza de Vaca regarding the prowess of the region's natives and
their bows and poisoned arrows. The better educated and more experienced Spanish recruits undoubtedly knew of occasions in Europe when
a beavor meant the difference between life and death on the battlefield,
especially when enemy archers were about.[50] In any event, there were a
surprising twenty beavors on the expedition.[51]

Somewhat similar to the use of beavors were gorgets; one is noted
specifically, and others among Coronado's men may be implied by the
occasional mention of neck pieces or other nonspecific armor (especially mail). Although by the eighteenth century, gorgets had shrunk to
mere ceremonial decorations of rank (later to be used as ostentatious
Nazi regalia), in the fifteenth, sixteenth, and seventeenth centuries they
actively protected the upper chest, the neck (when high-collared), and
(occasionally) the shoulders. Shrinking remnants of the days of full
body armor when they first appeared in the 1400s, gorgets could be
made of plate (two pieces, front and back) or of mail.[52]

But the torso also needed protection. According to the muster roll
there were about a dozen cuirasses and at least a half dozen corselets,
almost exclusively belonging to the mounted contingent.

The cuirasses and corselets in the sixteenth century were steel
breastplates, although both had started off being made of leather. A
cuirass, as the term was used, usually included a backplate.[53] The cuirass
of the sixteenth century was tested to be musketproof, whereas the
lighter corselet was only pistol proof.[54]

But armor need not be solid or plate metal. Spain, like the rest of Europe, had a long tradition of using mail for body protection, but the Spaniards seemed to retain its occasional use longer than other Western countries.[55] By the sixteenth century, for reasons of economy and weight, mail apparently had a resurgence among adherents, especially mounted men, as reflected in the statistics of the Coronado Expedition, where forty of the men-at-arms had mail coats or jackets, which also might include hoods (coifs).[56] In military theaters in which the opposition lacked crossbows and did not have powerful longbows, mail still was defensively effective.[57] However, although a shirt of mail weighed less than plate armor, it placed all its weight on the wearer's shoulders and was just as subject to rust.[58]

A few other pieces of purely European armor were listed in the muster, such as a couple of gauntlets for mounted men and several knee pieces for infantrymen. Gauntlets—if plate, probably laminated at the wrist—were to protect the sword hand and wrist.[59] The knee guards (some probably full shinguard greaves) were usually used to protect the forward leg of pikemen, but in Coronado's force they would be used similarly by an arquebusier, a crossbowman, and numerous swordsmen undoubtedly for protecting the lead leg.[60]

Nonetheless, for this army, much of the armor was the lighter stuff that was popular and practical both in Europe and in Mexico. According to the muster roll, about fifty of the horsemen and about five of the footmen wore buckskin jackets. Sword-and-buckler men in particular might wear, in addition to a helmet, either a stiff leather jerkin or a studded jacket or brigandine, a vest with small plates of iron or horn stitched between two layers of canvas.[61]

Then there was that even-less-expensive and less-elaborate protection. This was the local version of light armor, adopted from the Indians, which consisted of a quilted jacket made of cotton or maguey fibers, stuffed with a thick padding of cotton. When properly made, these jackets were capable of stopping numerous arrows.[62] One of De Soto's captains serving at the same time as Coronado's force came out of an Indian fight in Florida having survived over twenty arrow hits.[63] However, at the outset, only about a half dozen of Coronado's mounted men wore this armor of the country, according to the muster roll.

At least in the view of those who were departing from semitropical portions of New Spain, the lighter, nonsteel protection was a reasonable adaptation to accommodate local climate and geography. By contrast, the luckless army of Narvaez, headed for Florida, had been "recruited in Spain rather than the Spanish Caribbean, [and] the men wore hot, heavy breast- and back-plates as well as metal helmets." Therefore, at least prior to battle, these weighty pieces seemed more of an impediment that caused painful chafing than an advantage in combat.[64]

Somewhat similarly, it can be argued that the horses of Coronado's mounted men were subject to military adaptation to the climate regarding armor. During the Reconquista of Spain, it was unusual "to find one [man-at-arms] whose horse had no covering, or the neck of whose horse was without steel mail."[65] By the late fifteenth century, this equine barding was in the form of plate armor.[66] However, and this would affect the employment of cavalry in the Coronado Expedition, such armor, along with the saddle, would add over seventy pounds to be carried by the mount.[67] As the Portuguese found in North Africa, this additional metallic horse furniture could cause heat exhaustion in the horses in a desert climate.[68] Whether or not such horse armor was employed, a Spanish war horse would be expected to be "stout and strong" in order to accommodate a "high-peaked Moorish saddle, with its shoe stirrup often of solid bronze."[69]

Horse armor is listed only once in the muster roll. Coronado, for his twenty-two or twenty-three steeds, took along "three or four sets of horse armor."[70] One might assume that if he took the paraphernalia all the way to Cibola, the captain general shared his extra sets of bard with a couple of his officers.

While armor usually is considered defensive in nature, soldiers, of course, need offensive, man-killing implements. The weaponry of the Coronado Expedition reflected both European requirements and variations seemingly adapted for local conditions.

To start with the relatively big guns, six small cannon were in the weaponry.[71] The only real certainty about these weapons, other than the fact that they were provided by Viceroy Mendoza,[72] is that much remains historically uncertain. In an age in which calibers of artillery pieces were not standardized, there is a chance that this bronze ordnance, "numerous small cannons," had "varying sizes of bores ranging from three to six inches."[73]

The mountings of this ordnance will be discussed at length later, but the guns would have had to set on some sort of carriage or stand. While most nations in the sixteenth century did not paint their gun carriages, "[i]n the first half of the century Imperial and Spanish gun-carriages were sometimes painted black, with their metal-work in red."[74]

As for artillery personnel, on the battlefield (as contrasted with siege emplacements), the majority of pieces, of whatever size, were served by three men: the gunner, the gunner's mate or mattross, and a laborer. The gunner ladled the powder and sponged the bore between discharges, and the other two members of the gun crew provided the muscle in aiming the gun. One of these two also covered the vent hole, probably with a very heavy leather glove, during the dangerous procedure of ladling the powder. The mattross brought the lighted match, on a linstock, to the primed vent hole while the gunner moved back several yards when ignition was to occur.[75] While some soldiers (especially men-at-arms) still tended to look down on artillerists, such technicians, handling large amounts of powder and carrying lighted matches, courted danger even before an army came face to face with the opposition.

Presumably these ordnance pieces carried with Coronado were produced in Spain, although this need not be true.[76] They might even have been local products; as early as 1522–1524, Hernando Cortes, in addition to setting up a manufactory to make gunpowder, had used the copper-casting skills of the Aztecs and other native Mexicans to cast cannon.[77] Similarly, Diego Almagro (the younger) was having artillery and other arms and armor manufactured in Peru at least as early as 1541–1543.[78]

Wherever they were cast, there has been a reasonable assumption by most historians that the six guns were all the same caliber—more or less—in this era of ordnance inexactitude. As will become apparent in a discussion in chapter 8, it might be significant regarding their battlefield employment that the six guns were called *versillos* in the Coronado documents.[79] *Versos*, or *emseriles* or *pedereros*, was the Spanish name for an early type of swivel gun (nominally breechloaders), known by the English as fowlers, bases, and murderers.[80] "Versillos" would be a diminutive form of "versos," but that does not necessarily mean "smaller"; it might be a regionalism or a term of affection.[81]

But classifying something a swivel gun is open to technical interpretation. Such breech-loading guns, forged out of iron rather than cast and called hailshot pieces, were being made in Flanders as early as 1470.[82] Despite their obvious obsolescence, such forged iron swivel guns, sometimes integrated with bronze parts, still were being used on shipboard at the time of the Spanish Armada.[83] It is possible, but not likely, that Coronado's guns were of this primitive ilk. However, it also apparently has been assumed that these versillos were not breechloaders.

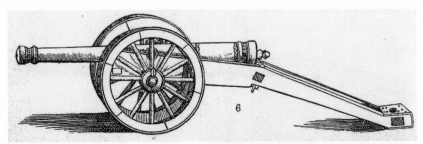

Top, a falconet. Right, A sixteenth-century engraving of an artillery park. (*Author*)

In any event, because of their diminutive caliber, these pieces with Coronado most often have been called falconets by knowledgeable military historians, using the standardized nomenclature established by the French later in the sixteenth century.[84] A falconet was the smallest piece in the French system, having a barrel about the size of a small modern recoilless rifle (although considerably heavier, from about three hundred to five hundred pounds)[85] and often with wheels only up to a man's waist.[86] It should not be assumed that the small caliber meant they were only defensive weapons. On shipboard such falconets were not only used to repel boarders, they were considered offensive man-killing weaponry, used to clear enemy decks, like the stereotypical swivel guns.[87] Because of this confusion or technical vagueness regarding Coronado's "cannon," they usually will be referred to as falconets in this volume.[88]

However, artillery has not captured the popular mind when the general reader thinks of the conquest of the New World. The conquistadors are best known for introducing hand firearms into the New World,

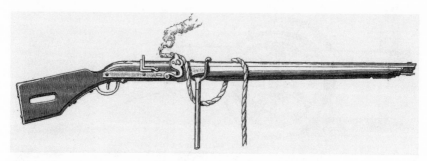

An artist's rendering of a sixteenth-century matchlock gun. (*Author*)

weapons that supposedly terrified the natives. The firearms initially carried by the Spanish marksmen were arquebuses. In an era where the production of weaponry and the creation of art intersected, many of the early firearms were manufactured in Italy and sold for export.[89]

But not everyone appreciated this new art form, especially men-at-arms who could be killed by the penetrating power that exceeded that of crossbows and longbows. The French knight Bayard, who would be killed by an arquebus in 1524, believed it wrong "that a man of spirit should be exposed to be killed by a miserable stone or iron ball against which he cannot defend himself."[90]

About 1510 to 1520, these firearms had advanced to the stage where the soldier did not manually have to apply the burning match (or fuse) to the touchhole for the powder to ignite. This advancement, the matchlock, incorporated a trigger mechanism whereby the match, held in place by a serpentine clamp, snapped into the priming pan and set off the chain-reaction explosion.[91]

These matchlocks were more rudimentary than the more mechanical wheel locks, a design that may not have been invented until about 1550–1560.[92] Being rudimentary, matchlocks were relatively inexpensive weapons.[93] Being rudimentary, they also could be repaired in-country, sometimes with parts produced by native artisans.[94]

However, this primitive nature had at least one disadvantage: the match obviously would not be kept burning on a long march; it would have to be ignited by flint and steel.[95] Therefore, the arquebus was not brought into action quickly; it was not useful in a sudden, unexpected ambush or attack. And when trouble was expected in "rain, mist, or wind," the touchhole priming would have to be held under the armpit and the lighted match held within a cupped hand.[96]

While the contemporary accounts usually do not specify whether arquebuses were lightweight ones or heavy ones requiring extra support when firing, this distinction is often not historically important. As a practical matter, the lighter and heavier arquebuses were identical and the technicalities usually did not affect their tactical employment. Both types used the matchlock system for igniting the powder to send the lead ball toward the enemy.[97] Although aiming an arquebus in the sixteenth century was less than precise, an unlucky man as far as five hundred paces away could be killed by a scratch shot fired by a lucky marksman.[98]

Later in the sixteenth century, after 1520, Spain was the innovator again in expanding the use of an even heavier firearm, the musket. This weapon, when firing, needed the support of a forked stick near the muzzle.[99] While still a matchlock, the musket had increased killing power and supposedly could send its ball through one armored man-at-arms and into the body of an unlucky cavalryman riding behind.[100] Again, contemporary chroniclers often were not discriminating in identifying whether weapons were arquebuses or muskets.[101] Thus, although original Coronado documents may say arquebus, this does not necessarily foreclose musket.

Therefore, either type could have accompanied Coronado, although the twenty-five listed in the muster were said to be arquebuses (and probably were).[102] The Spanish .66- to .72-caliber arquebus (imprecise in its bore) was more infantryman friendly at ten pounds, half the weight of a twenty-pound Spanish musket.[103]

In Europe, whether arquebusiers or musketeers, Spaniards with firearms would more likely not wear either helmets or breastplates.[104] But this did not always hold true with arquebusiers in the Americas.[105] As of 1540, and this is reflected in the muster roll, an occasional helmet still would be found among otherwise-unarmored arquebusiers, even in Europe.[106]

Arquebusiers, when on the march, would either have individual rounds of powder and shot in a dozen wooden tubes attached to a bandolier (called the Twelve Apostles) or carry their basic issue of black powder in a wooden flask on a shoulder strap and their ball ammunition in a haversack.[107] Often, at least in the latter part of the sixteenth century, the powder flasks were issued by the government, being all painted black, with stripes, and carrying the quartered crest of Castile and Leon.[108]

Coronado's force, not unlike other Spanish expeditions of the 1540s, was not limited to arquebuses or muskets when it came to hand-held projectile weaponry. The little army had almost as many crossbowmen as arquebusiers listed in the muster: twenty-one.[109] As will be seen, the use of the crossbow by Coronado's army has become an archaeological blessing.

In the Middle Ages, crossbows, also called arbalests in the early years, were made of laminated horn or whalebone.[110] Even with this primitive construction, the bolts or quarrels (then like miniature arrows with metal projectile points and fletching) of these weapons proved lethal to armored men-at-arms, so the European baronial class sought the help of the pope in banning the use of such egalitarian ordnance.[111] It was not until the latter part of the fifteenth century that steel bows, with wooden stocks, came along.[112] This powerful bow had a killing range of well over three hundred yards, although the deadly accuracy of a William Tell was only guaranteed at sixty-five to seventy yards.[113]

While the makeup of the bowstrings apparently is not certain, one expert has concluded that the medieval and Renaissance crossbows used "several dozen turns of thin twine, of pure hemp or flax" such as "sail-makers sewing twine." Such a string would resist being stretched out.[114] Oiling would help prevent damage from the elements.[115]

As for the crossbow string being stretched prior to firing, this also was subject to mechanical innovation that meant crossbowmen did not have to have the supposed Herculean physiques of longbowmen. Although there are no hints as to the methods used by Coronado's crossbowmen, the available technologies to draw the crossbow string included contrivances such as the early cord-and-pulley system, the primitive belt hook, the more advanced screw–and-handle method, and the more practical goat's-foot lever (cranked like a manual automobile jack).[116] While it is not unlikely that Coronado's marksmen used the goat's-foot lever or its equivalent, it also is possible they employed the more sophisticated mechanism eventually favored by the famous Genoese crossbowmen, a crank windlass.[117]

Despite innovations such as the crank windlass, the crossbow in Europe saw a noticeable decline in use even during the relatively brief span of the Italian Wars. Presaging the extinction of the crossbow as a military weapon, during the fighting in Italy in 1521, Gascon crossbow-men of the French army found themselves being out of range when they came under the fire of imperial arquebusiers.[118] Reportedly, crossbow-

A sixteenth-century woodcut depicting crossbowmen target shooting. Note the dog retrieving a quarrel. (*Author*)

men disappeared in regular set-piece warfare in Europe by 1522 or 1525, although the weapon was employed defensively by those in fortifications until about 1530–1535.[119]

Indicating that the disappearance of the crossbow was influenced by such tactical considerations, when European *expeditionnaires* confronted Ottoman forces, "who were armed and disciplined after the European fashion,"[120] the Europeans abandoned the old technology. Therefore, the Germans, Spanish, and Italians taking Tunis in 1535 were noticeably lacking crossbows.[121] Similarly, the Portuguese opposing the Ottomans in Abyssinia in the 1540s, like their Turkish opponents, relied on the arquebus when it came to firing projectiles.[122] While the crossbow remained a favorite European hunting weapon, it, like the English longbow, was virtually unknown in warfare after 1572.[123]

However, for various reasons, including the fact that they were not facing opponents using gunpowder, the Spaniards invading the New World did not quickly abandon the bowed weapon. Among other conquistadors, Cortes had a company of crossbowmen with him in Mexico, and Francisco Pizarro had crossbowmen with him in both his first (1524) and second (1532–1533) expeditions to Peru.[124] Crossbows still were part of the Spanish conquistador arsenal in 1566–1568 when Juan Pardo explored what is now the Southeastern United States.[125] Probably, as was the case with the English and their beloved national weapon, the longbow,[126] occasional but noted successes with crossbows discouraged a complete abandonment of the technology. Nonetheless, from the first, the Spaniards in the New World worked to increase their reliance on hand-held firearms.

Surprisingly, the crossbow continued to have several battle advantages equivalent to those of the arquebus. First, unlike with the English longbow, neither the crossbow nor the arquebus required a lifetime of practice to become proficient.[127] In addition to needing less training to gain competence, the precombat physical stress would be less for a crossbowman than for a bow archer. Like an arquebusier, the crossbowman could be ready to fire without having "to hold the draw weight" as an archer would have to do. And, like an arquebusier, a crossbowman would need little room to maneuver left and right for a shot, perhaps less.[128]

The crossbow even had some advantages over matchlocks. First, and this would especially apply to frontier wars, where resupply would be more of a problem, crossbows represented a less-sophisticated technology. Presumably, some damage to crossbows could be more easily repaired in the field by not-so-skilled soldiers.[129] Second, ammunition—the bolts or quarrels—could be more readily manufactured in the field, a situation not so applicable to firearms requiring gunpowder.[130] Third, crossbows could throw firebombs into a besieged fortress.[131] Finally, unlike the arquebus, a crossbow was silent when fired, and there was no explosive recoil.[132]

However, a crossbowman, compared and contrasted with an arquebusier or musketeer, would have to accept certain limitations. First, the speed of fire was much slower than in the case of a bow archer, and it might have been slower than that of a trained arquebusier.[133] Second, the trajectory of a crossbow's bolt is not as flat as a bullet. Like a regular arrow, the crossbow would have to be aimed high to accommodate more of a gravitational drop than with a firearm, depending, of course, on the distance to the target.[134] This would make accuracy more of a problem than with even problematic arquebuses.

But if military crossbows saw their eclipse during the sixteenth century, other ancient weapons, although on the wane, were hanging on. These other weapons were hafted weapons or pole arms of various types.

Pikes, in Renaissance Europe, developed into both a defensive weapon against cavalry and an offensive weapon against other compact groups of the enemy.[135] However, against an enemy who was able to shoot missiles into the ranks of the pikemen and then disperse in retreat, the pike was not the best of choices, although the defensive armor usually worn by pikemen in Europe was a point in their favor.[136]

Another disadvantage was that it took longer to train a pikeman than an arquebusier or a musketeer, and a pikeman had to have a more impressive physique to begin with.[137]

Adding to the physical demands, pikes got longer as the sixteenth century wore on. While this change enhanced their defensive and offensive capabilities, it also meant they became heavier and more unwieldy. Pikemen on the march in Europe had to stow their pole arms in baggage wagons.[138] Nonetheless, especially during the Italian Wars of the first decades of the sixteenth century, a healthy percentage of pikes still were needed to protect arquebusiers (who lacked a subsequent invention: the bayonet). Indeed, in wet weather, the pike was by far the more reliable weapon.[139]

Recently, based on the recovery of an apparent ferrule (metal butt tip) at a Hopi village, there has been speculation that the men of the Coronado Expedition, even the infantrymen, carried lances, not pikes.[140] Especially during the first conquistador period, even up to 1550, with the crown providing some weapons and the individuals sometimes being individually responsible, pikes definitely still were in use by the Spaniards, whether in anticipation of European or native opponents.[141] To insist there were no pikes with Coronado, particularly when half-pikes and modified pikes would have been available, is pedantic.[142]

As for the halberd—a combination of a short pike and a hatchet blade—this colorful weapon (so often seen in modern Shakespearean plays) "was not adopted by the Spaniards," according to historian F. L. Taylor, when speaking of the Spanish military establishment in Europe.[143] However, this must be an overstatement, at least regarding Spain's colonial forces of the sixteenth century, for numerous period illustrations, from both European and native Indian artists, show the occasional halberd in use.[144] In addition, a sixteenth-century cartouche on a map shows Spanish halberds in use at the port city of Cadiz.[145] Finally, an early history of the conquest of Mexico states that in addition to cannon, arquebuses, crossbows, and swords, the Spaniards also fought with halberds.[146]

Therefore, it is not surprising that at least one arms historian determined that the halberd "was regularly used in their [the Spaniards'] conquest and settlement of Mexico and was naturally part of the military equipment carried on the expeditions of De Soto, Coronado and Juan de Onate."[147]

But there probably would not have been as many halberds as pikes, for, while the halberd's popularity began to drop as early as the first quarter of the fifteenth century, the pike continued to gain in reputation well into the seventeenth.[148] Nonetheless, the possibility of one or more halberds being taken along by Coronado's men, most of whom apparently were individually responsible for providing their own arms and armor, cannot be discounted.

Steel swords, of course, would be carried by all or many of the Spaniards, although those carried by the men-at-arms are not even especially noted in the muster roll.[149] To the militant Spanish upper class, the classic sword represented the trinity of strength, justice, and the Christian cross.[150] As early as 1525, even the youngest members of the Spanish militia were noted for walking around with swords as sidearms.[151] With such a national demand, by 1500 the Spanish cities of Toledo, Valencia, and Bilbao were manufacturing centers for edged weapons, with Toledo in particular being known for the quality of its sword blades.[152] While Italy might have set the fashion for armor, it is clear that Spanish swords long were imported into Italy.[153]

The edged weapons carried by Spanish soldiery would have included both the two-handed and rapier-type swords, with the rapiers sometimes supplemented with a buckler (a shield, sometimes called a target).[154] It has been said that sixteenth-century Spaniards had a "national love of the sword and buckler."[155] Regarding Coronado's infantrymen, of the approximately fifty swords mentioned in the muster roll, only one was a two-handed weapon.[156]

The Spanish and the Italians, in the early days of the sixteenth century, led the way with the rapier, a sword with a more stylish guard and a lighter (but still appropriately long) blade that originally was good for both thrusting and cutting. However, eventually, the hacking gave way to thrusting, and the rapier often was employed with a dagger or buckler in the other arm, or, in the absence of those auxiliary implements, a cloak wrapped around the nonsword arm.[157] The muster roll notes about a dozen daggers, almost exclusively among the footmen.

Spanish gentlemen in particular were pictured carrying the lightweight rapiers, and the stereotypical engraving on the blade (in Latin) was, "Draw me not without reason and sheath me not without honor."[158] Pizarro's rapier used in the conquest of Peru was produced in Valencia, with an ornate hilt and handguard and a rigid and diamond-shaped blade.[159]

Therefore, the Spanish core under Coronado was a formidable little army by itself, especially keeping in mind that the muster roll was but a mere minimum for both the weaponry and the men. Muster rolls of colonial eras are almost inherently partial lists.[160]

But as well equipped as it was, the Coronado Expedition was not a typical military force compared with detachments then operating in Europe. This deviation from the European norm held for the composition of the force's personnel and their weaponry.

In the relative dearth of firearms and comparative plenty regarding crossbows, Coronado's force was unlike Spanish armies then operating in Europe. There, Spain's successful military prowess was one in which "[t]he most important result of this mental and physical resiliency was the development of the use of firearms by the footsoldier."[161] Seemingly, in this case, Spain exhibited a typical belief of a first-rate power, one that has so often resulted in disaster: that unconventional wars in the backwaters against a more primitive foe deserved second-rate materiel.

But this convenient conclusion may not be warranted. Perhaps it was the Spanish in New Spain who were demonstrating that military adaptability so admired (and previously mentioned) by historian F. L. Taylor. Skepticism about Coronado's force being short-changed in the ordnance area may be appropriate because neither firearms (including artillery) nor crossbows were the weapon really feared by the indigenous people with whom the Spanish came into contact during the sixteenth century. There was another offensive weapon to be counted.

The Coronado Expedition, also unlike the Spanish forces in Europe, was not populated mostly with infantrymen. The majority of the Spaniards in the contingent were mounted men, and this was not just a recognition that the west of the North American continent was a land of wide open spaces yearning not to be fenced in. Cavalrymen were the not-so-secret weapon of the conquistadors.

As indicated, while the sixteenth century saw the decline of the mounted knight and the rise of the despised man who fired missiles or who poked with pikes, such men-at-arms still were, in effect, the tanks of the era. Even in Europe, "[n]o other troops could develop the driving power of a squadron of charging men-at-arms."[162] The war horses of the conquistadors, perhaps even slightly more massive than the average coursers upon which mounted European knights relied, probably were from fourteen hands, three inches to fifteen hands, two inches high, which is a lot of persuasion.[163] When the Aztecs first saw the "deer" upon which the Spaniards were mounted, they thought the animals were "as tall as the roof of a house."[164]

Regardless of size, war equines were all the more impressive in the New World, where there were no pike-wielding infantry squares. An Italian participant in the fighting between the Spanish and the natives, Girolamo Benzoni, wrote that when it came to the horse, the Indians "dread this very spirited animal more than all the arms the Spaniards have used against them." According to this observer, the Indians admitted this fact "publicly [and] it is not the valour of the Christians, nor their arms, artillery, lances, swords, or cross-bows that have subdued them, but the fear, the fright, inspired by their horses."[165] Benzoni had spoken to a native chief in Nicaragua who said his fellows successfully battled the Spanish one day, "But at last, most of us were so frightened by the impetus of the horses, as to take flight."[166] According to Benzoni's way of thinking, while the Spanish seemingly never failed when they had horses, they certainly never succeeded when they were without them.[167]

Nunez Cabeza de Vaca, who had actually traversed the region Coronado was planning to enter, agreed with the general military efficacy of equines. For combat in the open field, he believed that unlike crossbows and arquebuses, "the horses will best subdue, being what the natives universally dread."[168]

As for the weaponry of these terrifying mounted Spaniards, it has been mentioned that those pieces would include swords and lances. Although the origins are obscure, wheel-lock cavalry pistols perhaps had been introduced as early as 1515–1534.[169] They appeared in regular European warfare sometime in the 1540s.[170] However, although a mounted German gentleman adventurer serving with the Spanish in South America during 1538–1539 possessed wheel-lock pistols,[171] probably no such weaponry would have been available to any of Coronado's men-at-arms. Unlike the Germans, Spanish horse furniture that provided for pistol holsters dated only from about 1547.[172] It was only later in the sixteenth century that the Spanish mounted men began to discard the lance and replace it with the wheel-lock pistol.[173]

Finally, Coronado's column took along some dogs, presumably mostly the notorious war dogs of the conquistadors. War dogs were mixed breeds of wolfhounds, deerhounds, and mastiffs, greatly favored by the Spanish for guard duties and to run down or torment natives.

A print showing a Spanish mounted attack on native warriors in Peru
in the 1530s. (*Author*)

Sometimes these dogs wore their own quilted armor and studded collars.[174] When the Aztecs observed the hounds of Cortes, they considered them "enormous, with flat ears and long dangling tongues," with
eyes of "a burning yellow."[175] In a cosmic-justice sort of way, the use of
these devastating creatures against the Aztecs was righteous, for
Mesoamerican civilization was cannibalistic regarding humans and
apparently had dog meat on its regular cultural menu.[176]

Fortunately, such dogs with Coronado, although eventually contro-
versial, never gained the notoriety of the dogs with other Spanish leaders, such as De Soto. With the Coronado Expedition, there was no
early need for such hounds.[177] However, since dogs sometimes were
trained to retrieve crossbow bolts, the dogs with the expedition occasionally might have been used for that, especially on the open prairie.[178]

In summary, the Spanish field force of Francisco Vasquez de
Coronado was, at least on paper, a tidy, efficient, and well-outfitted little army that could deliver quite a punch in battle, especially because
this campaign, unlike that of De Soto, would not see much of the
indigenous guerrilla tactics so successful in swamps and forests. While
the men in both the horse and the foot undoubtedly possessed fewer
pieces of European-style armor than would be the case when Spaniards
were facing European or Ottoman opponents, this was a period of tran-
sition when metal armor was losing its importance. A Spanish histori-

an, writing less than a half-century later, wrote that Coronado's expedition was "a good and well equipped army," a result of the "faultless preparation of the viceroy Don Antonio de Mendoza."[179] In addition, in this case and unlike many other expeditions, the European ordnance and sinews of war apparently had a more-or-less constant presence with Coronado's army, perhaps only increasing in proportion, as there were steadily increasing Spanish casualties and occasional reinforcements.[180]

However, the fact that the army was relatively numerous and so well appointed had a potential downside. In 1536, when the Spanish force of Diego de Almagro left Francisco Pizarro's little army in Peru and returned to Chile, it was believed that this led the natives of Peru to chance a revolt.[181] Likewise, the citizens of New Galicia believed that the expedition was taking too many of the best men of the province, and, therefore, they were apprehensive by the time this well-equipped army was scheduled to depart. The citizens knew that the nearby sierras contained many angry Indian fugitives who had been chased into hiding by Guzman.[182] Not-so-much-later events in New Galicia would show this worry to have been justified.

# SIX

# Indian Warrior Allies

Accompanying Captain General Coronado and his Europeans was a significant contingent of allied Indian warriors—auxiliaries. While some modern scholars feel the term *auxiliaries* tends to diminish the historical role of these fighters, from a military standpoint the nomenclature is quite appropriate. The Indian soldiers were auxiliaries every bit as much as were other supporting allied troops in other wars and campaigns. From antiquity to modern times, these friendly fighting forces, usually serving the direct interest of another nation that pays most of the tariff, have been given the technical military title "auxiliaries." These fighting men, noncitizens of the assisted and larger power—although often trained to an equally professional level—provided a less expensive and more flexible method of combat support.[1] It was not uncommon for sixteenth-century European armies to have auxiliaries recruited outside the regular framework that were considered valuable, if sometimes ill-disciplined, additions in battle.[2]

In addition, the military term of art "auxiliary" certainly is more positive a title than "mercenaries."[3] Even supposedly full-fledged allies may be seen as auxiliaries when their leaders are not equally seated at the highest-level command council table—although wise diplomacy may forestall them being so labeled in that case.

In the event, since much ink has been spilled regarding Indian allies (called by the Spanish *Indios amigos*) without enough care being taken to separate those serving as warriors and those employed as camp followers or servants, an attempt to distinguish those functional groups is made herein. Therefore, the Mexican Indian soldiers most often will be identified as warriors or auxiliaries.

As for the numerical strength of the Indian fighting contingent, Castaneda, seemingly excluding other Indian hangers-on and camp followers, estimated "about 800 natives of New Spain" were collected with the "more than 300 Spaniards."[4] This estimate of relative strengths in a well-organized and government-sponsored expedition in the latter part of the early conquistador era does not appear questionable, especially when the potential opposition was not seen as a major military power.

Further, this guesstimate of eight hundred by a participant was accepted, with a slight boost, by scholar George Hammond about seventy-five years ago. He thought the "auxiliary force" contained "more than eight hundred Mexican Indian allies, armed with anything they could manage."[5] Another Spanish borderlands historian, Arthur S. Aiton, who was familiar with the later testimony of Viceroy Mendoza and Coronado, equivocated and said there were "eight hundred Indian allies" at Compostela but "over a thousand native allies paraded" at the review held for the viceroy.[6] On the other hand, a third Coronado student of the era of Hammond and Aiton thought there were "three hundred Indian allies" in addition to the "more than a thousand Indian and negro servants and followers."[7] Perhaps most perplexing, when one remembers the heroics of American Indians in two world wars, was Herbert Eugene Bolton's statement in 1936 that Coronado and his "300 Spanish horsemen" were accompanied only by "1,000 Indian servants."[8]

The only other persuasive and primary mention of the number of armed friendly Indians, besides Castaneda's, came years after the expedition, in 1547, when Coronado—this time trying to help his mentor Mendoza out of a legal jam for mismanaging funds—testified that Mendoza's estimate that thirteen hundred Indian volunteers accompanied the expedition was correct, "a few more or less."[9] This helpful testimony, of course, occurred after Mendoza apparently had helped derail similar charges against his protégé, and it does not really distinguish between auxiliaries and camp followers.[10]

In the event, like Topsy, Castaneda's reasonable statistic of eight hundred allied warriors has grown over the years among most historians—or at least gotten blurry. That indefatigable researcher and translator, Richard Flint, is a case in point. In 1997, he put the range between "800 or 1,300" and dismissively opined about the significant variation, "whichever figure for number of Mexican Indians may be more accurate . . . , it is clear that the membership of the expedition was predominantly Mexican Indians."[11]

However, the exact number later became important to Flint. Just six years later, he had reconsidered, now relying on the testimony supporting Mendoza's estimate by an accused codefendant, Coronado.[12] When Flint accepted this thirteen-hundred number, he already had suggested regarding Coronado's veracity in testifying that the captain general possessed "either a faulty memory" or committed "outright obfuscation" or evidenced an ignorance of the "daily conduct of the expedition he led" when he testified in his own defense in 1544.[13] Nonetheless, Flint in 2003 accepted the thirteen-hundred number without hesitation and unabashedly stated that the Indian allies in the expedition "composed at least three-fourths of it."[14]

Since then the number for Flint has held steady at "at least 1,300 natives of central and western Mexico," five hundred of whom Flint hypothesized joined the expedition after Castaneda made his first-person estimate.[15] Since discovering hearsay recollections that there might have been upwards of five thousand in the "Indian component of the expedition," Flint fortunately has held fast to the thirteen-hundred count.[16] But once again, while Flint implies that he is talking about the fighting contingent, he specifically makes no clear distinction between fighters and camp followers.[17] Subsequent scholars, however, have not been so careful in reading even Flint's estimates, assuming that all of the thirteen hundred were warriors, thus inflating the expedition to a "huge armed force of at least seventeen hundred men."[18]

From a logistical standpoint alone, an estimate of more than a thousand allied Indian warriors, over and above any native camp followers, would seem excessive for an expedition that continually had difficulty feeding itself. Therefore, Coronado's estimate of thirteen hundred, if it was honest testimony in a legal proceeding in which Viceroy Mendoza was being criticized for spending too much money and not treating the Indians right, apparently was taking into account both the Indian warrior allies and the camp followers. Indeed, Spanish historian Mota Padilla, who relied on some original sources no longer available, said (not unlike Castaneda) the expedition had "more than a thousand Indian allies and Indian servants," as well as others handling the stock.[19]

In any event, the raw number for the auxiliary troops, whatever it was—and it was certainly larger than the European fighting contingent—was not determinative of relative combat effectiveness within the army. Armament, horseflesh, and European discipline would count heavily in that area. While the European contingent was made up of sixteenth-century soldiers—those trained to work as a unit—the auxiliaries still were traditional warriors—fighters who relied on individual courage and ability.[20] Nonetheless, these friendly Mexican men added significantly to the overall fighting capability of Coronado's army and would help overawe potential opposition before trouble could occur.

According to the orders of Viceroy Mendoza, because of prior abuses, these auxiliaries were not to be employed as bearers and porters, but were only responsible for their own possessions and supplies.[21] This prohibition reportedly was followed to the letter. Indeed, the expedition obviously had so many pack animals because of this limitation.[22] This was a stark contrast with the contemporary expedition of De Soto into Florida and the American Southeast. On one occasion, according to an eyewitness, after two captains had been sent out to round up Indians, "a hundred men and women were taken. . . . They were led off in chains, with collars about the neck, to carry luggage and grind corn, doing the labor proper to servants."[23]

The disastrous De Soto Expedition also was one of a number of exceptions to the usual Spanish reliance on the combat abilities of their local allies. This general reliance should not be wondered at. Although much has been made of these Indian allies' aiding those Spanish attempting to conquer their native domain—as if the issue were a revelation—such a divide-and-conquer strategy is as old as warfare itself. While examples may be found in the Bible, the recruitment of disaffected (or enlightened) native allies was to be practiced by colonial powers other than Spain in such disparate locales as North America, Africa, and New Zealand.

As for the Spanish, in their Reconquista of Spain, they occasionally exhibited as much common sense as their well-known severity. They encouraged large numbers of Spanish-native Moors to join the Christians in fighting against other Muslims (especially those reinforcements coming from North Africa).[24]

This type of military policy naturally found its way to the New World. "It is fair to say that from the moment the *conquistadores* first landed in the Americas they found Indians willing to serve them, and

Indian auxiliaries took part—as warriors, porters, interpreters, and scouts—in every 16th century campaign."[25] Of course, to say the Spanish had Indian warrior allies in every particular military action or contest in the Americas, no matter how small, would be too broad a claim and would overly dilute the terrible effectiveness of these armored European intruders.[26]

But regarding most of their adventures and endeavors, it is hard to imagine the Spanish building their considerable empire in the New World without native assistance. In the conquest of Mexico, Cortes had the assistance of tens of thousands of Indian auxiliaries who hated their Aztec opponents. For example, when Cortes was marching toward Mexico City to retake it, according to a contemporary historian, the brigantines he had built for an amphibious assault were "carried on the backs of 8,000 [Tlaxcalan] men, who were escorted by 20,000 [Tlaxcalan] soldiers, with 2,000 more bringing provisions and supplying services."[27]

So common was the use of Indian auxiliaries, this standard operating procedure regarding the recruitment of native allies later became a sort of cynical template for success in the Americas. A Spanish historian of the late sixteenth century advised, "Advantage should be taken of the enemy by setting those of one district against the opponents and foes of another, if it should become necessary, as was done by Don Hernando Cortes in the conquest of Mexico and by Francisco de Ibarra in New Vizcaya."[28]

In the conquest of Mexico, as would be the situation in many other locales, there was not any sense of the allied warriors' betraying their race in serving the Spanish, for the Aztecs had subjugated the other tribes and used them as human resources when it came to their ritualistic human sacrifices. Indeed, during the desperate fighting with Cortes, some Aztecs even attempted to aid the invaders in the hope of bettering their individual situations.[29] Throughout Central and South America, similar mixed motivations existed for other Indians joining the Europeans.[30]

In addition, while the motivations of these so-called Indian Conquistadors have received considerable and long-deserved attention, one motivator not often addressed was the fact that many of the Indian allies, starting with the Tlaxcalan, had become Christians. The famous occasion known as the vision of the Virgin of Guadalupe only accelerated these conversions among the indigenous population.[31] While the fanaticism of the Spaniards is well known, similar religious fervor must have existed within the allied ranks.[32] This situation naturally would serve to spur native enlistment and to fortify their courage under fire—especially for the Coronado Expedition.

In any event, those natives joining the Spaniards in their northward march were only continuing a regional program that had been used by the notorious Nuno de Guzman's devastating campaign into New Galicia from 1529 to 1531, when he had the aid of about eight thousand Tlaxcaltecs, Huexotzinca, and Aztecs.[33]

However, what was different about the Indian warrior auxiliaries joining Coronado was the relatively small number of participants. That they outnumbered the Spanish soldiery is clear, but, unlike other such expeditions, the multiplier was only two or three, not the supposed hundredfold of other campaigns. While students of the topic might assert that such lesser numbers simply were a byproduct of imported Old World disease decimating native populations,[34] in Coronado's case it was a situation of both perceived military requirements and the availability of so many unemployed Spanish adventurers. In other words, the Spanish seemingly were well established in Mexico, the viceroyalty appeared militarily secure, there was no report of a vast standing army in Cibola and, if anything, an outlet was needed for newly arrived and ambitious European immigrants. While reportedly (according to Coronado), many thousands of Indians would have been glad to accompany the expedition if there had been room,[35] an inordinately large number of armed allies was not needed when the Spaniards were expected to lead the way, and the invasion prospect was not seen as desperate.

But even in a second echelon of a real military force, these allies would have to be about as well armed, albeit without firearms or crossbows, as the typical sixteenth-century peasant armies of Europe.[36] According to Ian Heath, a dedicated student of sixteenth-century military affairs across the globe, the Indians who aided the Spanish in subduing the Aztecs and, later, in expanding Spanish hegemony within the growing boundaries of New Spain often continued to use their traditional warrior clothing, their style of shields, and their own weaponry (particularly the bow) up until the 1580s. However, changes were taking place, and by the Mixton War of the 1540s, the natives often wore a mixture of indigenous and Spanish clothing.[37] Therefore, picturing Coronado's *Indios amigos* as wearing the bright and new animal-skinned livery (including animal-head headgear) of the Mexican conquest era probably is extrapolating the evidence too much, especially for an expedition far from home and with clothing wearing out.[38]

A redrawing of a codex illustration showing Nuno de Guzman
and his Indian allies during his
devastating campaign against
other native peoples in New
Galicia. (*Author*)

Regarding that traditional outfit, when the Spanish tackled the
Aztec Empire, they faced an enemy whose armories and arsenals had
(in archaic English) "bows, arrows, slings, launces, dartes, clubbes,
swords and bucklers, and gallant targettes more trimme than strong,
skulls [helmets] and splintes [shin guards], but not many, and al made
of woode, gilte or covered with leather." Although made of wood, the
weapons were "very harde and strong" and the arrows had flint or bone
heads—coated with "venemous" material, often proving fatal to enemies.[39] Since the fighting *Indios amigos* of Cortes used the same type of
ordnance, it reasonably has been assumed that Coronado's auxiliaries
were similarly fixed.[40]

As for native tactics that might have been employed successfully by
their European allies in battle when directing the auxiliaries, those
regarding the use of bowmen likely were at the forefront. The Indians
of Mexico did not employ their bowmen statically as did England; the
native bowmen often were used as mobile units in battle, moving in and
out as needed.[41]

Regarding the weapons borne by these native allies, there is some
room for debate. Richard Flint wrote about the documentary record,
"There is no evidence that European equipment was provided to the
Indian allies."[42] Herbert Eugene Bolton carried this historical-record
vacuum to its logical extension, writing, "The Indian allies doubtless
carried their native implements of war, including cotton armor. . . . [I]t
may be surmised that [their weapons] included bows and arrows, clubs,
spears, light javelins, and slings—all of which had been in use by the
Aztecs and Tarascans at the time of the Spanish conquest."[43]

In addition, often the natives used weaponry in which the Europeans possessed no skill; the favorite weapon of the Mixtec Indians was the atlatl, a hand-held spear-thrower that could increase the velocity of the projectile by up to 60 percent.[44] Thus, since historians have known about the likely presence of so many non-European weapons in the hands of the natives, these same writers have presumed that there was no possibility for them to have possessed European weaponry.

But the thinking should be expanded. While it certainly is correct that there is no mention in the Coronado sources about the provision of European-style weaponry to the native allies, that does not foreclose the possibility. The Indians of the vast area of Florida, who certainly were not under Spanish subjugation, early on supplemented their native arsenals with captured European weaponry. Although bows and arrows were their mainstay weapons, they did "possess and are skillful in the use of other arms such as pikes, lances, darts, halberds, slings, clubs, broadswords, sticks and the like, if there are more such weapons."[45]

Ian Heath has noted that although friendly or subject Indians initially were prohibited from possessing metal weapons, the traditional obsidian-bladed sword, the *macana,* was soon replaced by the European-style blade. Some Indian allies, including Tlaxcaltecs and Aztecs, were using Spanish swords by 1524. While permission to carry such weapons was not regularly granted even upper-class and Hispanicized Indians until after the Coronado Expedition, one cannot say that none of Coronado's auxiliaries were so armed.[46] Thus, for example, when that previously noted partial blade supposedly belonging to Juan Gallego was found in Kansas near the turn of the twentieth century, there was no assurance that such a lost item, assuming it was authentic, was not a broken and discarded weapon that was appropriated by a Spanish auxiliary.

When it came to military specialties, some of the better-connected auxiliaries almost certainly filled adviser roles, while they or others would attempt to be interpreters as the force headed beyond Mexico proper. As for the lower ranking Indian warriors, although these allies were not used as beasts of burden, as was too often the case on other expeditions, they also were much more than mere "grunts" or "cannon fodder." Especially those who were trail-seasoned likely would have been able to impart important wilderness skills to their Spanish brothers in arms.

Many of the warriors certainly were employed as huntsmen for the expedition. More experienced with life in the bush, they likely would supplement the rations of the Spaniards in addition to providing for themselves. But there had to be more when it came to other food groups. The Aztecs long had raised maize (corn) and beans.[47] Also, the Indian lands of Mexico were the culinary birthplaces of such foods or spicy additives as chocolate and vanilla.

Scurvy was a curse that marched with armies every bit as much as it sailed with navies, but there is relatively little mention of that debilitating malady in Coronado literature, and it comes near the end of the endeavor. Even before the sixteenth century, it was recognized that a fresh diet seemed important in treating the disease, with the English (later to be called limeys) specifically recognizing the importance of limes, oranges, and the juice of other fruits in treating the disease.[48] The Spanish with the expedition, in particular, had national traits and geographic factors on their side in resisting scurvy. Not only was sixteenth-century Spain full of experienced mariners used to combating the disease, but individual Spaniards were aided by their southern European culinary traditions and the fact that they were marching out of a land in which the natives had grown chili peppers for a score of centuries.[49] "They have a kind of pepper for seasoning that is called *chilli*, and nothing is eaten without it," wrote an earlier chronicler since called the Anonymous Conquistador.[50] Native auxiliaries would be invaluable in searching for such indigenous plants, which could be used to enhance flavor in the cookpot and which, probably unknowingly, added important vitamins.

As for providing for the expedition after it had left any bases of supply, some of the indigenous allies accompanying Coronado must have provided other important dietary help for the column in addition to hunting down wild meat on the hoof or snaring lesser prey. While the European soldiers certainly would have made use of any wild onions they came across, the Indians would have more experience in determining which berries were edible.

The Spaniards already had learned from the indigenous people about the importance of prickly pear in the diet, for Spanish sailors in the New World had seen that prickly pear fruit successfully combated scurvy.[51] Nunez Cabeza de Vaca had discovered that the plant was "of agreeable flavor" and "[t]he natives live on it three months in the year, having nothing beside."[52] As indicated, prickly pear has many medicinal qualities, including acting as an antiscorbutic by serving as an excellent source of vitamin C, and the Aztecs long had used that cactus as food.[53]

In addition to prickly pear, the marching Spaniards probably availed themselves of the edible parts of the yucca plant, which was gathered by tribes in the American Southwest.[54] While the roots of the so-called Spanish bayonet are not edible, parts of the plant growing above ground are.[55]

More epicurean knowledge would come once the Spaniards arrived at Cibola, representative of the pueblo culture, and found a lifestyle that was particularly agrarian. Wild foods that the Puebloans (especially the Hopi) were eating at the time of the entrada included prickly pear fruit, cactus buds, sunflower seeds, and grass seeds.[56] These items supplemented their regular crops, such as multicolored corn, beans, and squash.[57]

Once the expedition reached the Great Plains, there was first-hand observation of the Indians there regarding the fine dining provided by the American bison. In addition, the Spanish might have been made aware of the use some plains Indians made of the inner bark of the cottonwood tree, which was chewed and proved a source for salicylic acid (the ingredient of modern aspirin). In addition, the cottonwood bark, boughs, and leaves could serve as acceptable horse feed.[58]

Thus the caloric and vitamin assistance of the Indian allies was important, in addition to the information obtained once the force was among the peoples of the unknown lands. While such native knowledge was perhaps not a prerequisite to success on every occasion, certainly many exploratory expeditions throughout the world, from Australia to the Arctic, came to grief when such information was lacking or ignored.

But the Coronado Expedition was a military invasion, and not a mere foraging foray. The bottom-line question regarding the indigenous auxiliaries was, "Would they fight?" While, unfortunately, the Spanish chroniclers of expeditions rarely mention the role and effectiveness of their native allies, seldom are there complaints about their abilities. Such omissions, like Sherlock Holmes's noting when a dog did not bark, are telling negative evidence. Certainly, if blame could have been laid at the feet of the native warriors at the conclusion of the disappointing campaign of Coronado, such finger pointing would have occurred at some time by some witness.

Therefore, one Coronado historian undoubtedly was inaccurate when he relied on a factual premise and came up with his seemingly logical, but historically unsupported, conclusion. "The Indian allies the army took along were probably ineffective," wrote Duncan Robinson in 1940. "Used to the warm climate of Mexico, they suffered terribly when the army encountered its first typical plains blizzard."[59] Robinson had to be wrong. Not only did some of the fighting take place in warmer seasons, even that taking place in winter and early spring 1541 was partially motivated by the hope of getting warmer clothing—quite an incentive, especially for Mexican Indians with chilblains or frostbite.

On the other hand, more recent historians, rightfully reacting against omissions by past Eurocentric scholars, have waxed poetic as to the heroic contributions of the Indian allies. Certainly, general praise is called for when addressing their role. "Indeed, without them Spanish conquest of the Americas could never have taken place at the speed that it did, and might not have been possible at all," opined Ian Heath.[60]

Nonetheless, when it comes to very detailed examples of individual actions, some of this praise has been excessive and without much historical support. This is especially so regarding the Coronado Expedition. Historian Stan Hoig said the Indian warriors, perhaps close to two thousand of them, provided Coronado "with a dominating force" in the battles with the natives.[61] Regarding the Battle of Hawikuh in July 1540, Flint and Cushing Flint believed their "numbers probably explain the relative ease with which that fabled pueblo was taken."[62] As will be seen, both of these conclusions are entirely speculative and go against what is known about the battles and about the tactics employed during the fighting.

The contemporary Spaniards recognized the importance of their Indian allies, but they might on occasion have given their European fighting men precedence when it came to basic supplies of food and clothing. Such discrimination could be logically concluded based on the casualty statistics once the Coronado Expedition entered the harsher lands to the north. During this portion of the march, only one hungry Spaniard, but "several Indian allies" and "two negroes," were fatally poisoned "from eating some herbs because they were out of food."[63]

On the other hand, when a little corn was obtained, according to Coronado, it was used to relieve "the friendly Indians" and only some of the Spaniards.[64] In addition, specific occasions are mentioned when the Spaniards actively looked after their fellow warriors. During the march to Cibola, the Spaniards saw that their comrades "were in great danger" because of the cold. The men-at-arms let the auxiliaries ride their lead

An early eighteenth-century illustration of the Spanish attempting to change Peruvian natives from enemies to allies. (*Author*)

horses with the hidalgos walking.[65] And, as is well known, the Tiguex War was occasioned by the requisition of winter clothing for the Indian auxiliaries in particular.

There is no doubt that the Indian auxiliaries were extremely important to the mission of Coronado's army. There certainly were occasional problems, as when the lack of discipline of the auxiliaries (especially relating to dealings with the local tribes) caused friction. But regarding raw numbers and individual skills, these fighting allies helped prevent the expedition from being a total disaster.

In addition, while the loyalty of many of the Spaniards with the captain general would be tested and strained to the breaking point, no such problem would be laid at the door of their friendly Indian auxiliaries. One historian who speculated that Coronado's native allies did not do much of the fighting at least noted (more correctly, if not completely accurately) that "none forsook" Coronado by deserting.[66]

# SEVEN

# A Colorful Accompaniment of Women, Servants, Slaves, and Other Camp Followers

The European fighting contingent in the Coronado Expedition included non-Spaniards, and there was an even bigger contingent of Indian warrior auxiliaries. However, this military endeavor was much more diverse than that, both as to ethnicity, gender, and individual functions.

During the sixteenth century, European armies "did not consist entirely of front-line soldiers, for a large number of servants, drivers, grooms, traders and women and children followed in the train of the troops."[1] As previously noted, and with mounted troops especially, farriers and blacksmiths would be included with the support personnel.[2]

But farriers and blacksmiths, like chaplains and scribes, might be enrolled members of the military force. There were others who were allies or auxiliaries of the pacific variety, clearly civilians and clearly providing supporting roles to the fighting men. As with a modern army, lack of a direct combat role did not equate with nonessential services. An army must be fed. An army also somehow needs to mend its tattered socks, shoes, and other clothing; to bed down; and to treat the sick, injured, or wounded. In addition, most soldiers need to find new equipment or clothing when continued repair is out of the question.

While a Spanish army marching in Europe would have regulation sutlers who would extend credit to soldiers, sell items to them, and bid for items during estate sales,[3] this probably was not the situation with the Coronado Expedition. However, two Coronado scholars have opined that individual soldiers may have been unofficial sutlers or unit wheeler-dealers who loaned money or marketed items to their comrades.[4] If honest, these individuals would be less of a curse to the command than those comrades who performed more predatory activities such as gambling.

But most of those performing support services would have been true camp followers and not soldiers. In addition, many of the camp followers would not have been volunteers but would have been servants. While some of the accompanying servants (or slaves) were Indians, many with Coronado would have been of African descent. One historian of the expedition estimated that there were "almost a thousand camp-followers, black and red, with the baggage and supply train of horses and mules . . . and accompanied by a commissary 'on the hoof' of cattle, sheep, and swine."[5]

There probably were not that many camp followers, although the number certainly was both impressive and cumbersome. A more reasonable calculation would be about four hundred to six hundred of various ethnicities, which more closely would fit into the estimates that the total Indian cavalcade (including warriors) was about thirteen hundred.

While some of these camp followers undoubtedly were European, it is well documented that people of African lineage accompanied the expedition. While they were important participants, it is imprecise for modern historians to assert that they therefore made this an "Indian-Spanish-African" endeavor, for the expedition served only particular Spanish military and political goals. In addition, the majority of the Africans were not volunteers and certainly were not decision makers; most of them were slaves or servants.

It is known that there was "a free negro interpreter"[6] in the expedition, and other free blacks likely served in various capacities. In addition, in those days of strident Roman Catholicism, it is safe to assume that all the Africans (along with all the Europeans, and most, if not all, of the accompanying Indians) were at least nominal Christians, even if some still were considered "Moors."[7]

But even the indentured Africans would not have been inactive members of this military force. Based solely on what occurred during many wars in which a slaveholding society was involved, it is certain that some of these indentured Africans, including full-fledged bondsmen, occasionally wore any armor provided by their masters, bore excess weaponry willingly supplied by those same hierarchical superiors, and participated in some of the guard duty and even fighting, perhaps with the occasional promise of eventual freedom as a reward.[8]

This general tendency to make use of Africans was enhanced during the conquests of the Spanish Americas. The Spanish colonies initially were places where much of the hard slave labor was performed by indigenous people, for "the black slaves of Spaniards in the colonies tended to function more as personal auxiliaries" such as servants and clerks "just as in the Conquest they were personal auxiliaries of individual Spanish conquistadors."[9] Thus, during this era, the poor Indians, seemingly an inexhaustible and readily available population, were worked to death, not the more valuable Africans.

But while some of these African servants obviously served as pages to men-at-arms and as mere armed retainers,[10] some went even beyond this. There "were servants who were, by necessity, armed; by fighting and surviving they usually earned their freedom and became conquistadors in their own right."[11]

Indeed, despite their original lowly status, some of these black Christians became full-fledged members of Spanish military forces. One was Juan Garrido, who, after being baptized a Christian in Spain, joined in the conquests of Puerto Rico, Cuba, and Mexico, apparently among other endeavors. He died a free man in Mexico City around 1547.[12] Another of the best documented examples was Juan Valiente, whose owner allowed him to participate in the subjugation of Guatemala, where he earned some fame and wealth before being killed in an Indian fight in 1553.[13] Others, less known, had adventures similar to those of Garrido and Valiente.[14]

But not all blacks who became respected conquistadors started out as servants or slaves. Juan Beltran was born in Spain a free man, apparently of mixed black-Spanish heritage, just a couple of years after the first voyage of Columbus. He was an infantryman under Pizarro and became a trusted resident of Peru. He retired to Spain, apparently taking along his common-law native wife and illegitimate daughter.[15] A few other such free mulattoes voluntarily served with Spanish forces.[16] It is not impossible that one or two of those listed in the Coronado muster roll were of mixed black-white blood.

Therefore, during the sixteenth century, "Negro slaves and freemen alike often fought for the Spanish, and not only in emergencies—the guards of the mule-trains attacked by Drake in 1573 included Negroes, for instance, of whom at least one was armed with an arquebus."[17] Almost certainly, some of the African servants watching the horse herd of Coronado performed armed guard duty at night.

Nonetheless, while honest historians must concede that the full-fledged participation of some Africans performing military duties undoubtedly occurred during the Coronado Expedition, they must also acknowledge that its occurrence would be only occasional—probably rare—and likely reserved for exceptional bondsmen of great physique or perceived high intellectual ability and loyalty. While accounts of any battlefield heroics of these black men seemingly have not been preserved, reports of a few notable actions—including those occurring during a great Texas hailstorm—have been.[18]

The record also is not empty concerning some of the African servants or slaves accompanying the Coronado column running away, which occurred when the advance party on its way to Cibola suffered a rugged trail and little food.[19] This certainly was not a rare happening during the settlement of the Americas. In fact, the first reported African slave to abscond and head into the bush for a life of wild freedom occurred on the island of Hispaniola in 1502.[20] These escaped "Cimaroons" (so called from the Spanish word for *runaway*) often formed guerrilla bands that were effective in raiding their former plantations and in killing their late Spanish masters. While later supplied with arms by English and French sea corsairs, Cimaroons on Hispaniola in the 1540s used homemade spears and arms taken from slain Spaniards.[21]

As for African bondsmen specifically fleeing to the indigenous population and successfully going native, this probably occurred during the entrada of Francisco Coronado, but it also probably was rare. In addition to the salutary lesson of Esteban, which demonstrated a definite ethnic antipathy between some of the locals and Africans, there also was the fact that the Indians of the Southwest would not then have seen much advantage of taking on outsiders not easily assimilated, whether white or black, free or slave, servant or priest. In the Caribbean, some escaped black slaves merely exchanged Spanish masters for native Carib masters.[22]

Not all the camp followers with the expedition were black or involuntary, and not all were male. Female camp followers in a European military force of the era would attend to both the upper class male

A French print showing peasants on the march to greet Charles V. This gives a sense of how camp followers may have appeared in Coronado's time. (*Author*)

members of an expedition and to the other ranks, "but on a smaller scale" for the commoners. "The[se] women of the camp—or of the army—did duty as sutlers and as housekeepers, probably for more than one man at a time, cooking their food, washing their clothes and so on."[23] While these liaisons were unlikely to "be regarded as one of marriage" neither "was it prostitution or brothel keeping; it was more a kind of 'permanent relationship' with several men."[24]

In the sixteenth century, with the presence of women there usually would be at least some children. Even young children marching along with the army "could make themselves useful by guarding the animals, and the boys from a very early age helped to look after the horses and polish the weapons."[25]

A relatively large number of the women of the Coronado Expedition would have been natives assisting the Indian warrior allies. The Spaniards, as will be noted, also had their female assistants of native blood. And there were nonindigenous women with the expedition as well, perhaps more numerous than previously thought.

There was ample reason and precedent for the presence of European women with the borderlands expedition of Coronado. While many know of the services of Dona Marina, an Indian woman who served Hernan Cortes as an interpreter and a mistress,[26] fewer know that there were Spanish women attached to the Spanish army of Cortes attempting to recapture the Aztec capital in 1521. These women made themselves more than useful by acting as nurses for the sick and wounded, by filling in as substitute sentries for the battle-weary men, and in some instances participating in the actual combat. According to historian Francis MacNutt, "[S]ome of them [were] described as 'wives' of the soldiers" and, while "[l]ittle has been said of the courage and devotion of these obscure heroines," the names of five of them are a matter of record.[27]

Not surprisingly, other European women with Cortes were killed by the Aztecs during the fighting—in particular, five Spanish women who had arrived with Narvaez and who were slain after the Spanish were driven out of Mexico City.[28] This exposure to combat occasionally meant women were in fighting roles. During the struggle for Chile, a woman named Ines Suarez "distinguished herself in a defence of the town of Santiago against the Indians in 1541."[29] Similarly, also in 1541, during the Mixton War, Beatriz Hernandez, the wife of one Captain Olea, participated in the fight for the defense of Guadalajara.[30]

Considering the secondary position of the Coronado Expedition to the Cortes conquest, the Spanish female companions were nonetheless almost as well represented—at least statistically—when it comes to whom is identified. According to Flint and Cushing Flint, "Only two women who accompanied their husbands on the expedition are known by name, Maria Maldonado and Francisca de Hozes. Both were well remembered by former expedition members who later wrote chronicles of the undertaking."[31] Flint and Cushing Flint also note two other native wives whose names are subsumed into the known identities of their husbands (as often occurs in history and genealogy).[32] "These four," the authors write, "are surely not even the tip of the iceberg of women who traveled to Cibola, performing tasks . . . disdained by the conquistadores."[33]

One must not forget that these women, like the men, had ambitions. A few probably dreamed of establishing the *encomienda* lifestyle with a husband. Some certainly had lofty motivations that bespoke their religious faith.

While there is no documentary evidence of combat participation—for fortunately the desperate straits of Cortes were not replicated in the American Southwest of 1540–1542—the women accompanying the Coronado column were nonetheless important to this military endeavor. Certainly most of the women performed historically feminine roles.

Whether Spanish or Indian, they would have had kitchen duties, if for no other reason than that employment usually improved the fare for all concerned. They also would have been laundresses, tailors, and seamstresses. Maria Maldonaldo was recalled by an expedition member as one who acted as an amateur seamstress for the men and who "did many other excellent things."[34] While an army, according to Napoleon, marches on its stomach, the seats of breeches and the toes of stockings tend to show the wear.

But such sartorial maintenance might have been more warlike than patching trousers, reflecting the skilled piecework for which women have long been renowned. Based on what women did in Europe when living in a city that produced armor, it can be presumed that the females with Coronado also helped maintain helmets and breastplates, by sewing worn linings and replacing leather straps.[35]

In addition, women, like other camp followers (whether male or female), would maintain both the hygiene of a camp (through active participation in field sanitation) and the cleanliness of encamped individuals (through combing out lice, for example) during this era. It has been concluded that when the camps of European forces contained women, less disease occurred.[36]

Also, when it came to the fighting, which did occur during the expedition of Coronado, at least some of the women accompanying the force undoubtedly were (in modern military terms) a unit providing combat support. These would have been the women who eventually helped collect the fallen on the battlefield and who would provide nursing assistance to the wounded after battle. Again, Maria Maldonaldo was remembered as one who cared for the sick.[37] As Florence Nightingale and Clara Barton recognized, there is little that is as much comfort to a seriously wounded or dying man than the presence of a sympathetic and gentle female attendant.

In keeping with this supposed civilizing aspect of women on the frontier, some of the European women probably provided evening entertainment in the form of singing around the cook fire. And as acknowledged by Flint and Cushing Flint, in addition to being cooks, seamstresses, and nurses, the women (both European and native) also served "as companions and lovers and the makers of field households."[38]

These companionships might have been more than expedient natural liaisons, for the more intimate services sometimes were hardly unofficial when it came to Spanish soldiery, a fact unaddressed by previous Coronado scholars. Unlike Henry VIII's English army of the era— which, according to a contemporary Italian observer, "did not take wenches with them" on campaign—Renaissance forces on the continent "reflected totally different social attitudes."[39] Thus, in the Italy where many Spaniards learned the art of war, "[p]rostitution was an accepted feature of . . . society and so was the military brothel."[40]

Militarily, the presence of prostitutes was sometimes seen as being as important as having enough ammunition. At one point, when an imperial force under Charles V (made up of Germans, Italians, and Spaniards) decided to streamline its advance by getting rid of excess baggage and superfluous camp followers, the soldiery had to make do with only three assigned whores per company.[41] On the other side of the line, Francis I, the French king who wasted so much of his national treasure fighting the Spanish in Italy, spent a portion of that royal money on female "camp followers" for his military retinue.[42]

Of course, men being what they are, the presence of female attendants, particularly when among the courtesan class then called *filles de joie*, often complicated matters for the command. In 1473, a directive issued to regulate a Burgundian military force (organized in the Italian style) warned about soldiers becoming too possessive of particular women, resulting in jealous dissension among the men.[43]

Nevertheless, despite the obvious drawbacks, the Spanish imperialists proved to be quick learners of the lifestyle of the Italian campaigns. Erasmus, obviously referring to the forces under Charles V, among others, complained in 1530 that they "cart harlots around with them."[44] When the Spanish sent a force to Vienna to fight the Turks during the Muslim attack of 1532, they were openly accompanied by courtesans.[45]

At least by the latter half of the sixteenth century, the Spanish army in Europe provided prostitutes for the soldiery as part of the camp-follower establishment. In the 1550s, the Spanish forces in the Netherlands reckoned that there should be five such women per company of two hundred men.[46] When the Duke of Alba marched north to Flanders in 1567 to suppress the Dutch, his army included two thousand prostitutes, "as regularly enrolled, disciplined, and distributed" as the Spanish cavalry and artillery.[47]

Naturally, the presence of chaplains and clergy with the Spanish forces, an almost obligatory situation in this age of militant Roman Catholicism, eventually put a crimp into this situation, but only in degree.[48] By the end of the sixteenth century, the use of these military whores, called *femmes publiques*, was reduced to three women per company. In addition, the regulations prohibited underage females and hypocritically mandated that the women operate "under the disguise of being washerwomen, or something similar, performing a servile task."[49] Thus, even back then, such activity generally was a story "the soldiers wouldn't tell."[50]

Of course, all this means only that it is possible authorized prostitutes were on the expedition. It is also possible that Coronado's field force contained no such contingent of professional women—at least officially. Diego Lopez, one of Coronado's defenders at the official investigation held several years after the expedition, testified that the captain general "did not permit blasphemy, living in concubinage, or excessive gambling."[51] But concubinage in this case probably meant unofficial liaisons with native women. It also may be a relevant fact, supporting either theory regarding the presence or absence of prostitutes, that Spain prohibited single women from immigrating to the Americas in 1541.[52]

In addition, without contrary evidence, it ought to be assumed that the clergymen accompanying Coronado were not licentious themselves and would disapprove of illicit liaisons between the soldiery and the camp followers. Reportedly, Friar Marcos, in addition to obviously being jealous of Esteban's popularity with the Indians during the reconnaissance north prior to the expedition, also did not approve of Esteban's taking "the women that were given him."[53]

In any event, scholars, especially those in the arena of women's studies, must be open to the idea that some of the females, whether European or native, traveling on this epochal voyage were at least part-time prostitutes, and not just "liberated" free spirits. The possibility is only enhanced by the fact that a later sixteenth-century historian of conquistador activity, including Coronado's, advised, "Concubinage must not be allowed in the army. On account of this offense God our Lord often permits defeats in war, and does not grant favors or victory."[54] This historian, Baltasar de Obregon, did not mention the euphemism "concubinage" with respect to Coronado's column, nor did he brand the expedition a complete failure. But among other Spanish failures he did attribute the destruction of the San Geronimo settlement planted by Coronado in Sonora to the licentiousness of the Spaniards toward the native females.[55] Again, if concubinage meant taking up with Indian women and taking advantage of their unsophisticated ways, some commanders (and some priests) would see a military brothel as a functional substitute and a necessary evil.

Be that as it may, numerous women in various capacities shared the adventures and sufferings of the expedition heading into unknown lands. These females certainly benefitted the undertaking's supply system, the commissary, and the hospital. And, based on what Spanish soldiers expected in Europe, the military veterans with Francisco Vasquez de Coronado might not have satisfied all their dreams with mere visions of gold.

# EIGHT

# The March North into Sonora

Viceroy Mendoza, although not putting himself in field command, took an active part in planning the expedition, and he made some important and positive decisions regarding the movement of the army into the little known north country. One determination was to accommodate his Indian allies. According to Castaneda, since "it would be rather hard for the friendly Indians in the country if the army should start from the interior of Mexico itself, he ordered them to assemble at the city of Compostela, the chief city in the New Kingdom of Galicia, 110 leagues from Mexico, so that they could begin their journey there with everything in good order."[1]

While this would allow his native auxiliaries to arrange their affairs and schedule their own leave-takings, it also was a clever logistical move used by army and naval bureaucrats, for it probably saved expenditures from the military chest by making these allies responsible for their own travel to Compostela. When Mendoza reached Compostela, "he found the whole company assembled, being well treated by Christobal de Onate, who had the whole charge of that government [of the province of Nueva Galicia] for the time being."[2]

The viceroy held a review of his forces.[3] "All were very glad when he arrived," recalled Castaneda, "and he made an examination of the company and found all those [officers] whom we have mentioned." It was apparently during this review that Francisco Vasquez de Coronado officially was appointed captain general at an installation ceremony and when Mendoza "assigned the captains to their companies."[4]

The next day, February 22, 1540, the Spaniards, "captains and soldiers together," gathered for and heard mass.[5] Presumably, during the mass, there was a ritual called the blessing of the flag by the priest, a formality that went back at least to the Middle Ages.[6] The banner subject to this particular honor, a color that would serve as a religious emblem for the force, would be presented by either Mendoza or Coronado to the safekeeping of a responsible ensign (or color-bearer).[7]

After mass, Mendoza faced the whole force and "made them a very eloquent short speech" that (undoubtedly based on mutinous disasters that had attended other attempts at conquest) wisely extracted an important oath of allegiance. The viceroy told

> them of the fidelity they owed to their general and show[ed] them clearly the benefits which this expedition might afford, from the conversion of those peoples as well as in the profit of those who should conquer the territory, and the advantage to His Majesty and the claim which they would thus have on his favor and aid at all times. After he had finished, they all, both captains and soldiers, gave him their oaths upon the Gospels in a missal that they would follow their general on this expedition and would obey him in everything he commanded them, which they faithfully performed, as will be seen.[8]

Presumably there was some sort of recognition of the Indian warrior allies who were to accompany the expedition, particularly of their leaders. Such attention, if it occurred, would have been very politic and a demonstration of good leadership by the viceroy.

When the army set out the next day, it was a scene out of the Middle Ages—or a Renaissance civic festival. Coronado certainly was well attired, for he was taking along "many fine clothes for himself" in his baggage, according to Lorenzo Alvarez, an expedition member.[9] As for Coronado's force, it marched out of Compostela "with its colors flying," according to Castaneda.[10] On this first day's march under the eye of the viceroy, the command, at least the Spaniards, might even have approached what an eyewitness said about the Spanish army heading to Flanders from Italy in 1566: "[It was a] fine company of gallant and valiant soldiers on the march . . . so well appointed as to uniforms and arms that one took them for captains rather than private soldiers. . . . One would have said that they were princes, so stiff they were and so arrogantly and gracefully they marched."[11]

Certainly there also were some musicians encouraging the step, for each Spanish military company in sixteenth-century Europe had two drummers and a fifer. While the drummers provided the beat for the appropriate step, the fifers were allowed to play any tune that did not interfere with the cadence.[12] In this rudimentary age, such military musicians, although not actual combatants, were considered trained specialists and a boon to any army, including armies in the Americas.[13]

If the pageantry on this occasion was reminiscent of medieval times, it also was a scene not unlike the one when the 7th Cavalry departed Fort Lincoln in the Dakota Territory to fight the Sioux in 1876. In Custer's case, his wife accompanied him but left the column and headed home on the second day, while the regimental band accompanied the expedition for a couple of weeks more before separating.[14] With Coronado's army, according to Castaneda, "The viceroy, Don Antonio, went with them for two days, and there he took leave of them, returning to New Spain with his friends."[15] It is known that at least some musicians, drummers for the foot and trumpeters for the horse, marched north.[16]

In Coronado's retinue there were many in addition to the European backbone of the force. It likely totaled about seventeen hundred souls, most of them not Spanish males. Probably, part of the considerable pack train followed close to the Spanish vanguard, attended to by servants and slaves. While horses normally would carry less, a pack mule of the era would be expected to carry two hundred to four hundred pounds, depending on the size of the beast.[17]

Most of the Indian auxiliaries would have marched behind the Spaniards, although others would be used as scouts, flankers, and interpreters hanging close to Coronado and his staff. Also, some of the allied chiefs might have been marching along on foot with this advance guard. Making their keeping up no problem, the mounted Spaniards undoubtedly dismounted and walked every so often to conserve their horses.

After the fighting men in the column would come the camp followers, including women, children, servants, and slaves. Probably most of the pack train was with this part of the column, along with extra mounts. Unless an attack seemed imminent—an unlikely possibility in this prehorse era regarding natives who later would take up raiding—a baggage train normally would bring up a military column's rear.[18] As for that baggage, the Coronado Expedition was well fixed when it came to its six hundred-plus train of packhorses and mules.[19] A 1620 column of eleven thousand Spanish troops marching to the Netherlands had but 673 pack mules.[20]

Finally, bringing up the rear of this traveling community and mixed menagerie would be the meat-on-the hoof livestock, an important and ready source of protein brought to the New World by Europeans.[21] While most of these critters would have been sheep or goats, there were anywhere from 150 to a more likely 500 head of Spanish cattle, apparently of the red, dun, or brown Retinto breed.[22] The Spanish sheep apparently were what is now called the Navajo-Churro breed, whose two types of wool (rough and soft) were perfect for rugs or blankets.[23] Castaneda recalled an amazing five thousand "rams and ewes" in the column.[24]

While everyone behind Coronado and his mounted officers would be eating some dust even on a windless day, the cloud occasionally raised by the herds of animals and their tenders would have been immense and asphyxiating. The pace and the daily mileage of the main army necessarily would be limited by these tail-end slowpokes, particularly the sheep.

Certainly, as they set off, the personnel in the army were in high spirits. Their troubles would only be beginning as they became trail worthy (and trail weary).

The expedition set up camps as each day closed. As noted, Lope de Samaniego was camp master or army master, and he would have been in charge of riding ahead to locate sites for camping with water and forage, to designate where tents would be set up, and, hopefully, to point out where the latrines would be located. If proper drainage was accounted for, this would be a low-lying area that military men traditionally have called "the sinks."

Although much disease then was blamed on bad air and vapors, there was some understanding in the sixteenth century about hygiene and sanitation. Europe, mimicking ancient times, had rediscovered privies between the thirteenth and fifteenth centuries.[25] In better military circles, offal and animal waste were kept out of camps and buried. It also was known that herds should water and do their business downstream from a command's water supply.[26] The Landsknecht armies in Europe used women and boys among the camp followers whose responsibilities included "cleaning and sweeping the shitting places."[27] Of course, it was a question of discipline when it came to making sol-

A woodcut of a wagon and field tents. (*Author*)

diers use the designated areas to perform their necessary business, and the Spanish of this era were not noted for being particularly fastidious in that regard.[28]

Fortunately, the Coronado Expedition (which had plenty of servants and camp followers to do any dirty work) would be moving into generally healthful climates—desert and high plains—and some of the command's advance would be up streams, with the herds to the rear. In addition, there usually would be plenty of room to camp and more than enough fresh, bracing, and occasionally violent breezes, keeping any bad air and vapors at bay.

As camp master, Samaniego also was in charge of making sure everyone had food at the end of the day. Regarding the provision of rations, the Spanish forces of the sixteenth century, like armies in more modern eras, had considerable logistical tails.[29] However, in Europe, as the sixteenth century progressed, the Spanish could send contractors ahead of a marching army to arrange for food, to contract for local wagons and carts, and to organize camping places.[30]

Obviously, with an expedition of this size, heading into the foreign wilderness, that newer methodology of supply could not be employed. Food and a large amount of other materiel would have to be transported, or collected from local natives who were not given vouchers and who would have had no use for money in any case. This, of course, was the traditional method of armies, even as medieval times became Renaissance times in Europe. "[E]verything necessary for the soldiers was requisitioned on the spot, with or without compensation. The troops made for a village or group of villages (usually oblivious to their impending fate) and quartered themselves wherever they chose."[31]

It was hoped that the column could be resupplied by ships sailing up the west coast of Mexico into the Sea of Cortes (what later would be called the Gulf of California). Nonetheless, such important items as ammunition (including good gunpowder) and duplicate parts for the firearms and other weaponry would have to be carried as unit, rather than individual, baggage.[32] Extra crossbow strings also would be included in this important classification of supply.[33] As with any force, "An army without its varied supplies, which the trains care for and provide, would soon be neither useful nor ornamental."[34]

In addition, the expedition almost certainly would have heavy-duty stuff to be used by blacksmiths, such as a primitive anvil and a supply of iron and copper.[35] Likely there were sharpening stones for keeping blades keen. Ready-made horseshoes, important for rough country, also would have to be hauled.[36] While apparently not as well-supplied as the heartless De Soto Expedition, the Coronado column took along chains, manacles, and collars to imprison recalcitrant natives—and ill-disciplined soldiers.[37]

For transport of this military column, there is specific mention in the chronicles of packhorses and pack mules. The first days of the march were trying when it came to unseasoned men functioning in unfamiliar jobs, complicated by the enlightened directive that their native allies were not to be employed as pack animals. "As each one was obliged to transport his own baggage and all did not know how to fasten packs, and as the horses started off fat and plump," reported Castaneda, "they had a good deal of difficulty and labor during the first few days, and many left many valuable things, giving them to anyone who wanted them, in order to get rid of carrying them."[38]

Ultimately, although animals might become broken down, the regular marching built up the men's endurance. While terrain would make a difference, by the time the Spaniards reached the level ground of the Great Plains, they would average five leagues daily, about thirteen-and-a-half miles, and consider that an easy march. A forced march by then would be six or seven leagues, approximately sixteen or eighteen miles. If necessary, the Indian allies would be able to make eight or nine leagues in a day, about twenty-five miles.[39]

Thus the army soon became trail seasoned with all the on-the-job training, especially in transport, and this also began to build both personal physiques and unit integrity. "In the end necessity, which is all powerful, made them skillful, so that one could see many gentlemen become carriers, and anybody who despised this work was not considered a man," wrote Castaneda.[40] This leveling was unusual for sixteenth-century Spaniards, for "to partake of such menial activity was anathema to Spanish officers and gentlemen."[41] In this case it was more like the English, whose Francis Drake once said, "I must have the gentleman to haul and draw with the mariner, and the mariner with the gentleman. . . . [L]et us show ourselves to be of a company."[42]

And there was plenty of work to do and personnel to look after. According to historian Mota Padilla (writing in the eighteenth century), the expedition had "more than a thousand horses [cavalry mounts] not counting pack-animals, and others loaded with six field-guns, powder, and shot, and more than a thousand Indian allies and Indian servants, and horse-handlers, cowmen, and shepherds."[43] At least one subsequent historian obviously picked up on this, stating that the pack train was "laden with light mountain guns."[44]

Nonetheless, even this list by Mota Padilla is a somewhat ambiguous assertion and does not necessarily foreclose the possibility that there were wheeled vehicles in the column, although that negative inference certainly is the more readily drawn one. An unextraordinary number of carts would be less likely to invite comment in recollections than an extraordinary number of pack animals.

In addition, also despite the seeming implication by Mota Padilla, the falconets more than likely were on gun carriages, although they conceivably could have been designed to fire from a stationary type of wooden frame, with or without small wheels. Therefore, they could have been disassembled and carried in carts or wagons.[45] Indeed, artilleryman Juan Troyano, in one nonverbatim transcript of later testimony, said he moved up "some artillery wagons" from Cibola to Tiguex during the troubles at Tiguex.[46] However, one of the two top Coronado scholars believes another Troyano version is correct, wherein he merely said he moved up some "artillery pieces."[47]

As for wheeled gun carriages with limbers pulled by horses, they, although novel, were used in the first phase of the Italian Wars (1494–1525), during which the practice became more common.[48] Early on, smaller versions of these artillery pieces, called *knallbuchsen* (pop guns) by the Germans, began to appear.[49] These diminutive guns presumably invited battlefield mobility even more.

In addition to artillery, other wheeled vehicles could have accompanied the expedition north, despite the known references only to packhorses and mules. The tumbrel, of course, "is nearly as old as man him-self," and "[t]he waggon is nearly as old as the land over which it trun-dles."[50] Even in Europe, while packhorses were convenient in the six-teenth century when there were mere trails and narrow bridges, rough roads accommodated carts, and wagons were used on better roads.[51]

Looking at Europe to resolve this Coronado transport question, the Spanish military in Europe, at least in mountainous regions, primarily relied on pack mules, and did so during their later sixteenth-century marches north to the Low Countries.[52] However, such things as anvils and heavy medical chests would not have to be taken along on such columns in settled Europe. In addition, the Spaniards also used wagons and four-wheeled carts for logistical purposes in less-rugged country.[53]

In addition to being able to haul heavier and bulkier loads, wheeled vehicles have other advantages over pack animals, as any student of B-western films can attest. Even in Renaissance times, wagons could be corralled before battle in order to defend the supplies kept in the rear.[54] Here, the noncombatant camp followers, such as artisans, peddlers, prostitutes, and servants, might huddle among the supply guards, hop-ing not to be attacked.[55]

Nonetheless, the contemporary documentary evidence known so far implies the exclusive use of pack animals and implicitly forecloses the presence of carts or wagons. But the route north between the coast and the mountains, although difficult, apparently could have been improved to accommodate simple wheeled conveyances. Coronado scholar Herbert Eugene Bolton, while indicating that the first leg of Coronado's journey up the west coast of Mexico proceeded along a trail that started out as single-file jungle track, assumed that the expedition, using "a host of native laborers," had to have widened this into a sort of road to accommodate all of the traveling stock.[56] Indeed, since the trail north could accommodate horses, this was an indication that it was not the worst of tracks. The Spanish had to use human carriers exclusively only when the terrain was very rugged and not fit for stock to travel.[57]

Thus it is possible that Coronado, like British General Edward Braddock two centuries later campaigning in Pennsylvania, improved this wilderness track sufficiently to accommodate carts or even wagons. The Spanish certainly were capable of such engineering feats.[58]

The problem with assumptions like the one that Coronado used pack animals exclusively is that so much is left unsaid about this expe-dition and other such endeavors. While an early historian of explorations in New Mexico later advised taking along heavy cannon (culverins) to subdue any recalcitrant pueblos, he did not hint at how they might be transported up the trail.[59] This historian of the conquistadors also was silent about wagons and carts, suggesting only that "[o]ne should take along pack horse and mules that are used to the hardships of the road."[60]

Given the overwhelming weight of the documentary evidence, it is not surprising that most scholars do not imagine wagons or carts accompanying Coronado north.[61] Nonetheless, such a well-appointed expedition ought to have had a few carts. In addition, those small artillery pieces had to tag along somehow. As will be argued in a later chapter, the expedition almost certainly had to have made some wheel ruts, even if they were from the relatively diminutive falconets.

A good percentage of the Europeans in Coronado's force were decently outfitted for conventional warfare, but the artistic scenes (by Frederic Remington, N. C. Wyeth, and others) of the Spaniards plodding along in the sunny Southwest wearing their steel equipment is unlikely, especially after their first festive day on the road. When the Spanish, Italian, and German army of Charles V invaded North Africa and marched through enemy territory to besiege Tunis, a Landsknecht wrote his German hometown that "it was so hot that the armoured men nearly suffocated and thought they would die of the heat, and when one went to help the other by loosening the armour, he would burn his fingers on the metal."[62] And, by the late medieval times, it was recognized that heavy physical exertion while wearing armor could cause heat prostration or worse.[63]

Even in more temperate Europe, soldiers on the march were prone to insist that their armor be stowed in baggage carts.[64] And because the Spaniards were the sixteenth-century originators and fashion trendsetters when it came to broad-brimmed hats for military men,[65] wearing steel—especially "steel pots"—on the road would have been tiresome and hot to no purpose.[66] Nonetheless, to the extent that the men-at-arms are portrayed in art at the forefront, this would have been appropriate in case there had to be a quick deployment for battle—and it also was a question of status.[67]

Thus, unless a threat seemed imminent—and Coronado's force probably always had scouts riding in advance if not along the flanks—much of the bulky equipment and heavier sinews of war probably were with the baggage train. In Europe, which had plenty of deadly summertime heat and humidity, the heavier muskets "were carried on the march by beasts of burden."[68] Presumably, for most of Coronado's men, their lances, pikes, halberds, heavy swords, arquebuses, crossbows, and steel armor usually would have been with the baggage, although reasonably accessible.[69]

As for halberds, arquebuses, and crossbows carried by the men while marching (before contact with any enemy), presumably they would have cloth covers on them until actually needed—a rust-preventative practice in use by the end of the medieval period.[70] Many of the men perhaps carried with them waterskins, as apparently was done during the Tunisian campaign of 1535.[71] Regarding sidearms such as light swords and daggers, most military men on active service would feel naked without having them on their persons, and the Spaniards of the sixteenth century would have been more adamant, especially when it came to swords.[72]

The lesson to have their weapons at the ready, even before they reached the unknown lands to the north, was imparted on Coronado's column with violent suddenness. When the army reached Chiametla, south of Culiacan, it paused to collect food in the area, a military necessity that is never endearing to the local population, as the Spaniards well knew from their experiences during the Reconquista.[73] A Spanish crossbowman "indiscreetly" chased some "enemies" into a village, and the army master, Lope de Samaniego, who was in charge of the foraging, followed with more men.[74] The crossbowman, who had been captured by the Indians and who had cried out for help, was rescued.[75] However, Samaniego, "thinking himself secure, raised the visor of his helmet just at the time when an arrow was shot from one of the thickets, entering one eye and piercing his brain."[76] In addition, "five or six" of the army master's squad were wounded.[77]

Diego Lopez, a member of the foraging party and an alderman from Seville, took charge of the foragers and sent word back to the main command about the death of Samaniego. The army was shocked with the news, but that did not prevent "[s]everal sorties, by which food was obtained and several of the natives taken prisoner."[78] According to Castaneda, the Spanish "hanged those who seemed to belong to the district where the army-master was killed."[79] As a salutary lesson, the bodies were "left swinging from various trees."[80]

This act of retaliation—hanging "those who seemed to belong to the district"—was only the beginning of an almost continuous method of guerrilla warfare practiced by both sides in the North American fighting between the indigenous and invading peoples for 350 years, to the end of the nineteenth century.

Don Garcia Lopez de Cardenas, "a gentleman of much valor," was appointed master of the camp and the army.[81] Then, having foraged, retaliated, and appointed Samaniego's replacement, the expedition was just about to continue its march north when Captain Melchior Diaz and Juan de Saldivar arrived back at Chiametla. They had been on their Mendoza-mandated reconnaissance to Chichilticalli, a locale considered the edge of the northern wilderness (and about five hundred miles from Culiacan). According to Viceroy Mendoza, who ultimately received a written copy of the report, Diaz found the northern country toward Cibola "cold and . . . with heavy frosts."[82] The cold had been so intense that a couple of the Spaniards were disabled and some of the Indian warriors with Diaz died of exposure.[83] This should have raised a red flag for the captain general regarding a hungry future, but, instead of changing plans to meet this possibility, he apparently relied on the advancing summer season and Alarcon's supply ships.

While Coronado certainly was privy to the findings of Diaz and Saldivar, only rumors of their pessimistic opinions probably leaked to the rest of the expedition.[84] But according to Castaneda, Friar Marcos reassured everyone "that what they would see should be good, and that he [de Niza] would place the army in a country where their hands would be filled, and in this way he [de Niza] quieted them so that they appeared well satisfied."[85]

Diaz's report, in addition to its less-than-generous opinion of the country, also contained important military information, although it was second-hand from Indian informants claiming familiarity with Cibola. As for this intelligence regarding the Cibolans and their defensive capability, Diaz, who already had experience fighting natives, wrote:

> [T]here are seven villages, a short day's travel from each other. . . . Their houses are built of stone and mud, rudely constructed. . . . Most of the houses are entered from the terraces, with ladders to the streets. The houses [mostly] are three and four stories high. . . . Ten or twelve adjoining houses are served by one ladder. . . . On the ground floor they have some slanted loop-holes as in the fortresses in Spain.
>
> The Indians say that when the inhabitants are attacked they all withdraw into their houses and fight from there, and that when they go to war they carry shields and wear some skins of the cattle of different colors. They fight with arrows, with small stone maces, they say, and with

other weapons, made of wood, that I could not identify. They eat human flesh and keep as slaves those whom they take prisoners in war.[86]

This detailed information (some of it inaccurate), even if it were known outside of Coronado and his staff, would not overly concern Spanish adventurers who hoped for wealth and fame more than they feared fighting. With its lifted spirits from Friar Marcos's oratory, Coronado's army headed north to Culiacan, "making detours into the country to seize provisions."[87] Presumably, since the Spanish core of the expedition had a large number of gentlemen-at-arms and was operating in potentially dangerous territory far from home, desertion was not a problem.[88] Certainly the Coronado chroniclers do not raise the issue while the army was marching toward its mysterious goal.

Because the expedition reached the outskirts of Culiacan on Easter eve, the townsfolk requested that the visitors not enter until Monday. Coronado consented to the delay, and the army went into camp and presumably celebrated mass on Easter and rested.[89]

Obviously, the municipal leaders and Coronado came to an agreement that encompassed more than a mere delay when it came to entering Culiacan. In fact, because he was their governor, the townsfolk apparently wanted to give him a proper welcome, something that would have been inappropriate on a holy day.[90] According to Castaneda,

> [T]he army started in the morning to go to the town and, as they approached, the inhabitants of the town came out on to an open plain with foot and horse drawn up in ranks as if for battle, and having its seven bronze pieces of artillery in position, making a show of defending their town. Some of our soldiers were with them. Our army drew up in the same way and began a skirmish with them, and after the artillery on both sides had been fired they were driven back, just as if the town had been taken by force of arms, which was a pleasant demonstration of welcome.[91]

This sham battle recently has been described by one historian as "a unique, farcical event."[92] Even one of the premier Coronado scholars has hinted that the "mock battle" merely was part of a ceremonial entrance into Culiacan.[93]

However, this exercise was neither unique nor farcical nor an elaborate but empty ritual. Up to very modern times—until they were replaced by autumn maneuvers, elaborate war games, and regular field exercises—sham battles were held for entertainment and for military training. Even a fifteenth-century revision of Vegetius's military treatise

A German print showing a Renaissance tourney. (*Author*)

*De Re Militari* noted that soldiers not only had to be "trained in the use of arms," they also, "through regular training and exercises," had to know "how to act and react together."[94] Such obviously was the case with Coronado's force at Culiacan, a unit that included many military veterans who were familiar with the tradition of mock combat.

That tradition was quite old. The Romans practiced cavalry maneuvers in what they called war games—training exercises that were imitated by Carolingian mounted men in the ninth century.[95] Then, during the Middle Ages, a practical reason for jousting tournaments was developing and maintaining skills for warfare. These popular contests, which many churchmen opposed, were dangerous even when blunted weapons were employed against opponents. Tournaments, in addition to knight-on-knight jousts, might also include mock battles called melees.[96] These training exercises, held in Spain up to the late fifteenth century, included light horsemen imitating a mounted bullfight to add to their skills.[97]

Medieval tournaments, even if not resulting in fatalities, often were ruinously expensive for the participating would-be heroes because the tournament entrants were expected to host celebrations and to wager on outcomes. In addition, such low-brow infantrymen as archers and crossbowmen were excluded from participation in these knightly affairs.[98] For Europe as a whole during the late fourteenth and fifteenth centuries, these extravagances, like knighthood itself, entered a period of decline and did not even purport to be team training for warfare.[99]

However, the sixteenth century, in which "collective training . . . [was] as important as individual prowess,"[100] saw modern adaptation and advancement on the theories regarding these contests. Being collective events, it was not just men-at-arms who participated—infantrymen also took part.

Thus, while still popular, festive events, these latter-day sham battles, occurring as early as the first two decades of the 1500s, were more inclusive as overall training exercises. In these contests, opposing forces attempted to capture a fortified position or to force an "enemy" from a fake village set up for the exercise. This was a more-valid attempt to replicate real-world battle situations regarding terrain and fortifications.[101] Indeed, in spring 1518, prior to launching another campaign into war-torn Italy, Francis I of France held such a sham battle, complete with a fake wooden village and wooden cannon shooting inflated balls at the attackers.[102]

Some military forces even regularly scheduled these exercises. The army of Venice, during the 1500s, instituted maneuvers in spring and fall—training exercises that seemed to be the precursors of what European armies would be doing regularly prior to the First World War.[103] The sham battles conducted by the Venetians also included mock assaults on castles.[104]

Although military service in the Spanish colonies did not become mandatory for physically fit and free males sixteen to forty years old until October 1540, militia duty had been expected from the locally settled Spaniards from the beginning. This was especially true on the frontier; when Nuno Guzman waged war in New Galicia in 1529, and conscription was enforced. Many of the militia officers and other ranks in these militias were veterans of European conflicts in Italy and the Low Countries.[105]

Thus, somewhat surprisingly, a sixteenth-century training maneuver—obviously also a morale booster for the expedition members and a form of entertainment for the locals—was performed on the frontier of New Spain by the army under Francisco Vasquez de Coronado. It not only prepared the expedition, especially the officers, for any anticipated opposition, but it had the added advantage of providing exceptional training for the militiamen of Culiacan.[106]

However, as is true in present-day combat training, there was always a danger in such exercises, even if the ammunition consisted of blanks and gunwads instead of actual ball ammunition. During the sham battle held by Francis I in 1518, while, "it was the finest combat ever seen and the most like real war, . . . some were killed and others wounded," noted a French eyewitness.[107] The risk was greater when it came to firing artillery pieces, even diminutive falconets. Gunners, when sponging out a hot piece or ladling powder into the mouth of a sponged bore, were advised to stand to one side of the barrel to avoid the results of a premature explosion, which could drive a rammer or a ladle into a gunner's body.[108] This danger was one reason why sixteenth-century battlefield guns took anywhere from two to three minutes to fire each round.[109]

But even standing to one side was no guarantee of safety. As Castaneda related, the one exception to the "pleasant demonstration of welcome" that day after Easter was "the artilleryman who lost a hand by a shot, from having ordered them to fire before he had finished drawing out the ramrod."[110] The unfortunate cannon cocker has been identified as expedition member Francisco Munoz.[111]

Coronado's army lay over at Culiacan "several days, because the inhabitants had gathered a good stock of provisions that year and each one shared his stock very gladly with his guests from our army," recalled Castaneda.[112] The visitors were, indeed, treated like guests. While the regular soldiers were "well lodged and entertained by the townspeople," the officers, "gentlemen and people of quality" were taken into the apartments of the well-to-do locals.[113]

The column also used this all-too-brief period of hospitable relaxation to further winnow excess baggage. "Some of the townspeople were not ill repaid for this hospitality," recalled Castaneda, "because all [of the gentlemen and people of quality who were with the army] had started with fine clothes and accoutrements, and as they were obliged to leave their fine stuff, . . . many preferred giving it to their hosts" rather than putting it on Alarcon's ship "that had followed the army along the coast to take the extra baggage."[114]

By the time the expedition got under way again, the army was well provisioned "with more than six hundred loaded animals, besides the friendly Indians and the servants—more than a thousand persons."[115]

However, one of the Spaniards, named Trujillo (or Trugillo or Truxillo), was not among this northbound throng. Trujillo was bucking for the sixteenth-century equivalent of a Section 8 discharge. According to Castaneda, he "pretended that he had seen a vision while he was bathing in the river." The devil, this shirker claimed, had told him to kill the captain general and marry his wife. For Friar Marcos, and other priests in Mexico when they heard the tale, this was proof that hell was against the expedition's goal of saving pagan souls and provided fodder for numerous sermons and homilies.[116]

While modern Catholic theologians still might wonder whether this slacker was being recruited for demonic possession, his contemporaries, like the seasoned soldiers many of them were, had no doubts that he was shamming. "The general ordered Truxillo to stay in that town and not to go on the expedition, which was what he was after when he made up that falsehood, judging from what afterward appeared to be the truth," wrote Castaneda.[117]

The incident of giving a weakling and a whiner what he wanted, while unimportant overall, no doubt was recalled by the ordinary soldiers of the expedition when they much later began to have doubts about the leadership of the captain general.[118] Nonetheless, the expedition undoubtedly was better off without Trujillo, and he probably would not have long survived at the hands of his not-amused comrades; hence his risky gamble with the growing influence of the Inquisition.[119]

As it turned out, Trujillo was not the only one who would not be close enough to the captain general to commit mayhem on his person— or to protect him. Coronado decided that his army, a bulky and cumbersome array of mankind and animals, was too slow for an exploratory campaign into generally unknown territory. Therefore, not yet being in the face of the enemy, the captain general made an important military decision to split his command. He and an advance force would proceed posthaste to Cibola. The rest of the army would follow at its own pace, set up camp at Corazones, and then await orders from Coronado.

# NINE

# The Garrison Left at
# San Geronimo

The policy of sending scouts in advance of an invading force is as ancient as the Old Testament. During medieval times, it was a "wise commander [who] would dispatch some of his troops to reconnoitre the line of march, reporting on the strength of garrisons and the defences of towns along the route of march."[1] The need for reconnaissance being applicable to all ages, it naturally held true in the sixteenth century. An English soldier of fortune of that century, Roger Williams, advised that a "commander that enters the enemy's countries ought to know the places that he doth attempt; if not, he ought to be furnished with guides, especially in coming to besiege a town."[2]

While Francisco Vasquez de Coronado was aware of the importance of reconnaissance, he also knew that the road ahead already had a reputation for being dangerous. As a proud Spaniard, he naturally believed that a commander should be at the front. Therefore, just before leaving Culiacan and hitting the trail, Captain General Coronado made a seemingly wise command decision. "[T]he general started ahead with about fifty horsemen and a few foot soldiers and most of the Indian allies," wrote Castaneda, "leaving the army, which was to follow him a fortnight later, with Don Tristan de Arellano in command as his lieutenant."[3] It should be noted that Viceroy Mendoza had agreed to this dispatch of an advance guard.[4]

According to Rodrigo Maldonado, Coronado was careful when he "took with himself [some] of the men-at-arms they had. . . . The general did not take with him [all] those he [previously] selected, because in choosing, he left other persons among the *caballeros*, captains, and men-at-arms who remained, both captains and men-at-arms, with as much competence and courage for whatever might be presented as those he took with him." Thus, Maldonado assured his interviewer, those Coronado selected were not any "more outstanding than those who remained."[5]

Since there supposedly was no distinction regarding courage or abilities, it is likely Coronado took those who were among the best equipped, whether horse or foot. Also indicating that he realized his reception at Cibola was likely to be unwelcome and he needed all the up-to-date military technology available, he took Hernando de Alvarado, chief of artillery, and his assistant, Juan Troyano.[6] If there had been any wagons or carts with the army used to carry provisions, Coronado almost certainly left all behind with Arellano.[7]

As for the large number of Indian allies taken along, the total could have been anywhere from 450 to 600, depending on their total representation within the main army.[8] However, historians Richard Flint and Shirley Cushing Flint have hinted that at least nine hundred Indians were with the advance, using the methodology of taking Castaneda's estimate when he said "most" of the Indians went with the advance, but then obviously basing the result on the thirteen hundred estimate of Indian allies and not on Castaneda's estimate of eight hundred.[9]

Taking a relatively large number of allies along did not necessarily reflect a belief that their overwhelming presence would be necessary or even helpful, especially when rations were a concern. It more likely indicates Coronado's recognition that since they were indigenous auxiliaries, they would be more likely to get bored, give up, and walk home if they were not taken along on the initial adventure. Any Spaniards left behind were less likely to desert as quickly, especially since there still was that hope of wealth.

Coronado, with his advance force, departed from Culiacan on April 22, 1540.[10] It was a "lightly equipped," enthusiastic bunch, and, probably reflecting their desire to save pagan souls rather than to reform soldierly lives, all the friars went with the advance, "since none of them wished to stay with the army."[11] On May 26, the captain general "reached the valley of Corazones and rested there for several days."[12]

Mendoza, after the Mixton War, envisioned a line of presidios to protect against the raids of wild northern tribes. However, it was not until the latter part of the sixteenth century (and after that discovery of rich silver deposits) that this line of presidios, not unlike American Army posts of the nineteenth century, began to be built.[25]

In those future years, when there was perseverance, "the Spanish presidio evolved from a simple garrisoned fort with a purely military mission into the nucleus of a civilian town, a market for the produce of neighboring farms and ranches, and an agency for an Indian reservation."[26]

However, in 1540, the immediate problem in leaving a garrison town behind was that it would be seen by natives as diminishing the main expedition. "If he [an invader] left fortified places behind him, he must block them by detachments, whose loss would enfeeble his striking force," wrote a renowned student of the sixteenth-century military.[27] "On the other hand," he continued, "if the garrison left behind was too weak, it would hardly serve its purpose. If such a fort in the rear was too undermanned, it would tempt opponents to rise against the garrison."[28]

Thus Coronado had to balance his options in the matter of garrisoning San Geronimo sufficiently, but not too much. It was the classic military dilemma, where a commander does not want to employ too few troops to do the job but also does not want to risk too many to be missed if disaster strikes.

In authorizing the establishment of a post at San Geronimo, Coronado knew that to the north beckoned a territory that was only vaguely known, but definitely hostile, based on what had occurred to Esteban and to Friar Marcos de Niza. This region certainly would have been intimidating on paper if the Spaniards had been provided with accurate statistics.

It was estimated during the early twentieth century that at the time of the Spanish *entrada*, the various Indians falling under the pueblo lifestyle numbered approximately twenty thousand, situated in about seventy separate communities. These pueblos, including those of the Tiguex in the southern portion, mostly hugged the lengthy Rio Grande valley. The Hopi towns were located off to the northwest, and the Zuni, linguistically different, were to the east of them. Other Puebloan tribes were to the east of the Rio Grande, including those living on the upper Pecos River.[29] While these numbers would indicate that Coronado needed a bigger army if permanent occupation was the goal, the strength of the opposition also made securing that line of communications and supply extremely important.

# The Invasion of Zuni

Leaving Arellano with the bulk of the expedition, including the majority of the Spanish soldiery, to set up the San Geronimo garrison and probable supply depot, Coronado headed north toward Cibola. This excursion would take about eighty days, which about matched the rations taken.

Although this was an advance guard, Coronado decided to make it strong enough to be a respectable strike force. Castaneda estimated that the captain general "started ahead with about fifty horsemen and a few foot soldiers and most of the Indian allies."[1] This recollection apparently placed the number too low.

There are other, more contemporaneous and more generous estimates of the horse and foot taken along. Captain Juan Jaramillo thought Coronado had "70 horsemen" with him.[2] Another expedition member, part of the advance force, wrote that there were eighty horsemen and twenty-five infantrymen.[3] However, in addition to the cavalry and the infantry, the third combat branch also was represented, for the chief of the artillery was taken along as well as "part of the artillery."[4] Whether this meant two or three or four of the falconets were taken along is unknown. The artillery complement numbered probably two, but perhaps three pieces, keeping in mind both the presence of the captain of artillery and the relative smallness of the entire advance party of Spaniards.[5] Probably the horsemen and footmen taken up the trail were among the best armed and armored, with many of the arquebuses and crossbows.

Coronado later wrote Mendoza, "[I]t was fortunate that I did not employ the whole army in this undertaking, because the hardships have been so very great and the lack of food such that I do not believe this enterprise could have been completed before the end of this year, and even if it should be accomplished, it would be with a great loss of life."[6] Nonetheless, with the auxiliary contingent, there probably were about 550 to 600 in this considerable reconnaissance in force.

The advance column first headed toward Corazones, where Vaca had extolled the generosity of the natives. However, it was no easy picnic for the Spaniards, their Indian allies, and the accompanying Africans. The advance guard already was seeing problems with provisions, for the sheep taken along as food on the hoof soon fell behind and many of them perished.[7]

According Coronado's report, "Ten or twelve of the horses had died of exhaustion by the time we reached the valley of Corazones, because they were unable to stand the strain of carrying heavy burdens and feeding little. For similar reasons some of our negroes and several of the Indians deserted, which was not a slight loss for the expedition."[8]

Unfortunately, the corn at Corazones was not yet ripe. A little corn was obtained from another valley by barter, which, according to Coronado, "relieved the friendly Indians and some of the Spaniards."[9] However, Coronado apparently punished any Spaniards who stole corn on their own.[10] It is possible that on this march north, "several Christians"—Spaniards—were killed by poison arrows of local Indians who had turned unfriendly.[11]

According to Castaneda, who did not participate in this hungry advance and would not recall these significant hardships, the march north was otherwise militarily uneventful, although it generally became more melancholy regarding morale. He wrote:

> The general and his force crossed the country without trouble, as they found everything peaceful, because the Indians knew Friar Marcos and some of the others who had been with Melchior Diaz when he went with Juan de Saldibar to investigate. After the general had crossed the inhabited region and came to Chichilticalli, where the wilderness begins, and saw nothing favorable, he could not help feeling somewhat downhearted, for, although the reports were very fine about what was ahead, there was nobody who had seen it except the Indians who went with the negro, and these had already been caught in some lies.[12]

In addition, the somewhat renowned "red house" made of red earth of Chichilticalli was found to be "one tumbledown house without any roof, although it appeared to have been a strong place at some former time when it was inhabited, and it was very plain that it had been built by a civilized and warlike race of strangers who had come from a distance."[13]

But the food and forage situation was no better at Chichilticalli. Although the column badly needed rest and recuperation, only two days were spent at the red house. The command virtually staggered forward, with Coronado recalling that "[t]he horses were so exhausted that they could not stand it, so that in this last desert we lost more horses than before; and several Indian allies and a Spaniard named Espinosa besides two negroes, who died from eating some herbs because they were out of food."[14]

Undoubtedly further depressing Coronado, when Melchior Diaz arrived with the results of his reconnaissance, he had not given much hope to the captain general of obtaining food easily at Cibola. As for the so-called Kingdom of Cibola itself—the land of the Zuni—while the Spaniards seemed to think there were seven "cities" there, that number is not beyond debate. After Coronado and his army arrived, the count varied from observer to observer, from five to seven. In 1540, there may have been but six occupied Zuni pueblos.[15] Captain Juan Jaramillo thought that in "this province of Cibola there are five little villages" besides the main one.[16]

Nonetheless, despite all the daunting information (some of it inaccurate), the vanguard of the expedition continued on "through the wilderness" in probably a general north-northeasterly direction. This leg of the march took fifteen days, north through much of what is now Arizona, and the command reached the Zuni River.[17]

This was about "eight leagues from the village" of Cibola, where the Spaniards saw the "first Indians from that country." But these two natives "ran away to give the news."[18] Considering the challenges and the distance, the advance to that point should rank as an epic military march. The column was entering into what is now New Mexico.

A pulp magazine writer, R. Edgar Moore, backed by imagination rather than solid research, nonetheless probably was accurate when he wrote of the Coronado column as it approached Cibola (also known as Hawikuh, with various spellings), "The cavalrymen and foot soldiers were on constant guard now, for they were penetrating deep into the

Northern Mystery. Despite the brilliant sunlight the horsemen took to wearing their cuirasses again in case of sudden attack, and at night the soldiers slept on their arms."[19]

But Coronado, or one of the veterans advising him, showed some good sense. Master of the army Lopez de Cardenas was sent to guard a strategic position—what he called "a bad pass"—that controlled the approach to Cibola.[20] Coronado later explained the occupation of the pass to Mendoza:

"After this I ordered the maestre de campo to go and see if there was any bad passage which the Indians might be able to defend, and to take it and protect it until the next day, when I would come up. He went, and found a very bad place in our way where we might have received much harm. He immediately established himself there with the force which he was conducting."[21]

That night, as the vanguard was camped in this pass, according to Coronado, "[t]he Indians came . . . to occupy that place so as to defend it, and, finding it taken, they attacked our men. According to what I have been told they attacked like valiant men, although in the end they had to retreat in flight, because the maestre de campo was on the watch and kept his men in good order."[22] Coronado later would testify that some of the Spanish horses were wounded by arrows during the skirmish.[23]

There were indications that some of the Spaniards with Lopez de Cardenas were green and that most, if not all, were on edge. According to Castaneda, "[S]ome Indians in a safe place yelled so that, although the men were ready for anything, some were so excited that they put their saddles on hind-side before; but these were the new fellows. When the veterans had mounted and ridden around the camp, the Indians fled. None of them could be caught because they knew the country."[24] Cardenas later credited "two mounted men who were on guard duty" with frustrating the supposed attempt to kill all the Spaniards.[25]

Like most of the sites of the Coronado Expedition, the exact location of this first, historic skirmish between these disparate cultures in the American Southwest is unknown. One archaeologist has estimated that it occurred anywhere from "6 to 12 miles southwest of Hawikku."[26]

The next day, as the column advanced into what is now New Mexico, they saw a "settled country in good order"—probably indicating that there was ample evidence of cultivation—but when they actually viewed the hilltop village of Cibola or Hawikuh, they found it to be "a little, crowded village, looking as if it had been crumpled up together," wrote Castaneda, undoubtedly relying on what he was told by members of the advance column. "There are haciendas in New Spain which make a better appearance at a distance."[27]

Hawikuh, it is believed, had been occupied since 1400 by the Zuni and, before that, it may have been the community of other people since about 1000 AD.[28] But the tired and hungry Spaniards were not impressed by matters of archaeological antiquity. "[S]uch were the curses some hurled at Friar Marcos that I pray God may protect him from them," noted Castaneda generously.[29]

But Marcos was not the only one who should have had a guilty conscience that day. The Zuni, whether they were sorry or not, supposedly had recognized the connection with the death of the "Black Mexican" a year before when they learned of the approach of Coronado's expedition. The Zuni, according to their oral tradition, had "always felt in danger and went about watching the bushes." Now, true enough, many men of Sinaloa had come back, and "[t]hey wore coats of iron and even bonnets of metal and carried for weapons short canes that spit fire and made thunder."[30]

Nonetheless, to the residents, Cibola was home and worth defending. Also, largely forgotten by a century of tourists, the Puebloan people were not Quakers. While not a marauding warrior race such as the Apache, "[t]he Pueblo Indians were able fighters. . . . There were occasional battles between two or more of their villages."[31] In addition, while "the pueblo dwellers preferred to live in seclusion and peace, and . . . fought best on the defensive," they reportedly were warlike enough to take the scalps of fallen enemies.[32]

The men of Cibola Pueblo, in particular, were not ready to submit to these "men of Sinaloa" wearing iron and spitting fire, for they were the most militant of the lot when it came to the Seven Cities. The old-time Zuni of the several communities of Cibola were honest enough to recognize that they all were generally "bad tempered and quick to anger."[33] However, the Zuni of Hawikuh had an especially noted reputation for aggressiveness among the Zuni of the other pueblos. These other Zuni believed that those of Hawikuh could be aroused every bit as easily as a hive of bees.

In one of their folk tales, when an arrow was shot into the middle of the community plaza by a couple of Zuni boys as a prank, the Hawikuh residents "all poured down" out of the pueblo looking for the "enemy." In fact, it was generally conceded throughout Cibola that even if those of Hawikuh took casualties in defending their city, still "many, many" would keep coming on. Only "until many were killed or wounded" would "the remainder [decide] to flee."[34]

Adding some logic to the stubbornness of the Zuni of Hawikuh, one must remember that the pueblo lifestyle was not merely a socialist exercise in communal living. The Puebloan architecture, as hinted at by Diaz's reconnaissance report, was an example of defensive military engineering every bit as much as European castles, chateaus, and manor houses.[35] Doorways, even small ones, did not usually appear on the ground level of old-time pueblos. Windows on any level were nonexistent. The first-story apartments or storage rooms were entered through trapdoors in their roofs, and chimneys were limited to small vent holes by the fireplaces and outlets on the roofs.[36] Therefore, for all of their disappointing appearance to Spanish eyes, the cities of Cibola were formidable fortresses every bit as much as were the contemporary wooden palisades of the Indians that other Europeans found on the Eastern Seaboard.

But the Spaniards and their allies had traveled a long distance to reach Cibola. In addition to having made this very considerable effort, as Coronado later informed Viceroy Mendoza, "that was the place where the food was, of which we were in such great need."[37]

An immovable object, a remnant of ancient and pagan times, was about to meet an irresistible force in the form of sixteenth-century Spanish steel and medieval Roman Catholic faith. Ironically, because the agrarian people of Zuni lived in settled, yet heavily fortified, communities, the Spanish way of European warfare would prove to be effective, albeit risky.

# ELEVEN

# Modern Tactics Versus Antiquity: The Battle of Hawikuh

The Coronado Expedition, persuasively demonstrating that it was a military endeavor, had its share of blood-and-thunder action. The first significant battle occurred at the Cibolan pueblo of Hawikuh on July 7, 1540. While the contemporary chronicles often are eloquent in their omissions and contradictions, much of the story of the Battle of Hawikuh can be pieced together.[1] In addition, using information regarding known military doctrine of the age, other gaps can be filled in circumstantially with reasonable certainty.

According to Pedro de Castaneda, who was not there but who would hear the war stories of his comrades, the Zuni people of the seven villages of Cibola had gathered together at Hawikuh (also called Cibola) to meet—but not to greet—the Spaniards and their allies. "These folks waited for the army, drawn up by divisions in front of the village."[2] Adding to the tension in a manner later used by Hollywood directors, smoke signals apparently rose to the sky from points around Cibola.[3]

There, before the pueblo of Hawikuh, the Zuni warriors stood, probably indicating as much a warning and deterrent as an effort to take the fight to the enemy standing beyond their homes. Historian F. W. Hodge estimated the town then claimed nine hundred residents in two hundred terraced homes.[4] Reportedly, the adult male Cibolans already had evacuated their women and children from the city.[5]

As for Coronado, true to his instructions and probably true to his desires, he showed restraint and made an effort to give diplomacy a chance. As Coronado explained in his letter to the viceroy, he sent some horsemen forward, under the command of the master of the camp, Garcia Lopez de Cardenas. Also in this detachment were Friars Daniel and Luis and Coronado's personal secretary and notary, Hernando Bermejo (or Vermizzo). The contingent was to assure the Zuni that "we were not coming to do them any harm, but to defend them in the name of our lord, the emperor."[6] It is not unlikely that a trumpeter also accompanied the group, for trumpeters in the sixteenth century, like drummers in the eighteenth century, were used to convey diplomatic messages or offers regarding truces.[7]

These individuals read the *requerimiento,* a standard advisement mandated by King Ferdinand of Spain in 1511. The document declared that the papacy held the world for God and that the pope had awarded the hemisphere to the Spanish. Through this formal reading and announcement, the people addressed were told they were now subject to Spain and to the Christianity of the Roman Catholic Church. If they refused submission to Spain and acceptance of the new religion, they would be considered rebels, have their property forfeited, and be made slaves of the Spanish.[8] While the *requerimiento* rightly has been lambasted and lampooned as containing legalistic and theological language that was beyond the ken of most of the addressees (even if there was a proper interpreter), like the act of drawing a line in the sand, its basic meaning was apparent: peace or war, surrender and submit or fight.

In addition, while the *requerimiento* was tailored for pagan towns in the New World, throughout history it had been customary for would-be conquerors to summon a town to surrender before there was an investment in bloodshed by the attackers.[9] By the sixteenth century, it still was the formal law of war that if attackers had to breach and enter the walls, then there would follow "an awful time of pillage and every form of cruelty and disorder, as was ever the way in those days when a city was taken by storm."[10]

As Coronado explained in his letter to the viceroy:

Meanwhile I arrived with all the rest of the cavalry and footmen and found a large body of Indians on the plain who began to shoot arrows. In obedience to the suggestions of your Lordship and of [our majesty], I did not wish that they should be attacked, and enjoined my men, who were begging me for permission, from doing so, telling them that they ought not to molest them, and that the enemy was doing us no harm, and it was not proper to fight such a small number of people.[11]

However, this legalistic and conciliatory stance on the part of the captain general only encouraged the Zuni. "[W]hen the Indians saw that we did not move, they took greater courage and grew so bold that they came up almost to the heels of our horses to shoot their arrows," wrote Coronado to Mendoza.[12] Later, when called on to defend his actions, the captain general estimated that the number of Zuni warriors was high enough to be worrisome—"[s]ome three hundred Indians with bows, arrows, and shields."[13]

According to historian Mota Padilla, who used some primary sources, "more than two hundred Indian warriors came out" of the pueblo, and although they were warned "to keep the peace, they made lines on the earth that no one should pass, and when our people attempted to do so, they let fly a shower of arrows, and began the attack."[14] This use of archers to attempt to break up the formation of an advancing enemy, analogous to putting out skirmishers, should not have surprised the Spanish. The Aztecs had used such standard battlefield tactics.[15]

"[T]hey wounded Hernando Bermejo's horse and pierced the loose flap of the frock of father Friar Luis, the former companion of the Lord Bishop of Mexico," recalled an apparent member of the Spanish party.[16] Lopez de Cardenas later testified that the Cibolans "lodged another [arrow] in the clothing and armor of the said notary."[17] Coronado, in later justifying his actions, claimed Brother Luis actually was hit.[18]

This growing defiance was too much of a provocation for Coronado, especially when the friars gave their approval for counterviolence. "On this account I saw that it was no longer time to hesitate, and, as the priests approved the action, I charged them."[19] With their battle cry of "Santiago!" (Saint James), the Spaniards were soon among the Zuni.[20]

Mounted Spaniards had a reputation for being impetuous and almost irresistible in the attack, especially in the Americas. In 1520, when a vast army of Aztecs blocked Cortes's force of Spaniards and Tlascalan allies on the plain of Otumba, it was only the desperate strategy of Cortes and his troop of men-at-arms attacking in the center, where the Aztec command post was located, that won the bloody day.[21] And, at the fierce battle for the Alabaman village of Mauvila, in 1540, the horsemen of De Soto caused such destruction on the open ground that the much more numerous Tuscaloosa Indians were forced back into their village to be slaughtered.[22]

However, as cavalrymen know, a reckless hell-for-leather charge has its risks. During the last campaign of the Reconquista of Spain, one such cavalry charge was drawn into a Moorish counterattack that was a strategic setback.[23] Fortunately for Coronado's men-at-arms, the Zuni, like most Indians during the conquistador period, had neither the tactical nor technical ability for such a counterstroke.[24] It was only Coronado's apparently cautious effort to limit the risk or to stem the bloodshed that caused the Spaniards to halt their charge prematurely.

As Coronado's report recalled the brief skirmish on the plain and its panicky aftermath on the part of the defenders:

> There was little to do, because they suddenly took flight, some running toward the city, which was near and well fortified, and others toward the plain, wherever chance led them.
>
> Some Indians were killed, and others might have been slain if I had allowed them to be pursued. But I saw that there would be little advantage in this, because the Indians who were outside were few, and those who had retired to the city, added to the many who had remained there in the first place, were numerous.[25]

While Coronado was vague about the Indian casualties on the plain, others were not. Mota Padilla later estimated that "more than twenty were left on the field, [and then] they barricaded themselves in their quarters."[26] Lopez de Cardenas, later defending his actions, estimated "that not more than ten or twelve of the Indians were killed."[27]

As for the Spanish casualties, according to Coronado, "Two or three . . . soldiers were hurt in the battle which we fought on the plain, and three horses were killed, one belonging to Don Garcia Lopez, another to Villegas, and the third to Don Alonso Manrique."[28] Another witness, without mentioning human casualties, confirmed that the Zuni "killed three horses and wounded seven or eight."[29] All the soldiers and all the horses recovered, noted Coronado.[30]

But this little military victory did not solve any of the Spaniards' immediate problems. Apparently in following up the withdrawal of the Zuni into their city, some of the Spaniards closest to the pueblo attempted to force an early entry into the stronghold on the heels of the retreating Indians before a defense could be organized, a standard albeit difficult military stratagem.[31] However, according to an anonymous member of the advance party, "Because of the great injury they were doing to us from the flat roofs, we were compelled to draw back."[32]

The Zuni still held their fortress, and that meant a quick assault was in the offing, for a siege was not an option. As Coronado wrote, "As that was the place where the food was, of which we were in such great need, I assembled my whole force and divided it as seemed to me best for the attack on the city, and surrounded it. As the hunger which we suffered would not permit of any delay, I dismounted several of these gentlemen and soldiers."[33]

During the sixteenth century, when there was time, it was the practice of commanders to exhort and harangue their troops before they went into battle.[34] If the captain general followed this military custom, he probably did so at this point, albeit briefly, for hungry men are not patient.

Friar Marcos, who had lost most of his credibility with the army, also was listened to on this occasion, for he said, regarding the justness of the upcoming battle, "Take your shields and go after them."[35] Thus, presumably while many of their numerous Indian allies and a few of the mounted men-at-arms were encircling the pueblo, the Spaniards prepared to take their sustenance by use of their full force.

Because the Puebloans of Hawikuh demonstrated some understanding of basic warfare, the Spaniards, experienced on so many battlefields by 1540, also put their individual and collective knowledge to work. In fact, the Spanish of the era had a reputation for assaulting citadels "under showers of bullets, stones, unslaked lime, molten lead flaming hoops, and whatever else desperate townsfolk could lay hands on."[36] Although the captain general was without notable battle experience, with the inclusion of veterans of Spain's Italian Wars (and other conflicts), it must be presumed that Coronado's forces did not proceed to assault the rude fortress willy-nilly, no matter how famished they were.[37]

In order to be successful, even against primitive Puebloans, and to limit casualties, the attack on Hawikuh undoubtedly followed some basic European rules of warfare and must have employed some standard techniques.[38] These techniques were required since the Zuni city was militarily formidable. In fact, because of its relatively rudimentary stage of development, the town had certain defensive advantages. Since it had neither wheeled vehicles nor large domesticated stock, there was no need for entryways on the ground floor. Hence, battering down a main fortress door would not be an option for the Spaniards; they would have to climb walls under fire.

The two or three or four artillery pieces were brought out and probably set up in front of the Spanish horse and foot, as was the custom in Europe at the time. Fortunately, Captain Hernando de Alvarado, the chief of the artillery, had the experienced soldier Juan Troyano assisting him at Cibola. Troyano, a Spanish veteran of the Italian Wars, apparently served as a de facto command sergeant major of the expedition, for one of his comrades later said that Coronado and his captains acted on military matters only after consulting him.[39] Troyano, according to another comrade, "was in charge of [the] half a dozen *versillos* supplied by the viceroy."[40] A modern historian concluded that this professional soldier, a man of many talents, was also gifted with picking up languages, including those of Native Americans.[41] Therefore, Troyano probably also was the de facto battery commander of the ordnance present the day of this initial battle.

However, these Spanish *versos* were small guns, equivalent to the French and English falconets, "the smallest listed artillery piece of its day, firing a 1 or 1 1/4 pound shot."[42] As indicated, that shot might be made of iron, lead, or stone—or the projectiles could have been scrap such as nails.[43] In the event, these falconets, with bores of but two inches and their approximate one-pound balls, were hardly siege guns.

As previously discussed, these heavier weapons with the expedition have been translated and classified as *versillos* or *pedereros*—swivel guns. Also noted previously, the name swivel gun conjures up a picture of a small, antipersonnel gun, often a crude breechloader in the sixteenth century, with the barrel's trunnions supported by a rotating, U-shaped yoke and peg mount.[44] Of course, these man-killing *versos* often had their metal U-shaped yokes set into the gunwales of Spanish ships in the sixteenth century.[45] As such, they were not mounted on carriages.

Therefore, Richard Flint in particular has determined that these small artillery pieces used at Hawikuh were swivel guns designed to fire from a stationary type of wooden frame—a base—presumably without even small wheels.[46] Certainly, especially in the early years of European artillery, before true field guns, even light siege artillery was mounted on immovable wooden stands.[47] However, this theory does not mean that Coronado's guns could not have been disassembled and carried in carts or wagons.[48] It there were such carts or wagons, the guns could have been fired while in the vehicles, a tactic that was employed as early as 1419, when dissident Hussites had seven small cannons shooting from wagons.[49]

Militarily, it would make sense for the Spaniards with Coronado to place these artillery pieces on moveable gun carriages. During the Italian Wars, at the Battle of Ravenna on April 11, 1512, "the Spaniards for the first time turned the cannon [with them] into a field-arm, by mounting it on carriages and driving it to the front among the attacking lines." In turn, this method was thereafter adopted by their Venetian opponents.[50] Soldiers everywhere welcomed, if not demanded, this mobility in battle. Even the Chinese—who (although presumably the inventors of gunpowder) did not keep advancing their technology as to firepower—mounted guns on wheeled carriages as early as the late fourteenth century.[51]

There was this same desire for mobility in the Americas. Even the earliest colony established by Columbus had "carriage-mounted *falconeta*-type artillery."[52] One historian of the conquistadors, noting that often little was written about the use of artillery, has concluded that the guns of the conquest period were on wheeled carriages, perhaps without limbers, and likely pulled along by Indian porters, maybe with the barrel pointing in the direction of travel.[53] Viceroy Mendoza, in fact, in protesting that there were occasions when the Indians had to be employed as manual laborers, noted that much of the country was too rugged for carts and "artillery had to be dragged by hand."[54] There was no mention of pack animals by Mendoza regarding the transportation of guns.

There is contemporary or near-contemporary support for the idea that Coronado's guns were on wheeled carriages. A Flemish painting by Jan Mostaert, presumably showing the attack on the Zuni and with some highly inaccurate details, has two falconets on such gun carriages in front of the infantry attack.[55] This painting apparently was commissioned for the government of Charles V, so it would be based on some official reports.

There also is substantial circumstantial evidence supporting the theory that Spanish ordnance in the Americas would be mounted on wheels, transported as wheeled artillery, and employed in battle on these wheeled carts or carriages. First, the contemporary native codex illustrations of the army of Hernando Cortes fighting the Aztecs show Cortes's artillery pieces mounted on wheeled gun carriages.[56] Perhaps more persuasive, when Cortes was fighting to regain possession of Mexico City, the Spaniards, according to an early historian, removed one of their heavy cannon from one of their lake-borne brigantines "and mounted it on a heavy cart to use against the enemies."[57]

This mounting of guns on carts was standard procedure for other expeditions outside of Europe bereft of normal logistical support and supply. When a Portuguese expeditionary force arrived in Abyssinia in 1541, it brought swivel guns and other artillery to fight Somali Muslims invading the Christian kingdom. Even though the Ethiopian countryside was ruggedly mountainous, the European artillerists built carts to mount the guns (which, like Flint opined about Coronado's guns, also had bases) and to transport powder and ball.[58]

While this artillery-transport topic has not been addressed in detail, most Coronado scholars undoubtedly would be satisfied to assume that the guns were carried on the backs of some of the abundant pack animals. Indeed, the historian Mota Padilla supports this methodology, saying that pack animals were "loaded with six field-guns."[59]

Nonetheless, the evidence regarding the artillery of Cortes as well as the known mounting of such swivel guns on carts in Abyssinia, a country as rugged as much of Mexico and the American Southwest, allows some debate on this point, especially since those falconet barrels could weigh anywhere from three hundred to five hundred pounds. And, as will be seen, the existence of small-wheeled cannon, on carts or on carriages, might explain the subsequent—and significant—engineering exploit on the Pecos River in 1541.

Also relating to the military engineers and pioneers who would feature in the building of that bridge, it is obvious their presence with the Coronado column meant that tools other than wheels also likely were present at the attack on Hawikuh. Among such construction implements, axes, for example, would be more than useful in such an attack. While there is no mention of such weapons (or tools) being included in the inventory of Coronado's equipment, it is known that at least one "Spanish battle-axe" accompanied the contemporary De Soto Expedition.[60] As L. Frank Baum's Tin Woodman could verify, such an instrument would prove invaluable in cleaving a wood door in twain. Although the pueblos of the era were without such doors, an axe also could demolish adobe, at least with patience. Certainly, since the expedition had bridge-building capabilities, Coronado's main pack train, even if it carried no battle-axes, contained such tools as woodsmen's axes, carpenters' adzes, and mattocks. Although it is possible that no such tools accompanied the captain-general's advance column, since the guns were brought along some sort of hand tools would be present.

In addition, that most basic of siege machines, the scaling ladder, had been part of military equipment since before the second millennium BC. At the great siege of Constantinople in 1453, of which Spaniards would be all too aware, the Turks employed two thousand ladders in their assault.[61] While it is clear that later in its conquests Coronado's army used such ladders, there is no mention of them regarding the attack on Hawikuh, although Coronado mentioned a single scaling ladder (belonging to the inhabitants) on "the wall on one side."[62]

Nonetheless, it is hard to imagine that Spanish ladders were not employed at Hawikuh, even though this assault was an initial learning experience for many of the Spaniards. Certainly Coronado was on notice that absent a friendly welcome, ladders would be needed. Friar Niza, among his hearsay exaggerations, had reported that the Cibolans were said to climb up into their terraced buildings by ladders.[63] In addition, the reconnaissance report of Melchior Diaz specifically had advised that there was a paucity of ladders to be found at the multistoried pueblo.[64]

Especially during this era, military men assaulting buildings several stories high necessarily would have a plan for gaining the height; even the valiant and vainglorious Spanish saw no honor in dying before coming to grips with the enemy.[65] Some technique for scaling would be employed if for no other reason than to avoid being stoned to death like trapped animals in a pit.[66] At the time, it was well known that absent breaches made by siege guns or mines (explosives placed under a fortress wall by tunneling), the least expensive alternative (in money, if not in lives) in capturing a citadel was the use of scaling ladders.[67]

Indeed, the Spanish in particular often employed scaling ladders. During the last stages of the Reconquista, a strike force of Spaniards performed a *coup-de-main* against the Moorish citadel of Alhama de Granada by marching three successive nights before surprising the garrison by placing their ladders against the fortress and swarming over the walls.[68] As for in the Americas, as will be detailed below, Hernando Pizarro's forces used scaling ladders when assaulting an Inca fortress during the revolts of 1535–1536.[69]

For Coronado's force, any ladders likely would have been simple wooden affairs. Perhaps they would be fancy enough to have iron hooks on top for grappling a wall and sharpened iron points at the bottom for securing the ladder into the earth.[70] It is not impossible that the equipage brought from Mexico included previously made and transportable scaling ladders, to be assembled when needed.[71] Such ladders were recommended in the military works of Roman writer Flavius

Renatus Vegetius; an illustrated edition of Flavius had appeared in 1475 with virtual blueprints for such ladders.[72]

However, it is unlikely that any scaling ladders used by this advance guard of the Coronado Expedition were either prefabricated or fancy. More likely they were put together as the army was waiting to advance through that "bad pass," not then knowing whether the Zunis would capitulate peacefully.[73] If the ladders were made in the immediate area of Hawikuh, they likely were made of pinyon or juniper, which were the trees the Zuni used to construct their pueblos.[74] It should be noted that some archaeological work has found period nails, which could have been holding together ladders, "distributed on the western edge of the site with some clusters near passageways that permitted access to the interior portions of the pueblo."[75]

As for the basis for their own ladders, apparently minimally employed, the Zuni likely used "a heavy log with the stub ends of the limbs remaining."[76] Obviously, an attacking force with a few tools also could make similarly primitive log ladders with relative ease, or just nail crossbars onto such logs.

In any event, the second and major attack on Hawikuh began. "I ordered the harquebusiers and crossbowmen to begin the attack and drive back the enemy from the defenses, so that the natives could not injure us," reported Coronado later.[77] This was according to long-standing military doctrine; missile troops were "of use to open a battle, to provoke the enemy, to damage their defenses, to inflict wounds, to kill from a distance, and to disrupt their ranks," advised Aelian's book on warfare.[78] It is likely that Coronado also used bowmen within the ranks of his Indian auxiliaries to dart in, fire their arrows, and then quickly withdraw.[79]

Presumably, the falconets opened the ball by peppering the pueblo with shot, using small, jagged pieces of iron as canister if the range was short enough.[80] In addition, the Spaniard's Indian allies who were not archers also were put into position for the upcoming assault, undoubtedly set to follow behind their better-protected Spanish friends, who would provide mass and momentum to any entry into the pueblo.

Once again, pulp writer R. Edgar Moore likely was accurate in his imaginative description of a scene seemingly reenacted from ancient times. "Sharp yells split the air as they [the Cibolans] pulled up the ladders leading to the upper tiers of the city. Suddenly the air was filled with the waspish sound of winging arrows."[81] Based on how the Zunis

remembered, in their oral tradition, killing Esteban one year previously, their defensive weaponry
also included rock-throwing
slings and war clubs, in addition
to their short bows and arrows.[82]
While arrows and clubs were universal weapons, the Spanish in
particular had experience defending against stone slings when
fighting the Moors during the
Reconquista.[83] In the Americas,
the Spaniards learned to fear the
slingshots of the Incas, which,
David-and-Goliath-like, could
stun a man even wearing a helmet.[84]

A nineteenth-century interpretation of a Spanish arquebusier. (*Author*)

The standard procedure for an assault of a fortified town, employed
in ancient times by Alexander the Great and certainly used regularly
since late medieval times, was for a bombardment to precede the attack
and for multiple threats or feints to be made at various points on the
defensive line.[85] In sixteenth-century Italy, the combatants also
employed the time-honored procedure of besiegers "dividing the attention of the garrison between several breaches."[86] Finally, during the
actual attack, usually at one point while the feints were made elsewhere,
missile throwers (whether archers, crossbowmen, or arquebusiers) were
supposed to lay down a base of fire to keep the heads of defenders down
as the attackers climbed up their scaling ladders.[87] The shootists, especially arquebusiers, generally were not expected to participate in an
actual assault against the walls.[88]

The assault itself was the job for men with armor, in this case dismounted men-at-arms.[89] This also was standard doctrine, notwithstanding the beliefs of some soldiers and many historians that it was the
ordinary soldiers who were to lead the way and to act as sacrificial "cannon fodder." Those leading the way "should be the best soldiers in the
army, excelling all others in stature, strength and military skill." These
best warriors provided an attack with "its power, impetus and momentum from the mass of men that presses forward from the rear."[90]
Indeed, "being among the first to enter in the assault of a fortified

place" might qualify a medieval man-at-arms for an additional device on his heraldic crest.[91]

While their native allies also would be subject to similar bravado, the Spaniards, especially the hidalgos, would claim the status of being at the fore as a point of honor.[92] Thus, the dismounted men-at-arms being armored (as probably most of them in the advance party were), they would be the ones to declare, "Follow me!"

The weapon of choice for these sixteenth-century storm troopers would be swords and rapiers (and perhaps short pikes or halberds), which could be thrust forward in a tight place or formation.[93] Those immediately behind the first rank were also to be top-notch men "of great use in emergencies."[94]

The Spanish in the New World generally followed the dictates of the standard military theory, and this included threatening a citadel at several points.[95] In 1535–1536, when Hernando Pizarro's Spaniards were assaulting an Inca fortification in Cuzco, they found one particularly obstinate Indian defender, who brained with his heavy cudgel anyone climbing up the walls. Consequently, Pizarro ordered "that three or four ladders be set up, so that while he was rushing to one point, they might climb up at another, for . . . it was he alone who was fighting." The Spaniards succeeded in gaining the upper level "at two or three places" and the fort was captured.[96] Similarly, during the last campaign (1540–1542) to subdue the Yucatan, the Spanish and their Indian allies attacked the fortified Mayan town of Sihochac in three columns at different points. A "tactic [that was] proved successful time and again."[97]

Thus Coronado logically would not initially concentrate only on one defensive position on the pueblo and would order feints at multiple points, perhaps with the falconets wheeled about and extra ladders at least being carried to these secondary positions. He noted that he attempted to use his crossbowmen and arquebusiers to drive the enemy "from the defenses" or "from the walls."[98] Archaeologists have discovered three lead balls that could have come from arquebuses, or the falconets. Two were found on the north side of the pueblo site and one was discovered on the south side.[99]

Coronado later reported, "I assembled my whole force and divided it as seemed to me best for the attack on the city."[100] However, Coronado's report to Mendoza also egocentrically mentioned only one point of actual attack. "I invested the wall on one side, where I was told that there was a scaling ladder and that there was also a gate."[101] Recent archaeology, finding that the heaviest concentration of nails was on the west side, "suggests that the Spanish attack was on the pueblo's more vulnerable western side instead of on the steeper eastern side."[102]

While the evidence supports the conclusion that Coronado was assaulting the city pursuant to then-current European doctrine, standard military theory was only as good as the technology, which initially showed some promise. The artillery firing at the Zuni, according to a Spaniard present, "began to do them harm."[103] Artilleryman Troyano later recalled his bombardment "killed some of" the Cibolans.[104]

However, the Zuni Indians undoubtedly learned to take cover whenever the falconets belched flame, just as the Aztecs had quickly learned to duck or scatter when they saw the Spaniards aiming their artillery and arquebuses or notching the quarrels of their crossbows.[105] Thus, the noticeable effectiveness of the cannonade did not continue, for the firing had to go on, certainly intermittently, into the afternoon.[106] In addition, since the pueblo was either mud adobe or stone faced with mud, such artillery had its limitations if the guns were using solid balls in the hope of reducing walls to rubble.[107]

Thus, while the European contingent with Coronado was close to being an up-to-date sixteenth-century military force, the lack of real siege artillery made it more like a medieval army when it came to taking a fortified town, even a Southwestern pueblo.[108] In any event, at Hawikuh, the falconets were found somewhat wanting on this particular occasion.

The modern hand arms of the Spanish reportedly did not perform up to expectations either, although, like the falconets, they also did the Zuni defenders some initial harm.[109] The arquebuses apparently could not keep up a constant and well-aimed fire, for, as Coronado later wrote, the arquebusiers "did nothing at all: for they came thither so weake and feeble, that scarcely they coulde stand on their feete."[110] This observation by the captain general indicates that the exhausted arquebusiers were not provided with rests or support sticks for their firearms—but they should have been.[111] It also was here that the eighty-day forced march, undoubtedly hard on the mounts of the men-at-arms, demonstrated itself just as hard on the infantry. Such a sustained effort inevitably would "seriously impair" a shooter's "shooting capacity"; "[m]en who have been overmarched, or whose health and comforts have not been attended to whilst on the march, can never be expected to maintain their stamina should an engagement occur."[112]

In addition, the expedition did not have enough arquebusiers to offer the option of having them fire by squads, giving some a pause during reloading while keeping up a sustained fire. Firing by squads had occurred in 1527 during the assault on Rome.[113]

In any event, even in the best of circumstances, these early handguns had their limitations. The barrels could become overheated if the firing was too sustained.[114] Also, the men behind the barrels had their limitations as well, even if rested. A sixteenth-century observer of military affairs wrote that arquebusiers "were afraid to take a proper aim, for their weapon was like a short petard, heavy and clumsy. . . . Indeed, it was more terrifying to the firer than to those for whom the shots were intended, and it's sheer bad luck on anyone who was hit, for he was unlikely to have been the one aimed at."[115]

Even the crossbows had problems at Hawikuh, according to Coronado. Of course, tired and careless crossbowmen could trip and discharge their weapons prematurely—accidents every bit as deadly as when occurring with a firearm.[116] But here there was an equipment failure. As Coronado wrote, "the crossbowmen suddenly brake the strings of their bowes."[117] Not only was the breaking of a highly tensioned string (or the steel bow) dangerous to the shooter,[118] but multiplied, it could affect the outcome of a battle. Thus, this weapons failure was not an unheard of battlefield problem; in a fight during the attempted conquest of Columbia in about 1540, the Spaniards were defeated when "the cords of several crossbows were broken."[119]

If only the arquebuses had been deficient at Hawikuh, with the crossbows fully operational, the Spanish tide of battle might have gone better. During a contemporaneous Spanish expedition down the Amazon River in 1542, the crossbows outperformed the firearms. On one occasion in that humid Brazilian weather, while the gunpowder for the arquebuses was rendered damp and useless, the crossbowmen of Francisco de Orellana successfully drove off an attack by angry natives.[120]

As for the defective crossbows of Coronado at Hawikuh, the bad strings presumably were due to the dry Southwestern climate. The effects of desert sun and air on the weaponry should have been counteracted by proper preventative maintenance, a military failure that seems apparent.[121] Perhaps if the deceased (and experienced) Lope de Samaniego had still been master of the army, this maintenance would have occurred.

A Zuni pueblo photographed in 1873. (*Library of Congress*)

In any event, the Spanish attack on the pueblo, which started off so well with the slaughter of the Zuni outside its walls, was stalled. Because of the problems with the arquebusiers and crossbowmen, "the people who were on top for defense were not hindered," wrote Coronado.[122]

This first battle certainly was not going as some romance writers would have it. Edgar Moore, writing for the Coronado quadricentennial and probably envisioning a people more primitive than anthropologists would rate the Zuni, assumed that with the firing of "[t]hat one volley . . . the fight was over. No longer was the air full of piercing death; the crash of rolling stones was stilled, and an awed hush supplanted the terrifying yells on the battlement. Cibola had fallen!"[123]

It would not prove that easy to scare the Cibolans with thundersticks and lightning. Artillery of the sixteenth century was supposed to panic those on the receiving end, of course.[124] Indeed, there were occasions when the unexpected explosions of artillery and arquebuses did panic a primitive enemy, as when the Spaniards invaded the Yucatan in the 1560s.[125]

But such shock and awe against a fortified town was asking a lot of the little falconets. Cibola did not fall after a single volley, and it was not so susceptible to mere noise and explosive flashes. Neither was Cibola to fall like Jericho, even though blaring trumpets probably surrounded Coronado, encouraging and directing the various detachments of the army.[126] Like a European counterpart, Cibola would have to be taken by storm.

The Spaniards and their allies, desperate for food, were up to the challenge. Since the Spaniards now realized they lacked artillery heavy enough to knock down walls and create multiple points of entry through breaches, they probably fell back onto standard assault doctrine, which required that "a torrent of projectiles [be] concentrated on one particular spot,"[127] as Coronado had indicated.

The ancient weaponry of the Cibolans also had drawbacks. Not only would the supply of rocks and stones to crush Spanish bones have been depleted, such attrition also would affect the arrows, especially since the Zuni, no less than the Spaniards, would have expended many of their missiles at too long a range in the excitement of battle, as would happen on European battlefields.[128]

The time had come for a do-or-die assault on the pueblo. As Coronado later wrote the viceroy, having assembled his whole force, "I dismounted with several of these gentlemen and soldiers."[129] He went to the Zuni scaling ladder that had been left along a wall.

Leading this rush, Coronado, in effect, entered the breach, as would be expected of a heavily armored man-at-arms of the era, whether in Europe or in the Americas.[130] He did this by attempting to climb up the Zuni ladder. While dangerous, it was, in this first encounter, a necessary show of courage for the captain general. Especially during a campaign's initial stages, according to a French soldier of the sixteenth century, "when the soldier shall see a captain who has behaved himself well and performed any notable thing at his first trial, all the valiant men will strive to be under his command, believing that so auspicious a beginning cannot fail of a prosperous issue."[131] It was this desire to be seen that inspired Coronado to wear his brilliant armor, a professional affectation that inspired one's troops—and provided a target for one's enemies.[132]

While Coronado proved to be heroic, he was not invulnerable. "As for myself," he recalled, "they knocked me down to the ground twice with countless great stones which they threw down from above, and if I had not been protected by the very good headpiece which I wore, I think the outcome would have been bad for me."[133]

One of Coronado's companions related more details about the wounding of the captain general after he had "decided to enter the city on foot":

> As he was distinguished among them all by his gilt arms and a plume on his headpiece, all the Indians aimed at him, because he was noticeable among all, and they knocked him down to the ground twice by chance stones thrown from the flat roofs, and stunned him in spite of his headpiece, and if this had not been so good, I doubt if he would have come out alive from that enterprise.[134]

But it was not only his quality armor that saved Coronado. According to Castaneda, "During the attack they knocked the general down with a large stone, and would have killed him but for Don Garcia Lopez de Cardenas and Hernando de Alvarado, who threw themselves above him and drew him away, receiving the blows of the stones, which were not a few."[135] Later, Coronado acknowledged "that if Don Garcia Lopez de Cardenas had not come to my help, like a good cavalier, by placing his own body above mine the second time that they knocked me to the ground, I should have been in much greater danger than I was."[136]

In addition to being knocked unconscious, Coronado said he suffered three wounds on his face and an arrow wound in a leg, while his body was covered with bruising.[137] Undoubtedly, his troops were concerned when he was carried off the field, probably to be attended to by the surgeon, not knowing whether he was fatally injured. Even back then it was known that "[t]he cure of the wounds of the head is not always to bee presumed upon, though small, nor yet dispaired of, tho[u]gh great."[138] In fact, as far as his men knew, they "thought the Indians had killed him."[139] As was demonstrated during the attack on Rome in 1527, the sudden battle death of a commander could break the spirit of the attackers or inspire them to fight harder.[140] During the heat of this battle at Hawikuh, the assumption that their leader was dead undoubtedly infuriated the Spaniards more than it demoralized them.[141]

Although Coronado was unconscious and could not relate exactly what occurred, it is illogical to think the Spaniards relied on a single Zuni ladder to carry the pueblo bastion. While the fury of the Spaniards, seeing their captain general laid out *hors de combat*, might have succeeded in forcing entry at this single point with a single ladder, it would have been tactically risky and a costly lesson Coronado's men would not forget and would not repeat.

Probably some of the Spaniards actually climbing up the ladder or ladders were swordsmen, holding bucklers above their heads—especially after their leader's mishap— to protect against the blows of stones and missiles, as was the custom in such an assault.[142] Presumably, these swordsmen, once they gained the roof, fought like those who were with Cortes in Mexico, where the Aztecs remembered them splitting heads to the shoulders, severing arms from torsos, and slashing open the abdomens of defenders.[143]

Behind those heavily armored men leading the way presumably would be a swarm of Indian auxiliaries climbing and pressing from behind.[144] In any event, an entrance was forced and the upper stories were gained. For defenders, whether European or more primitive, this would mean the jig was up.[145]

Current fashion would give credit to the Spaniards' Indian allies, simply because of their overwhelming numbers in the advance party, for bearing the brunt of the attack and winning a victory.[146] But because of a silent record regarding the employment of the allies during the contest, this is pure speculation that goes against both the military methodology of the day and simple logic.[147]

Such a politically correct scenario also would be unfair to the better-armored and better-disciplined Europeans who were expected to lead the way, whether in Europe or in the Americas. This standard tactical model actually has support, for Pedro de Castaneda wrote, "the first fury of the Spaniards could not be resisted, and in less than an hour they entered the village and captured it."[148]

Nonetheless, the Indian auxiliaries undoubtedly were an important part of the battle. It is not unlikely that their more-numerous presence tipped the scales against the Puebloans by crowding into the pueblo after a foothold had been gained, which would have been after their Spanish comrades had created a breach in the defenses and after the Zuni knew that for them the battle was unwinnable.

To give additional credit where credit is due, the people of Cibola, like the people of Rome, did not fight to the last ditch when they saw how things were going. The Zuni elected to withdraw from their city. "[F]or when the Indians saw that his grace [Coronado] was determined to enter the city, . . . they abandoned it, since [we] let them go with their lives," wrote a Spanish eyewitness.[149]

Of course, it also is possible that the Cibolans were able to escape because of the negligence of the ring of Indian allies who surrounded the pueblo and the Spanish horsemen who probably were riding around it. Both groups might have left their posts to join in the attack, a dereliction of duty due to insubordinate courage.[150]

Finally, Coronado may have decided early on, before he was struck down, that it was wise to let the Cibolans have an escape route. Since antiquity, it occasionally had been the practice not to surround a besieged city "but to leave a section open for those who wanted to escape, so that the final action might take place with less bloodshed."[151] Cortes in Mexico also apparently was aware of the military proverb "If your enemy runs away, build him a silver bridge."[152] Of course, this motivation for lessening the effusion of blood by leaving open a route of escape could be of benefit to the attackers in various ways. The Aztecs of preconquest times, who had the motivation to capture enemies for sacrifice rather than killing them all outright, also were well aware that leaving an escape route would mean defenders would turn to flee before fighting to the death.[153]

Lopez de Cardenas later expanded on this. He testified that he was part of an agreement with the Cibolans, saying that the defenders signaled they wanted peace, and they were allowed to abandon their pueblo and "went away without being harmed by the Spaniards."[154] This particular scenario, supposedly occurring when only members of the advance party would have been witnesses and presented in an inquiry in which Cardenas was charged with various acts of cruelty, strains credibility.

Because of the escape of much of the population, some historians have labeled this obvious victory on the part of the Spanish and their Indian auxiliaries as a battlefield toss-up. Bolton suggested that "from a military point of view the battle was a draw."[155] Also, apparently because of the dearth of casualties on the part of the victorious attackers, others have minimized the Spanish victory, one team of historians crediting the mass of *Indios amigos* in concluding that the "fabled pueblo" was overrun with "relative ease."[156] While Bolton's finding is just silly, the second conclusion misconstrues the criteria needed to demonstrate a real battle, especially a first violent encounter between cultures.[157]

The Cibolans, suffering significant casualties, were defeated, or conceded defeat, and retreated from their city thoroughly chastened. "After this the whole province was at peace," wrote Castaneda.[158]

After the withdrawal of its citizens, Hawikuh was occupied, although, as Pedro de Castaneda recalled, it was "taken with not a little difficulty, since they held the narrow and crooked entrance."[159] As will be seen, "with not a little difficulty" can be used to describe so much about the Coronado Expedition's campaign throughout western North America.

Despite the scale of violence, Spanish casualties were light in this early encounter, one in which the natives had no prior experience in killing such armored invaders.[160] In addition to the injury to the captain general, Cardenas, Pedro de Tovar, and Pablo de Melgosa, an infantry captain, suffered bruising. Others received more notable wounds: Gomez Xuarez had an arrow wound in the arm, and one Torres had been hit in the face with an arrow. Slight arrow wounds were suffered by "two other footmen."[161]

When it came to the wounded, the entire army of Coronado had certain technological and cultural advantages inherent to the care of their own casualties. First, European surgeons would have some knowledge regarding treating arrow wounds incurred in the warfare of the late medieval and early Renaissance periods.[162] Second, regarding wounds inflicted by swords, pikes, or firearms, "bullet-wounds were by far the most serious" for treatment by European surgeons.[163] A Spanish commander, in 1575, wrote about the casualties his unit suffered when fighting against fellow Europeans in the Low Countries: "Most of the wounds come from pikes or blows, and they will soon heal, although there are also many with gunshot wounds and they will die."[164] Of course, in the Americas, it would be some time before the natives would acquire gunpowder weaponry.

As for casualties among their Indian allies, the chroniclers, unfortunately, are again silent. Many modern historians would conclude that the Eurocentrism of the Spanish was all that prevented them from detailing the involvement, the courage, and the significant losses of these allies. While Eurocentrism—and national and class pride—certainly played a part in the inadequacy of the record regarding the natives, this does not solve the problem of a silent record. Like the possible presence of gun carriages and scaling ladders, any concise conclusions about the losses, if any, among the allies at Cibola are unfortunately just as speculative.

In any event, both sides seemed to get off relatively cheaply in this first major encounter, especially since the Zuni losses easily could have been much worse. In addition, the law of war from antiquity through the Middle Ages was that a town or fortress that refused a summons to surrender and was taken by storm was at the mercy of the besiegers. Common soldiers in the attacking force, who had paid the price of the resistance, sometimes disobeyed their commanders' orders not to sack a conquered city.[165] In this case, there was no dead captain general to avenge; plus, there was little enough loot and no townspeople left inside available for slaughter.

As for Coronado, he was modest in the report to the viceroy that he wrote as he recovered. "The Indians all directed their attack against me because my armor was gilded and glittering," he explained, "and on this account I was hurt more than the rest, and not because I had done more or was farther in advance than the others; for all these gentlemen and soldiers bore themselves well, as was expected of them."[166]

Modesty aside, Coronado undoubtedly had some self-satisfaction regarding his initial taste of combat. As a French professional soldier of the era commented about his first contact with the enemy while leading his hundred men, "My example upon this occasion may serve for something, wherein though perhaps there are no great matters performed, yet so it is that of little exploits of war great uses are sometimes to be made."[167]

But the important thing for Coronado's men, both Spaniards and Indian auxiliaries, was that they now had food. "They discovered food there, which was the thing they were most in need of," said Castaneda.[168] Another member of the expedition, proving himself wiser than King Midas and more poetic than Castaneda, wrote, "We found in it what we needed more than gold and silver, and that was much corn and beans and fowls, better than those of New Spain, and salt, the best and whitest that I have seen in all my life."[169]

Coronado's advance force soon discovered that the Cibolans had been particularly productive and especially thrifty in their agrarian pursuits. According to Mota Padilla, the Spaniards also "took possession of the outbuildings, in which they found sufficient corn, beans, and squash to last the winter."[170]

Hawikuh would not forget the Coronado Expedition. Neither would the Zuni forget Esteban. As one tribal member told a researcher in 1992, "even today, the Zuni dislike blacks. . . . I know it's wrong to feel like this but that's just the way it is. We've never forgotten Esteban. He was the beginning of the end."[171]

But those Zuni who were alive during the visit of Coronado also were careful not to provoke another visit by invaders from the south.

Apparently, after the Spanish finally evacuated the region, the Zuni left the "well built crosses" erected by the Spaniards at the pueblos alone, for they still were there forty years later.[172]

# TWELVE

# Melchior Diaz Seeks the Pacific Supply Ships

Although Coronado and his advance force were fully occupied with capturing Hawikuh and securing their food supplies, other events were occasioned by the activity of other players in this Southwestern America saga. These events were far from Cibola, and not all of them were on land.

Coronado attempted to secure his line of communications with the establishment of a base garrison at San Geronimo. While that post was extant, it was used as a springboard for the attempt to open another line of communication, this time between the expedition and the supply ships promised by Viceroy Mendoza. Although this attempt, like that of the establishment of San Geronimo, ultimately failed, it has provided historians with the stuff of high adventure, including adventure on the almost-open sea.

When thinking of seamanship during the sixteenth century, most students of history would probably first recall the exploits of Englishmen like Francis Drake and Martin Frobisher. This age of English predominance, however, occurred in the latter part of the era. During the beginnings of the century, the Spanish were tied with the Portuguese when it came to salty grit and navigational skill on the open seas. Indeed, the Spanish early on established a training school for the "systematic and scientific teaching" of maritime navigation, an accomplishment that impressed even the English.[1]

Also, while the British later, especially in the eighteenth century and especially in American waters, became the experts in combined operations, the Spanish led the way in Europe regarding land-and-sea military and naval cooperation during the post-Renaissance era. From their late fifteenth-century Reconquista, the Spanish "[i]n purely military terms . . . learned a great deal between 1481 and 1492, not only in the use of firearms but in the management of very large forces, as well as combined operations involving land forces supplied by sea while inside enemy territory." This expertise, earned from hard experience, made "the armies of Spain . . . a force to be reckoned with in early 16th century Europe and to an even greater degree on the other side of the Atlantic."[2]

As indicated, based partially on the report of Friar Marcos, it was hoped that the Coronado column could be resupplied by sea, a not-unreasonable belief on the part of Mendoza relying on the information he had available.[3] However, even as the army marched north, the reconnaissance patrols Coronado sent out seemed to call this hope into question, for the Sea of Cortes and the trail north kept diverging. It began to seem that east was east and west was west and never the twain would meet.

Meanwhile, Viceroy Mendoza at least was going to do his best to keep his part of the bargain that he had made to resupply his appointed captain general by sea. Pursuant to Mendoza's orders, on May 9, 1540, as Coronado was leading his advance guard toward Cibola, Captain Hernando de Alarcon set sail from a port on the west coast of Mexico with two small ships, his flagship the *San Pedro* and the *Santa Catalina*.[4]

The sea voyagers almost immediately ran into extremely rough seas, and those aboard the *Santa Catalina*, in the words of their doughty leader, "became unduly frightened, threw overboard nine pieces of artillery, two anchors, a cable, and many other things as indispensable for their undertaking as the ship itself."[5] The battered ships put into the small port of Santiago de Buena Esperanza, and Alarcon reports, "I repaired the damage I had suffered, supplied myself with the necessary things, took on board the people who were waiting for me, and set sail for the port of Aguayaval." This port was north of the latitude of Culiacan, and Alarcon learned "that General Francisco Vazquez de Coronado had left [there] with all his forces."[6]

Pursuant to the instructions he had received from the viceroy, Alarcon then added to his flotilla a ship he found at Aguayaval, the *San*

A late seventeenth-century Italian map of New Spain showing both California as an island at left (California Isola) and Quivara, center left, just below "Messico." (*Author*)

*Gabriel,* "which was carrying supplies for the army." Alarcon, who by now certainly deserved the title of either commodore or admiral (even if he never officially was given those titles), continued north with his little fleet, hugging the coast, "in order to see if I could find any markers, or Indians who would furnish me some information."[7]

Alarcon was determined to do his duty and outperform the efforts of Captain Ulloa, who had sailed the same waters for Hernando Cortes (hence the name the Sea of Cortes) in 1539. Alarcon, being more thorough than Ulloa, charted the coastline for potential harbors and hoped "to report on the secret of that gulf, . . . even at the risk of losing the ships."[8]

Finding the depth becoming dangerously shallow as they sailed north, Alarcon had his chief pilot take to a small boat in order to find a channel.[9] Although all three ships became stuck in the sands, and the strong current threatened to swamp the flagship, "a miraculous rise of the tide" set all three craft free. "Even though the sailors wanted to turn back," the Columbus-like Alarcon later wrote, "still I insisted that we sail on and proceed on the voyage we had started."[10]

Tacking the ships in order to continue north in the channel against a strong current, the Spanish sailors finally were rewarded with solving "the secret of that gulf." "Here we found a mighty river with such a furious current that we could scarcely sail against it."[11] Alarcon had found the mouth of the mighty Colorado River before it was dammed by electric-turbine progress and drained by international irrigation—but he had not yet found Francisco Vasquez de Coronado.[12]

Meanwhile, on the land side of this combined endeavor, after the capture of Hawikuh, Captain Melchior Diaz was sent south to deliver Coronado's order to the main army to march north and rejoin him. Then, as previously noted, in late September, Diaz took twenty-five of the best men remaining at San Geronimo de Corazones and, according to Castaneda, "took guides and went toward the north and west in search of the seacoast" in an effort to link up with Alarcon's ships.[13] In addition to guides, Diaz apparently also took some allied Indian warriors.[14]

After marching an estimated 150 leagues (about four hundred miles), Diaz and his mounted men and Indian allies came to the region of the Colorado River inhabited by the Yuma Indians, whom the Spaniards thought to be "exceedingly tall and strong men—like giants."[15] Mota Padilla, the Spanish historian, related that these giant Indians "got along well with our people," unlike some previous natives of the region who were "naked and very cowardly."[16]

In addition to the great men they found there, this party of Spaniards recognized the Colorado as "a very great river" (it was over a mile wide), which they called the Firebrand River. Diaz also learned from the Indians "that there had been ships at a point three days down toward the sea."[17]

Thus encouraged, the Diaz party followed the Colorado toward its mouth. However, according to Castaneda, when the Spaniards "reached the place where the ships had been, which was more than fifteen leagues up the river from the mouth of the harbor, they found written on a tree 'Alarcon reached this place; there are letters [buried] at the foot of this tree.'"[18] When Diaz dug up the dispatches, he learned the heartbreaking news that Alarcon, after waiting to hear of Coronado, had headed back to New Spain with his ships.[19]

While this sea-and-land hookup failed, it was through no failure of trying on the part of Alarcon. That salty sea dog, having gotten as close to the mouth of the Colorado River as he could with his ships on August 26, 1540, decided to attempt to go up the river in two of his ships' boats, leaving twenty men behind on the ships. Then the two boats, by sail, by rowing, and apparently by being hauled by men on shore with ropes, headed upstream.[20] While Alarcon was on his small-boat mission, the *Santa Catalina* probably "made a reconnaissance of the California coast."[21]

Captain Hernando de Alarcon. (*Author*)

Although their first confrontation with the natives was tense, especially when "about two hundred and fifty Indians [watched on shore] in warlike mood with bows and arrows and some banners like the Indians of New Spain,"[22] with the help of interpreters, Alarcon and his men spent the next several weeks among them. In addition to learning about their lifestyle, Alarcon made attempts to find out about Coronado's army.

Toward the end of his stay, Alarcon asked an old man "about Cibola and whether he knew if the people there had ever seen people like us. He answered no, except a negro who wore on his feet and arms some things that tinkled." When Alarcon asked why those at Cibola had killed Esteban, the old man said they killed him after he warned them he had many brothers with "numerous arms, and that they were not very far from there." According to this informant, Esteban died "so that he would not reveal their location to his brothers."[23]

Even later, Alarcon heard that some visitors from Cibola had arrived on the Colorado River and told the local Indians that at Cibola "there [were] other fierce people like us, of the same qualities and features as we, who had fought much with the men from Cibola, for they had killed a Moorish companion of theirs." The hearsay talk about Esteban indicated he had done no harm to the people of Cibola to merit his death.[24]

Because of this intelligence, Alarcon tried more than once to get his men to contact Coronado. "I consulted with my men, but there was no one who would risk going, although I offered many rewards in the name of your Lordship," reported Alarcon to Mendoza. "Only a

Moorish slave volunteered to go, although not very enthusiastically."[25] Alarcon's attempts to recruit local Indians to make the dangerous trip also were to no avail.[26]

After learning all he could, Alarcon returned downriver to his ships. This journey took only two and a half days, while the trip upstream had taken over fifteen.[27] Alarcon persuaded his crew to take him back upriver, telling them he hoped "Francisco Vazquez . . . perhaps, during the sixteen days I spent sailing up the river, he might have heard of me."[28] Alarcon did return to the Indian villages upriver, where he learned that his friend, the old man, had been approached by Indians of another tribe to join them in killing Alarcon.[29]

Finally, giving up on contacting Coronado or hearing from him, Alarcon returned to his ships, the wooden hulls of which were becoming rotten with boring sea worms, and departed for home.[30] He had been able to ascend the river a reported eighty-five leagues (260 miles) and had traveled thirty leagues (ninety-five miles) inland.[31]

Although Melchior Diaz and his men had failed to make contact with Alarcon, their adventures were only beginning. Not all of them would make it back to San Geronimo.

Diaz hoped to cross over the Colorado "to continue his discoveries farther in that direction."[32] Consequently, his party marched up the river looking for a suitable ford. After six days, having decided that the river could be crossed on rafts, the Spaniards asked the local Indians for help building them. While the rafts were being constructed, one of Diaz's men happened to see armed natives heading into hiding by a mountain on the other side of the stream.[33]

Fearing treachery, Diaz had one of the local Indians seized surreptitiously and, to obtain information, tortured—a not-uncommon method of obtaining prebattle intelligence in the sixteenth century.[34] According to Castaneda, the man confessed that he and his cohorts, although helping to "make the rafts with all zeal and diligence," planned "to catch them in this way on the water and drown them or else so divide them that they could not help one another." There would then be "an attack on both sides of the river."[35]

Having discovered the plot, "the captain had the Indian who had confessed the affair killed secretly, and that night he was thrown into the river with a weight, so that the other Indians would not suspect that they were found out." [36] Despite this Spanish attempt to form a secret counterconspiracy, the natives somehow figured out by the next day that the Spaniards knew their plans, "so they made an attack, shooting showers of arrows."[37]

But the Spaniards, going on the immediate offensive, gave better than they got in this little battle on the Arizona-California border. According to Castaneda, "when the horses began to catch up with them and the lances wounded them without mercy and the musketeers likewise made good shots, they had to leave the plain and take to the mountain, until not a man of them was to be seen." Upon the return of the pursuing Spaniards, the party "crossed all right, the Indian allies and the Spaniards going across on the rafts and the horses swimming alongside the rafts."[38]

Now on the south side of the Colorado (in Arizona), the small force headed south, looking for the western shore of the Sea of Cortes. The Spaniards encountered extremely rugged country and, to avoid this terrain and to find water, apparently headed more to the east.[39] Sometime during these wanderings, Diaz attempted to capture one of those gigantic Indians, in order to have a live show-and-tell for Viceroy Mendoza. This was a futile and unwise attempt, for it aroused "the enmity of these Indians."[40]

In addition to their horses, another of man's best friends traveled with the party. As Castaneda heard and recalled it, "one day a greyhound belonging to one of the soldiers chased some sheep which they were taking along for food."[41] Captain Diaz, a man of action, undoubtedly was not in a good mood that day. According to Castaneda, "When the captain noticed this, he threw his lance at the dog while his horse was running, so that it stuck up in the ground, and not being able to stop his horse he went over the lance so that it nailed him through the thighs and the iron came out behind, rupturing his bladder."[42]

Because of his wrath at a hungry or bored hound, Diaz suffered an awful wound that even today, if one is in the wilderness, would be a death sentence. The chroniclers do not mention what happened to the dog.[43] However, the captain was a tough frontiersman, and his men were devoted to him, so they attempted to get him back to civilization (and undoubtedly to a priest for confession) to die.[44] "After this the soldiers turned back with their captain. . . . He lived about twenty days, during which they proceeded with great difficulty on account of the necessity of carrying him."[45] However, their burdensome leader, no doubt in excruciating pain, was not the only major problem the Spaniards faced. As Castaneda related, the party had "to fight every day with the Indians, who had remained hostile."[46]

Eventually things got better for everyone—except Diaz. "They returned in good order without losing a man," wrote Castaneda, "until he died, and after that they were relieved of the greatest difficulty."[47] Reported Mota Padilla, "And so they buried him on a little hill, and above his grave they put a cross, and continued their journey with a feeling of grievous loss."[48] Diaz died January 18, 1541.[49] His surviving comrades reached San Geronimo.[50]

As with other aspects of the Coronado Expedition, dedicated experts have done their best to track the march of Melchior Diaz and his men. While it is as difficult to come up with Diaz's itinerary and mileage as it is to estimate the march of the main column, the mystery is not made simpler by the possibility that the captain might have made exceptional time before he had to be carried in a litter. During the era, at least in Europe, it was not considered exceptional for a horseman to ride fifty miles during a twenty-four-hour period.[51] However, a close student of this miniexpedition has detailed how difficult the going was, especially for horses, over much of the brush-covered desert route.[52]

In any event, the lonely grave of this bold and impetuous Spanish cavalier lies somewhere in the Sonoran wastelands on the road to Corazones, between Sonoyta and Caborca.[53] Archaeologists likely will never locate that site, but what about those cannon tossed off the *Santa Catalina* into the sea at the mouth of the Gulf of California?

Not only did the failure of naval resupply jeopardize the safety and comfort of Coronado's army, it ultimately added to the financial embarrassment of the Spaniards who were members of the expedition in this extreme case of misdirected and missing baggage. "[A]nd so all of this stuff was lost, or, rather, those who owned it lost it, as will be related farther on," wrote Pedro de Castaneda.[54] Nonetheless, while the freezing landsmen under Coronado undoubtedly blamed the sailors for stealing their property (as sailors are wont to do when it comes to their army brethren), it is hard to fault the abilities and efforts of Alarcon and his reluctant seamen. "[N]o explorer could have done more to carry out the orders of the Viceroy," wrote a US Army trailblazer familiar with the region.[55]

It also is impossible to conclude that Diaz and his men did not do their best militarily to link up with the navy. This planned union of surf and turf simply was one of those best-laid plans that went astray and was not to be. While location is important, that amounts to only three dimensions. The fourth dimension of timing might be everything to a rendezvous.

In addition, undoubtedly exacerbated by the failure to locate the supply ships and to make San Geronimo an important post for resupply, there was an ultimate failure regarding the prototype presidio left at San Geronimo. When the Diaz party arrived back in Sonora without their leader, Captain Alcaraz sent word to Coronado about the death of Diaz and the failure of the meeting with Alarcon. Alcaraz also informed the captain general that some of his soldiers at San Geronimo "were ill-disposed and had caused several mutinies, and that he had sentenced two of them to the gallows, but they had afterward escaped from the prison."[56]

Coronado responded by sending Captain Pedro de Tovar to San Geronimo to straighten things out. When Tovar arrived, he found that a Spaniard had been killed with a poisoned arrow, so Tovar ordered Alcaraz to conduct a minicampaign against the rebellious Indians in the neighborhood. The results were unsatisfactory, with, according to Castaneda, "seventeen soldiers dead from the poison." The results would have been even worse but for the assistance provided the Spanish by the warriors of Corazones. Seeing how exposed San Geronimo III was, Tovar moved the post north to the Suya valley.[57] He then returned to the north, taking with him not "the rebels and seditious men there" but "the most experienced ones and the best soldiers."[58]

Not surprisingly, the mutinous spirit at San Geronimo III continued, and those with "the bad dispositions" held daily meetings, complaining that they were isolated and that Spanish forces were bypassing them. These "worthless" fellows gained control of the garrison and proclaimed Pedro de Avila as their captain. Those in revolt left San Geronimo and withdrew to Culiacan, leaving a sick Captain Alcaraz "with only a small force."[59] When these deserters reached Culiacan, however, they were recognized for what they were and arrested by the local officials, who worried about the increasingly exposed frontier to the north.[60]

Eventually, certainly as part of the Mixton War, the Indians around San Geronimo, noting the weakness of the garrison, first stopped trading with the Spaniards and then rose in revolt.[61] Supposedly, much of the bad feeling with the natives had occurred because of the brutality of Alcaraz and his forcing sexual relations with the Indian women.[62] Although the weakened Spanish garrison was on the alert, the Indians attacked the settlement early one morning, killing and plundering. Some of the Spaniards retreated south with some of the horses, fighting a rearguard action. During this withdrawal, Alcaraz was mortally wounded. Apparently, counting their captain, a total of three Spaniards were killed in the uprising, as well as many of the servants and twenty of the horses.[63]

The survivors stumbled south, and they found some sanctuary and were fed in Corazones. Eventually the Spaniards managed to make it to Culiacan, where they, unlike the deserters, were welcomed by the citizens.[64]

San Geronimo III was abandoned, without Coronado being any the wiser, and the needless death of Captain Diaz contributed to this failure to maintain the post. Nonetheless, because of Diaz's active participation in several notable chapters of the Coronado Expedition, quite a bit of romance has been associated with him, and most historians seem to accept his heroic if bloody role. He even has his defenders who proclaim him particularly ethical. One student of Diaz said he was a staunch foe against the enslavement of Indians "by Diego de Alcaraz and other miscreants in high office."[65] However, Diaz also has his detractors, including a couple of scholars who compared him with Nuno de Guzman, another of the "inhuman slavers."[66]

Some of Diaz's contemporaries also had criticism for him. After he was dead and after all the desert dust of the expedition settled, he received some implicit military second guessing during the inquiry into the conduct of the endeavor. In a situation not unknown in the modern military, many of the witnesses at the investigation blamed the uprising at San Geronimo on the deceased Alcaraz. Further emphasizing this tendency to blame the dead, a few of the witnesses alleged it was Diaz, not Coronado, who decided to appoint Alcaraz as commander in his stead when Diaz went traipsing off on his important mission to contact Alarcon.[67]

# THIRTEEN

# Reconnaissance West and the March East into Tiguex Territory

So in summer 1540, and after a fashion (and a little fighting), "Cibola [was] at peace"[1] Coronado reportedly ordered that his force do no further injury to the Zuni. He even punished some of his Indian allies who stole items from the locals.[2]

But of the province of Cibola, regarding the report of Friar Marcos de Niza, Coronado wrote Mendoza, "I can assure you that he has not told the truth in a single thing that he said, but everything is the opposite of what he related, except the name of the cities and the large stone houses."[3] Coronado, to protect the cleric from the wrath of the soldiery, sent Niza packing back to New Spain with Captain Juan Gallego, who was carrying dispatches.[4]

The captain general had to be concerned about the status of the expedition at this point. Certainly, he needed gunpowder; the falconets alone burned three pounds of the stuff for every shot.[5] But the main army would bring more powder, crossbow bolts, and other supplies.

The continuing worry was food. Not only had the Zuni villages proved less than spectacular to European eyes, the issues about provisioning would not be abated indefinitely. While the maize found at Cibola solved the immediate problem of the Spanish and their Indian allies, demands soon would increase. This was especially true since Coronado was told by the Cibolans about a similarly sized province to the east called Tiguex. The whole army would be needed to seek out that potentially hostile land.[6] Coronado could not afford to rest on his laurels regarding the expedition, or even to pause in his efforts.

First of all, as plentiful as it first appeared, the food in this so-called Kingdom of Cibola was not inexhaustible, especially to a sixteenth-century military column. According to an eminent student of the period, "An army could only live for a short time on the plunder of an invaded district. . . . Even in a richly-cultivated region an invader could not live for more than a few days on mere plunder—all the more so because mercenary bands were most wasteful pillagers, and spoiled in one week resources that should have lasted for three."[7] While there is no real evidence that Coronado's force was extravagant or wasteful, Cibola was not set up to host such a number of out-of-town visitors.

Second, increasing that number of visitors, the main army was marching up from the south under Arellano. But because Coronado and his advance force had not left behind them bad blood, "Everything went along in good shape," wrote Castaneda, "since the general had left everything peaceful, because he wished the people in that region to be contented and without fear and willing to do what they were ordered."[8]

Fortunately, with the main army traveling at a slower pace with its on-the-hoof commissary, the march was not as hungry as had been the forced march with the advance column. Indeed, one of the worst incidents for the main force came when the local natives shared their well-known prickly pear preserves. While some scurvy prevention undoubtedly was obtained when the members of the expedition satisfied themselves, it came at a price. "They gave this preserve away freely," recalled Castaneda, "and as the men of the army ate much of it, they all fell sick with a headache and fever, so that the natives might have done much harm to the force if they had wished." But this was just a twenty-four-hour malady, and the army continued on to Chichilticalli.[9]

These beneficial and adverse experiences with local cuisine were not unique in military annals. When invading Germans reached the Ukraine in 1942, local food provided important sustenance. First it was the watermelon, which, according to one German soldier, "saved our lives." There were also apricots being dried by the locals in the arid climate. Neither of these crops caused diarrhea in the hot summer weather.[10] However, when the Germans availed themselves of beehives being kept in the Caucasus Mountains, trouble developed. According to the same German soldier, an entire company "had not been able to resist eating the delicious honey from the numerous hives they found in the village. . . . Most of them were rolling around on the ground as if drunk or drugged." It turned out the bees pollinated the rhododendron flowers, which resulted in narcotic-like honey. Fortunately for the Germans, as was the case with Arellano's men, the effects were gone within forty-eight hours.[11]

The Spaniards under Arellano, as they continued to march, saw in the rugged country some Rocky Mountain or bighorn sheep that still inhabited that region. But these could not be added to the larder of the army, for, being "used to the rough country, . . . we could not catch them and had to leave them," wrote Castaneda.[12]

In Cibola and awaiting the arrival of so many extra stomachs, Coronado had to cast about for more-prosperous and productive lands and for any other potential sources of supply. While the viceroy's instructions dictated that he seek "other lands and provinces" to conquer,[13] necessity also was a motivation to that same end. Coronado wrote Mendoza, "I have determined to send men throughout all the surrounding regions in order to find out whether there is anything, and to suffer every extremity rather than give up this enterprise, and to serve his Majesty, if I can find any way in which to do it, and not be lacking in diligence."[14] Later, Lopez de Cardenas, the master of the camp, was more blunt: "[A]s the said general and his people saw that the land was sterile and that they had been deceived, they decided to explore in order to see if they could find a better land where God, our Lord, and his Majesty would be served and they themselves benefitted."[15]

Throughout the operations in the American Southwest, Coronado made it a virtual policy of sending out numerous minor expeditions under his captains. This delegation of authority to cover more territory in a lesser amount of time was quite appropriate. Indeed, even in Europe it was not uncommon for an army to send out flying columns to forage for supplies.[16] But such a situation, while it "enabled junior officers to show their mettle," also resulted in occasional conflicts with the natives, brief periods of fighting that centuries later would be called subalterns' wars.[17]

Coronado asked the Cibolans to tell the Spanish "about the provinces that lay around" Cibola "and got them to tell their friends and neighbors that Christians had come into the country, people whose only desire was to be their friends, and to find out about good lands to live."[18] Having seen how friendly the Christians could act, and undoubtedly not wanting them as long-term neighbors, the Zuni told the visitors about the Hopi pueblos to the west.

As Castaneda noted, this western province also had "seven villages of the same sort as theirs, although somewhat different." The Zuni told the Spaniards that "[t]hey had nothing to do with these people," some twenty-five leagues from Cibola, whose "villages [were] high and the people ... warlike."[19] Obviously, the Zuni were recommending that the Spaniards visit some of their enemies, who happened to be Hopi, and show them the same imperial courtesies.[20]

Consequently, wrote Castaneda, "The general ... sent Don Pedro de Tovar to these villages with seventeen horsemen, and three or four foot-soldiers."[21] While Coronado obviously believed the Zuni that the other pueblos were there, he apparently was not impressed that they were that warlike. Nonetheless, in addition to probable Indian allies, Coronado also sent a secret weapon with the little squadron: Franciscan Friar Juan de Padilla, a fighting chaplain if ever there was one, for he "had been a fighting man in his youth."[22]

If the Spaniards had learned of the Hopi, the Hopi also were familiar with the reputation of these invaders. "[T]hey had heard that Cibola had been captured by very fierce people, who travelled on animals which ate people." Castaneda recalled, "This information was generally believed by those who had never seen horses, although it was so strange as to cause much wonder."[23]

The Hopi perhaps supposed that such warriors and beasts would announce themselves well in advance with mighty roars, making extra vigilance unnecessary. During this cultivation season, the Hopi did not go on trading visits to other tribes but only commuted between their individual pueblos and their fields on valley floors. Therefore, they had no advance warning of the approach of Tovar and his party. "When they reached the region," said Castaneda, "they entered the country so quietly that nobody observed them." In addition, as the Spaniards neared the first pueblo of the cluster of Hopi villages, called Awatobi, they came after nightfall "and were able to conceal themselves under the edge of the village, where they heard the natives talking in their houses."[24]

However, in the morning, when the Spanish were discovered below "and drew up in regular order, while the natives came out to meet them, with bows, and shields, and wooden clubs, drawn up in lines without any confusion," the Hopi quickly recovered their sense of confidence. Once again, the standard scenario was played out, as the Spanish sent forward an interpreter to alert the natives of the benefits of submission and the consequences of resistance. Then the Hopi, although a "very intelligent people," drew lines on the ground and insisted that the Spanish must "not go across these lines toward their village."[25]

While the Spanish waited and continued to try to talk, "some men acted as if they would cross the lines, and one of the natives lost control of himself and struck a horse a blow on the cheek of the bridle with his club."[26] This act of bravado, apparently equivalent to the Great Plains habit of counting coup, was too much for Friar Padilla, who thought these continuing preliminaries were a waste of time. He turned to Captain Tovar and said, "To tell the truth, I do not know why we came here."[27]

With this mild expression of exasperated rebuke, along with the obvious clerical approval for what was to follow, it was the Spaniards' turn to lose control of themselves. When Tovar's mounted men heard Padilla's comment, "they gave the Santiago [war cry] so suddenly that they ran down many Indians and the others fled to the town in confusion." But, as quick as some of the Spaniards were, the Hopis in the pueblo were even quicker, for before all of the men-at-arms could get into the melee, these other Hopis rushed out with presents, "asking for peace."[28]

As the Indians "did not do any more harm," Tovar immediately told the members of his force to desist in their assault and to rally around him.[29] Although there apparently arose among the Hopi a local oral tradition about the fight that the defenders of the village killed five men in a nine-man advance party and that Coronado himself then "fell upon [the village] with his men and devastated and destroyed it,"[30] there apparently were no Spanish deaths and there was no bloody retribution on the part of the Spaniards.[31]

Instead, the people of the pueblo formally submitted to the Spaniards on behalf of the whole province and offered more presents, including food and some turquoise. Later, representatives from the other Hopi pueblos individually submitted their respective pueblos and allowed the Spaniards to enter them to visit and to barter.[32]

Since Tovar had authority from Coronado to only go as far as the Hopi villages, he returned to Cibola to give his report.[33] This report, as so many received by Coronado from his reconnaissance parties, was disappointing, for Tovar saw nothing more than additional pueblos as were found in Cibola.[34]

Coronado then ordered Garcia Lopez de Cardenas to take about a dozen men to reenter the country in order to find the river reported to be there, the Colorado.[35] Indicating how routine these side excursions were becoming to the seasoned army of invasion, especially as the Spaniards became proficient in sign language, Cardenas did not even bother to take an interpreter with him, "nor did he need one."[36] Cardenas was hospitably welcomed by the previously chastened Hopi before he headed across the desert to find the river, accompanied by Hopi guides.[37]

Cardenas was warned by his guides that the river was twenty days away. Sure enough, after twenty days, the party got to an elevated country "full of low twisted pines, very cold, and lying open toward the north, so that, this being the warm season, no one could live there on account of the cold."[38] The river was there, but it was at the bottom of a very grand canyon (*the* Grand Canyon), and it looked from above "as if the water was six feet across, although the Indians said it was half a league [well over a mile] wide."[39]

The party of Spaniards camped on the canyon rim for three days, having to go "a league or two inland every day late in the evening in order to find water."[40] Between these trips, they looked for a way down. In fact, according to an expedition member, "[a]lthough the men sought diligently in many places for a crossing, none was found."[41] Finally, a party consisting of "Captain Melgosa and one Juan Galeras and another companion," began to climb down "at the least difficult place" and disappeared from view. But the intrepid threesome found the canyon "very hard and difficult" and they were forced to give up, climb up, and rejoin their friends at about 4 p.m. "They said that they had been down about a third of the way and that the river seemed very large from the place which they reached, and that from what they saw they thought the Indians had given the width correctly."[42]

To the climbers, some of the rocks in the canyon, which had looked miniature from above, were seen to be "bigger than the great tower of Seville." Much like Zebulon Pike, who felt the mountain later called Pikes Peak was unclimbable, Castaneda pronounced the canyon "impossible to descend."[43] Another expedition member proclaimed it "utterly impossible to find a way down."[44]

Cardenas, being told by his guides that the water situation would only get worse if they continued west, decided to call the reconnaissance quits. Although they correctly guessed that the river they saw below was

View of the Grand Canyon from the South Rim. Coronado sent Garcia Lopez de Cardenas and a small patrol to seek the Colorado River. After nearly three weeks of marching they came upon the river at the bottom of a "very grand" canyon where rocks that appeared miniature from above were actually "bigger than the great tower of Seville." (*Library of Congress*)

the same one Alarcon and Diaz had reached—the Colorado—"the expedition did not have any other result."[45]

Herbert Bolton thought that this momentous occasion in history merited the erection of "a group statue in memory of all three [Spanish climbers into the canyon] at a suitable place on the brink of the stupendous and now famous gorge which they so gallantly pioneered."[46] Cardenas himself was less than impressed with this natural wonder of the world. As was the case with Tovar's reconnaissance, Cardenas could only tell Coronado that he had seen nothing encouraging. No trace of gold was found.[47] Later, when testifying about his efforts, Cardenas mentioned only his visit to the Hopi and not the big canyon he had seen, recalling only the "much thirst and hunger" the Spaniards endured.[48]

Meanwhile, Captain Hernando de Alvarado was sent on a reconnaissance to the east of Cibola. This was the result of a delegation of Indians—including "a tall, well-built young captain" called Bigotes (Whiskers) because he had a mustache—coming to Cibola in response to the Spanish declaration that villages in the region were to submit. The village of Cicuye whence they came (later to be called Pecos) was seventy leagues (215 miles) from Cibola.[49] These Puebloans not only told the Spaniards they were friends, they brought presents (including hides, shields, and headpieces) and told the visitors of the great hairy cows to be found on the plains.[50] Bigotes agreed to guide the Spaniards east.

Consequently, according to Castaneda, taking "twenty companions," Alvarado started on his journey. After five days, heading to the southeast, he reached the impressive pueblo town of Acoma, which sat on a mesa almost four hundred feet in altitude. The Acomans had a regional reputation of being robbers—marauding raiders who lived on spoils.[51]

The Acomans initially "came down to the plains ready to fight, and would not listen to any arguments," drawing lines in the soil, "determined to prevent" the Spaniards from crossing. But this was bluff, for when the Acomans realized the invaders would fight, "they offered to make peace before any harm had been done."[52]

What impressed the Spaniards when they were allowed to examine Acoma was its fortress-like nature. "The village was very strong, because it was up on a rock out of reach, having steep sides in every direction, and so high that it was a very good musket that could throw a ball as high."[53] There seemingly was but one entrance to the pueblo, and that entrance had limited access. Then one would have to go up steps and ascend a wall with handholds, subject to the "large and small stones [piled] at the top, which they could roll down without showing themselves so that no army could possibly be strong enough to capture the village," observed Castaneda.[54] Another expedition member agreed, saying the peaceful Acomans "could have spared themselves the trouble and stayed on their rock and we would not have been able to trouble them in the least."[55] Unknown to the Spaniards, there was an easier way up the mesa, but the Acomans wisely kept that route secret.[56]

Acoma Pueblo sketched by C. B. Graham during Lieutenant James W. Abert's 1846–47 expedition into New Mexico. (*Library of Congress*)

Alvarado and his men next traveled three days to the east and got into the province called Tiguex, which was peaceful and, in Alvarado's opinion, a suitable location for the army's winter quarters. He sent word back to Coronado who "was not a little relieved to hear that the country was growing better."[57] Coronado dispatched a party under Cardenas to the Tiguex pueblos to prepare the region for the quartering of the main army.[58] There were, in Juan Jaramillo's estimate, fifteen pueblos in Tiguex, terraced and made of adobe mud walls.[59] This winter preparation required that the Tiguexans give up an entire pueblo, Alcanfor, and move into the pueblos of their relations.[60] As expressed in the Declaration of Independence, being forced to accept troops into one's home is not conducive of good relations.

Meanwhile, Alvarado's party left the immediate Rio Grande valley and continued east, arriving at Cicuye (Pecos Pueblo), which was seen to be "a very strong village four stories high."[61] The population in 1540 was about twenty-five hundred, which would mean there was a strong contingent of males of fighting age.[62] Cool springs were located at the base of the pueblo.[63] It was here that much trouble for the Spaniards would develop, based on their lust for gold.

While the presence of Bigotes with the reconnaissance patrol had made their introduction at Tiguex peaceful, Bigotes's act of taking them to his home pueblo was even more pacific, and more exciting. Not only did the Pecos Indians come out of "the village with signs of joy to welcome Hernando de Alvarado and their captain [Bigotes]," they led the

Spaniards into the pueblo with drums and flutes. The locals also presented the visitors with cloth and turquoise.[64] At some point, Alvarado held out the promise that the army would assist the people of Pecos in a war against their native enemies.[65]

During this pleasant visit at Pecos, the Spaniards made the acquaintanceship of an Indian slave whom the Spaniards called Turk or the Turk because he looked like one. Turk, who apparently was from the Central Great Plains and who might have been a Pawnee, began to fill the Spaniards' heads with lofty dreams. Turk not only described large herds of buffalo, he also said there were large settlements vaguely to the east.[66] Revitalized about their prospects, Alvarado and his advance party returned to Tiguex, taking Turk along as a future guide and, unbeknownst to the Spanish, an imaginative storyteller.

On the way back to Tiguex from Pecos, Alvarado and his reconnaissance party apparently circled to the north. When he reported back to Coronado, he said he had seen many buffalo and, also to the north, a pueblo of about five thousand people. This was Taos Pueblo.[67] Taos was "a large and powerful . . . village" with a stream flowing through the area claimed by the pueblo. The residents crossed this river on wooden bridges made of large and trimmed pines.[68]

The main army had now arrived at Cibola. Cardenas had been sent to Tiguex to prepare the winter quarters. Giving orders to Arellano to follow with the main army in twenty days, the captain general again took an advance party, "thirty of the men who were most fully rested," and headed toward Tiguex.[69] After a cold and thirsty march, Coronado's group reached the province of Tiguex, had a look at the several pueblos, and apparently set up headquarters at the pueblo where Alvarado had located: Alcanfor, or Coofor.[70]

Coronado also got a morale boost at Tiguex after he had a chance to listen to the tales Turk was coming up with. The captain general "felt no slight joy at such good news, because the Turk said that in his country, there was a river in the level country which was two leagues wide, in which there were fishes as big as horses, and large numbers of very big canoes" complete with rowers and sails. Turk also said that the lord of that country took his afternoon naps under a great tree decorated with golden bells. The people of the land had plate dishes and table jugs and bowls made of gold.[71]

Turk—apparently either a pathological liar or just a very clever manipulator—was believed "on account of the ease with which he told it," because he refused to identify nongold objects as gold, and because he seemed to know about gold and silver.[72] However, the seeming dispositive proof Turk offered to the greedy and gullible Spaniards was the claim that he made against Bigotes. Turk claimed that when he had been captured, the people of Pecos under Bigotes confiscated the golden bracelets he was wearing.[73] Such a bold story seemed too detailed to be fictional.

Because of this tale, Coronado had Alvarado return to Pecos Pueblo, where he "was received as a friend," according to Castaneda. When the Puebloans were confronted by Turk, they denied all knowledge of any golden jewelry. Alvarado had Bigotes and another tribal leader named Ysopete clapped in irons. "The villagers prepared to fight, and let fly their arrows, denouncing Hernando de Alvarado, and saying that he was a man who had no respect for peace and friendship."[74] Alvarado had but twenty-four men-at-arms and four arquebusiers.[75] He therefore made a hasty retreat to Tiguex with his prisoners. Bigotes and Ysopete (the latter, like Turk, also believed to be a native of Quivira) would remain prisoners for the next six months and, as Castaneda saw it, "This began the want of confidence in the word of the Spaniards whenever there was talk of peace from this time on."[76] It also did not help that of the three prisoners—Bigotes, Ysopete, and Turk—at least one or two had dogs set upon them, apparently in an effort to learn the truth about the gold bracelets or the golden land of Quivira to the north.[77]

Objectively, with the benefit of hindsight, one might well ask why a head man like Bigotes was detained. Many members of the expedition, in addition to Castaneda, later reasonably concluded that this treatment resulted in bad feelings that would not go away. While not a particularly good reason in this case, there was at least a long-standing military theory that supported the taking of such hostages. As one of Pizarro's soldiers wrote to his father in 1533 about the situation in Peru when the Spaniards seized the Great Inca, "We have him prisoner in our power, and with him prisoner, a man can go by himself 500 leagues without getting killed, instead they give you whatever you need and carry you on their shoulders in a litter."[78] But Pizarro's tiny army was in a virtual state of war in an organized empire that had a very definite governmental-administrative-communication system in place. There was less of a military necessity for the actions of Coronado's command. However, in part because of such hostage taking, there would be future cases of military necessity.

In a way, things were moving too fast at Tiguex in the absence of the main army. With his thirty men, the twenty-eight with Alvarado, and with the at-least twenty with Cardenas, Coronado began his occupancy of Tiguex with only about eighty Europeans. He undoubtedly had at least a few Indian allies; that number probably would have been greater except for the fact that the weather was so cold.

The expedition was to find that even when in full force, it lacked the numbers needed to successfully occupy an enemy territory. In the closing days of the Spanish Reconquista, Portugal was considering the full-scale invasion of Morocco. One of the wiser voices among the Portuguese warned that unlike the situation in Spain, where there was a friendly population to support Christian endeavors, one "who seeks to conquer a foreign kingdom [like Morocco] must be quite certain that he has enough strength to dominate the countryside. . . . If his strength is small he will be unacceptably forced to rely on stockades and artillery to protect himself from a supposedly conquered enemy."[79] In the event, Coronado's Spanish vanguard in Tiguex might be deemed strong enough to handle potential trouble but not intimidating enough to forestall those same difficulties from natives who had become progressively less impressed.

# FOURTEEN

# Unwelcome Occupiers and the Tiguex War

Since Arellano had not yet moved up with the main army, Coronado's force, in early 1541, was split between Cibola and Tiguex for several weeks. This temporary numerical weakness of the Spaniards in Tiguex certainly would not have gone unnoticed by the people of that province. Even in Europe, when soldiers quartered themselves among towns during winter, "their presence was a source of continuous discomfort and growing bitterness for the town dwellers."[1] Or, as Niccolo Machiavelli put it more succinctly, quartered troops "live to their liking" but "not to the liking of those who lodge them."[2]

As for the living conditions for the intruders, they likely were similar wherever the Spaniards and their Indian allies were posted: primitive and boring. For the natives and the unwelcome visitors, it was a cold winter. Even in Europe, Spanish soldiers, like the Italians, suffered whenever they campaigned in northern climes in the off-season.[3]

In addition, during the enforced stay at Tiguex by only a small part of the army, there was little enough in the way of entertainment, especially for the virile Spanish soldiery, who had not come to the land of enchantment of New Mexico for rest and relaxation. Certainly, the contemporaneous armies of Europe, including those of Charles V, were known for getting drunk, playing at dice, swearing, quarreling, and brawling when out campaigning.[4]

With the rather miserable living conditions, these winter quarters at Tiguex demonstrated that trouble can germinate and grow even in the cold. The record is empty regarding the presence of alcohol among the expedition, although soldiers always have been resourceful regarding locating or manufacturing that class six type of military supply. Drunkenness was a serious problem with sixteenth-century armies in Europe.[5] Ironically, the apparent absence of any booze for the rank and file might have made the general misery more intolerable in this case.

It likely was during this cold stay in Tiguex that there were noticeable disciplinary problems among the Spaniards. Juan de Contreras, Coronado's personal groom, recalled that the captain general tried to protect the locals from a rapacious soldiery. "If any individual from the army disobeyed, committing any outrage or taking corn or property" from the Indians, "Francisco Vasquez imprisoned and punished that person." Contreras "saw that for very slight infractions individuals were kept in shackles for two or three" duty days.[6]

While the friars probably did their best to turn the soldiers' thoughts to better things, age-old underminers of discipline, such as gambling, certainly took place. For his part, Coronado, according to expedition member Diego Lopez, did not permit "excessive gambling."[7] Gaming that gets out of hand has always been a disciplinary concern with armies. "All the playing-cards possessed by the soldiers should be destroyed on leaving the towns and in places where they cannot obtain others," warned a late sixteenth-century history about taking expeditions into New Mexico. "If soldiers did not have cards they would not gamble away their valuables, arms, and horses. . . . They would occupy their time in fixing up their arms . . . and peace would be preserved if playing-cards were not present."[8] Apparently, in believing that the mere prohibition of cards will prevent trouble, such historians have never carved their own dice or wagered on scorpion fights.

But gambling primarily would sour relations between the members of the army and not normally affect relations with the occupied populace. There are other vices that impact those military-civilian relations.

As noted, it is open to debate whether official prostitutes accompanied Coronado's main column. Such a presence, according to Spanish ideas of the era, was intended to reduce the temptation for the soldiery to commit rape.[9] In either case, it certainly was true that the friars could not completely prevent carnal thoughts among the soldiery, especially with a seemingly subservient civilian population at hand. "Heavy punishment should be imposed in order that the soldiers may not dishonor the wives and daughters of the natives, especially those who are not yet baptized and those who have recently been converted," warned that same sixteenth-century history, which reads like a manual for successful field operations in occupied territories. "When they fail to keep and obey this just and Christian law of discipline and chastity, the natives usually revolt, because it is like poison which perverts their hearts and incites them to destroy and kill those who perpetrate these offenses."[10] As with gambling, Coronado reportedly attempted to suppress "living in concubinage."[11]

But the long-standing simmering problems with the local population at Tiguex centered on the requisitioning of supplies, both food and clothing. Provisions, warned that Spanish history, "should be acquired through proper and peaceful means, requested and bought from their owners in exchange for goods, all with their consent. . . . Provisions should not be taken by force," except "with Christian moderation" after other efforts had failed.[12]

Because the expedition was not prepared for northern weather, a situation exacerbated by the failure to link up with Alarcon's ships, there was a pressing need for winter clothing. Coronado later testified that "a certain number of Spaniards, soldiers, and Indian allies complained to [him] that they were naked and dying from cold and asked him to order some clothing, gathered from the surrounding pueblos with which they might protect themselves and not perish from the cold."[13]

Therefore, before the arrival of the main army from Cibola, "the general wished to obtain some clothing to divide among his soldiers, and for this purpose he summoned one of the chief Indians of Tiguex, with whom he had already had much intercourse and with whom he was on good terms, who was called Juan Aleman by our men, after a Juan Aleman who lived in Mexico, whom he was said to resemble."[14] Coronado, obviously anticipating the needs of the men with Arellano, said more than three hundred or more pieces would be needed, and he delegated his officers to start collecting from each of the Tiguex pueblos.[15]

Ironically, by demanding the clothing from a subject people, the Spaniards not only were acting as many European armies of occupation, they specifically were copying the harsh demands of their former enemies, the Aztecs. The Aztecs once required a conquered province to provide over fifty thousand cloaks *per month* to their overlords.[16] Such conduct by the Aztecs, of course, helped the Spanish acquire the Indian allies they needed to overthrow the Aztec Empire.

In addition, Coronado's men, being in bad straits themselves, lacked finesse in enforcing their demands. According to Castaneda,

> As they were in very great need, they did not give the natives a chance to consult about it, but when they came to a village they demanded what they had to give, so that they could take off their own cloaks and give them to make up the number demanded of them. And some of the soldiers who were in these parties, when the collectors gave them some blankets or cloaks which were not such as they wanted, if they saw any Indian with a better one on, they exchanged with him without more ado, not stopping to find out the rank of the man they were stripping, which caused not a little hard feeling.[17]

While not much of a defense, weak mitigating factors applied to the Spaniards and their seizure of Tiguex food and other resources. Just as the Spanish had certain expectations regarding finding real cities and a relatively advanced civilization (with precious metals and gemstones), they likely had high hopes about the availability of food and forage, if not clothing. When the Spanish arrived in Peru, they found a developed native state that included "great storehouses full of necessary things, which were for provisioning the [Inca] soldiers." These locally produced things stored for the native army included food and clothing.[18]

Therefore, Coronado and his army might have expected to find a prosperous land such as in the Low Countries or India, where plentiful supplies, if not purchased, could be appropriated without starving or freezing the inhabitants. But once again, Coronado had received only bad intelligence from Friar Marcos, even though the follow-up reconnaissance of Diaz had hinted at the true state of affairs.

Nonetheless, according to Castaneda, who seemingly wrote his account as a booster of the new lands, there was relative plenty in Tiguex when it came to food, for, "In one year they gather enough for seven."[19] As for Mota Padilla, he also wrote that the people of Tiguex had some "granaries of corn, which they keep two or more years, and is a perpetual sustenance, as are also beans and very large squashes."[20] Thus, it was more the demand for limited clothing that would set off trouble, although the Indians certainly did not appreciate the horses of the Spaniards grazing in their newly planted fields of maize.[21]

With the confiscations, Coronado may have been cognizant enough to recognize that things were going to get hot in Tiguex even during the cold weather. Juan Troyano, the artillerist, was sent back to Cibola to bring up "some [of the] artillery pieces."[22]

With a revolt already simmering, there only needed to be a spark to set off a powder keg of trouble. That occurred when one of the Spanish men-at-arms left his camp and rode to a pueblo a league away, the pueblo of Arenal, where reportedly "the greatest injury had been done" regarding requisitions. When he arrived, the Spaniard espied "a pretty woman."[23] This man-at-arms, later identified in several documents as the well-connected Juan de Villegas,[24] then had the audacity to call "her husband down to hold his horse by the bridle while he went up; and as the village was entered by the upper story, the Indian supposed he was going to some other part of it."[25]

The husband heard "some slight noise" above him and Villegas climbed back down, "took his horse, and went away." The Indian climbed up "and learned that [Villegas] had violated, or tried to violate, his wife." Gathering some elders from the pueblo, the husband went to complain to the occupying authorities about what had happened.[26]

Although the master of the army, Cardenas, later testified it was he who made the investigation into the incident,[27] Castaneda recalled that it was Captain General Coronado, acting in a classic military fashion, who "made all the soldiers and the persons who were with him come together" and conducted a lineup. The complaining witness was unable to identify an individual from this rank of foreign-looking soldiery (another situation that has faced commanders in other eras). Castaneda, sounding like a soldier who knew, opined that the violator had perhaps "changed his clothes" in the meantime.[28]

However, the husband insisted that while he might not be able to identify the man, he could identify his horse. Sure enough, when taken to the stables, he "found the horse, and said that the master of the horse must be the man." However, either Villegas or the man who had lent him his mount, "seeing that he had not been recognized," denied the dirty deed. Apparently, even with this disputed evidence, no further investigation was conducted, and neither the aggrieved husband nor his assaulted wife got "any satisfaction."[29] This incident, according to Castaneda, was the breaking point.

Coronado's troops should have been aware of basic human nature, if not aware of previous examples touching on this area of military-civilian affairs. Francisco Pizarro, the hardly sensitive conqueror of Peru, had ordered his soldiers not to molest the wives and concubines of the captive Inca emperor, "realising the reverence in which [these women] were held." Likewise, Hernando De Soto, when campaigning in Peru, also enforced this prohibition, "knowing that if anything were to incense [an Inca chief] to rebellion it would be the rape of his women."[30] Even an early royal patent for the discovery of the newfound lands in North America, issued by the English in 1501 to some enterprising Portuguese, granted the patentees the power to punish their sailors who committed "any attacks on the virtue of native women."[31]

In addition, a number of the Spanish conquistadors, especially when they relied on native assistance so much, were not unaware that smoothing civilian-military relations was militarily important once a transgression had occurred. While he refused to compromise when it came to matters of suppressing paganism and idolatry, Hernando Cortes, before the major outbreak of Aztec resistance, once hanged one of his Spaniards for the theft of two Mexican-owned turkeys, "so anxious was he to appear just to the natives."[32]

Although it would be historically hypocritical to impose modern notions of ethics and justice on a field force of sixteenth-century Spaniards marching through the hinterland of North America, a military analysis of such a sexual assault is not confined to any particular century. The failure of Coronado (or Cardenas) to resolve the case in any way to the satisfaction of the local population clearly was an error in judgment. Not only did the issue go to the general discipline of a military force in an unfriendly environment, an individual member of the command had created a problem that obviously jeopardized the several missions of the Spanish expedition. This would have been a problem for an occupation army if it had occurred anytime in history, even if the occupied territory was inherently friendly.

For example, during the Second World War, US Army Private Eddie Leonski brutally murdered three inoffensive local women in Melbourne, Australia, an allied nation playing host to US forces in the Pacific. While some Australians would have preferred to have their own courts handle the affair,[33] the more important practical consideration was that the American Army did not allow the case to fester. In a court-martial prosecution that some believe was a virtual railroad ride on the track of political expediency (despite Leonski's unquestionable factual guilt), the soldier was arrested, tried, convicted, and hanged within a mere six months in 1942.[34] "Everyone in the U.S. Army thought it a tragedy that an American was involved because the people of Australia gave us an excess of goodwill and hospitality," recalled the judge advocate officer who prosecuted Leonski. "This case had Melbourne by the throat. It had to be dealt with fairly but harshly."[35]

In the event, Coronado, who already had written Mendoza that the people of Zuni loved their women "better than themselves,"[36] neither acted fairly to the people of Tiguex nor reacted harshly to his own men during the brief window of opportunity open to him. He certainly did not appear to keep a promise he made at some point that he would hang any Spaniards committing rape.[37] His indecisiveness left the unresolved sexual assault as fuel to be added to an already volatile situation. According to Castaneda, the resultant explosion did not even wait twenty-four hours: "The next day one of the Indians, who was guarding the horses of the army, came running in, saying that a companion of his had been killed, and that the Indians of the country were driving the horses toward their villages. The Spaniards tried to collect the horses again, but many were lost, besides seven of the general's mules."[38]

Lopez de Cardenas, the master of the army, also later recalled that one of the Mexican Indian horse guards was killed.[39] However, according to the recollections of Coronado, a total of two Indian auxiliaries or servants were killed by arrows when the horse herd was raided.[40] At least one Spaniard thought that four or five allied Indians had been killed.[41]

While the Spaniards did not act decisively to try to prevent this outbreak, they knew that something had to be done to protect their most fearsome weapon, their horses. "When the horse is dead, the man-at-arms is lost," the Spaniards learned from their fighting in Europe.[42]

Because this was a serious matter even without considering the loss of Coronado's mules, "The next day Don Garcia Lopez de Cardenas went to see the villages and to talk to the natives." [43] With him went "seven or eight mounted men." They followed a trail of dead horses, pincushioned with arrows, and rounded up what equine survivors they could.[44] At one of the villages, horses were confined behind a palisade. There was "a great noise inside, the horses being chased as a bull fight and shot with arrows." The few Spaniards could do nothing, since the Puebloans stayed within their fortified village and would not descend to the plain.[45]

From the perspective of the poor horses, it should be noted that one sixteenth-century soldier wrote that wounding them with arrows, unlike shooting them with bullets, caused the animals great pain, desperate rearing, and terrible panic.[46] Certainly the Spaniards, who could be callous to much human suffering and the suffering of the horses of other armies,[47] were affected by the suffering of their four-footed companions.

On the other hand, the Tiguex people obviously also recognized the military importance of depriving enemy men-at-arms of their mounts as well as military transport. Coronado estimated that anywhere from thirty to fifty horses were stolen in the raid.[48]

In attempting to cripple an enemy force by killing or maiming its horses, the Indians, who at this point in history had no special use for such animals, actually were emulating a tactic occasionally used in European warfare of the period. However, even when occurring between "civilized" armies, this often-effective animal cruelty was considered negatively as "bad war."[49]

And war it was. When the people of Arenal killed the horses, they cut off their tails and sent them around to the other pueblos as an invitation to revolt.[50] The people of Tiguex obviously acted in concert in finally resisting the invaders because one pueblo, apparently deemed indefensible, had been abandoned,[51] and when Coronado sent Cardenas around to the various other pueblos to assess the situation, according to Castaneda, "He found the villages closed by palisades. . . . They were all ready for fighting. Nothing could be done, because they would not come down onto the plain and the villages are so strong that the Spaniards could not dislodge them."[52]

The details of the resultant Tiguex War, like much of Coronado's expedition, are vague and confusing and must be cobbled together as a matter of the best guess. It is certain that various pueblos revolted and came under Spanish attack in turn. Undoubtedly, this is why historian Mota Padilla recalled these contests as "several wars [that] broke out."[53] It often is unclear which battles occurred around which pueblos, for there were at least a couple of contemporaneous names for each pueblo, and many of the pueblos have long since moved or otherwise disappeared.

Coronado called a council of war with his captains, along with "the friars who were with the army," to deal with the crisis. "[I]t was decided, by the agreement of all, to wage war on the Indians," according to Lopez de Cardenas.[54] Part of the reasoning was the traditional fear of an advancing army leaving "enemy castles in the rear" which could jeopardize the overall campaign.[55] In addition, both Friar Juan de Padilla and

Friar Antonio de Castilblanco gave their approval, Friar Padilla saying "that it was not permissible for them to kill anyone, but that he would approve and consider appropriate whatever the general should do."⁵⁶

However, the Spaniards first offered the people of Tiguex the opportunity to submit and "accept peace." If they did not, Coronado intended "to do them what harm he could."⁵⁷ Needless to say, the hostile population refused to submit.

Coronado decided that Arenal Pueblo, where the sexual assault reportedly had occurred, should be surrounded by Cardenas and "all the rest of the force."⁵⁸ Presumably, since combat was anticipated, the clerics with the army conducted mass and heard confession from the soldiery, a solemn preparation that probably had not occurred before the desperate assault on Cibola the year before.⁵⁹ Coronado might have used this occasion to once again conduct a harangue to encourage the men then gathered for the coming combat.

Before the rest of the army actually arrived to begin a siege, Captains Juan de Saldivar, Velasco de Barrionuevo, Diego Lopez, and Pablo de Melgossa raced ahead with a strike force.⁶⁰ This party of "sixty horsemen, a number of footmen, and some of the Indians from Mexico" was under the command of Cardenas. Apparently, before they arrived at the pueblo, Cardenas, with "a few of the captains who were with him, separated from the other people and for a period of two hours summoned them [of Arenal] to peace." Although this peace parley presumably was sincere, it also was a distraction, for the majority of the members of this strike force apparently approached the pueblo unobserved from another side.⁶¹

After the two hours of negotiations (and stealthy positioning), Cardenas "waged war and ordered his men to attack them," and the force likely hidden on the other side rushed the pueblo.⁶² These Spaniards and Indian auxiliaries "took the Indians so much by surprise that they gained the upper story, with great danger, for they wounded many of our men from within the houses," wrote Castaneda.⁶³

This strategic toehold on the top of the pueblo, accomplished by the time the main force arrived, was the result of a classic *coup de main* of siege warfare.⁶⁴ But it was at a cost, for, according to Cardenas, by the time his men gained some of the terraces, "some Mexican Indians were killed and thirteen or fourteen Spaniards were badly wounded."⁶⁵

Nonetheless, even with the toehold being particularly tenuous, the defenders of Arenal were caught between two enemy positions, a desperate situation in any fight. But it continued to be desperate also for the Spanish. "Our men were on top of the houses in great danger for a day and a night and part of the next day," reported Castaneda. "[A]nd they made some good shots with their crossbows and muskets."[66] Meanwhile, other Spaniards and allied Indians fought a prolonged battle inside the pueblo, taking "the houses of these natives one by one," according to Cardenas.[67] On the plain outside the pueblo, Spanish horsemen "with many of the Indian allies from New Spain smoked them [the defenders] out from the cellars [kivas] into which they had broken, so that they begged for peace."[68] One historian gave the Indian auxiliaries particular credit for entering the "subterranean passages" and burning out the defenders.[69]

Thus, this first pueblo of Arenal, reportedly a small one, fell, according to Mota Padilla, "after some battering."[70] The defenders, according to Coronado, had "wounded more than forty Spaniards and Indian allies."[71] However, what followed this hard-fought and stand-up fight set the whole district aflame.

According to Castaneda, the Indian defenders, because they were losing the fight, "begged for peace." Two of the Spaniards on the roof, Pablo de Melgosa and Diego Lopez, "answered the Indians with the same signs they were making for peace, which was to make a cross. They then put down their arms and received pardon."[72]

Cardenas, when later facing accusations regarding his conduct during the expedition, was adamant that he never accepted any sort of a surrender through the use of a cross or otherwise. Although he earlier had asked for submission, "Once hostilities started, he never summoned them again until the fight was over, nor did he observe that the Indians asked for peace." But Cardenas, evidencing a selective memory, also claimed that he did not recall how many, if any, Indian defenders had died in the capture of the pueblo.[73]

Castaneda believed that Cardenas did not know about any terms of submission and thought the Indians had surrendered at discretion only "because they had been conquered." In addition, Cardenas had his orders from Coronado to take no prisoners and "to make an example of them so that the other natives would fear the Spaniards." Castaneda sadly concluded, "Nobody told [Cárdenas] about the peace that had been granted" the Indian defenders, and the few soldiers who knew about it and "should have told him about it remained silent, not thinking that it was any of their business."[74]

While this Pontius Pilate attitude on the part of Pablo de Melgosa and Diego Lopez sounds plausible (and is not unknown in military circles), others present added believable details during the expedition investigation. Juan Troyano, the professional soldier and artillerist, agreed that the defenders, being "sorely pressed . . . communicated by signs to the captains and Spaniards that if they were assured of safety, they would offer peace." When the captains and Spaniards responded with the sign of the cross, they said such a submission would mean "no harm or hurt would be done to them."[75]

While Troyano did not say whether Cardenas was informed of the promise, he did testify that Coronado came on the scene, presumably to discuss the disposition of the prisoners, and had the hostages Turk and Bigotes brought along to see whatever justice was to be administered.[76] Cardenas acknowledged that Coronado sent Turk, Bigotes, and Ysopete "to the scene of the battle so that they might see the power with which the pueblo was taken, and the punishment that he inflicted on the said Indians . . . in order that they . . . counsel others not to rebel, but to come and make friends."[77]

Melchior Perez was another witness who specifically recalled the events. For his part, Perez testified that Cardenas not only knew what had transpired, he participated in the bargain. Because Perez suspected that Cardenas "would not keep his word," he said to him during the negotiations, "Lord do not show them the cross unless you expect to fulfill." To this Cardenas replied "that he had made" the suggestion of the cross "incorrectly."[78] There was no love lost between these two conquistadors, and the best defense that Cardenas had regarding this testimony was that Perez (as well as Troyano) was his personal enemy.[79]

While the details of how the surrender came about are not carved in stone, what followed is mostly undisputed, except for the total casualty list among the captured Indians. According to Castaneda, Cardenas "ordered two hundred stakes to be prepared at once to burn them alive."

> Then when the [surrendered] enemies saw that the Spaniards were binding them, about a hundred men who were in the tent [where they were being held] began to struggle and defend themselves with what there was there and with the stakes they could seize. Our men who were on foot attacked the tent on all sides, so that there was great confusion around it, and then the horsemen chased those who escaped. As the country was level, not a man of them remained alive, unless it was some who remained hidden in the village and escaped that night to spread

throughout the country the news that the strangers did not respect the peace they had made, which afterward proved a great misfortune.[80]

Other Spaniards did not make the carnage to be as great. Juan de Contreras thought Cardenas only had time to burn fifteen prisoners before the others resisted.[81] Rodrigo Ximon thought twenty or thirty had been killed at the stake.[82] Juan Troyano recalled forty or fifty burned alive.[83]

Coronado later testified that he knew nothing of what happened to any prisoners taken at Arenal, including any display of them for the benefit of Turk and Ysopete. He had only ordered Cardenas "not to raise the siege of said pueblo until it was completely subjugated." However, Coronado had heard that some of the prisoners kept in the tent of Cardenas "had revolted and offered resistance and that some of them had been killed."[84] Considering the testimony of others, his is less than convincing.[85]

However, perhaps it is to Coronado's credit that he at least denied participating in such a scheme of retribution. First, even in the Middle Ages it was considered consistent with the concept of a just war to keep promises made to an enemy.[86] Second, certainly by the early fifteenth century, the killing of captured opponents was frowned upon in Christian Europe.[87] By much of the seventeenth century, the mass execution and slaughter of prisoners would be generally unacceptable under the rules of war as they had by then developed, even if it involved no breach of faith to those captured.[88] Such massacres also were seen, by then, as usually militarily counterproductive.

As for the interim period, the situation regarding killing captives during most of the sixteenth century was a thorny, muddled issue, and generally fell somewhere within three camps: wholehearted enthusiasm, mere distaste, and outright condemnation. Even those taken prisoner who were not considered rebels were at risk. While members of the nobility often were held for ransom, a leftover courtesy from the Middle Ages, "In the sixteenth century all others were frequently massacred. Only the fear of reprisal prevented the killing of prisoners."[89] Indeed, there are many occasions throughout that violent century when whole regiments of helpless European prisoners were unmercifully annihilated by other Europeans, sometimes depending on the nationality or point of origin of the victims.[90] Of course, as was demonstrated by the Thirty Years' War of the seventeenth century, civilians often were no better off.

A sixteenth-century woodcut showing two prisoners being burned at the
stake. (*Author*)

Of course, the fact that massacres were rather commonplace did not
make them ethically or morally right, even in that century, at least for
those who thought much about it. But not everyone thought much
about it. According to one historian, during this era "especially the
Turks and the Spaniards, increasingly used atrocities against civilians as
a calculated policy of terror."[91]

As for the particular punishment imposed at Tiguex, death by fire,
that certainly was not an unknown punishment, especially for the
Spanish in the New World. When Cortes caught some Aztec nobles
conspiring to kill him, he had them condemned and burned publicly, a
"novel form of justice imposed in the kingdom of Moctezuma."[92]
Despite not being uncommon in Europe and elsewhere, being burned
at the stake always has been an especially horrendous way to die, and
purposely so. It certainly was no coincidence that in the Low Countries
in 1535, Charles V issued an edict that decreed that only heretics who
recanted were to be executed by the sword (males) or buried alive
(females); those who stubbornly held to their Protestant beliefs were to
be burned alive.[93] When Girolamo Savonarola, the excommunicated
Dominican friar who railed against the corruption of Pope Alexander
VI's Rome, was sentenced to death after his 1498 trial in Florence, he
was relieved that he would suffer death by hanging before his body was
consumed by flames.[94]

Of, course, the intention of this highest degree of punishment had
long been to get everyone's attention, even when involving a single victim. Hence the well-remembered martyrdom of Joan of Arc in the fifteenth century. Increasing the toll did not make the practice any more
acceptable, even in olden days. Thus the public revulsion that turned
Bloody Mary's England irretrievably Protestant in the sixteenth century
when she had three hundred dissenters burned alive.[95]

In addition to the general issue of taking no prisoners or summarily executing those taken, if there had been a breach of the implied terms of surrender by Cardenas in slaughtering the then-defenseless survivors of the pueblo, then that was not even considered appropriate behavior in the wild and dangerous sixteenth century. Regarding the exact details of the atrocity at Tiguex, the testimonial evidence leads to the reasonable conclusion that there was such a dishonorable violation of a promise of mercy extended to the Puebloans and accepted by them by the quick abandonment of their defensive position.

Supporting the direct testimony obtained during the investigation of the expedition, the character of many contemporary Spaniards fit well within the charge of breach of faith made by the people of Tiguex. Starting early in the sixteenth century, the arrogant Spaniards gained a nasty reputation for not keeping their word when making life-and-death bargains with foreigners, traitors, rebels, heretics, or pagans (as defined by the Spanish), especially when those unlucky folk were captured or otherwise fell into their power.[96] In the words of William H. Prescott, the Spaniards unfortunately mingled "the fanaticism of the Crusader . . . with the cruelty of the conqueror."[97] While other countries, including Spain's enemies, occasionally demonstrated analogous behavior,[98] the historical proofs of this well-deserved Spanish reputation are both numerous and notorious and span the entire sixteenth century.

Of course, the first example of betrayal is a subtle one, wrapped up with claims of rebellion and national necessity, and one of which most nations of sixteenth-century Europe would approve. When the Muslim ruler of Granada negotiated a surrender to Ferdinand and Isabella in November 1491, at the end of the Reconquista, the articles of capitulation seemed to guarantee the rights of the Muslim residents of Granada. However, Spain viewed the agreement as a mere temporary expedient, and by 1500–1501, the conversion of the Muslims of Granada to Catholicism was made mandatory, with exile being the only alternative, a choice earlier offered the Jews of Spain.[99] This was only the beginning of the efforts resulting in a Spain of one faith.

But the best-known example to sixteenth-century Europeans and to students of the conquests of the Americas is the mutual agreement entered into by Francisco Pizarro and his royal prisoner, Atahualpa the Great Inca of Peru. Atahualpa received a promise not to be killed and to be freed if he was able to fill his cell with golden treasure. Perhaps not imagining that such an offer could be fulfilled, Pizarro agreed to the oral contract. In due course the room was filled, and on July 26, 1533, the Great Inca was garroted to death, only avoiding being burned at the stake by an eleventh-hour agreement to be baptized a Catholic.[100] Naturally, there are many other factual complications, and the Spaniards would plead military necessity for the homicide, but certainly the bargain, sealed with the promised consideration, was not honored.[101]

Throughout the rest of the sixteenth century, whether in their dealings with the French,[102] the English,[103] the Flemish,[104] or the Dutch,[105] the Spanish expanded on their reputation for not honoring treaties, terms of surrender, or solemn agreements regarding safe conduct. Occurring in both the New World and the Old, these cold-blooded violations of covenants made in the name of expediency saw victims who usually were heretical Protestants but occasionally were devout Catholics.

Therefore, not only is the on-the-spot evidence compelling that Cardenas or his subordinates accepted the surrender of the Tiguex warriors with at least an implied promise of Christian mercy, the smoky and bloody results comported with a Spanish tendency that became policy: Even solemn promises did not have to be kept when dealing with religious or political dissidents, rebels, and avowed enemies.

As for the complicity of Coronado himself, he had ordered that no prisoners be taken, although holding out the promise of mercy undoubtedly was not part of the captain general's plan regarding the attack on the pueblo (and he perhaps was not informed afterward that such a promise had been at least implied). At best, much like Colonel John M. Chivington at the Sand Creek Massacre three hundred years later in the Colorado Territory, Coronado encouraged the mercilessness up front and then did not even attempt to reassert his command over his subordinate officers and a vengeful soldiery when he had the chance.

While the ethics of these sixteenth-century situations seem clear enough, this uncompromising attitude had real-world implications in a military sense. The Spanish tendency to dishonor agreements was a salutary lesson that stiffened the resolve of Spain's enemies. Thus, such bloody conquests were Pyrrhic victories; for example, in the Netherlands, the "atrocities made it clear to the rebels that surrender to the Spaniards was not an option."[106]

These enemies, who ultimately would respond like angry bees around a greedy bear at the honey tree, included French corsairs and privateers (both Catholics and Protestant Huguenots) attacking Spain in the New World, the rebelling Flemish and Dutch during their Eighty Years' War against the Spanish occupiers, and the ambitious English prior to, during, and after the 1588 sailing of the Spanish Armada. The people of Tiguex would also prove to be apt students when confronted with Spanish perfidy and in drawing pertinent military lessons about whether to resist.

# FIFTEEN

# Military Miscalculation: Siege Warfare

The Spanish and their Indian auxiliaries acquitted themselves well in the capture of Arenal, exhibiting bravery and sound tactical decisions. The fact that the defenders were slaughtered was not in itself a strategic misstep, for since the time of Alexander, a salutary lesson or two like that often meant subsequent sieges became unnecessary when submissions would be accepted with the promise of clemency.[1] But clemency promised must be delivered.

Therefore, the details of the follow-up massacre at Arenal proved a public-relations debacle that undid most of the glory and all of the usefulness, for the people of Tiguex would not believe in any future promises of mercy. There was no going back to the more-limited warfare of Cibola. "After this occurrence," according to Mota Padilla, "the Indians fortified themselves in the other pueblos."[2]

Of course, not all the rebellious Indians stayed holed up in their pueblos all the time. Apparently, groups of Tiguex warriors roamed the area, attacking and clubbing to death any Indian auxiliaries found in the countryside foraging.[3]

Things looked so grim for the invaders that Coronado even traveled to Pecos Pueblo with Bigotes to enlist support against the people of Tiguex. Pecos politely refused to become an ally of the Spaniards, and Coronado apparently returned to Tiguex with Bigotes.[4] However, it is possible that members of Pecos Pueblo were enlisted to make copper crossbow boltheads and arrowheads for Coronado's Spaniards and auxiliaries.[5]

As for the warlike preparations of the Tiguex people, this reinforcing of their communities included the main pueblo since called Moho, the village under the leadership of Juan Aleman. Probably based on how the natives had seen that the Spaniards conducted war—and how falconets, arquebuses, and crossbows could hit defenders on a roof—these Puebloans dug loopholes into the walls of their houses.[6]

The people of the province of Tiguex were not in any mood to compromise short of war, for they now said "that they did not trust those who did not know how to keep good faith after they had once given it, and that the Spaniards should remember that they . . . did not keep their word when they burned those who surrendered in the village."[7] The Tiguexans also undoubtedly remembered who had been in immediate command when the burnings and the slaughter at Arenal had taken place: Don Garcia Lopez de Cardenas.

This very hostile—and very logical—response of the people of Tiguex was not unlike that of their supposedly more-civilized counterparts to be found across the Atlantic. In 1549, when the Englishmen of Norwich rose in rebellion against excessive taxes and being forced to become Protestants, the Earl of Warwick led a force to suppress the rebellion. His first action was to "seize sixty men and [have] them hanged in the market place below the castle." Afterward, when Warwick offered the rebels "pardon for all who would disperse," the locals refused: "the hangings . . . on Warwick's first day in Norwich gave the peasants no confidence in the nobleman's words."[8]

From the Spanish viewpoint, Cardenas, master of the army, having brought about the capture and destruction of Arenal, was one who got results, and he therefore was "one of those" delegated by Coronado to attempt to gain the submission of the other pueblos in revolt.[9] This diplomatic mission, of course, included Moho.

With about thirty men-at-arms, Cardenas went to Moho. Although the residents of the village "were hostile," according to Castaneda, "they talked with him about a peace, and [said] that if he would send away the horsemen and make his men keep away, Juan Aleman and another captain would come out of the village and meet him."[10] Since the occupants of Moho likely would have been aware of the *coup de main* Cardenas had orchestrated at Arenal, this cautious condition probably made sense even to him.

Especially by the end of the Middle Ages, the meeting of enemies under truce conditions was believed by Europeans to be standard enough to be safe.[11] However, in this case, undoubtedly demonstrating more Spanish courage than sense, Cardenas also did "everything . . . as they required . . . in order to give them confidence, on account of his great desire to get them to make peace." He even took off his arms, handing his sword to his men.[12] However, he did not take off his helmet as requested, and he may have concealed a dagger in his clothing.[13]

When Juan Aleman came out to parley with two other Indians, his ostentatious embrace of Cardenas was more like a bear hug, pinning the Spaniard's arms to his sides. Meanwhile, the others drew out wooden clubs from behind their backs and gave Cardenas "two such blows over his helmet that they almost knocked him senseless."[14] Four other Indians may then have reinforced Juan Aleman and his group.[15] Dazed, Cardenas was dragged or carried to the pueblo; however, his bulk frustrated the Indians' attempts to get him inside a doorway.[16]

While apparently unexpected by Cardenas, such acts of treachery often go hand in hand with war—as do occasional acts of chivalry. During the siege of Malaga in 1487, the besieged Muslims sent a fanatic into the Spanish lines by stratagem. After allowing himself to be captured, this Moor asked to have an audience with King Ferdinand and Queen Isabella. While waiting, he saw a couple of well-dressed Spanish nobles, whom he took to be the royal couple, and attacked them with a hidden dagger, wounding both. After he was cut down during this double-assassination attempt, the fanatic's body was sliced into pieces and catapulted into the besieged city.[17] Perhaps even more to the point, the Duke of Burgundy, John the Fearless, in 1419, was hacked to death when he met the representatives of the King of France in order to discuss peace terms, an act of treachery that brought about years of bitter warfare.[18]

Thus, the perfidy by the Tiguexans was particularly treacherous under the traditional law of war, for it occurred during a discussion supposedly protected by a literal or symbolic flag of truce. This sort of violation had been seen as a breach of the law of war since ancient times,[19] and that viewpoint certainly was not restricted to Europe and more-formal warfare. In 1837, during the Second Seminole War, General Thomas Jesup received almost universal condemnation outside of the American South for seizing Chief Osceola and his band during scheduled discussions under a white flag of truce.[20]

As noted, such treacherous activity will invite retribution in the future from the aggrieved party. Indeed, Coronado, while denying any knowledge of any atrocities on the part of the Spaniards at Arenal or Moho, later asserted, "At both places the Indians tried to kill the Spaniards through trickery."[21] Understandably, there was no Spanish recognition that the conduct of Cardenas at Arenal was in any way connected to the responding conduct of the Indians at Moho.

This duplicity at Moho, with the springing of the trap, happened in mere moments. Fortunately for the master of the army, two of his men-at-arms had refused "to go very far off, even when he ordered them, and so they were near by and rode up so quickly that they rescued him from their hands." However, Juan Aleman and his cohorts, after they dropped Cardenas, were able to dart back into their village. As the rest of the Spaniards rode up to carry their wounded leader off, they were met with a "great shower of arrows which were shot at them [and] one arrow hit a horse and went through his nose." Although unable to do the Tiguex bowmen any harm, "many of our men," according to Castaneda, "were dangerously wounded."[22]

Because Juan Aleman and his fellows obviously attempted to capture Cardenas alive, the Spaniards believed they had intended "to commit some atrocity" on the camp master.[23] Cardenas, somewhat recovered from his assault, left a small covering party at the pueblo and took most of his men to another pueblo "about a half a league distant, because almost all of the people in this region had collected into these two villages." [24] However, the Spaniards had no better luck at this second pueblo in getting submission, for the Indians answered the demand "by shooting arrows from the upper stories with loud yells, and would not hear of peace," and Cardenas returned to Moho.[25]

There Cardenas apparently made a brief show of an attack, but he soon ordered his men to return to the Spanish camp at Alcanfor. As the Spaniards drew off on horseback, the Tiguexans, in a dangerous show of bravado, issued out on the plain. Cardenas, who had expected this, quickly charged back with his mounted men-at-arms "and caught several of their leaders," apparently killing them. The rest of the Indians returned to "the roofs of the village and the captain returned to his camp."[26]

Coronado now knew that he had a full-scale war on his hands if he wanted to reassert Spanish authority in Tiguex, and Moho was the major population center of the uprising. However, because the operational situation involved a static fortress, the Spaniards were able to apply their traditional European methods regarding siege warfare with confidence.[27]

Castaneda recalled, following the attempted seizure of Lopez de Cardenas: "After this affair the general ordered the army to go and surround the village. He set out with his men in good order, one day, with several scaling ladders. When he reached the village, he encamped his force near by, and then began the siege."[28]

Thus, while their use at Cibola was problematic, scaling ladders undoubtedly were used in the attacks at Tiguex. Once again, it is unknown whether these basic siege implements were constructed on-site or had been brought along from Cibola (if not from New Spain). Presumably, they were constructed on-site; therefore (unlike the situation around Hawikuh), they probably were constructed out of nearby cottonwood trees. Although the resilient cottonwoods are a blessing for the arid American West, they do not provide the best building material, for the wood does not hold nails well.[29] Of course, the ladders could have been lashed together.[30]

The people of Tiguex would have been busy while Coronado's men were building ladders. Because of the respite between the seizure of Cardenas and the starting of the siege, the people of Tiguex "had several days to provide themselves with stores."[31] With the recognition that Moho could therefore withstand a lengthy siege, the scaling ladders were put to almost immediate use, and the Spaniards and their Indian auxiliaries, as at Cibola, tried to take Moho by storm. Complicating any attacks, this particular pueblo reportedly was on "a circular sierra [mountain]."[32]

But the scaling ladders were not the only offensive technical method employed. The attackers "attempted to open a breach," but when their "makeshift battering rams" broke through the outer coating of the pueblo's wall, it was seen that there was an inner structure of palisaded tree trunks and woven branches.[33]

Unfortunately for these frustrated attackers, the Tiguex certainly also had used those several days of preparation to gather up plenty of rocks. According to Mota Padilla, much injury was done to the Spaniards by the stones thrown from the rooftops and by arrows shot from the improvised loopholes.[34]

"[T]hey threw down such quantities of rocks upon our men that many of them were laid out," recalled Castaneda, "and they wounded nearly a hundred with arrows, several of whom afterward died on account of the bad treatment by an unskillful surgeon who was with the army."[35] Of course, military medicine was primitive during the sixteenth century. Boiling oil often was poured into wounds—a procedure meant to cleanse the wound but only making it worse. Amputations were all too common, and often there was only liquor to use as a sedative.[36] In addition, Coronado's soldiers believed the wounds festered because the warriors of Tiguex kept rattlesnakes in wicker baskets so their arrowheads could be covered with collected venom.[37]

The Spanish and their Indian auxiliaries, during this first assault, were able to occupy a position on one of the roofs, but, unlike the struggle for Arenal, they "were forced to abandon this on account of the many wounds that were received and because it was so dangerous to maintain ourselves there." Although there was a second attempt to seize this toehold, the attackers finally withdrew from the interior of the pueblo.[38]

After this costly initial attack of the campaign against Moho, the siege continued, "during which time several assaults were made."[39] "One day," recalled Castaneda, "when there was a hard fight, they killed Francisco de Obando [or Ovando], a captain who had been army-master all the time that Don Garcia Lopez de Cardenas was away making the discoveries."[40] Ovando was killed as he tried to squeeze into an opening in the pueblo wall; he was grabbed by the defenders, pulled in, and killed with an arrow.[41] His body could not be recovered, and it remained inside. This was urban warfare at its worst.

Also killed during this particular attack was "Francisco Pobares, a fine gentleman."[42] Pobares, attempting to obstruct one of the loopholes with mud, "was shot in one eye by an arrow, at which he fell dead."[43] More fortunate was Juan Paniagua, "a very good Christian and noble person" who recited his rosary regularly. An arrow wounded him on the eyelid, but he believed it was his faithful recitation to which "he owed his life."[44]

During an assault on one of the points of the pueblo, according to Mota Padilla, "A ladder was put where, at all costs, some climbed up; but designedly the Indians had many parts of the roofs exposed to the sky and not connected with the others." With fire from the different positions, architectural enfilades of which a European military builder would be proud, the defenders "did much damage, so that they wounded more than seventy."[45] Among those wounded in this attack were at least three Spaniards, one Carbajal, Alonso de Castaneda, and one

Benitez.[46] During the fighting at Tiguex, some of the wounded were quartered in Coronado's tent "so that they might have better care."[47]

Apparently confined to another tent during the fighting at Tiguex was Turk, who was chained "under lock so that no one could speak to him" and in the personal custody of one Cervantes. At one point, jailor Cervantes saw "the Turk talking with the devil in a pitcher of water." After the attack that cost Captain Ovando his life, Cervantes denied to the Turk that any Spaniards had been killed, but Turk answered, as Castaneda heard the story, "You lie; five Christians are dead, including a captain." Because of this intimate knowledge, Cervantes was convinced that the Turk was a consort of the devil.[48] Thus was planted in the minds of the Spanish soldiery a barracks rumor, supporting both the idea that the clairvoyant Turk may have known what he was talking about when he said there was gold and silver in Quivira and the suspicion that his real intent was to serve a devilish purpose by destroying the crusaders.

In any event, with this costly assault, Coronado had the recall sounded and apparently decided henceforth to rely almost entirely on siege tactics to force a surrender. While the inmates had plenty of corn, it was known that Moho suffered from a lack of water, for it had no well and overlooked the river that was beyond the pueblo's defensive perimeter.[49] Throughout history, besiegers normally attempted to cut off water from a city under siege.[50] This offensive strategy was unnecessary for the Spaniards at Moho, with the exception of not allowing nighttime water sorties toward the river. However, the defenders, at one point when they especially were suffering from thirst, were relieved by a heavy spring snowfall that provided sufficient water to continue resistance.[51] Also, according to Castaneda, the defenders attempted to dig "a very deep well inside the village, but were not able to get water, and while they were making it, it fell in and killed thirty persons."[52]

The besiegers also had their problems. Mota Padilla wrote that Coronado's force was "lacking [in] artillery," meaning siege artillery.[53] But the Spaniards did have their little falconets, probably mounted on some sort of wheeled carriages. Obviously, these were ineffective, based on the later comment of Castaneda's that a "piece of heavy artillery would be very good for [the] settlements [discovered] . . . in order to knock them down."[54]

While it is unknown for sure why the falconets were no good, their limited calibers obviously did not make them logical ordnance to take a city by siege or by storm. If they were the old-fashioned breechloading swivel guns, forged rather than cast, they might have had more than a normal chance of bursting during firing. In addition, the buildings of Tiguex were either adobe or of a reinforced wattle-and-daub construction. Such natural elements sometimes make the best defensive redoubts. In 1500, when an army of Danish knights and mercenary infantry used their artillery against the north German Dithmarschers at the Battle of Hemmingstedt, the Danish guns were ineffective in reducing the redoubt of the peasant force of German defenders, for "the few [cannonballs] that were fired sank into the muddy walls of the redoubt and the powder was soon wet."[55]

In any event, the artillery of the sixteenth century seldom was a deciding factor on the field of battle, and this applied to the frontier assaults on the pueblos in Tiguex. Field pieces of the era had to be placed on the flank of an attacking force or in the front.[56] Once the infantry and cavalry moved forward, however, the heavy ordnance had to cease fire, for firing over the heads of one's own force was not safe. Therefore, generally "artillery was only able to get off a few salvoes before . . . the advance of its own army blocked its line of fire."[57]

But the Spanish may have improvised other siege machines to aid the little falconets. Once again, while there is little evidence that the Spaniards had carts with them, if they had any, these likely were used in the attack. As previously noted, during the 1512 Battle of Ravenna, the Spaniards placed arquebusiers into "small, low, two-wheeled vehicles, built of light wood and capable of being propelled by the soldiers themselves."[58] This employment solved both the problem of providing protection for the arquebusiers—placed in front of the other attacking infantry—and the problem of arquebuses being too heavy to handle (a difficulty that actually had been seen during the exhausting fight at Cibola).[59]

Because the siege dragged on for two months, the desperate Spanish "attempted many foolish acts," according to historian Mota Padilla. One of these attempts "was to build some engines with timbers, which they called swings, like the old rams with which they battered fortress in times before gunpowder was known." Unfortunately for the attackers, these rams "did no good."[60]

Another foolish attempt was "to make some wooden tubes tightly bound with cords on the order of rockets; but these did not serve either."[61] This curious reference to rocket tubes does not appear else-

A nineteenth-century
reconstruction of a Roman
swing battering ram.
(*Author*)

where, but apparently was based on a source document relied on by Mota Padilla.

The Chinese used rockets in ancient times, and the British employed them in the late eighteenth and early nineteenth centuries. While these particular pyrotechnics probably were not standard weapons in every European arsenal during the early years of the use of military gunpowder, they did exist to an extent that Coronado's Spanish veterans of European warfare either would have seen them or heard of them:

> By the beginning of the 15th century, rockets were widely known in parts of Europe, as evidenced by a German military report in 1405 in which several types of rockets were mentioned. During the 15th century, both cannons and rockets were used on the battlefield; however, the accuracy and range advantages of the cannon over the crude rockets became apparent and the rockets were gradually discarded. For the next three centuries following the year 1500, rockets became obsolete as weapons and their use was limited to signals and fireworks displays.[62]

The Chinese used wooden, hand-held rocket launchers as late as 1500, which was illustrated in Chinese training manuals beginning in the fifteenth century.[63] Thus, Mota Padilla might have been right about the attempted use of rocket tubes and rockets by Coronado's besieging army.

However, because Mota Padilla, by training a lawyer, was writing about seemingly unfamiliar military matters in about 1740 (before the general reintroduction of rockets as weapons), there is a chance he misinterpreted his source material.[64] What he thought was a reference to rocket tubes might have been to staves bound into very imperfect barrels or kegs, to be employed as jerry-built petards.[65] Proper European petards, used to blast away obstructions, were heavy buckets filled with explosives and often moved up to a fortress gate or wall by a party of soldiers, acting as a forlorn hope, who laid the mouth of the bell-shaped container against the gate and attempted to scurry away once the match on the dangerous thing was lit. But the petard, introduced sometime in the sixteenth century, quickly went out of fashion by the end of the seventeenth.[66]

In any event, and in fairness to the ingenuity of Coronado's soldiers, whatever these unsuccessful field-built contraptions were, they likely were constructed out of the inferior wood available, including cottonwood. Probably such also was the case with "some small machines for slinging" that Castaneda recalled also were used ineffectively against the Indian settlements "to knock them down."[67]

However, during a prolonged siege, such field-expedient attempts would, if nothing else, constructively occupy the time of the besieging force and tend to keep the soldiery focused and out of mischief. Besiegers perhaps also were detailed to the mountains to get better lumber.

More could be assessed about the battles and siege of Moho if it were known for sure the location of the pueblo. Matt Schmader, Albuquerque's resident archaeologist, thinks the site of the pueblo at Piedras Marcadas, near Albuquerque, is a likely candidate.[68] Although others disagree with this assessment, archaeological work indicates there was a significant siege or battle there. The sketchy details, based on dug relics, support the conclusion that the Spaniards and their allies used typical methods in their siege operations. Of the thirty-two leaden balls discovered in this archaeological digging (many apparently spent and smashed) and the twenty-one copper crossbow boltheads found (also some broken), many were concentrated outside the location of the old walls.[69] Schmader believes the distribution of artifacts indicates a large battle around the pueblo.[70]

Schmader also thinks that the evidence found at Piedras Marcadas supports a conclusion that there was a fight for the central and adjoining rooms of the pueblo. "I think the Pueblo people barricaded themselves inside this roomblock and fortified it. The Spanish attacked from south to north, hurled themselves against the walls, but they couldn't break through."[71] This does not mean the Spaniards actually attempted to hurl themselves against the walls Superman-like. Historian Mota Padilla wrote that the Spaniards attempted to smash through the walls with "some make shift battering rams, during which time much damage was done to our people by stones from the roofs and arrows from the loopholes."[72] This would be in addition to the Spaniards' attempting to use their ladders to climb over the pueblo walls onto the roof, as indicated by Castaneda.

Other clusters of relics seem to indicate fighting, including at what would have been the southeastern corner of the presumed central plaza and inside an aboveground kiva.[73] Historians think the pattern hints that the Spanish methodology was to drive the Indians into the central plaza and kill them there.[74] This conclusion might be influenced by how the Spaniards were known to have attacked the Aztecs and the Incas in their cities; it might not hold so true in attacking a pueblo.

Also at the Piedras Marcadas site is an apparently caved-in pit that archaeologist Schmader believes is the collapsed well—but others disagree.[75] Finally, the presence of so many large caret-head nails (with triangular, not flat, heads) of the period found at the archaeological dig[76] would support arguments regarding the presence and use of the ladders (and the presumed destruction of one or more during the attack), as well as the ineffective battering rams, rocket tubes, and slings. But nails also were long used as canister rounds, including during the sixteenth century, so this also might be evidence of falconets being used at close range.[77]

In any event, at this fertile site near Albuquerque, according to British battlefield archaeologist Glenn Foard, who visited Piedras Marcadas, such archaeological work will advance "understanding of the way in which European technology of war was actually applied in the Americas."[78] But it appears at present that applying the tentatively known archaeological record reinforces the conclusion that the Spanish used standard sixteenth-century techniques.

However, the story of the struggle for Moho also contains some nonarchaeological elements related to the better side of human nature. There were a few occasions of chivalry during the closing days of the siege—a siege that by then had consumed about six weeks. Although it "was impossible to persuade them to make peace, as they said that the Spaniards would not keep an agreement made with them," the men of Tiguex recognized that the Europeans were loath to kill women and children.[79] According to Castaneda, the defenders asked to speak to the besiegers and told them "that, since they knew we would not harm women and children, they wished to surrender their women and sons, because they were using up their water. . . . So they gave up about a hundred persons, women and boys, who did not want to leave them."[80] The Spaniards' allowing noncombatants to leave Moho was a bad decision, according to the military textbook, although it demonstrated a humanitarianism not often seen when a siege involved such serious fighters as the Spanish. Besiegers usually did everything to inflate the population of a city under attack, encouraging noncombatants to flee to such a target and then preventing any exodus. A swollen population would starve all the sooner.[81]

At the time of the evacuation of the defenders' family members, recalled Castaneda, "Don Lope de Urrea rode up in front of the town without his helmet and received the boys and girls in his arms, and when all of these had been surrendered, Don Lope begged them to make peace, giving them the strongest promises for their safety." The adults left in the pueblo told Urrea to go away—they still did not trust "people who had no regard for friendship or their own word which they had pledged." One Tiguex warrior notched an arrow, threatening to shoot Urrea and telling him to put on his helmet. Urrea, for his part, said he trusted them not to hurt him while he remained before them helmetless. Finally, the Spanish gentleman, after an arrow had been shot and planted between his horse's forefeet, put his headpiece on and slowly rode back to the siege lines. The warriors of Tiguex, "[w]hen they saw that he was really in safety," only then sent volleys of arrows toward their enemy.[82]

Herbert Bolton later extolled the courage of Urrea, writing that his "coolness and chivalry were long remembered."[83] But Urrea acted as a Spanish man-at-arms—who also was trying to save the lives of his comrades—ought to have acted. Even more impressive than the humanity of the Spanish on this occasion was the chivalry demonstrated by the Tiguexans, for Urrea's stubbornness exceeded the traditional terms of such a brief truce.[84] The more-primitive people had refused to take advantage of Urrea's vulnerability, demonstrating that Coronado was not the only "knight of pueblos and plains."

Castaneda claimed that there was another example of the honor of those defending Tiguex. As mentioned, when Francisco de Ovando was killed inside the pueblo of Moho, his body was not then recoverable. Supposedly his remains were not mutilated, for "when the village was captured, he was found among their dead, whole and without any other wound except the one which killed him, white as snow, without any bad smell."[85] On the other hand, Cardenas, who then was refuting his reputation for bloodthirstiness, testified that Ovando had been dragged into the pueblo alive and that the Tiguexans had "killed him, committing great barbarities with him, and cutting him into pieces."[86]

Ovando was among the highest ranking officers of the expedition killed in battle, and historical controversy regarding the state of famous human remains during the brutal Indian wars is not unheard of; often the controversy had political or ethnic overtones. For example, there was an almost immediate disparity of opinion whether General Custer's body was mutilated gratuitously at the Little Big Horn in 1876, with the discussion being affected by the emotion of the time.[87]

In any event, even after the exchange of gallantries between Captain Urrea and the warriors of Tiguex, the bitter siege continued after the noncombatants left. Apparently, some of Moho Pueblo was burned over the heads of the defenders during this last stage of the fighting.[88]

As for the final capture of Moho, it happened quickly and bloodily a fortnight after the noncombatants had been evacuated. As related by Castaneda, "Fifteen days later [the defenders] decided to leave the village one night, and did so, taking the women in their midst. They started [just before dawn], in the very early morning, on the side where the cavalry was."[89]

While the Tiguexans were stealthy, the Spanish sentries also were negligent that night. The Indians came upon "two soldiers who were not very alert; of these, one disappeared, and the other was found with his heart pierced by an arrow."[90] Nonetheless, the withdrawal from Moho finally was discovered, and, "The alarm was given.... The enemy attacked [the Spanish in camp] and killed one Spaniard and a horse and wounded others, but they were driven back with great slaughter until they came to the river, where the water flowed swiftly and very cold."[91]

Meanwhile, the rest of the army came to the assistance of the mounted Spaniards in cutting down those attempting to ford the Rio Grande, and "there were few who escaped being killed or wounded," recalled Castaneda.[92] "This ended that siege, and the town was captured, although there were a few who remained in one part of the town and were captured a few days later."[93]

"Two hundred of the besieged died in the fights" involving Moho, according to Castaneda.[94] As for the Spanish, according to Coronado, in addition to Captain Ovando, "four or five other soldiers" were killed, and many soldiers were wounded.[95] A member of the expedition later thought that seven Spaniards were killed and more than seventy or eighty wounded in taking the pueblo.[96] Presumably, those Spaniards and Christian Indian allies killed in the fighting were interred nearby under the supervision of the Franciscan friars accompanying the army.[97]

The Spaniards' official attitude about their significant casualties probably was summed up by Sir Roger Williams, a sixteenth-century professional soldier (who fought for both the Dutch and the Spanish in the Low Countries): "There can be no brave encounter without men slain on both sides. True it is, the fewer, the better conduct; but the more dies, the more honor to the fight."[98] This, of course, meant that when Cibola had fallen the year before, there was little glory.

But such a vainglorious attitude regarding war would not mean that the victors in a siege were happy about their fellows who were dead— quite the contrary. As is typical when a town is captured by assault, the victorious soldiery undoubtedly was in no mood to be generous to those who had been so obstinate.[99] The Indians deserved punishment, testified Diego Lopez, "because they had killed many Spaniards [and] important persons in the army."[100] While no fiery massacre similar to that occurring at Arenal is recorded, there was some awful retribution.

Not only did the Spanish consider the people of Tiguex to be rebels, the fact that they were pagans would have offended the Spaniards' sense of Catholic solidarity and religious superiority. Even when campaigning in Flanders, the Spanish "acted 'as if they were in enemy territory, beginning to live at discretion,' and they continued on their way 'confiscating everything, rightly, wrongly, saying that everyone is a heretic, that they have wealth and ought to lose it.'"[101]

Probably catering to the typical demand for revenge, Coronado apparently ordered or allowed brutalities to occur. Of those captured at Moho, Alonso Sanchez testified that they were "stabbed and lanced."[102] According to Coronado's page, Alonso Alvarez, Coronado directed that dogs attack some of the prisoners and specifically ordered that other prisoners be maimed. "[A]fter the pueblo's capture, two or three Indians were set upon by dogs and another nine or ten had their hands and noses cut off," testified Alvarez. Alvarez said he heard the order given for the mutilations and heard Coronado order those so crippled to be displayed to the pueblo people.[103] Another expedition member saw hands chopped off but did not know by whose order.[104]

An early seventeenth-
century print showing
the brutal assault on
Cuzco during the Inca
uprising in the 1530s
after the initial Spanish
conquest. (*Author*)

Like burning prisoners, cutting off hands was not unheard of in the
sixteenth century. Cortes had ordered the hands of fifty Aztec spies
hacked off—an intentionally salutary lesson that was novel even for that
cold-blooded Indian nation.[105] In 1536, when on an expedition in
Yucatan, Captain Francisco Gil summoned local Indians and then
killed twenty leading citizens by burning them at the stake. But one
Indian noble was sent back to his people with his nose and one hand
cut off.[106] Also like burning people at the stake, this punishment of
maiming was intended to be barbaric and to deter others.

Of course, such drastic treatment for those seen in rebellion hardly
started in New Mexico—or even in Mexico. In 1487, when Malaga fell
into Christian hands during the Reconquista, the Spaniards not only
treated the captured Muslims harshly by selling them into slavery,[107] the
*renegados* and the *conversos*—respectively, Spanish Christians who converted and fought against their countrymen and those who only converted to Islam—were treated as traitors and rebels and were killed at
the stake or by other methods.[108]

Perhaps more to the point in viciousness, in 1049, when William the
Bastard, later to be known as William the Conqueror, captured the
rebellious Norman town of Alencon, William ordered that the hands of
the defenders be cut off.[109] While the slaughter or execution of perceived traitorous rebels was unexceptional in Europe until the nineteenth century, the cutting off of limbs or members was considered
exceptional punishment during the later, reputedly more enlightened,
centuries. The very recollection of such a deed, even perpetrated during
medieval times, seemingly concedes the heinous nature of the punish-

ment. Indeed, Emperor Maximilian, and the rest of Christendom, was not adverse to reporting and propagandizing when similar atrocities were committed by the Ottoman Turks.[110]

But Coronado later indicated that he had no knowledge of atrocities at Moho, just claiming that "the defenders were overcome and pacified."[111] While his testimony appears disingenuous, it could have been true. Sixteenth-century rulers and commanders were wont to issue orders about the rules of just warfare, but their soldiers were just as wont to do whatever they wanted, whether in Europe or in the Americas. "The Sack of Rome [by an imperial army of Spaniards, Germans, and Italians in 1527] merely established an unnecessary and cruel record of what was self-evident, that imperfectly disciplined warrior bands could make decisions at their own discretion and act against their commanders or ignore their commands."[112] But, once again, most of the witnesses who testified about the expedition were adamant that Coronado was in charge, and everyone knew that fact.[113]

The fall of Moho and the punishment of its inhabitants did not end the Tiguex War. Two of Coronado's captains, Don Diego de Guevara and Juan de Saldivar (or Zaldivar) were tasked with capturing the third major pueblo the local population decided to defend.[114] As with the entire war, archaeologists and historians are divided on which sites are which pueblo battlefields. Similarly, even the name of this third holdout pueblo has long eluded historians—and there will be no revelation here. Richard Flint noted that according to Rodrigo de Frias, three pueblos—Pueblo de las Cruz, Pueblo de la Alameda, and Pueblo del Cerco—were destroyed and burned around this time.[115] For his part, Herbert Eugene Bolton, a historian trapped in what he perceived to be the less-romantic atomic age, simply called the third embattled village "X."[116] Herein, this last bastion will be called Third Pueblo.[117]

The warrior inhabitants of this pueblo obviously started off with high morale, believing they could resist the assaults of the Spaniards. After the defenders declined the summonses to surrender, the Spaniards, according to Captain Saldivar, were obligated to make "war and, using ladders, reached the flat roofs."[118] Saldivar, seemingly duplicating his heroic role at Arenal, entered one of the rooms of the pueblo to aid Don Lope de Urrea "and another soldier, whom [the Indians] had surrounded and were trying to kill." For his efforts, Saldivar suffered three arrow wounds on his face and head.[119]

However, the defenders of Third Pueblo were so cocky that they made that most common of mistakes in war: they underestimated their enemy. Throughout this siege, some of the warriors of Third Pueblo "used to come out every morning to try to frighten our camp," wrote Castaneda.[120] In this offensive harassment of the Spanish, the Tiguex of this pueblo were demonstrating sound military theory, even by European standards. In the more-advanced forms of warfare conducted in Europe, it had long been an accepted tactic to have sorties issue forth from a besieged fortress, since those (usually nighttime) attacks would harry and exhaust the enemy and sustain morale for the besieged.[121]

But sorties and sallies naturally imposed some risk for those defenders caught outside a citadel.[122] For example, during the Italian Wars, Chevalier Bayard, the renowned French knight, heard from a spy about such a sally outside a castle in order to forage. The French were able to spring an ambush on the foragers.[123] The Spanish themselves, during the siege of Velez-Malaga, in the last stages of their Reconquista, had frustrated a major nighttime sortie by their Muslim opponents.[124]

In their case, the Tiguex people were undone by their own regularity—and by bad timing. On the day the people of Third Pueblo decided to evacuate their village at dawn and flee, at the end of March 1541, the Spaniards sent out spies to watch for the daily sortie and also sent out enough troops to set up an ambush. When the scouts saw the people leaving the pueblo and heading "toward the country," the soldiers left the ambush and "pursued and killed large numbers of them." Meanwhile, those in the main Spanish camp rushed into the now-undefended pueblo "and they plundered it, making prisoners of all the people who were found in it, amounting to about a hundred women and children."[125]

Supposedly, those left in Third Pueblo "sued for mercy," according to expedition member Cristobal de Escobar.[126] If nothing else, this final episode of the siege reinforces the conclusion that while the men of Tiguex did not trust their own lives to the Spaniards, they did not believe that the foreigners would kill their wives and children.

The Tiguex War pretty much ended with the fall of Third Pueblo, although there was some additional devastation of the province. One expedition member estimated that "twelve or fifteen Spaniards died and [of] wounded [there were] more than sixty."[127]

Later, much was made of the Spaniards' burning down not only the pueblos in open revolt and placed under regular siege but about a dozen others. Claims were made that the arson occurred because the Spanish needed firewood and warmth during the harsh winter.[128] However, later testimony was almost unanimous that these potential fortresses also were razed so there would be no further resistance.[129] While not necessarily a good reason—especially when Coronado was trying to placate the Indians of Tiguex—such a strategy was a valid military consideration. Whether in Spain or elsewhere in Europe, monarchs in particular found it convenient (and militarily expedient) to level the castles of truculent noblemen.[130]

But for the people of Tiguex, the burning of their pueblos was the last straw, and little or no rebuilding took place while the Coronado Expedition was there. According to Castaneda, "The twelve villages of Tiguex, . . . were not repopulated at all during the time the army was there, in spite of every promise of security that could possibly be given to them."[131] According to a nineteenth-century US Army officer, this reluctance was more than understandable, "for no more barbarous treachery was ever shown to a submissive foe than had been shown to these Tigueans by these faithless Spaniards."[132]

The Tiguexans, like the Zuni, would not forget the Coronado Expedition. Forty years later they recalled that during the siege, Coronado had "pressed them so hard that those who did not die at the hands of the Spaniards [or] Castillas . . . died of hunger and thirst. . . . Finally the people surrendered and put themselves at his mercy."[133]

# The Mixton War Rearranges
# Viceroy Mendoza's Military Priorities

The Coronado Expedition certainly was a historically important event when viewed through the lens of exploration. The expedition also saw some real warfare with attendant horrors. However, to the Spanish of the New World, it is a mere historical footnote when compared to what was going on in northwestern central Mexico during the same period. This epochal event for New Spain was the Mixton War, a struggle that almost saw the Spanish and Christianity ejected from much of Mexico.[1] The contest, while not completely unexpected, unfolded with a suddenness that well-nigh undid all of the efforts Viceroy Mendoza made on behalf of New Spain. It also had the potential to destroy the Coronado Expedition upon its return to civilization.

The Spanish residents of Governor Coronado's province of New Galicia had been concerned when they saw so many available defenders head north into the unknown, although, as it turned out, only a couple of the expedition's men-at-arms were actual residents of New Spain. Unfortunately for these worried colonists, their safety concerns nonetheless proved well founded, even if the expedition was but transferring newly arrived Spaniards to the northern wilderness. Just as they did when the US Army withdrew from the western American frontier in 1861 to fight the rebels in the East, the original native occupants of the land were watching these armed Spaniards parade through and were considering what seemed to be the obvious ramifications.[2]

Consequently, in spring 1540, only about a month after Coronado's army headed north, trouble began in New Galicia. It started with the murder of a prominent *encomendero* (one granted an *encomienda*) and was followed by murderous attacks on priests and other landowners. In this uprising, the abused Indians on the estates were aided by their wilder brethren coming down from the mountains.[3]

At the time, the trouble appeared as spontaneous and not coordinated with other events. Indeed, there was evidence that the actual outbreak was due to Indians getting drunk, going on the initial killing spree, and then deciding to continue the uprising in earnest.[4]

However, there was much more to the Mixton War than a murder raid by unhappy and drunken natives. Neither was this the more-typical native uprising due to general dissatisfaction. In addition to the undeniable grievances about treatment they received at the hands of Spanish *encomenderos*, there was a definite religious aspect behind this uprising of the local Indians. By their wild and unconquered brethren to the far north, the Indians of New Galicia had been exposed to a revised resurrection of their ancient pagan beliefs—beliefs that now "promised everything from sensual pleasure to immortality to those who would desert Christianity, and threatened unbelievers with dire penalties." Part and parcel of this cult was that it mandated the "declaration of unrelenting war against the Spaniards and all Christians in the New World."[5] The pagan altars for human sacrifice reappeared in the fortified mountain villages of the hostiles, and baptized Indian backsliders were doused with water to wash away the stain of Christian salvation.[6]

Thus, in such a primitive messianic and millennium type belief, usually incorporating magic and pagan rituals, the white European intruders somehow would disappear and the good old days be restored. "Such a desperate religious reaction often was the harvest when a people's insular sense of superiority and their entire belief systems—apparently obsolete—were cast aside within the time frame of a single generation."[7] This violent reaction has been seen worldwide, especially in the Americas. For example, in the Arizona Territory in 1881, there was an explosive uprising based on the end-of-the-world preaching of a medicine man named Noch-ay-del-Klinne. This excitement was followed in 1890 with the almost identical rustic theology of the Ghost Dance religion, which resulted in the bloodshed at Wounded Knee, South Dakota.[8]

There have been other manifestations of this type of desperate, last-chance faith in other hemispheres. In 1857, in South Africa, a suicidal, end-of-the-world prophecy ultimately resulted in the starvation of many Bantu.[9] In the 1860s, there were the dances of New Zealand's Maori Hau-Hau cult, which resulted in a bloody rebellion.[10] In the Philippines in 1904–1905, a violent, messianic craze faced American soldiers defending the new colonial ambitions of the United States.[11]

In the sixteenth-century rebellion and uprising known as the Mixton War, the Spaniards of New Spain were confronted with thousands of courageous and treacherous foes who had a religious fanaticism temporarily matching their own, as well as equaling Spain's Turkish opponents in the Old World.

But the Spanish made the initial mistake of underestimating both their enemies' abilities and the spread of the fanaticism. The Spaniards, for example, did not know that part of the plan of the proselytizing leaders of the faith was that many of its adherents, supposed friendly allies of the Spaniards, keep their new-found religion disingenuously concealed until an appropriate time.[12] Adding to a false sense of security on the part of the Spaniards was the fact that, initially, many of the Indians to the south were willing to stand neutral and join the cause only if they saw the Spaniards could be defeated.[13] Such proof was not long in coming.

A respectable little force of seventeen mounted Spaniards under Miguel de Ibarra, backed up by fifteen hundred Indian allies, proceeded to the rebellious area. Ibarra, also accompanied by a couple of Franciscan friars, hoped to avoid hostilities, something that seemed all the more possible since other Indians joined him on his march. When the force approached the town of Tepestistaque, which was a *penol,* or fortified hilltop, the recent Indian recruits expressed their true colors to the other Indian allies, and most of these previously enrolled allies therefore deserted. Warned of an impending ambush, Ibarra executed several of the treacherous latecomers but nonetheless hoped that no battle would occur.[14]

A battle did take place, however, when the insurgents came out of their mountain fastness and attacked the Spanish force. After four hours of bitter fighting, the battered Spaniards and their few remaining Indian allies still held the field. The next day, with the approval of the friars, Ibarra withdrew. Passing through a rear that was now aroused against him, Ibarra and his force reached Guadalajara.[15]

The uprising spread, with more fortified *penoles* established by the hostiles and many more attacks on Spanish *encomenderos* and their African retainers.[16] In order to end these bloody disturbances without resort to an all-out war, Viceroy Mendoza authorized New Galicia's acting governor, Cristobal de Onate, to bring the rebellious tribes and communities into line. Consequently, Onate and a force of fifty horsemen, some Spanish footmen, Indian allies, and artillery, headed to the greatest of the *penoles* at Mixton.[17]

When Onate's efforts to parley with those in Mixton failed utterly, he began to deploy his small army before the *penol* prior to assaulting it. However, before the Spanish were ready to attack, those in the fort and many more Indians on the outside surrounding Onate fell on his force. Onate and his men managed to extricate themselves and conduct a fighting withdrawal to Guadalajara, but not before more than a dozen Spaniards, a half-dozen Africans, and three hundred allies were killed.[18]

With such an early and signal success, it was small wonder that other lukewarm Indian communities now went over to the insurgents. Many Spanish towns, including two Coronado passed through—Compestela and Culiacan—were cut off and surrounded. Meanwhile, Onate began to prepare Guadalajara for defense and urgently asked the viceroy for help.[19]

Mendoza, as part of his schemes for exploration and exploitation for the benefit of himself and Spain, had imposed on a well-known conquistador, Pedro de Alvarado, to allow Mendoza to become a partner in Alvarado's plan to sail to the Philippines. However, with much of New Spain now threatened, Alvarado, who had a reputation as a decisive (and brutal) man of action, generously agreed to postpone sailing and to use his men to put down the rebellion. He marched with his contingent to Guadalajara.[20]

But Alvarado was so experienced and so enthused that he refused to listen to the cautionary advice of Onate. Without waiting for reinforcements from Mexico City, and refusing the assistance of Onate's smaller contingent, Alvarado marched on the strong *penol* of Nochistlan, leading a force of one hundred men-at-arms, one hundred Spanish infantry, and about five thousand Indian allies. He reached Nochistlan on June 24, 1541, and almost immediately launched his attack. It was a disaster, for once the assault stalled, the rebel Indians poured out of their fort and counterattacked.[21]

Alvarado himself displayed his usual courage, but he was mortally wounded. His army was demoralized and virtually put to rout, with-

A 1595 engraving showing Pedro Alvarado's losing attack on the native *penol* stronghold of Nochistlan. Alvarado was mortally wounded in the assault. (*Author*)

drawing toward Guadalajara, covered by Onate's small contingent, which had followed behind Alvarado's thousands.[22]

Now all the wavering Indians cast their lot with the insurgents. A great Indian army, perhaps as large as fifty thousand but likely closer to fifteen thousand, moved against Guadalajara.[23] On September 29, 1541, the insurgents launched a determined attack on the fortified city, capturing the undefended church and setting it afire. But with an effective use of their artillery, the Spaniards and their allies beat back the initial assaults, killing hundreds.[24]

Nonetheless, the defenders were so hard pressed that they were on the brink of a fatal despair. Onate rallied them, threatening to open the gates for the enemy if he heard any more defeatist talk. He also began to lead a series of sorties against the attackers, sallies that drove back the Indians while losing only a single Spanish soldier. When the Indians gave up and withdrew, they supposedly had lost an incredible fifteen thousand dead.[25]

Whatever the true numbers of those involved and those perishing, so amazing was the successful defense that the Spanish soon reported a supernatural reason for the lopsided victory. This was that Saint James himself had appeared and ridden a white horse out of the burning church leading an angelic army. Those pagan Indians not killed outright by these reinforcements supposedly were blinded and maimed by the heavenly host.[26]

Certainly, nationalities other than the Spanish in eras since the sixteenth century have come to analogous conclusions regarding the direct intrusion of otherworldly saints into worldly contests.[27] However, since the Spaniards fighting the Mixton War themselves put out the eyes and apparently cut off the hands of many whom they captured, the story of saintly and angelic assistance might have been a convenient explanation for any follow-up investigation about atrocities against the irreligious natives.[28]

In any event, although this heroic defense ended an immediate crisis, much more had to be done. As Guadalajara was withstanding its siege, Viceroy Mendoza took to the field, marching out of Mexico City with an army of about 450 Spaniards and perhaps thirty thousand Indian allies.[29] Whatever the exact number of auxiliaries, this might have been the largest number of Indian soldiers ever to accompany a conquistador army, and they included Tlaxcaltecs, Tarascans, and Otomi.[30]

Even with Mendoza having raised such numbers, the situation still was considered so critical that some of the native allies were issued and authorized the use of firearms and horses.[31] Probably encouraging this potentially dangerous move was the fact that many of the local militia serving as mounted cavalry under Mendoza were poorly trained, so they were converted to infantry.[32]

Mendoza's army first captured the *penol* of Cuina, defended by ten thousand Indians, after a siege of about two weeks. Once the Spanish and their allies entered the town, the slaughter was immense. More than two thousand insurgents were reported captured and branded as slaves.[33]

Following a linkup with Onate's force, Mendoza moved to capture Nochistlan, the fatal field of battle for Pedro de Alvarado. This offensive involved another siege, with the Spanish artillery being used to batter down the defenses. Nochistlan was captured after several days, but many of the defenders were allowed to escape and return to their *encomiendas*.[34]

Finally, Mendoza and his army marched to the strongest of the *penoles*, Mixton. With perhaps one hundred thousand rebels still under

A [sixteenth-century Spanish] map in Latin of "Hispania Novae." Guadalajara is just to the northwest of Mexico City, identified with a cathedral near the center. (*Author*)

arms, a siege of three weeks seemingly made little initial progress. But having suffered such casualties already, the sunshine soldiers and summer patriots among the hostile Indians—especially those who were previously Christianized—began to waver once again. As occurred so often in warfare in Renaissance Europe, many of the warriors changed sides wholesale and joined the Spanish forces.[35]

When the final assaults were made against Mixton—again supposedly with the active intervention of Saint James—there was a "great slaughter" of the defenders. Thousands of the insurgents, seeing that the game was up, "cast themselves," Masada-like, "down the cliff" to avoid capture and enslavement. Others were more fortunate, for the friars with the Spanish army supposedly inveigled so that many of the defenders were allowed to walk away and go home before the final fall of Mixton. As for those actually captured, there were over ten thousand.[36]

Although the destruction of Mixton did not immediately end the war, its fall broke the backbone of the revolt. Virtually all those in rebellion submitted to Spanish authority by early 1542.[37] Mendoza and Spanish Mexico had weathered a horrific crisis.

While New Spain was fortunate regarding the outcome of this second war for the conquest of Mexico, Coronado and his expedition were no less lucky. If the war had been lost—even if Mexico City had remained secure—then the force would have been left to its own devices and had much difficulty getting back home. It would have had to cut its way through thousands of aroused insurgents flushed with victory.

The expedition also was lucky that Mendoza had acted with such alacrity in suppressing the rebellion. If the war had dragged on longer, there was no telling when the lines of communication between the expedition and Mexico City, once severed, would have been reestablished. Just as the impending threat of the Spanish Armada in 1587 (and the resultant defensive measures taken by Queen Elizabeth) had prevented supplies, reinforcements, and information from getting to the English colony at Roanoke, Virginia,[38] there was a similar threat to the distant army of Coronado.

As it was, while Coronado was effectively cut off from the outside world during the actual fighting, it was a brief period occurring after Tiguex had been subdued, which was not noticed—the expedition was not left on a dead vine. In addition, although the war prevented Alarcon from attempting another voyage up the coast to resupply Coronado, geography still likely would have prevented that eventuality.[39]

Coronado certainly knew something bad was going on, for after Don Garcia Lopez de Cardenas suffered a broken arm (and learned that he had a significant inheritance awaiting him in Spain), Cardenas led a group of a dozen Spaniards south to get to Mexico City. After they reached the destroyed San Geronimo post, they quickly retreated back to Tiguex, carrying word of general trouble back to the captain general.[40] But the line of communication soon was reopened. After the major fighting in the war ended, Captain Juan Gallego was returning to Coronado from Mexico City with twenty men-at-arms, "reinforcements of men and necessary supplies for the army."[41] When Gallego reached Culiacan, he found twenty-two men from San Geronimo, including those who had deserted and those who followed them more honorably.[42] These he added to his force, promising to intercede with Coronado on the behalf of the deserters.[43] The Spaniards, once again, were accompanied by a number of Indian allied warriors.[44]

Gallego then proceeded to march this small force through "200 leagues with the country in a state of war and the people in rebellion," according to Castaneda. Gallego led the way with an advance force of about a dozen Spanish horsemen and some of his auxiliaries, leaving two-thirds of his little army to travel with the baggage train. There were clashes with the rebellious Indians almost every day, but Gallego soon made the natives dance to his tune.[45]

To accomplish this effective result, whenever Gallego's van would approach a village, he would charge into the community with but six or seven of his countrymen, killing the rebels and setting fire to the houses. By the time his train caught up, all they were able to do was to take whatever loot they could find. With these lightning attacks without warning, the natives in the towns ahead soon fled at the mere rumor of his approach.[46]

But not all were able to get away as Gallego kept up his rapid pace. Near the town of Corazones, where the Spaniards were joined by some Indian volunteers, his advance guard apparently was able to surround a village, and the Spaniards killed and captured a large number of people. The captives were hanged "to punish them for their rebellion."[47]

During all this advance north, only one Spaniard was wounded, apparently by a poisoned arrow on his eyelid, and he lost that eye. The allied warriors from Corazones were so amazed with the success of these forays conducted by the Spaniards that they "held them to be something divine rather than human."[48]

In any event, in effect if not intent, the active prosecution of the Mixton War, including Gallego's march, provided security for Coronado's line of communications and for his return home. Certainly, the busy insurgents had no chance to harass the Spanish-led army far to the north. With the success of Mendoza's campaign, Coronado was kept from having to face additional foes in his rear, other than the ones who had destroyed San Geronimo and who were no match for any returning force.

Finally, there was an additional aspect regarding the Mixton War that did touch directly on the Coronado Expedition, at least in an historical sense. Due to the death of Alvarado, his partner, Viceroy Mendoza, took over the fleet and sent some of the ships to the Philippines as planned, but he sent the rest of the fleet up the coast of upper California under Juan Rodriguez Cabrillo. Thus, while Cabrillo and the commander who succeeded him upon his death missed San

Francisco harbor, they did explore much of the Pacific coast.[49] In August 1542, California natives told these explorers, through signs, the belated news "that Spaniards were five days from here."[50] These would be the Spaniards under the late Melchior Diaz—by then long gone.

# SEVENTEEN

# Building the First Bridge
# across the Pecos

C oronado, being in blessed ignorance of the details of the Mixton troubles going on way to the south, still had a desire to march throughout the new country, looking this time for golden Quivira instead of golden Cibola. But first Coronado returned to Pecos Pueblo. As related by Castaneda, "During the siege of Tiguex the general decided to go to Cicuye [Pecos] and take the governor [of the pueblo] with him in order to give him his liberty and to promise them [the people of Pecos] that he would give Whiskers [Bigotes] his liberty and leave him in the village, as soon as he should start for Quivira."

Among the other villages or pueblos located during the Spaniards' reconnaissances of the region beyond Pecos were the ruins of a pueblo not far from the present town of Galisteo. It was "entirely destroyed and pulled down, in the yards of which there were many stone balls, as big a twelve-quart bowls," according to Castaneda. Through the lenses of his military perspective, Castaneda thought that the stone balls "seemed to have been thrown by engines or catapults, which had destroyed the village." When Castaneda made enquiries, he found that a native people from the north called Teyas, which meant "brave men," had unsuccessfully besieged the vacated village some sixteen years before. He concluded that "they must have been a powerful people" and "they must have had engines to knock down the villages."[1] Certainly, Castaneda was not alone in hearing vague rumors of a military power in the region and operating in the not-too-distant past.

This "mystery of the village that had been bombarded by round shot has never been solved," wrote historian A. Grove Day.[2] Presumably, these stones were naturally produced spherical rocks and not evidence of a long-lost Celtic warrior race in the Americas.[3] Nonetheless, with such imaginative conclusions regarding indigenous warfare, it was no wonder that there seemed a possibility that Turk's tall tales were true. If nothing else, Castaneda's opinion demonstrates that the Spanish still did not know what lay ahead, at least militarily.

After the conquest of Tiguex, before the army moved from the region, it left four of the bronze falconets behind at the "fine village" of Chia (Zia). Chia had not been involved in the Tiguex War and had remained peaceful. The artillery pieces were left behind for the people of Chia "to take care of" because the guns "were in poor condition," according to Castaneda.[4] The nature of the falconets' malady was not described. Presumably, being bronze, none had burst during the fighting, but if the weapons had been poorly cast that might have been a fear, especially if any of them bulged out due to excessive charges.[5] Even bronze artillery—which could have been produced in Spain, Flanders, Austria, Germany, Italy, France, Sicily, or elsewhere—could have been poorly cast.[6] Another possibility is that the gun carriages had collapsed or were in danger of that happening.[7]

Although the presence of the falconets apparently was never mentioned again in the documents, presumably the remaining two guns continued on with the expedition. The four surplused falconets might have been left in New Mexico. If so, perhaps a lucky archaeologist might dig them up some day.[8]

In any event, "when the river [Rio Grande], which for almost four months had been frozen over so that they crossed the ice on horseback, had thawed out, orders were given for the start for Quivira, where the Turk said there was some gold and silver."[9] "The Turk," remembered Castaneda, also "had said when they left Tiguex that they ought not to load the horses with too much provisions, which would tire them so that they could not afterward carry the gold and silver."[10] Presumably, there was some recollection among the Spaniards who had assaulted Cibola of the relative importance between food and loot.

As the army prepared to leave Tiguex, Coronado spoke with some Zuni representatives from Cibola "and charged them to take good care of the Spaniards who were coming from Senora with Don Pedro de Tovar." Coronado also entrusted the Zuni with letters to give Tovar, informing him of the plans of the main column and further telling Tovar to look for additional letters buried under crosses that the advancing army would erect.[11] These actions would tend to keep the Zuni quiet, since they would believe Coronado's command was not isolated.

The expedition finally got under way in spring 1541, about late April or early May. The force reached Pecos Pueblo, about sixty-five miles from Tiguex, and Coronado fully liberated Bigotes, which pleased the populace.[12] Either out of gratitude or simply to speed their departure, the chief of Pecos and Bigotes presented the Spaniards with another supposed native of Quivira named Xabe, who agreed with Turk that there was some gold and silver there, but not as much as Turk promised.[13] Reportedly, Turk also confidentially told the people of Pecos that he would make sure that the members of the expedition would return so weakened by starvation that they could easily be overcome and killed.[14]

The Spanish being ignorant of such duplicity at Pecos, Turk remained the main guide, "and thus the army started off from here."[15] One noted scholar, the late David Weber, certainly exaggerated a bit when he wrote, "[Much of] the route of Coronado . . . can be accurately reconstructed because the sites that he visited remained occupied by Indian peoples and because landmarks stand out in sharp relief in the Southwest."[16] Surely Weber was speaking only of the first half of Coronado's march into the American Southwest, for, once the captain general left the pueblos behind, even an approximate route is anybody's guess—a guess slowly being supplemented by occasional archaeological discoveries.

Still, there are just too few campsites and battlegrounds known with exactitude to connect the dots and define the main trail of the expedition.[17] Plus, Coronado sent out so many small parties that their exact whereabouts were not always well documented. Even Castaneda's account is frustrating as a road map, a shortcoming no doubt caused by the years between the doing and the telling, but also probably due to the Spanish penchant for keeping discoveries secret and safe from the prying eyes of competitors, especially England and France.[18]

In any event, the command started off toward the area later labeled "Land of Unknown Spaces" on some early maps.[19] Leaving the pueblo in supposed peace, "the army started from Cicuye [Pecos]," and pro-ceeded "toward the plains, which are all on the other side of the moun-tains, [and] after four days' journey they came to a river . . . , and they named this the [Cicuye] river."[20] This stop would be the only occasion on which the expedition went to the trouble of building a bridge.

Presumably, this river in springtime flood was the Pecos. However, not all historians, over a period of 150 years, have agreed on what river was bridged. Early American historians or travelers believed the stream was the Rio Grande.[21] Several more recent writers have guessed the Canadian River.[22] Indeed, one long-time Coronado scholar, Albert Schroeder, maintained that opinion for thirty years, insisting that the location "could not have been on the Pecos River."[23] However, but-tressed by recent archaeological findings in the Texas Panhandle, it is a good bet that after Coronado's expedition left the Pecos pueblo (then called Cicuye), it apparently marched down the river (also called Cicuye) that ultimately would be called the Pecos.

While many historians have concluded that the bridge was across the Pecos, the exact location of the bridgehead also has been a subject of debate. Herbert E. Bolton, among others, accepted the site as Anton Chico.[24] However, the further refinement by Richard Flint and Shirley Cushing Flint probably is correct in locating the Guadalupe County crossing site "below La Junta (the confluence of the Pecos and Gallinas rivers). That point is approximately ten miles east-southeast of where Canon Blanco joins the Pecos."[25]

In the event, instead of fording the stream, which, according to Castaneda, then had "a large, deep current, which flowed from" the direction of Cicuye, Coronado decided that the engineering project was called for. "They had to stop here to make a bridge so as to cross it," wrote Castaneda. "It was finished in four days, by much diligence and rapid work." Once the job was done, "the whole army and the animals crossed."[26] Typically, there is no additional contemporary information regarding the method of construction of the bridge. In the words of one historian, it "could have been anything from an actual wooden structure to a low water crossing."[27] Another historian of the expedition agreed that "[t]he bridge may have been a ford that had to be built up because of the high water the Spaniards encountered there."[28] However, most have decided Castaneda called it a bridge for a reason.

If any of Coronado's men-at-arms or soldiers were qualified military engineers, artillerist Juan Troyano would be among them. One of his acquaintances on the expedition recalled that Troyano, a certified veteran of the Italian Wars, was "a man of excellent skill and judgment" and that he knew "something about building bridges."[29] Another compatriot recalled that Troyano was "personally extremely valuable on the expedition."[30] It requires minimal speculation to conclude that Troyano was the Colonel Nicholson of the expedition, supervising the building of the Pecos River bridge as the fictional Nicholson did for the one on the river Kwai.

While the local Indians would know where passable fords were during various seasons of the year, "It is doubtful whether the early Indians had any knowledge of bridging more advanced than such simple foot logs" as were used at Taos.[31] Therefore, Richard Flint certainly was correct in concluding that the bridge was not of an indigenous design but was a product of European engineering.[32] However, there would have been indigenous input, for, in locating the appropriate place—likely where there normally was a firm-bottomed ford—any willing local natives undoubtedly would have been consulted regarding native trails.

Plus, some Spaniards undoubtedly rode ahead to reconnoiter likely spots.[33] Then, of course, pikes or lances would have been used to test the depth of the water and any mud.[34]

For simplicity's sake, a location "sufficiently firm to support the load" and where "the depth and scouring action of any water in the gap" would not be too great would be optimal. For a conventional bridge, a bottom too "soft and muddy or sandy and shifting" would require piles to be driven—a military bridging situation "resorted to only as a last resort."[35]

As to the specific design of the bridge, that also requires speculation. The Spanish army certainly had experience in northern Europe in building temporary bridges for the passage of troops. These bridges could be in the nature of Bailey bridges (portable pontoon bridges of the Second World War supported by boats) or bridges requiring piles to be driven into the riverbeds.[36] During the brief Schmalkaldic League War of 1547, in which Charles V defeated dissident German Protestants at the Battle of Muhlberg, the emperor's veteran Spanish and Italian troops quickly threw a pontoon bridge across the river Elbe under fire.[37]

This bridge building by Spanish military engineers carried over into the New World—sort of. When the army of Cortes was preparing to evacuate Mexico City, his carpenters dismantled timbers in an Aztec palace and made a portable bridge to be dropped into the gaps along the causeway out of the city.[38] However, under the press of battle (and the weight of the fleeing Spanish and allied army), the temporary bridge collapsed and was abandoned.

On the other hand, a few years later, when Cortes was exploring south toward Honduras, the Spaniards reached a broad river with a strong current (and even stronger alligators). Instead of attempting to ford with their horses, Cortes requested that his Indian allies build a bridge, undoubtedly under Spanish supervision. That structure, which Cortes estimated would last ten years, reportedly lasted fifty.[39]

Even though more detail is known about the bridges constructed during the ventures of Cortes, such information still is limited. With one Cortes bridge, it was related that Indians on rafts and in canoes were used to sink "the beams one by one in the mud."[40]

Contemporaneous with the Coronado Expedition, the command under De Soto was struggling through the swamps and forests of the America Southeast. More often than not, according to De Soto's secretary, the Spaniards typically "had no need of a bridge" and "they waded through the water up to their necks, with clothes and saddles on their heads."[41] However, early on, while morale and discipline still were high, the expedition, in a single day, "built a bridge of pines . . . and the next Sunday, they crossed that stream with . . . much . . . toil."[42]

Coronado's bridge was a less-ambitious engineering feat than that of Cortes in Honduras but took longer (lacking many handy Southern pine trees) than the one built by De Soto. The general area in which the bridge probably was built—although things can change over five centuries—has a Pecos River with high banks fifty to a hundred yards apart. Since there currently is some vegetation along the Pecos, presumably, in 1541, there were a fair number of mature cottonwoods (a soft hardwood) and saplings along the stream and otherwise within hauling distance for construction purposes.[43] While notorious for not being a first-rate construction material, cottonwood would serve for an exploratory expedition with axes.[44]

Flint and Cushing Flint suggest that the bridge built was a pontoon or floating bridge.[45] Such bridges have long been used for the movement of troops and, taken out of environmental context, that guess is not illogical. While cottonwood probably would not be the easiest wood to work with (or the most buoyant) in providing pontoons, a floating bridge presumably would make up for a soft river bottom.

However, because the river was in springtime flood, perhaps at times even bank-full, a wooden stringer bridge, supported by trestles or "bents" that could be dropped into place by block and tackle anchored on the bridge abutment or the previously raised trestle would have been the logical choice.[46] While potentially dangerous work, such bridges were long the bread and butter of military engineers in the era before the Bailey bridge. They can be constructed by disciplined troops even when the "carpentry work [is] handled by inexperienced labor" and when the stream's "current is swift and deep and scouring action is considerable."[47]

Nonetheless, military engineers would not necessarily be unanimous in suggesting a trestle bridge to support the stringers. Trestle bridges, according to a British military engineer of the nineteenth century, are not practical if the river to be crossed is "subject to be suddenly swollen during the period that a sure communication across them is required." This expert, Sir Douglas Howard, believed that a pile bridge was better for the crossing of "rapid but shallow rivers, in which boats, or floating bridges of any kind, cannot be used: or to bridge shallow, muddy creeks or gullies." Even if there was a soft river bottom, that problem could be solved simply by using "piles of considerable length."[48] Such projects did not require modern machinery, for the construction of pile-supported military bridges goes back at least to the ancient Romans.[49]

Whatever specific method of construction was employed to secure the bridge—and the available materials and limited skills exhibited by the expedition members seemingly would argue against a pile bridge—Coronado's men completed the work in four days. This would be much too long if they had hauled a ready-made bridge from Mexico but sounds reasonable for constructing a stringer bridge—whether supported by trestles or piles—with locally obtained materials. Coronado had a considerable number of men available to locate and cut timber as his engineer organized the actual builders. Like Cortes, he could have his Indian allies assist to "fell trees, fashion long beams, and drag them . . . for building a bridge."[50]

While the various work would have been done by different teams at the same time, in order of placement the builders first would assemble and erect an abutment on the western bank. Then, in the case of a trestle bridge, the trestle bents—previously assembled—would have been erected in the streambed. Next, the stringers—the lengthwise supports for the walkway—would have been secured to the initial abutment, to the trestle bents, and to the abutment on the far shore. The flooring and any side rails would have been secured to the stringers. Finally, the engineer would have had his men erect additional bracing to the bents and between the bents.[51] The construction of a pile bridge would be similar, and the pile driving, in theory, could be done by hand with heavy wooden mallets.[52]

Archaeologists and historians, in debating the location, express some hope that remnants of the structure might be found. This may prove to be but a pious hope.[53] If the bridge was constructed of local materials, only stone shore abutments would have much chance of surviving the centuries, and there certainly have been floods washing the banks away. In addition, cottonwoods do not provide the most durable of building timber. It is said that it starts "to rot the minute it hit[s] the ground."[54] Finally, even if Richard Flint's guess is right, finding the exact archaeological location of the bridge site will also be hindered by the fact that there have been considerable reclamation efforts in New Mexico's Guadalupe County and along the Pecos, dating back at least to the 1930s.[55]

Nonetheless, while it is clear that a bridge was built, probably across the Pecos, the question that cannot be sufficiently answered is: Why was it built? Of course, the waggish answer is: To get to the other side. But this witticism avoids answering the real question. The river was in spring flood stage, but even swift rivers can be forded by determined soldiers—albeit with some risk and some difficulty—with sufficient preparation.[56] Downstream, the flow might not have been so turbulent, and in four days, water depth and speed could rise or fall quite a bit. And, as Flint and Cushing Flint have observed, this was the only known occasion when the expedition went to the extraordinary trouble of building a bridge during a two-year march that saw many rivers.[57]

It is true that the expedition had a lot of camp followers, including women and probably some children, although Castaneda, in his typical selectivity, only notes the passage of the army and the animals. Bolton pointed out the obvious fact that "sheep with watersoaked wool are very poor swimmers."[58] Somewhat similarly, steel armor obviously could not be worn safely when fording a river, as some of De Soto's doomed men found out.[59] While these would seem to be valid reasons to build a bridge, there probably were others, including a desire to preserve possessions and to "keep their powder dry," since it was then known that any real hope of resupply was slim.

But there might have been less-obvious rationales. Once again, while the expedition probably was transporting most of the arms, equipment, and rations with the pack horses, there might have been some wheeled transport. While the lumber pickings were slim around Tiguex, there certainly was down time in which some carts could have been constructed, perhaps with materials from the various failed siege machines. Of course, since the expedition would later see Indians with dog travois,[60] those primitive carriers might also have been constructed.

The little army presumably still had two of the falconet cannon, probably being hauled with crude limbers or in carts. It goes without saying that bridges are helpful for the passage of rivers when it comes to artillery, and the heavier the guns the stronger should be the bridge.[61] In Coronado's case, the guns were not that heavy.

And, as previously discussed, the presence of other wagons and carts, although also unmentioned in the documents, is not impossible. Therefore, especially with the high banks of the Pecos, fording the river with wheeled conveyances would have been especially unfeasible during the spring runoff.

In addition, there would be other legitimate military reasons for constructing this first bridge over the Pecos. The expedition, having gotten away from Tiguex, was probably well served by stopping for several days in an open area to rest, recuperate, and (especially) reorganize. This would be true even if a pause had been made at Pecos Pueblo, a place in which there were prying eyes and even a soldierly temptation or two.

The construction of a bridge in the bush, in which the majority of the command could meaningfully participate, would have given purpose to the stop and would have forestalled immediate disciplinary problems. Soldiers are not exempt from the old cliché, "Idle hands are the devil's workshop."[62]

Finally, the pioneering involved in building a bridge in the wilderness was not without other, real-world, training benefits. So far, Coronado's force had been required to assault several pueblos. While they were not European fortresses, those attacks had highlighted some shortcomings with the army. The little falconets had been inadequate as siege guns, and four of them had been left as worthless in the rear.[63] In addition, attempted siege machines—at least a battering ram and some rock-throwing slings—also had been found to be wanting.

While Coronado and his men undoubtedly now were a little more skeptical about finding cities of Oriental splendor as they trudged onto the Great Plains, stranger things had happened. Indeed, they had seen the impressive, seemingly impregnable fortress at Acoma. In addition, as Coronado had found (and as the British would be reminded in Afghanistan in the 1840s), even cities made out of mud were not to be held in contempt.

Consequently, Castaneda later would report that in the future, "heavy artillery would be very good for settlements like those which Francisco Vazquez Coronado discovered, in order to knock them down." For not only did Coronado not have heavy guns, he also had "nobody skilful enough to make a catapult or some other machine which would frighten them, which is very necessary."[64]

Castaneda's implicit suggestion regarding classic siege machines was no more than part of the then-recent Continental European military tradition, for, while the last mobile assault tower was used in France in 1356, the ballistic machines (such as catapults) continued to be employed successfully until at least 1450, until gunpowder artillery entirely supplanted them.[65] But that did not mean that the construction of such machines out of antiquity were not occasionally attempted in the sixteenth century or later.[66] Indeed, Cortes, in his efforts to recapture the Aztec capital, had permitted the construction of a catapult to fling huge stones at the Aztecs.[67] The conquistadors were nothing if not capable of thinking outside the box, especially when it came to applying classical military solutions.

Therefore, it is not very speculative to conclude that one purpose of the great Pecos bridge-building project was to practice pioneering skills in case catapults or siege towers were needed to be built to take another, more substantial, city. An initial exercise in bridge building would increase these skills. After a column of Cortes's constructed a particularly challenging bridge in Honduras, the next bridge it had to build was done much more quickly and efficiently, for not only did everyone know what to do, "This time no one shirked."[68]

Certainly, neither Coronado nor his men wanted, for the want of a nail (or two), a city—especially full of golden treasure—to be lost. At the very least, the project kept the disillusioned expedition busy, and it got everyone on the Pecos's farther shore, positioned to leave New Mexico and enter the Panhandle of Texas—a terrain of plains, weathered cap rocks, eroded arroyos, and deep canyons.[69]

# The Expedition Enters the Cap Rocks and Canyons of the Llano Estacado

O nce it crossed the Pecos River, the army marched east. After eight days, the members of the expedition were treated to what was for most of them their first view of the American bison (invariably called cows by the Spaniards). Two days later, the army reached the lands of the Plains Apaches (now called the Jicarilla Apaches), "who lived like Arabs" and who "live[d] in tents made of the tanned skins of the cows." Although as of yet without horses, these Apaches "travel[ed] around near the cows, killing them for food." At this point in their history, dogs helped in moving villages, pulling the travois of the Apaches.

The Spaniards found the Indians "very intelligent," for they did not flee upon seeing the army, and they spoke to the advance guard, which included Turk and Coronado. Probably the honesty of Turk's interpreting was assured by the fact that the Spaniards now were becoming proficient in the sign language of the plains. The Apache vaguely described the region, claiming they knew of a big river to the east (perhaps the Arkansas or the Mississippi), which was traversed by canoes.

After parting with these Indians, the expedition continued on its way in a somewhat northerly direction. More Plains Apaches were seen, as well as "such great numbers of cows that it already seemed something incredible."[1]

The army was now on the Llano Estacado, the Staked Plain of eastern New Mexico and the Texas Panhandle, where "[t]he risk of traveling without a guide has been tried with fatal results."[2] Indicating how dangerous the area could be even for hidalgo huntsmen, Don Garcia Lopez de Cardenas broke his arm, presumably when his horse fell into a prairie dog hole chasing some bison, while another Spaniard off hunting got separated from the command and never was seen again.[3] Several Spanish hunters may have gotten lost and died or been killed by Indians.[4]

Because Turk claimed there was a substantial community called Haxa only a day or two to the east, Coronado sent a reconnoitering party of ten men under Captain Diego Lopez. Off they went, "lightly equipped" and with "a guide to go at full speed toward the sunrise for two days to discover Haxa, and then return to meet the army, which set out in the same direction the next day."[5]

Meanwhile, the advance guard of the main army kept coming across huge herds of buffalo, and the men-at-arms killed many bulls, undoubtedly with their lances.[6] At least some of the hidalgos probably had experience hunting boars—in Europe considered the most dangerous and most honorable game. Like participation in tournaments or jousts, hunting on horseback was considered capital training for soldiering.[7] Some of Coronado's Spaniards were so skilled they were able to lance rabbits running among the buffalo.[8] While none of Coronado's men were killed in this reckless hunting, the slaughter of the bison was not without cost, for three saddled horses got caught up with a herd and were lost.[9]

But it was not all dangerous field sports for the army. Coronado, becoming concerned about Diego Lopez, sent a dozen riders off looking "for traces of the horses" of the reconnoitering party. But according to Castaneda, "It was impossible to find tracks in this country, because the grass straightened up again as soon as it was trodden down."[10]

Finally, Lopez and his men were found by Indian auxiliaries who were foraging for berries. Haxa, of course, had not been located—since it apparently never existed except in the imagination of Turk. Lopez reported "that in the twenty leagues they had been over they had seen nothing but cows and the sky."[11] This cows-and-sky tag certainly was as good a description of the old-time Llano Estacado as there ever was.

Although the Spaniards were having serious second thoughts about the reliability of Turk—especially since another supposed citizen of Quivira, Ysopete, had been warning the Spanish that Turk was a liar— Coronado was not ready to give up. He sent a larger reconnoitering

Frederic Remington's
well-known late nine-
teenth-century recreation
of Coronado's Expedition
moving into the
American Great Plains
region. (*Author*)

party out under the command of Don Rodrigo Maldonado. So as not to let the terrain get the better of him, Maldonado had his men occasionally make "piles of stone and cow-dung for the army to follow."

After four days the company reached "a large ravine" and discovered a large village on the canyon floor, a village that had fond memories of Cabeza de Vaca and his companions.[12] Somewhat encouraged by having found something, Maldonado, according to Castaneda, "sent some of his companions to guide the army to that place, so that they should not get lost."[13]

When Coronado's column reached this plains settlement, the residents—supposedly assuming that these Christians would bless their possessions in the manner Cabeza de Vaca and his companions had (without taking any of those items blessed)—brought out a large stack of tanned buffalo hides and presented them before Coronado, according to Castaneda. Coronado, for his part, reportedly thought that these hides were a tributary gift, and he posted guards around the stockpile of valuable skins before any distribution.[14]

At this point there was evidence of a breakdown in discipline in the disappointed army, for, when word got out that the captain general was going to give his staff and personal friends first choice of the hides, the Spaniards broke ranks, "made a rush, and in less than a quarter of an hour nothing was left but the empty ground."[15] Castaneda also wrote that when the locals saw what was going on, they also rushed in and took back what they could. As for the women of the village, they "were left crying, because they thought that the strangers were not going to take anything, but would bless them as Cabeza de Vaca and Dorantes had done when they passed through here."[16]

While no violence erupted over this informal requisitioning (or theft)—as had occurred at Tiguex—it amply was demonstrated that what comes around, goes around. The army, setting up camp in this ravine (which must have been well watered), met up with a disaster that was not man-made. As described by Castaneda, "a tempest came up one afternoon with a very high wind and hail, and in a very short space of time a great quantity of hailstones, as big as bowls, or bigger, fell as thick as raindrops, so that in places they covered the ground two or three spans or more deep."[17]

The fact of this terrific storm, as much as the directional descriptions provided by the chroniclers, virtually locates the expedition on the Llano Estacado of Texas. In this Panhandle region, the southern end of which contains what is called Hail Alley, "plains northers swoop down with the rush of a predator. Atop the Llanos one can see them approaching for miles across the flat, but they cover ground with startling speed."[18]

Despite the force of the aerial assault, the black servants or slaves with the expedition performed heroically that day, protecting what horses they could from the deadly hail, although Castaneda was ambiguous as to whether the Africans were wearing borrowed armor or were using armor (or packhorse bags carrying stowed armor) to shield their four-footed charges.[19] The vast majority of the horses broke away, but some of the Africans "dashed up on to the sides of the ravine so that they got them down with great difficulty."[20]

Many such weather disasters in the sixteenth century were ascribed to God's will when they destroyed an expedition, and the subscribers to this theory included the losers and the beneficiaries.[21] However, in this case, Castaneda seemingly just thought that the sudden storm was a matter of luck—and mostly good luck, despite the destruction. He wrote:

"If this had struck them while they were upon the plain, the army would have been in great danger of being left without its horses, as there were many which they were not able to cover. The hail broke many tents, and battered many helmets, and wounded many of the horses, and broke all the crockery of the army, and the gourds [used by and acquired from the Puebloans]."[22]

As Castaneda observed, it certainly could have been worse. Indeed, this sixteenth-century setback someday could prove to be a historical blessing. As an incentive to the few archaeologists who have not thought about it, the shards of this crockery must have survived in the Texas Panhandle somewhere. Such ordinary Spanish earthenware pottery has been discovered at the very first colony established by Columbus in the Caribbean, and some similar stuff, which accompanied the 1588 Armada, was found after almost four centuries submerged in the cold saltwater off the coast of Ireland.[23]

In the event, after this fortunately minor disaster struck, the command had to spend time recuperating. In addition to salvaged equipment being dried out, it is likely the army's gunpowder had to be carefully spread out and "dried in the sun or in pans over the fire," as commentary regarding later expeditions recommended.[24]

Meanwhile, the persistent Coronado continued to dispatch reconnaissance patrols "to explore the country," and they found villages occupied by Indians called the Teyas, presumably the Caddoan people from whence Texas derives its name.[25] Some of these natives traveled a while with the army, and when questioned (with Turk sequestered from them), they said that Quivira was, indeed, to the north, but that the Spaniards "should not find any good road thither." Thus there was a growing belief that Turk had been lying.[26]

The army eventually moved to another canyon, one "a league wide from one side to the other, with a little bit of a river at the bottom, and there were many groves of mulberry trees near it."[27] While this might have been Palo Duro Canyon, it just as likely was Blanco Canyon, where the Jimmy Owens archaeological site is located. "The army rested several days in this ravine and explored the country."[28] There is evidence that the expedition lay over at Blanco Canyon, for many relics have been found, especially copper crossbow boltheads (which are metallurgically expedition specific) and nails.[29]

But details of the army's advance into Texas remain vague. As Hubert Howe Bancroft wrote 125 years ago, "the records, as might naturally be expected, are far from being sufficiently minute to enable us to fix the exact route followed."[30] Certainly the column reached the vicinity of Yellow House Canyon and where Lubbock now is, although earlier historians have opined reconnaissance even farther southeast along the Brazos into central Texas.

Coronado estimated that the army had wandered about 250 leagues—perhaps 650 or 700 miles—since leaving Tiguex. Once again, provisions were getting scarce. The captain general called an officers' council in order "to decide on what they thought ought to be done."[31]

According to Castaneda, "They all agreed that the general should go in search of Quivira with thirty horsemen and half a dozen foot-soldiers, and that Don Tristan de Arellano should go back to Tiguex with all the army." The men selected by Coronado to go with him were those he thought "to be the most efficient, and [with] the best horses."[32] Friar Padilla (with his assistants) also went along.[33]

Although the rest of the army—still craving riches and not adverse to further military action—was not happy with this arrangement, Coronado set off for Quivira, with Ysopete as a willing guide and with Turk in chains; Xabe, another supposed citizen of Quivira, remained with Arellano.[34] Coronado agreed to send back some express riders to keep the main army informed of his progress.[35]

Arellano and his companions remained in the Panhandle a fortnight, hunting for their rations and waiting to hear whether Coronado found anything that demanded the presence of the rest of the army. As Castaneda later recorded:

> It is estimated that during this fortnight they killed 500 bulls. The number . . . was something incredible. Many fellows were lost at this time who went out hunting and did not get back to the army for two or three days, wandering about the country as if they were crazy, in one direction or another, not knowing how to get back where they started from, although this ravine extended in either direction so that they could find it. . . . It is worth noting that the country there is so level that at midday, after one has wandered about in one direction and another in pursuit of game, the only thing to do is to stay near the game quietly until sunset, so as to see where it goes down, and even then they have to be men who are practised to do it.

Also to aid those who were lost, at dusk the main army would take roll and then "fired guns and blew trumpets and beat drums and built great fires." This helped some to regain the camp.[36]

After the two weeks, Arellano and the main army, according to plan, packed up and started marching back to Tiguex. It was apparently during this march that the main column had contact with an Indian woman who had met some Spaniards to the east, presumably De Soto's army.[37] As for Arellano's force, more or less retracing its steps, it hit the Pecos River thirty leagues (ninety-three miles) below the bridged river crossing.[38] When the force reached Pecos Pueblo, it found the village "ready for war and unwilling to make any advances toward peace or to give any food to the army."[39] Undoubtedly, the people of Pecos were disappointed that the Spaniards were not in a condition to be over-whelmed, as Turk had promised.

Further showing that things were not as peaceful as hoped, when the main force arrived back at Tiguex in July 1541, the Spaniards noted that several of the pueblos had been repopulated. But upon seeing the return of the army, the inhabitants once again headed to the hills or set up nonpueblo villages that presumably could be quickly evacuated if threatened.[40]

Arellano did what he could to prepare for Coronado's hoped-for return. Assuming that Tiguex once again would provide winter quarters, he went about collecting provisions to see the army through.[41] There also is archaeological evidence that tents with fire hearths were erected near Bernalillo.[42] To further occupy their time, Arellano sent out reconnaissance parties, including one under Captain Francesco de Barrionuevo, that went up the Rio Grande to the north. Among villages visited was the "large and powerful . . . village" of Taos, which would have been a second visit to this future tourist location by Coronado's soldiers. While these sixteenth-century visitors thought Taos to be a fine pueblo, they also thought it high in altitude and "very cold."[43] This probably saved Taos Pueblo from being considered as a site for quartering any Spaniards or Indian allies.

# NINETEEN

# Coronado's Flying Reconnaissance in Search of Quivira

O nce again, the captain general had decided to divide his force and head into the unknown. But this time he would be leading more of a flying column than was his advance guard in the march to Cibola. According to his later letter to the emperor, "With only thirty horsemen that I took with me as escort, I traveled forty-two days after leaving the army."[1] Because Don Garcia Lopez de Cardenas's horse had thrown him and he injured his arm, he did not go with Coronado.[2] Even if the remaining two falconet cannon still were with the army, and even if there were any carts or wagons still (if ever) accompanying the expedition, it is reasonably certain that Coronado did not slow himself down hauling such impediments toward Quivira.

In addition to basic hunger, part of Coronado's reasoning for taking such a small contingent obviously was the fear of scurvy, for he noted that the corn was gone and the army already was on a strictly meat diet. "For if they had all gone ahead [with me] the death of many men could not have been avoided," he opined, "as water was scarce and there were no other provisions except the food that they got by hunting the cattle."[3]

Supporting this grim assessment regarding scurvy, the main army under Don Tristan de Arellano, returning to the Rio Grande valley of New Mexico, suffered much on its return, although the herds of bison saw them through, and the grasslands sufficed for their mounts. "On the way they endured great hardships, because most of them had nothing to eat but [buffalo] meat, and it made many sick. . . . Every day it was necessary to go hunting. As a result of this and of not eating maize in all this time, horses fared very badly."[4]

Thus, if Turk's original plan had been to have the expedition perish on the southern Great Plains, it would not have been an impossible dream. The region was one in which the Spaniards learned that buffalo chips had to be piled up in lieu of rock cairns in order to retrace one's steps.[5]

History reports on even experienced military commands getting lost and meeting parched disaster on the seemingly endless Llano Estacado. In 1877, during a particularly severe drought, a company of the 10th US Cavalry's buffalo soldiers under Captain Nicholas Nolan became effectively lost there. Among the casualties of this disaster were four enlisted men who died miserable deaths. The rest barely escaped with their lives.[6]

While in buffalo country, Coronado noted how "very brave and fierce" the animals were, undoubtedly based partially on the fact that several of the Spaniards' horses were killed during the hunting. He also marveled at how the bison could go "many days without water." Finally, he commented that the buffalo chips, in a land without timber, could be used to fuel cook fires, a fact sodbusters learned later.

In any event, traveling and hunting for those forty-two days after splitting up with the main army, Coronado and his little force then headed still farther north, obviously cutting across what would become Oklahoma, "so as to give [Charles V] a true account of what was to be found in it." In his letter to his liege lord, Coronado succinctly summarized this impressive quick march:

> It was the Lord's pleasure that, after having journeyed across these deserts seventy-seven days, I arrived at the province they called Quivira, to which the guides were conducting me, and where they had described to me houses of stone, with many stories; and not only are they not of stone, but of straw, but the people in them are as barbarous as all those whom I have seen and passed before this; they do not have cloaks, nor cotton of which to make these, but use the skins of the cattle they kill, which they tan, because they are settled among these on a very large river.

It is believed that these native people were the Wichita Indians and that Coronado had reached the Arkansas River in Kansas. While relatively primitive, these folks still garnered some respect, for Coronado noted they were tall and the women were well-proportioned.[7]

They also posed a potential military threat to the little party of Spaniards, for the Quivirans, in the era when Coronado's force was among them, are thought to have been armed with bows approximately five-feet tall, made out of the wood of the bois d'arc (Osage orange or horse apple) tree. Sometimes they went into battle with a small shield worn on the left forearm.[8]

However, little is known from contemporary Spanish sources about the fighting ability of the Quivirans because, fortunately for Coronado, this was one leg of the expedition when there was no battling between Europeans and natives. The little force spent a total of twenty-five days among the people of Quivira, conducting reconnaissance in the region. Although he thought the country well watered and with good soil, Coronado reported to the emperor that there was no sign of gold or other precious metals.[9]

Reasoned tradition has it that the farthest north—beyond the Arkansas—Coronado or his men got was a hill at Lindsborg, Kansas, where a piece of mail was found in 1915.[10] But it is possible that some of Coronado's scouts, like the party of Zebulon Pike in 1806, wandered north across what now is the Kansas-Nebraska line.[11]

It was at Quivira that Coronado finally learned he had been led astray by his Indian guides "because they wanted to persuade me to go there with the whole force, believing that as the way was through such uninhabited deserts, and from lack of water, they would get us where we and our horses would die of hunger."[12]

Coronado, in the latter part of August, in deciding whether to winter in Quivira or return to Tiguex, consulted with the members of his flying reconnaissance column. Because of the slim prospects in the region and because there was a well-founded fear that snows would close the trails, according to Juan Jaramillo, "it seemed to us all that his grace ought to go back in search" of the main army and plan on returning to Quivira in the spring "to conquer and cultivate it."

Gathering what dried corn and fruit (probably wild berries, plums, and wild grapes) they could, Coronado and his party prepared to leave. In the village of Quivira, according to Juan Jaramillo, "The general raised a cross . . . at the foot of which he made some letters with a chisel, which said that Francisco Vazquez de Coronado, general of that army, had arrived here." For the journey homeward, Coronado would be accompanied by several guides from the village.

Not everyone would leave Quivira with Coronado and his party. Ysopete was left at Quivira, apparently at his own request. The Indian

A sixteenth-century drawing of men-at-arms in a quick march. (*Author*)

called Turk also stayed behind, although his final lack of movement was even more involuntarily than were most of the last days of this wretched and chained captive. According to Jaramillo, when Turk saw that his lies had been discovered, "one night he called on all of these people [of Quivira] to attack us and kill us. We learned of it, and put him under guard and strangled him that night so that he never waked up."[13]

With the full knowledge of Coronado, who testified that he gave the order after Turk had confessed his plot, Diego Lopez garroted Turk.[14] Likewise, Diego Lopez freely admitted that it was his job, as master of the camp, "to carry out justice, once he found out what wrongs El Turco had committed and was continuing to commit."[15] Turk was buried among the Spanish tents, away from the prying eyes of Quivira.[16]

While, ethically, one may criticize many of the actions of Coronado and his subordinates, the demise of Turk ought to be on the lowest rung of claimed atrocities.[17] Throughout history, treacherous guides have fared particularly poorly when their perfidy has been discovered. Often depending on a hearer's particular biases, most of these double-dealers have died unsung and unlamented.[18] As for Turk, his duplicity included getting Pecos Pueblo and other innocent natives involved in gratuitous problems with the Spanish, which garners him little sympathy.[19]

Coronado's party set off from Quivira going more or less in the direction whence they had come, according to Juan Jaramillo.[20] However, another member of this reconnaissance party (recalling the difficulty of traversing the trackless Llano Estacado) wrote, "We went back [to the Rio Grande] by a more direct route, because in going by the way we went we traveled 330 leagues, and it is not more than 200 by that which we returned."[21] It is this latter recollection that might provide Coloradoans with the glimmer of hope—however unlikely—that Coronado or his outriders clipped the very southeastern corner of the Mile High Centennial State before reentering northeastern New Mexico.[22]

Meanwhile Arellano, concerned that Coronado was overdue, had backtracked from Tiguex with forty men-at-arms to Pecos Pueblo. If anything, he found the people of Pecos even more truculent than before, although they probably did not know that even then, Coronado's reconnaissance force was approaching Pecos from the north or east. "[T]he people came out of the village to fight, which detained him [Arellano] there four days, while he punished them, which he did by firing some volleys into the village," according to Castaneda. "These killed several men, so that they did not come out against the army, since two of their principal men had been killed on the first day."[23]

Perhaps indicating that Arellano was considering the continuation of full-scale military action at Pecos, evidence was found almost a century ago that the expedition was manufacturing crossbolt heads and arrowheads from sheets of copper at the pueblo.[24] But, as noted previously, perhaps that piecework had been done during the Tiguex War, with the Spaniards getting assistance from the artisans of Pecos. In the event, by the time Coronado's party arrived, it found Arellano keeping the Pecos people at bay and the road open.[25] However, supporting the conclusion that Coronado merely felt the subjugation of the pueblo not worth the cost, the people of Pecos successfully kept the Spanish from capturing their pueblo.[26]

Thus, Coronado saw that the region's natives had reached the limits of their willingness to submit to Spanish dictates. Also, on his return to Tiguex, he undoubtedly was advised that it was going to be another tense winter.

In writing his report to his king, Coronado also realized how devoid of practical benefits his expedition had been. While noting that he had done his best, he wrote after he had returned to Tiguex:

> As I have been obliged to send captains and soldiers to many places in this country to find out whether there was anything by which your Majesty could be served, the diversity of languages spoken in this land and the lack of people who understand them had been a great handicap

to me, since the people in each town speak their own. And although we have searched with all diligence we have not found or heard of any towns, except those in these provinces, which do not amount to very much.[27]

Of course, in a military sense, as in a business sense, a negative intelligence report can be important. It can reorder priorities and determine what is not worthy of further investment of blood or treasure. Ultimately, Coronado—and almost everyone else—determined that the country was not worth a second visit, at least for a long, long time.

Although Coronado would not return to Quivira, Friar Juan de Padilla thought this northern land worthy of occupation by the church. He imposed upon Coronado to allow him—along with "a Spanish-Portuguese and a negro and a half-blood and some Indians from . . . New Spain"—to return and stay among the natives around Quivira as missionaries. This concession on the part of Coronado, while a sincere attempt to propagate the faith, was ultimately meaningless. Reportedly, Padilla was murdered after the army departed the Southwest, while the Portuguese named Campo and the Indians of New Spain were allowed to escape south.[28]

Later, Viceroy Mendoza, not knowing of the futility of this attempt at missionary work, very much approved of Coronado's decision to let Padilla and his compatriots stay behind and proselytize the Indians at Quivira and elsewhere.[29] In any event, while one might not be sure about Esteban, Friar Padilla came to be recognized as a bona fide Christian martyr of the American West.

# TWENTY

# Heading for the Stable:
# A Mutinous Army Marches Home

A lthough there fortunately was not much to relate about the expedition's second winter at Tiguex, it was another dreary season. Unlike warfare in Europe, there was little fear of an enemy army—this one with minimal clothing and unsophisticated weaponry—launching a surprise attack against those in winter quarters.[1] Consequently, the record is sparse regarding any martial excitement. While well-disciplined forces, including the Spanish of the era, might try to fill such down time with physical exercise and sports, including footraces and ball games,[2] there is a dearth of information regarding any available entertainment, or even particular vices—probably a demonstration of a dispirited force rather than evidence of laziness or a general reformation of character.

A member of the army recalled of the sojourn on the Rio Grande, "We spent two very cold winters at this river, with much snow and thick ice." In a quote probably not used by the New Mexico division of tourism, he thought Quivira—in modern Kansas—"a better country . . . and not being so cold, although it is more to the north."[3] Indicating that the expedition now was having serious morale problems, another expedition member later recalled that "mass was not being said in the camp; nor was there anyone to say it."[4]

Meanwhile, the reinforcements from San Geronimo III arrived, under the command of Pedro de Tovar. These new men were disappointed that nothing had been found at Quivira and were hopeful that the spring would bring a new campaign. Tovar also brought dispatches from Mexico City. One letter informed Master of the Army Cardenas that he had inherited the family estates in Spain. Because of this (and his injured arm), Cardenas was given permission to lead a party of invalids back south.[5] As has been related, Cardenas soon returned to the main army because of the destruction of the post at San Geronimo III and the dangerous fallout from the Mixton War.[6]

Thus, there were many stresses for Coronado. Once again, "because the soldiers were almost naked and poorly clothed, full of lice," he tried to obtain clothing from those people of Tiguex who still would communicate with the Spanish. This resulted in Coronado's being forced to "pacify" some unfriendly villages. In addition, there was a feeling among the soldiery that the best of the material collected went to the captains and their friends—and that guard assignments were made inequitably.[7]

In early spring 1542, as the army ostensibly prepared to return to Quivira, Coronado went horseback riding with Captain Maldonaldo. The two engaged in an informal horse race, and the girth for Coronado's mount broke. The captain general fell under the hooves of Maldonaldo's steed and suffered a serious concussion. The injury "laid him at the point of death, and his recovery was slow and doubtful," recalled Castaneda.[8] As another of his expeditionaires wrote, he "was sick a long time."[9]

All the members of the expedition seemed to agree that this serious injury knocked the stuffing out of Coronado and made him want to go home. "As a result [of the injury] he showed a mean disposition and plotted the return," recalled one of the captains.[10] "When the winter was over he was determined, regardless of any statements to the contrary, to turn back. . . . He longed for this more than anything else," wrote another member of the expedition.[11]

According to Castaneda, it was during his slow recovery that a morose Coronado decided that if he were to die soon, he wished to die at home with his wife. In effecting this desire, he enlisted the help of "the physician and surgeon who was doctoring him, and also acted as a talebearer" because of the mutterings that were going on among the soldiery. Obviously, in the expedition, there now were some "go-backs" and some "stay-behinds" when it came to attitude.

Apparently acting at the behest of Coronado, the surgeon met "secretly and underhandedly with several gentlemen who agreed with him." These unnamed hidalgos encouraged the soldiers to talk among themselves and in small groups about returning to Mexico. The men reportedly did not need much encouragement, since many already wanted to go home. The gentlemen also induced these dissidents to "send papers to the general, signed by all the soldiers, through their ensigns, asking for this."

Coronado, upon receipt of these petitions, apparently did not consider this mutinous behavior. However, "the general acted as if he did not want to do it," causing "the gentlemen and captains," only some of whom were in on the secret plan, to throw in their support for the return of the army by submitting signed documents in favor of the move. With this peer pressure, other gentlemen or captains provided their petitions. "Thus, they made it seem as if they ought to return to New Spain, because they had not found any riches nor had they discovered any settled country out of which estates could be formed for all the army."

Then, having "obtained their signatures," Coronado had the return to New Spain announced to the army. However, once the determination to head home was in the open, everyone began to compare notes about their participation in how it came about, and, in Castaneda's words, "the double dealing began to be understood, and many of the gentlemen found that they had been deceived and had made a mistake."[12]

Captain Juan Jaramillo later protested that "ten or twelve of us pleaded with him" to change his mind, but Coronado was obdurate.[13] While those who had reconsidered tried to get their signed recommendations back, Coronado supposedly feigned a physical relapse and posted "guards about his person and room, and at night about the floor on which he slept." Despite these precautions, Castaneda believed that the stay-behinds stole Coronado's chest where the papers and petitions were held. But those documents had been secreted elsewhere—in Coronado's mattress. Castaneda said there was a rumor in camp that the papers, nonetheless, had been recovered by those who submitted them.[14]

Although this entire scenario might seem far-fetched and too imaginative, there certainly has been a comparable situation in the history of the American West. In 1876, after another military column, under General George A. Custer, had been disappointed (and wiped almost unto annihilation), some of the officers supposedly created an analogous paper trail to justify actions already taken and to support decisions already made. With the apparent connivance of at least one of the non-commissioned officers, Major Marcus Reno and Captain Frederick Benteen got an enlisted men's petition written up that urged the retention and promotion of the surviving officers of the 7th Cavalry. There is a reasoned belief that much of this petition also was obtained secretly and underhandedly, with at least some of the signatures being forgeries.[15]

Assuming Castaneda's version is correct, Coronado had accomplished an end often sought by politicians and diplomats (if not by military commanders): he had gotten his way by surreptitiously floating a plan that others unknowingly adopted as their own inspiration. While the motivational and morale effects might have been short-lived, an idea to return home had been run up the flagpole and been saluted by enough expedition members to make it appear—at the time—to be a popular decision. Obviously, when it would come to justifying turning the column about and giving up, Coronado had covered his aspirations successfully.

In any event, according to Castaneda, "The general was very happy and contented when the time arrived and everything needed for the journey was ready, and the army started from Tiguex on its way back to Cibola." [16]

Contrasted with its march forward, the army on its return—at least the original Spanish members of that army—now looked more like Indians on the trail. Yet even after having appropriated, requisitioned, and stolen much native clothing, this did not mean that they looked like they actually had gone native and become accustomed to life on the borderlands.[17] While the hidalgos looked like combat veterans, Coronado's force also undoubtedly had more of a ragged, bedraggled, dispirited, demoralized look, and they eventually would begin to act in conformance to this.

Once it reached Cibola, the expedition paused for rest before starting the long march across the empty lands to the south. Certainly, the poor horses, undoubtedly as worn out as their riders and their packers, needed to recoup in greener pastures than offered by this part of New Mexico. "[M]ore than thirty died during the ten days which it took to reach Cibola, and there was not a day in which two or three or more did not die." Before the expedition finally reached the Spanish frontier at Culiacan, many more horses would succumb to either exhaustion, lack of forage, or some other malady.[18]

One native woman of New Mexico reportedly accompanied the withdrawing expedition, in contravention of the strict instructions given the army. This was the companion of artilleryman Juan Troyano, a woman whom that very professional soldier married and who remained with him the rest of his life.[19]

One wonders what happened to the bronze falconets as the army moved south. One prolific writer on firearms, Philip B. Sharpe, said, without a hint of a source, "[M]any are now reposing in historic museums throughout the Southwest."[20] That theory seems to have no factual basis. While the proper military procedure would have been to turn them back into some arsenal (getting signed receipts), in theory the guns could have been declared unserviceable and left behind as not being worth the trouble to bring back. Therefore, as noted, there is a chance that at least four of the falconets were buried in New Mexican soil to prevent them from falling into the hands of an enemy with more gunpowder than sense.[21]

Whether or not the falconets were left behind, the natives of Cibola were not averse to having other equipment left with them, for they followed the withdrawing column for several days hoping to pick up any discarded baggage. For some reason, the Cibolans also were not averse to the Indian members of the expedition remaining in the north, for they taunted those in the rear of the army with invitations to stay. Castaneda, for one, believed that the invitations were sincere and not malicious. Several Indian members elected to stay behind, as had others earlier.[22] Forty years later, when another Spanish expedition passed through, there still were several Mexican Indians from the expedition, who almost had forgotten their Spanish.[23]

While Friar Padilla returned to Quivira and martyrdom, two other Franciscans stayed behind. Friar Juan de la Cruz remained at Tiguex, where he reportedly was murdered in late 1542. Friar Luis Descalona or Friar Luis de Ubeda stayed to minister at Pecos, where he disappeared from history and Puebloan folklore, probably also being martyred for the faith.[24]

In addition to a few Mexican Indians, some Africans, and the friars, it has been conjectured that the Coronado Expedition left behind enough livestock to start the wild mustang horse herds and to lay the population groundwork for wild Spanish cattle, the ancestors of the Texas longhorns. Considering the lack of breeding stock noted in the documents, many historians have determined any Coronado equine bloodlines in wild mustangs to be unlikely.[25] Also discredited is the theory that any of the cattle taken along survived to breed and form wild herds on their own.[26]

While the indigenous population would have welcomed—for immediate killing, cooking, and eating—Coronado's column leaving behind horses, cattle, sheep, or goats, there were other life-forms, unknown but nonetheless unwelcome, that theoretically could have remained behind in the American Southwest. These would have been pathogens and assorted "germs." Diligent historians (although some seemingly would welcome positive discoveries) have found no proof that Coronado's Spaniards left behind pathogens that later ravaged the native peoples who came into contact with the army.[27] While plenty of bad blood was left behind, there were no bad germs.[28] European diseases would come later, along with European vices, in the natural course of events.[29]

As for the Spaniards, unlike a few *Indios amigos*, they did not have any alternatives to making the long march home. But their feelings of disappointment and dissatisfaction marched with them, and there undoubtedly was a growing sense that their captain general was no longer deserving of command.

While the hidalgos of the sixteenth century might have been noted for their inflated sense of honor and for their litigiousness regarding their personal rights, the more ordinary Spanish soldiery of the era gained a reputation for rising in mutiny when dissatisfied.[30] This problem of mutinous behavior for Spain came up especially during the long war in the Low Countries. "The least admirable trait of the very formidable Spanish troops of this later generation," wrote historian Sir Charles Oman, "was their proneness to mutinies or strikes on account of the non-appearance of their pay—a foible in which they rivalled the landsknechts and Swiss of the earlier years of the century."[31]

Thus, not just Spaniards were subject to fits of insubordination in the sixteenth century—and such ill discipline could be for seemingly trivial reasons (at least to historians). During 1512–1513, when Henry VIII sent troops to the Spanish-French border to assist the Spaniards and the Vatican forces fighting France, the English "expeditionary force of 7,000 soldiers . . . mutinied when they found that beer was unobtainable there."[32]

At least the usual cause of Spanish indiscipline was impecuniousness—and often resultant hunger. Therefore, it is not surprising that such behavior occurred well before the Dutch wars, in the case of New World conquistadors whose hopes of gaining treasure in the face of real danger seemed unattainable. Early on, Cortes faced a mutiny as he prepared to invade the lands of the Aztecs. According to Cortes's secretary, "He seized many of the conspirators and took their statements, in which they confessed it was all true. So, after a proper trial, he hanged Juan Escudero and the pilot Diego Cermeno."[33] As for the expedition of Hernando De Soto, in late 1540 he also faced down—with some severity—a mutiny by men who wanted to give up and go home.[34] And it was not only frightened expeditions on the march that saw mutiny, for in 1566, the famished Spaniards in the new town of Saint Augustine, Florida, rose up in a violent, albeit short-lived, mutiny.[35]

Compounding the morale problems for Coronado's army, two days north of Chichilticalli the southbound expedition met up with the hard-riding column of Captain Juan Gallego, who "was coming from New Spain with reenforcements of men and necessary supplies for the army, expecting that he would find the army in the country of the Indian called Turk."[36] According to Castaneda, Gallego was less than pleased to see that the plans to find a worthwhile country had been given up. Neither was Gallego mollified when he heard Coronado's reasons. Apparently, in camp that night, Gallego started "a little movement among the gentlemen toward going back with the new force which had made no slight exertions in coming thus far, having encounters every day with the Indians of these regions who had risen in revolt."[37]

Of course, even with their considerable efforts in making it to Chichilticalli, these new arrivals with Gallego did not have the same exhausted look as the rest of the army and hardly wanted to give up. They, as soldiers are wont to do, wanted to see some real action following their investment of time and trouble. While no man wants to be the last casualty in a lost war, those who still think they are invincible at least want to have some stories for the folks back home.

In the end, however, this active opposition to Coronado's withdrawal—a withdrawal now supported by many of those in the returning force who had gotten used to heading home—came to naught, and there was no open rupture within the ranks.[38] Neither did Coronado attempt to enforce an iron will in suppressing dissension like Cortes or De Soto.

In the event, the reinforcements under Juan Gallego fell into line. But Coronado's moral force as the leader of the army was slipping away;

according to Castaneda, "he had been disobeyed already and was not much respected." Coronado, perhaps feigning his condition, apparently kept to his bed when the army camped, and he always had a guard posted at his tent.[39]

It was well, however, that the army, including the reinforcements, kept together and maintained some professional discipline during its retrograde movement. As the expedition moved south toward Culiacan, it found evidence of the now-dying Mixton War and was in the position of having to mop up remaining resistance.[40] Castaneda recalled, "In several places yells were heard and Indians seen, and some of the horses were wounded and killed. . . . At one place . . . the hostile Indians wounded a Spaniard called Mesa," but "he did not die, although the wound of the fresh poison is fatal." In this case, quince juice applied to the wound reportedly saved Mesa's life, although he suffered from serious gangrene, which crept up the arm from the wrist wound.[41]

Having run this stressful gantlet of fear and fire, the army neared Corazones. The natives there proved themselves loyal friends to the Spanish once again, for they sent an escort out to meet the column. But there was not much of a rest at Corazones, for the provisions were failing and the rebellious state of the surrounding countryside prevented much foraging.[42] When two Indians killed a horse belonging to Don Tristan de Arellano, Arellano lanced one of them.[43] He also ordered that a captured Indian have his nose and one hand cut off before being released.[44]

As noted previously, many of the horses on this leg of the journey began to drop and not get up. It was not until the region just north of Culiacan was reached that the expedition was able to rest a couple of days and gather food.[45]

With this rest and refreshment, the army picked up its pace as it started again, but many in the expedition openly began to be insubordinate. One soldier who stole mats from his fellows was physically punished by Arellano.[46] "[S]ome began to disregard their superiors and the authority which their captains had over them," noted Castaneda, "and some captains even forgot the obedience due to their general."[47]

Technically, this was serious stuff, especially since the expedition members had sworn to obey their commanders. As indicated, the sixteenth century saw its share of mutinies on land and sea. Near the beginning of his world-encircling voyage, Francis Drake was presented with a mutiny led by one of the gentlemen on board, a mutiny intended to kill Drake and "overthrow" the enterprise. Drake solved the problem by conducting a court-marital and hanging the leader—after sharing holy communion and a good meal with his condemned friend.[48] As for Coronado, he was neither a sea captain nor a man like Drake—nor Cortes, nor De Soto. He had neither the intestinal fortitude to attempt such drastic action nor the isolated geography to get away with it; plus this was happening on the downslope of the campaign, and any such severity among potential constituents would be neither effective as a salutary lesson for the soldiery nor safe for the captain general.

Therefore, men began to drop out of the column and take breaks wherever and whenever they wished. Coronado attempted to reestablish unit cohesion and the chain of command by ordering the captains to be individually responsible for providing food to their companies from available village supplies under the administrative control of Coronado, since they were back in New Galicia and he still was governor with de jure authority.[49]

When the force limped into the town of Culiacan, which welcomed the returning expedition, Coronado again pretended he was sicker than he was and kept to his bed. This allowed him to meet his supporters out of sight of the rest of the army, and he pressed his friends to persuade the soldiers to hang with the army until they were back in New Spain. As incentives, Coronado made promises about gaining for the returnees favors and post-military-service employment from Viceroy Mendoza.[50]

But anything approaching a triumphal or impressive return to Mexico City was not to be. It was at Culiacan, probably where he joined the expedition, that Pedro de Castaneda apparently dropped out of the column. He was not alone in doing so.[51]

What was left of the expedition started out from Culiacan on June 24, 1542, heading south to Compostela at the beginning of the rainy season. The rough going through this unpopulated region, especially with the swollen rivers, was one last travail for the army. At one of the fords, a Spaniard was snatched by an alligator and carried away to be drowned and eaten while everyone else watched helplessly.[52]

Considering the times, it was not unusual that the Coronado Expedition, having outlived its reason for existence, did not stay together for a review for the viceroy. "Disbanding warriors was a widespread practice in the sixteenth century, when armies were recruited for the purpose of a particular campaign of several weeks or months."[53] But for Coronado, there was nothing approaching a formal mustering out with a sense of a job well done. In the rains and miserable conditions, Coronado's army simply melted away, as men dropped out to get home as best they could.

"The general proceeded," remembered Castaneda, "leaving the men who did not want to follow him all along the way, and reached Mexico with less than 100 men."[54] A Spanish youngster witnessed the arrival of the captain general, who appeared "very sad and very weary, completely worn out and shamefaced." For days afterward, the stragglers came staggering into Mexico City, exhausted and clothed in animal skins.[55] It was now sometime in late summer or early autumn 1542.

A seventeenth-century view of Mexico City. (*Author*)

The great adventure in the lives of Francisco Vasquez de Coronado, his captains, his men, his allied auxiliaries, and the various camp followers was over. Certainly for the arrogant hidalgos especially, the adventure was without pecuniary reward. As an early Spanish historian said about a later sixteenth-century expedition into the Yucatan that proved a financial bust, "[M]any or most of [the gentlemen] contracted heavy obligations for the amounts they spent on fancy dress, fine armor, and other things which forced them to borrow on their homes and lands for many years."[56] At least these many returning survivors—whether highborn or low, Spanish or native—still had their lives.

# TWENTY-ONE

# The Obligatory Spanish Inquiry into Conquistador Conduct

According to Pedro de Castaneda, although Coronado retained—for a time—his governorship of New Galicia, when he arrived back in Mexico City from his two-and-a-half-year expedition, Viceroy Mendoza "did not receive him very graciously" when he discharged Coronado from his duties as captain general. Castaneda thought Coronado's "reputation was gone from this time on."[1] Historian Herbert Bolton, always seeing the bright side for his knight of the pueblos and plains, wrote that Coronado, "For two more years, in spite of ill health . . . continued to exercise his office as governor, being occupied in the details of administration, making tours of inspection, coping with Indian uprisings, promoting public works, and playing cards with his friends." But Bolton also had to acknowledge that there were those, especially impecunious participants, who were disappointed in the failure of the expedition to find wealth, and these complainers supposedly provided the grist for an inquiry mill.[2]

The sixteenth-century Spaniards may have loved fighting, but they loved rules, regulations, and paperwork just as much. Plus, they seemed addicted to judicial inquiries, especially when the targets might provide the royal treasurer with income from fines. "To whom would it occur today to have a Judiciary Enquiry covering his past services put through the Court?" asked a veteran of the Second World War who had become an authority of the conquistador era.[3] However, while this official fastidiousness undoubtedly benefitted sixteenth-century Spanish lawyers and scribes, it also has been a treasure trove for historians, for nothing provides historical proof like a proceeding conducted under oath—even when perjury often is a participant.[4]

The lawyers got involved because the timing of the last several expeditions of the first—and greatest—conquistador era came when Spain and the Roman Catholic Church, both confident of their hegemony in the New World, were having second thoughts about all the new subjects and new souls under their respective authorities. While not concerned with giving back independence to any of the conquered peoples or granting freedom of conscience to the individuals, both Spain and the Vatican felt that the condition of the natives should be improved.

An indispensible participant in these reforms was Dominican brother Bartolome de Las Casas. He had seen firsthand the abuses suffered by the Indians in the Americas and, upon his return to Spain in 1539, resolved to end the dual curses of native enslavement and the encomiendas. He therefore laid his proposals before Emperor Charles V, who was then also the king of Spain, and his advisers making up the Council of the Indies. Instead of being allowed to return to the New World to minister to the Indians, Las Casas was asked to stay in Spain and help draw up what would be called the New Laws. The ordinances were issued in 1542 and 1543, just as Viceroy Mendoza was wrapping up the Mixton War.

While the New Laws were not as far-reaching as Las Casas desired, they did purport to stop—prospectively—the enslavement of Indians and the granting of encomiendas. In an obvious attempt to rein in corruption, government officials and churchmen also were ordered to give up their indentured Indians, and there was a restriction regarding the appointment of relatives to positions in the New World. Additionally, a system of tribunals was established to investigate past, present, and future abuses.

Not only were the Indians not to be exposed to further mandatory service for the Spanish colonists, but the paternalistic Catholic Church was to have a more-active role: the natives were to be converted into loyal vassals of Charles V and into good Catholic Christians subject to his holiness the pope.[5]

These New Laws initially caused much discontent in the new colonies. The conquistadors recognized that these new humanitarian rules were a threat to their livelihoods, if not to their effectiveness in performing the profession of arms. In fact, the New Laws were so disruptive that they helped cause the civil wars between Spaniards in Peru in the late 1540s.[6]

Elsewhere, the ordinances at least proved hard to enforce. However, for officials such as Viceroy Mendoza and Francisco Vasquez de Coronado, they proved very troublesome, for charges regarding abuses could be more easily brought by imported judicial officers who certainly had agendas of their own.

In September 1543, a judicial officer was appointed in Spain to look into the claims that "the expedition which Francisco Vasquez de Coronado made to the province of Cibola . . . committed, both going and returning, great cruelties upon the natives of the lands through which they passed." Coronado also had his critics regarding his civilian job as governor of New Galicia. Therefore, this official, Lorenzo de Tejada, also was authorized to look into Coronado's civilian conduct as governor of New Galicia.

With the arrival of Tejada, there began a lengthy legal process for Coronado. First there was the investigation regarding corruption surrounding his governorship. The numerous allegations made during this inquiry ranged from the trivial to the significant. When this proceeding, conducted in New Spain, was over, Coronado was absolved on twelve of the charges. As for the thirteen charges on which he was found guilty, he was fined. Regarding seven remaining and unresolved allegations, the issues were referred to Spain for resolution by the Council of the Indies.[7]

Then there were the historically more-serious charges regarding the expedition into the new lands, whereby the former captain general and his captains—especially Master of the Army and Camp Cardenas—faced numerous allegations relating to the expedition. These charges went to supposed abuses inflicted on the natives, from Bigotes to Turk, and encompassed the incidents such as the slaughter of the defenders of Arenal, including those in the tent of Cardenas. Over the years, historians have discussed and debated these charges against Coronado and his men.[8] Many of the allegations, being part and parcel of the military campaign, already have been set out and discussed herein.[9]

According to Coronado's greatest defender, Herbert Bolton, after the investigation of the alleged atrocities and war crimes, the matter was referred "to the Royal Audiencia of Mexico" and, after reviewing the case, "the judges on February 19, 1546, . . . completely absolved Coronado on all the charges." Cardenas, the man of action during most of the campaign in the new lands, was not so lucky. Bolton, calling the Coronado Expedition, on the whole, "quite exemplary—mild and gentle as compared with acts committed by Cortes, Pedriarias, Guzman, De Soto, or the Pizarros," concluded that "regardless of the evidence," Cardenas was made "an example for future conquistadores." The former master of the army was fined and spent time in a Spanish prison.[10]

A nineteenth-century American etching of Dominican brother Bartolome de Las Casas. (*Author*)

But Bolton was preceded by some who were not so sure about what went on in New Mexico in the 1540s. An earlier historian, who, if anything, was more intent than Bolton on justifying the ultimate introduction of his brand of Christianity into the region, reduced the troubles at Tiguex to an overly simplistic scenario. That writer, who had been the archbishop of Santa Fe, wrote in 1898 regarding the role of Cardenas in capturing and then burning Indians at the stake (a situation perhaps too reminiscent of the events of the Spanish Inquisition), "Unfortunately it happened that at the same time [that the Spaniards peremptorily requisitioned clothing from the natives] the soldiers mistook some peaceable Indians for rebels, and killed them." Then this writer summarized the rest of the Tiguex War, in which Coronado obviously made an attempt to minimize the carnage (and in which his soldiers and Indian allies demonstrated at least as much courage and persistence as brutality), as "the siege of Tiguex, or rather . . . the barbarous assassination of the Indians of that province."[11] Every age and every constituency, it would appear, has its own particular political correctness in which the agenda subsumes even obvious facts.[12]

Other historians since Bolton, while not disagreeing that Cardenas might have taken the fall for Coronado, have looked into things with more specificity than the former archbishop of Santa Fe and have not been so kind to the verdict regarding Coronado as was Bolton. "The resulting investigation record is one of testimony heavily weighted in favor of the former captain general of the expedition," wrote Richard Flint.[13] Stan Hoig, relying almost exclusively on the work of Richard

Flint, likewise concluded that because of "the demeaning facets of the Coronado Expedition," including Coronado's "excessive actions against native inhabitants," which came out during the investigation, the proof "regrettably tarnished" Coronado's "role in the annals of American history."[14]

While, as related in this volume, the evidence generally supports the allegations that the captain general authorized or allowed many of the atrocities or horrific actions of the expedition, Coronado's conduct ought to be put into fair context. While not a defense to specific acts, there is mitigation in the fact that the Coronado Expedition was, as Bolton claimed, mild compared to virtually every other conquistador endeavor during that era. For example, when Francisco de Montejo Pech invaded Guatemala in 1541, his army (which included many Indian allies) gained a reputation for abusing the natives of whatever social rank, and this abuse included sexual assault.[15] Other comparisons and contrasts—with the conquests of Cortes, Pizarro, and De Soto—already have been detailed, with Coronado coming off as either no worse or better.

Luckily for Coronado, Viceroy Mendoza to some extent anticipated the New Laws. As indicated in his instructions to Coronado, the captain general was to protect and defend the natives of the land "in order that no injury or ill treatment may be inflicted upon them" and "to bring its natives to the knowledge of our holy Catholic faith" and to bring the land within the authority of the royal crown.[16]

But the best defense of the charges against Coronado and his army was that the jurisdiction of his Spanish judges and critics was tainted by obvious hypocrisy. In other words, the expedition was held in judgment by those who not only stayed home during the endeavor but also benefited from it and who, in the main, could not stand up against such accusations and be held to be without sin, especially as aiders and abettors.

This hypocrisy was helped along at the time by the fact that the Coronado Expedition was a financial bust. A lot of high crimes and misdemeanors could be glossed over when a substantial one-fifth of the acquired loot went into Spanish royal coffers. Of course, in this Spain was not unique: later in the century, Elizabeth I would find her share of the spoils of Francis Drake and other marauding mariners sufficient to grant knighthoods for patriotism rather than to order up halters or gibbets for piracy upon a nation with which England was not then formally at war.[17]

The truth be told, with the restrictions of Las Casas, Cortes would not have been able to destroy the pagan foundation of the Aztecs and so quickly substitute an alternate system that, while certainly harsh, was not based on a theoretical tradeoff between sacrificial murder of other peoples and good crops.[18] Pizarro's amazing destruction of the Inca Empire—if anything more brutal and venal than what went on in Mexico—also could not have occurred with the enforcement of the Las Casas rules of engagement.[19] It was easy enough to impose, at least officially, the Las Casas paradigm after Hapsburg Spain had filled its coffers with ill-gotten loot and after the Vatican already had declared jurisdiction over the souls of those vast territories.

As for applying the new humanitarian guidelines to new conquests, those were in less prosperous lands that were not really threatened by competitor nations. Spanish steel already had seen to that. The New Laws only attempted to close the barn door after the stock had escaped, and neither Madrid nor Rome was going to give anything back.

Considering the fact that Coronado and his captains were tasked with carrying out the demands of empire and church—as uncompromising as those demands were—the injustice was not that they were held accountable for so little, but that they were accused at all. The accusers, after all, really were the institutions that benefited from the entire conquistador era.

But the greatest hypocrisy was the fact that Coronado and his men were accused of misconduct not considered judicable misconduct in Europe. "The behavior of Spaniards toward Indians in the early sixteenth century," wrote an eminent borderlands historian, "often seems cruel and repugnant by present standards. Nonetheless, it fell within the bounds of acceptable behavior for many western European males of the late middle ages, whose behavior toward one another was also cruel and repugnant by our lights."[20] A similar but more detailed assessment was made by a historian when he compared the 1527 sack of Rome with the conduct of Cortes in 1521 Mexico: "Spanish troops did not throw away the rule book and run amok when they left Europe behind. They brought the common culture and practices of soldiers, officers, and political leaders with them to this [Western] hemisphere."[21]

In fact, especially with the application and enforcement of the New Laws, the Spanish soldiery in the New World was to be held to a higher standard than those Spaniards in the sectarian warfare in northern Europe against heretics and rebellious non-Spaniards. For example, during the 1570s, in attempting to crush rebellion in the Low Countries,

> The Duke of Alba's Army of Flanders . . . captured and sacked several Dutch-held cities, treating the occupants with terrible ferocity and bringing the revolt to the brink of collapse, but . . . continuing difficulties in finding the money to pay his armies led to mutinies by the Army of Flanders in July and November 1576. Unlike Alba's earlier massacres, the resultant sacking and pillage of Aalst and the "Spanish Fury" at Antwerp—an orgy of killing, raping and looting in which 8,000 were slaughtered by soldiers "executing all such as they overtook . . . great numbers of young children, but many more women" . . . —were not deliberate acts of policy, but the result of the bloodlust of his mutinous soldiers.[22]

Things only got worse for the inhabitants of the Low Countries when the Duke of Parma—the illegitimate nephew of Philip II and a hero of the naval victory of Lepanto over the Turks—arrived in the Low Countries. Starting in 1578, Parma showed that his master, Philip II, was no longer going to play the nice guy:

> Parma surrounded the castle [defending the small Dutch town of Sichem] and reduced its walls but, seeking to make an example that would send a message throughout The Netherlands, he refused to accept its surrender and after overrunning the defences he ordered the commander hanged from the highest tower of the castle. . . . All the other officers and men were then hung by their feet from every window and tree, or marched through the castle hall between lines of Spanish soldiers and clubbed to death.[23]

After being promoted to supreme commander in the Low Countries by Philip II for his capture of Sichem, the Spanish commander did not change his conduct:

> Parma next led another savage onslaught on Maastricht, leaving 1,700 women and thousands of men butchered in the streets when the city fell, and when the town of Lierre was betrayed to him by its Scottish Catholic commander, Colonel William Semple, it was then reduced to rubble. Yrpes prepared itself for a siege by sending out of its gates all those inhabitants too young, too old or infirm to fight. Parma refused to allow them through his lines and, trapped without shelter, food or water, they remained encamped in no-man's-land, dying by hundreds, until the final storming of the town, when those who had survived were slaughtered like their menfolk.[24]

A [sixteenth-century] print of
atrocities commited by the
Spanish in the Low Countries.
(*Author*)

Many students of the conquistadors argue over the truth of the supposedly Las Casas-inspired Black Legend of Spain in the Americas, a
view admittedly advanced by Spain's European enemies. Yet one might
do well to ask the Dutch (traditionally Protestant) and the Flemish
(traditionally Catholic) whether Spain deserved the reputation of the
Black Legend.[25]

Of course, for the Spanish, as well as other Roman Catholics of the
sixteenth century, there supposedly was no legal hypocrisy in being concerned about the earthly welfare of New World pagans but not about
Old World Protestants (especially when they occasionally intruded on
the papal-authorized grant of most of the Western Hemisphere to
Spain). Las Casas, the Dominican friar and the great defender of the
natives of the New World, epitomizes this double standard.

At the same time that Las Casas compassionately argued that pagan
Indians were human and ought not to be forced to become Christians
(meaning Catholics)—because they were outside the jurisdiction of the
Church—he had no such sympathy for those who chose to be
Protestant (or were born Protestant). In his clerical view, while heresy
was tolerated before Western Christianity was institutionalized and
hierarchized into the Roman Catholic Church, it was only "because it
[the church] did not have the protection of rulers from among the
faithful."

"[H]eretics must be judged differently from pagans," argued the
legalistic Las Casas, "who must be attracted and invited to the faith
with kindness and mildness, but not forced." No such kindness and
mildness should be extended Protestants, wrote Las Casas, for "they are
rebellious traitors, disobedient enemies, and active workers against the
state. . . . Therefore, since heretics have come under the jurisdiction of

the Church (as has been proved), it can lawfully punish them by the hands of Christian rulers for the reasons we have frequently cited."[26]

As heretics, rebels, traitors, and dangerous enemies (even foreigners whose rulers then claimed to be outside the jurisdiction of Rome, Vienna, and Madrid), they could be subjected to all the awful punishments and torments unfairly imposed on the Indian pagans by Coronado and other conquistadors. Such was the legal opinion of a man now lionized as saintly.[27]

While current historians are correct that Coronado's army committed atrocities and probable war crimes, that is an easy conclusion. War by its nature is like the old-time punishment of flogging: it usually makes good men bad and bad men worse. However, what should be demanded of these scholars is answering the more difficult question: if the brutality was legal or acceptable in Europe at the time, did that make it any less legal or acceptable in the New World?

And, if it was not acceptable in either location, then the modern scholars of the New World must acknowledge that the native peoples were treated no worse than their European counterparts when the Spanish imported their art of warfare into the Western Hemisphere. Indeed, to the extent that the Spaniards (especially Coronado) regretted being brutal to the Indians (sometimes sparing women and children), the natives were treated better than their European counterparts, for the Spanish commanders and their priests had no guilty consciences when it came to activities in the Low Countries or crimes against Europeans in the New World. Again, while this does not make the conduct acceptable to disinterested parties, it does mean that the victims of the Coronado Expedition (or other expeditions) are only entitled to the same amount of historical sympathy and moral outrage as accorded European (or African, or Asian, or Indian, or Muslim) victims of Spain.[28]

In any event, while the Black Legend of Spanish conduct is amply supported in Europe and the Americas, there certainly were occasions when the color was one of many shades of gray. Also, empire building and war are always brutal and unsparing. This was doubly so during the sixteenth century, a period in which the Spanish were the best (and the worst) soldiers there were.[29] Wrote a French professional soldier of the time, "God [has] had need to be merciful to men of our trade, who commit so many sins and are the causers of many miseries and mischiefs."[30]

# Conclusion

*Assessing the Earliest Military Expedition*
*into the American Southwest*

Personally, Francisco Vasquez de Coronado may not have prevailed when it came to his expedition, but as a model military leader was supposed to do, he involved himself completely in his command, fighting side by side with his men, leading from the front rather than pushing from the rear. And he received honorable wounds in the service of his emperor and of his faith.

He also survived to return home to his beautiful wife. Although the days of his being a golden boy in New Spain were over, he remained reasonably active in local politics and was moderately prosperous. In September 1554, at about age forty-four, he died, apparently in bed, and he and his wife are buried in Mexico City.[1]

Merely by dying in bed peacefully, he proved himself a lucky conquistador. Ponce de Leon was severely wounded by an arrow in Florida in 1521 and died miserably (in bed) back in Cuba soon thereafter.[2] Both Panfilo de Narvaez and Hernando De Soto died in harness—vainly seeking their El Dorados in that same Florida—with Narvaez being lost at sea and De Soto dying of fever and being buried in the muddy Mississippi. Francisco Pizarro, who found his prize, was murdered by other conquistadors in Peru in 1541, while his half-brother, Gonzalo Pizarro, was beheaded in Peru in 1548 for treason against the Spanish crown.[3] Therefore, Francisco Vasquez de Coronado was most fortunate as a conquistador, even for one who lost most of his fortune and much of his reputation. He stayed out of prison and died in bed about a dozen years after he gave up soldiering.

But what of Coronado's expedition? How did it fare once the shouting stopped, and how ought it be judged by history in military terms?

One noted scholar of the Spanish Borderlands wrote eighty years ago, "Coronado, the pioneer, symbolizes the northward movement of Spain's frontiers in western America. . . . His odyssey to Quivira initiated on the plains a long procession of Spanish explorers."[4] While this might be the academic historian's perspective, the Spanish of New Spain did not seem to cherish much else about the expedition. Perhaps because everyone remembered only Quivira and the great herds of buffalo, even the fact that they had traveled through New Mexico generally was forgotten by the Spanish.[5]

Indeed, another scholar of the inland voyage concluded, "Contemporaries regarded Francisco Vazquez de Coronado's great *entrada* in search of the seven cities of Cibola as a failure in that no wealthy region was opened to conquest and exploitation."[6] This was viewing the expedition as a treasure-hunting venture, certainly not as a preliminary reconnaissance or an actual military campaign into a foreign domain.

Although not considered anything to brag about by contemporary Spaniards, more current conclusions often are just as dismissive. "By most standards, the Coronado expedition was a disaster," noted the author of one recent article, basing his assessment on the economics of the situation—as did sixteenth-century Spaniards. According to this cost-benefit analysis, the venture cost the equivalent of $30 million but "found nothing like the fabled Seven Cities of Cibola, which were rumored to exist on the Great Plains"[7]

These opinions, whether from grasping contemporaries or from economics-school historians, fail to look at the endeavor as the military venture it was. But even an evaluation based on the expedition's assigned missions is difficult, for Coronado was charged with the more modern military task of nation building as much as he was assigned to conduct a mere conquest.

Thus, when Viceroy Mendoza appointed Coronado as a new captain general, he specifically made the mission one of finding new lands, including the "provinces of Acus and Cibola, and the seven cities and the kingdoms and provinces of Matata and Totonteac." Coronado was authorized to act as an occupying force, with the power to punish "those who may be rebellious or disobedient." In addition, during his "discovery and pacification" of these lands, Coronado was to protect and defend the natives of the land and "to bring its natives to the knowledge of our holy Catholic faith" and to bring the land within the authority of the royal crown.[8]

The expedition failed in its mission insofar as it was to participate in nation building, which, as modern military officers are able to attest, can be a more-difficult assignment than winning an actual campaign during active warfare. As observed by historian Richard Flint, with the Coronado Expedition there was no permanent Spanish settlement that would equate with a true, long-term conquest.[9] Indeed, even the hoped-for establishment of Christian missions to educate and convert the native peoples came to naught, for those Franciscans left behind either were murdered or forced to flee once the military force was gone. This situation, again, is a phenomenon still seen today: after a successful conclusion of fighting, the expensive and just-as-dangerous work has only started.

But despite Mendoza's broad stated goals, it is presumptuous to look at the Coronado Expedition as a military migration, sufficient in and of itself to build a new dependency of Spain. True, if there had been thriving and rich lands to conquer and to occupy, then the expedition would have acted at least as a reconnaissance in force, to be succeeded by a follow-up wave of reinforcements, bureaucrats, and settlers. This is really what happened in Mexico and Peru, for the actual conquests of Cortes and Pizarro followed earlier parties that scouted out the respective country, if only in an outline form and if only to confirm hearsay about what lay inland. In addition, Cortes and Pizarro were followed by officious and meddling bureaucrats and government and church officials— the ones who gave gray hair to the conquerors.

If Coronado's expedition did not succeed in establishing new provinces or building new Spanish communities, it still was a military march of impressive proportions. But it was not just a lengthy march of thousands of miles; it was one that was able to return to its base, something not all conquistador efforts were able to claim. Indeed, Coronado, although not a professional man-at-arms, successfully divided his force on a couple of occasions, balancing military necessity and combat effectiveness with logistical limitations.[10]

A comparison with the contemporaneous expedition of Hernando De Soto is telling, although one must factor in the disadvantage that De Soto's army of six hundred or so Spaniards entered a geographic and climatic area that was the guerrilla-warfare graveyard to so many Spanish hopes, while Coronado's *entrada* saw terrain and topography not dissimilar to much of Spain. But neither force operated in a European environment, one in which (according to British General

Henri Bouquet, writing two centuries later) there was "country cultivated and inhabited, where roads are made, magazines [arsenals] are established, and hospitals provided." Instead, the armies of Coronado and
De Soto found, in Bouquet's estimate of fighting North American
Indians, a "vast inhospitable desart [sic], unsafe and treacherous . . .
where victories are not decisive, but defeats are ruinous."[11]

Nonetheless, Coronado avoided a ruinous defeat in the vast wilderness. As far as is known, he abandoned no living Spaniard or Indian
auxiliary or camp follower.

In contrast to this record was the contemporaneous expedition of De
Soto. Even discounting the fact that De Soto, unlike Coronado, did not
survive his search for gold and glory, the De Soto Expedition barely
avoided the fate of Narvaez. According to American historian Cyrus
Townsend Brady: "Three hundred gaunt, haggard, starving, broken
men, naked, shoeless, hatless, with neither equipment nor weapon, save
here and there a dulled sword which their feeble arms could scarcely
lift, were all that were left of the proudest, gayest, and most splendid little army that had ever debarked upon our shores."[12]

By comparison, the bedraggled army of Coronado, although shrinking to a mere company as members dropped out along the way to
Mexico City, was a victorious host coming home. Unlike many other
conquistador endeavors in the Americas, Coronado's expedition,
assaulting and besieging rough-hewn citadels, successfully applied for-
malistic military doctrine.[13] Thus, considering the fact that it engaged
in so much fighting and weathered at least one severe winter,
Coronado's force suffered amazingly few casualties and losses, although
these are subject to mere estimation.[14]

While Coronado's final tally of the returning personnel apparently
has not survived, Richard Flint and Shirley Cushing Flint, privy to the
most-trivial details regarding the lives of many members of the expedition, have concluded that "relatively few of the European members of
the expedition died."[15] While this is a vague statement—and might
mean anywhere from thirty to eighty Spaniards who died in hostile
action, from sickness, or getting lost in the mountains or on the Great
Plains—the total certainly was acceptable to sixteenth-century military
scorekeepers. It seems telling that none of the complaints later leveled
against the captain general went into wastage of Spanish lives.[16] Based
on deaths mentioned in the chronicles, along with a reasonable extrapolation of wounded or sick who likely died, it would appear that only

forty or forty-five Spaniards died during the thirty-month expedition, including those killed defending the San Geronimo camps.

Likewise, the reported deaths among the Indian auxiliaries were very low. Coronado, when testifying about Viceroy Mendoza's care and concern regarding the Indians accompanying the expedition, claimed that "thirty Indians did not die in the said expedition, including the stops and trip back and forth."[17]

However, even acknowledging that the Spaniards would have taken the lead in the assaults on the pueblos, this reckoning by Coronado (which apparently excluded the nonwarrior Indian camp followers) almost certainly must have been too low. A tally of those known to have died of battle and sickness, or to have deserted, taken from contemporary or first-person accounts, would add up to at least thirty-five or forty-five (taking into account a reasonable extrapolation). But even this estimation is based only on those losses that were noted, and the Mexican Indian contribution to the fighting often was ignored. Nonetheless, whether the auxiliaries suffered total losses of thirty-some to a hundred, when it came to sacrificing the lives of the Indian allies, the Coronado Expedition was no Guzman campaign.

Neither was it a Guzman campaign regarding the devastation and casualties among the native Indians resisting the invasion. Taking into account that there were fights or battles with the Zuni, the Hopi, the people of Tiguex, the people of Pecos, and the Yumans, the likely seven hundred to a thousand deaths among the warriors of the invaded provinces was significant and regrettable but no holocaust. Of course, while not a result of policy, certainly there were numerous deaths among the native women and children—from the fighting but especially from hunger and exposure resulting from the presence of the temporary occupiers.[18]

Coronado's expedition, militarily, was a fine testament to the organizational, logistical, and fighting abilities of Spanish leaders and soldiers. From beginning to end, the army under Coronado remained a potent fighting force, although once it returned across the dangerous frontier, it quickly realized that it had no further reason to exist. But this realization is common to most armies—including the United States forces returning from the American Civil War.

However, while Coronado's force traversed a lot of countryside and fought pitched battles and besieged respectable fortresses, it "only" won battles; it did not wage a successful war to its logical end. For unlike many other epic (meaning nondisastrous) military marches in North America—such as that of Doniphan through the American Southwest into Mexico; Kearney through the American Southwest and on to California; and Sherman across Georgia and the Carolinas to meet up with Grant—Coronado's expedition was not truly decisive in result. It did not crush an enemy into the dust, it did not end a significant war, it did not permanently transfer real estate from one realm to another. In fact, it did not even effectively enforce Spain's title to much of North America, as later filibustering efforts from France would prove.

But if the expedition of Coronado was a march, it also was an invasion—sort of. While its limited purpose (especially with limited personnel) was not to encompass a full absorption of unknown lands into the Spanish Empire, it was intended to lead to that eventual accomplishment. Thus the *entrada* was militarily analogous to a raid into a hostile region, to be followed by a full invasion of permanent personnel and colonists if needed or justified.

One eminent military historian, Edward Longacre, has proposed a formula regarding what a successful raid would entail. Although written in the context of American Civil War cavalry, many of the points fit the Coronado Expedition, at least up to that last winter at Tiguex:

> First of all, the officer in charge had to be bold and aggressive but also prudent, capable of exercising strict authority when necessary and allowing subordinates the discretion to launch secondary operations when desirable. He had to be adept at meeting unexpected turns of events, at implementing contingency tactics, and at fighting on the defensive as well as on the offensive, as conditions warranted. Likewise, his subordinate officers had to be enterprising and imaginative, as well as deeply committed to serving their commander faithfully in moments calling for unity of purpose and action. Then, too, the common soldiers had to be adaptable and resourceful, willing to endure the hardships of a long march in any sort of weather, capable of acting with individual initiative but also as members as a unified team, and able to wield axes and crowbars with vigorous precision.[19]

A successful raiding force, according to Longacre, also must have a detailed knowledge of the area to be traversed and know the location of any enemy forces and civilian communities within the hostile region, often relying on reliable guides and scouts.[20] Keeping in mind the exploratory nature of the mission of Captain General Coronado, even these requirements were met as best they could be.

While scholars might debate the impact of Coronado's army and whether it was a success as a raid, the important thing—as the Wright brothers learned early on about flight—was that Coronado was able to walk away from the rough landing. The army entered the target area, it dutifully performed its assigned (feasible) missions, and it got out with relatively few scratches. Narvaez and De Soto could only have dreamed of such a fine end to an expedition.

Unfortunately, also comparing the expedition to a wartime raid, the effort did not positively advance Spanish interests in the regions traversed and did not lay positive groundwork for subsequent expeditions. As was the case in other borderlands incursions, the civilians victimized would not care whether their losses were due to a real invasion or a mere raid.[21] Also, while the severity during the Tiguex War might be viewed as harsh military necessity, that fine legal point in the law of war would not impress victim peoples—whether American Indian or European. According to Elizabeth A. H. John:

> Pueblos had much to remember in the interval [before other Spanish ventures]. The Spaniards could not be trusted; they violated the laws of hospitality; they consumed precious stores like a plague of locusts. They set great store by an emblem of crossed sticks, which they trusted to protect them. Spaniards could be killed and so could their fearsome horses, but the price of resisting them was death and destruction.[22]

In summary, the members of the expedition came, they saw, they conquered—but they did not occupy, and they certainly did not win the hearts and minds of the people. This lack of permanency and lack of persuading the new "subjects" to adhere to the Court of the Holy Roman Empire and to the doctrines of the Roman Catholic Church are merely epitomized by the destruction of the settlement at San Geronimo III and by the ruthless slaughter of Friar Padilla. Certainly the Southerners who never got over Sherman's March to the Sea had nothing over the people of Cibola and Tiguex.

Especially after the Coronado Expedition, under the European model, the new lands explored were Spanish territory only by right of discovery, not by right of occupancy. While this may have given Spain a superior legal right as to other European powers, such a right, in the long run, traditionally is only as valid as it is militarily defensible. But even in 1720, when the expedition under Pedro de Villasur was slaughtered somewhere in Nebraska by French-backed Pawnee, Spain proved incapable of enforcing its claims.[23]

Therefore, militarily speaking, the Spanish and their Indian auxiliaries were not defeated in battle. But neither did they win a meaningful victory in the northern lands. At best, it was a successful raid into a foreign territory, and it had been intended to be much more of an event in the geopolitics of the Spanish and the Hapsburgs. Like Charles V's brief capture and brief possession of Tunis on the North African coast, it was to have been more than a mere raid.

But this shortcoming did not mean that all the members of the expedition were soured on such adventures. Over a dozen years later, Captain Tristan de Arellano, as Tristan de Luna y Arellano, was selected to lead a major expedition to settle Florida. Unfortunately for Spain, it was another dismal attempt to conquer that dangerous land.[24]

Neither did the ordinary expedition members think they had been militarily bested because of a failure to gain certain broad geopolitical goals; far from it. According to that chronicler of the expedition, Castaneda, those veterans, as they aged, "now when it is too late they enjoy telling about what they saw, and even of what they realize that they lost," and some of them "amuse themselves now by talking of how it would be to go back and proceed to recover that which is lost."[25] Juan Troyano, Coronado's opinionated artilleryman and bridge builder, wrote Philip II in 1568 that he thought a new expedition should be mounted to save those native souls who had been abandoned to paganism. As a man married to one of those natives, he also volunteered to accompany this new endeavor in order to look after the rights of the Indians.[26]

For his part, Pedro de Castaneda, when he wrote his important account of the expedition some twenty years later (while living in genteel poverty in Culiacan), seemed to have gained an appreciation for what he and his fellows had done, along with an understanding of the limited gains that had accrued for individuals and for Spain. "[M]ost people very often make things of which they have heard, and about which they have perchance no knowledge, appear either greater or less than they are," he wrote. "They make nothing of those things that amount to something and those that do not they make so remarkable that they appear to be something impossible to believe. This may very well have been caused by the fact that, as that country was not permanently occupied, there has not been any one who was willing to spend his time in writing."[27]

While Castaneda thus recognized the disappointing result of the expedition, he nonetheless had the pride of a veteran soldier in what he and his ordinary fellows had done:

> I am not writing fables, like some of the things which we read about nowadays in the books of chivalry. If it were not that those stories contained enchantments, there are some things which our Spaniards have done in our own day in these parts, in their conquests and encounters with the Indians, which for deeds worthy of admiration, surpass not only the books already mentioned, but also those which have been written about the twelve peers of France, because if the deadly strength which the authors of those times attributed to their heroes and the brilliant and resplendent arms with which they adorned them, are fully considered, and compared with the small stature of the men of our time and the few and poor weapons which they have in these parts, the remarkable thing which our people have undertaken and accomplished . . . are more to be wondered at to-day than those of which the ancients write, and just because, too, they fought with barbarous naked people, as ours have with [brave and valiant] Indians. . . . I have said all this in order to show that some things which we consider fables may be true, because we see greater things every day in our own times, just as in the future time people will greatly wonder at the deeds of Don Fernando Cortes, who dared to go into the midst of New Spain with 300 men against the vast number of people in Mexico, who with 500 Spaniards succeeded in subduing it, and made himself lord over it in two years.[28]

Thus for Castaneda and his impoverished fellows, their experiences were not unlike those of many veterans of almost any war of any era: while they never would seek to go through those particular travails again, they would not sell the memory of those experiences shared with their band of brothers for a million golden ducats. To them, the expedition had been a youthful disappointment, but certainly no embarrassing disaster of which they should be individually or corporately ashamed.[29]

As far as these ordinary Spaniards were concerned, they had done everything asked of them—and more. During battle, it certainly was not the thought of earthly wealth that motivated, but the desire to survive and to support "our people"—each other—in the fight. Once they had been soldiers, and they had emerged victorious—bloodied and without angels' wings, but victorious.

# Notes

## Introduction

1. See Albert L. Hurtado, *Herbert Eugene Bolton: Historian of the American Borderlands* (Berkeley and Los Angeles: University of California Press, 2012), 214–215.

2. See David Weber, *The Spanish Frontier in North America* (New Haven, CT: Yale University Press, 1992), 346–353. For the convenience of American readers, most of the Spanish names in this volume will be abbreviated or modified to conform with popular memories based on public school education, past histories, high school mascots, and automakers. Thus, for example, it usually will be *Coronado* and *De Soto*. While such names as Vasquez (Vazquez) and Cortes (Cortez) are anyone's call, consistency—hopefully not Emerson's foolish consistency—will be the watchword, albeit outside of direct quotations.

3. See Michael R. Oudijk and Matthew Restall, "Mesoamerican Conquistadors in the Sixteenth Century," in Laura E. Matthew and Michael R. Oudijk, eds., *Indian Conquistadors: Indian Allies in the Conquest of Mesoamerica* (Norman: University of Oklahoma Press, 2007), 43.

4. See, for example, Elizabeth A. H. John, *Storms Brewed in Other Men's Worlds: The Confrontation of Indians, Spanish, and French in the Southwest, 1540–1795* (College Station: Texas A&M University Press, 1975), xiv (discussing the Boltonian school).

5. Among the numerous horror stories of Spanish colonial documents being tossed into both European and American dustbins in the nineteenth century is the one in which many old documents in Santa Fe were used as kindling by one US territorial governor. See Frederick W. Hodge, ed., "The Narrative of the Expedition of Coronado, by Pedro De Castaneda," in J. Franklin Jameson, gen. ed., *Original Narratives of Early American History: Spanish Explorers in the Southern United States, 1528–1543* (New York: Charles Scribner's Sons, 1907), 373–374n1 (hereafter cited as Hodge, "Narrative by Castaneda").

6. For a mere hint of the impact of Flint and Cushing Flint in targeting the expedition for many others, the bibliography should suffice.

7. In attempting to resolve contradictions and seemingly irreconcilable differences between the documents and especially the bits of nonverbatim testimony, the author—who certainly is not infallible—will resort to his thirty-five years' professional experience of listening to witnesses, cross-examining witnesses, and (in particular) analyzing verbatim and nonverbatim testimonial transcripts and synthesizing plausible logical conclusions.

8. James D. Tracy, *Emperor Charles V, Impresario of War: Campaign Strategy, International Finance, and Domestic Politics* (Cambridge: Cambridge University Press, 2002), 8.

9. See, for example, Herbert L. Osgood, *The American Colonies in the Seventeenth Century* (New York: MacMillan, 1904), 1:396–526; 2:375–400. This historical school, of course, must rely on the sometimes questionable assumptions that official policies and statutes are both funded and followed.

10. David Eltis, *The Military Revolution in Sixteenth Century Europe* (London: Tauris Academic Studies, 1995), 1.

11. "Military history is also the study of weapons and weapons systems, of cavalry, of artillery, of castles and fortifications, of the musket, the longbow, the armoured knight, of the ironclad battleship, of the strategic bomber." John Keegan, *The Face of Battle* (New York: Dorset, 1986), 32.

12. John Sadler and Stephen Walsh, *Flodden 1513: Scotland's Greatest Battle* (Botley, UK: Osprey, 2006), 32.

13. A. H. Burne, *The Battlefields of England* (London: Penguin, 1996), xix–xx. Burne would then test his hypothesis against the records "to see whether it discloses any incompatibility with the accepted facts" and, if it did, he would repeat the process to refine the result.

14. Cf. Philippe Contamine, *War in the Middle Ages*, trans. Michael Jones (New York: Basil Blackwell, 1984), 236–237.

15. For example, during the very beginning of the archaeological renaissance now sweeping across peninsular Virginia regarding seventeenth-century Jamestown settlements, a respected—and refreshingly candid—archaeologist working for Colonial Williamsburg initially thought that the remains of a "patch box" found in an excavated pit was a relic for holding facial cosmetic patches. Only later was he informed that it was a patch box for holding bits of cloth needed to seat musket balls. See Ivor Noel Hume, *Martin's Hundred* (New York: Knopf, 1983), 130–135, 183.

16. For dates, the author will rely on the itinerary set out in George Parker Winship, "The Coronado Expedition, 1540-1542," *Fourteenth Annual Report of the U.S. Bureau of American Ethnology*, 1892–1893, Part 1 (Washington, DC: U.S. Bureau of American Ethnology, 1896), 341–344, supplemented by the chronologies in A. Grove Day, *Coronado's Quest: The Discovery of the Southwestern States* (Berkeley: University of California Press, 1940), 371–380, and in Richard Flint, tr. and ed., *Great Cruelties Have Been Reported: The 1544 Investigation of the Coronado Expedition* (Dallas: Southern Methodist University Press, 2002), 5–9.

17. Israel Sanz Sanchez, "Juan Jaramillo's 'Relacion': A Philological Reassessment of the Historical Approaches to a Document of the Coronado Expedition," *New Mexico Historical Review* 86, no. 1 (Winter 2011): 21.

18. When it comes to sixteenth-century Spanish, there are two schools of thought regarding literal translation versus free translation (to preserve "the spirit and vigorous" language of the original). See John E. Longhurst, tr. and ed., *Alfonso De Valdes and the Sack of Rome* (Albuquerque: University of New Mexico Press, 1952), 16n41.

19. See Winship, "Coronado Expedition," 470–563.

20. Hodge, "Narrative by Castaneda," 276. Thus, presumably, Hodge's version included revisions made by Winship in a 1904 edition of Castaneda. See Donald C. Cutter, *The Journey of Coronado, 1540-1543; Translated and Edited by George Parker Winship* (Golden, CO: Fulcrum, 1990), xxix.

21. See John Miller Morris, ed., and Pedro de Castaneda of Najera, *Narrative of the Coronado Expedition* (Chicago: R. R. Donnelly & Sons, 2002), lxxiii (prefers and uses the translation by New Mexico historians of the 1940s, George Hammond, Agapito Rey).

22. It also ought to be noted that while the 450th anniversary of the De Soto Expedition saw a healthy rebirth of continuing scholarship into that historic voyage, the scholarly output among the Coronado *aficionados* has been relatively more impressive. For this fact, Flint and Cushing Flint deserve a lion's and lioness's share of the credit.

23. Richard Flint has described his years of dedicated scholarship and publication (along with those endeavors of his wife, Shirley Cushing Flint) as an attempt not to "see the elephant" but to describe the Coronado "elephant" to the blind men of the East Indian parable. He therefore modestly lays claim to at least exposing "part of the elephant." Richard Flint, "What They Never Told You About the Coronado Expedition," *Kiva: The Journal of Southwestern Anthropology and History* 71, no. 2 (Winter 2005): 203–204, 213.

## CHAPTER ONE: THE MILITARY REVOLUTION OF THE SIXTEENTH CENTURY

1. Angus Konstam, *The Spanish Armada: The Great Enterprise Against England, 1588* (Botley, UK: Osprey, 2009), 74–76.

2. John Lothrop Motley, *The Rise of the Dutch Republic*, 3 vols. (New York: Harper & Brothers, 1883), 1:77.

3. *See* Judith Hook, *The Sack of Rome, 1527* (London and Basingstoke: Macmillan London, 1972), 288; E. R. Chamberlin, *The Sack of Rome* (New York: Dorset, 1985), 197–198.

4. John Calvin, *Institutes of the Christian Religion*, trans. Henry Beveridge, 2 vols. (Grand Rapids, MI: Wm. B. Eerdmans, 1981), 16, 20.

5. The Peasant Wars in Germany, the most serious occurring in 1525–1526, were known for the occasional brutality of the peasants against their social superiors and the wholesale massacre of tens of thousands of peasants (of both sexes and all ages) when the peasant forces were defeated in battle by armored men-at-arms and other professional soldiers. See E. Belfort Bax, *The Peasants War in Germany, 1525–1526* (New York: Augustus M. Kelley, 1968), 353–354.

6. See Motley, *Rise of the Dutch Republic*, 2:68–72, 3:63–67, 3:466–467. The uncompromising Reformed Christian theology of Calvin, epitomized by the clarion call to congregations of, "No popes, no bishops, no kings," did indeed spill over into secular political affairs, to the detriment of various monarchs. See Dorothy Mills, *Renaissance and Reformation Times* (New York: G. P. Putnam's Sons, 1939), 220, 242, 260.

7. See Hans J. Hillerbrand, *The Division of Christendom: Christianity in the Sixteenth Century* (Louisville, KY: Westminster John Knox Press, 2007), 190–191.

8. William Maltby, *The Reign of Charles V* (Basingstoke, UK: Palgrave, 2002), 43.

9. Ibid.

10. Martin Luther, "On War against the Turk (1529)," in C. M. Jacobs, trans. and ed., *Works of Martin Luther*, vol. 5 (Philadelphia: A. J. Holman Co. and Castle Press, 1931), 88. Erasmus, in 1530, also thought it should be a secular defensive war and not a crusade, but strangely claimed Luther did not believe in defending Europe against the Turk. See Norman Housley, ed. and trans., *Documents on the Later Crusades, 1274–1580* (New York: St. Martin's, 1996), 178–183.

11. However, in 1578, when the then more open-minded Portuguese made their regrettable decision to invade Morocco, their army included German Lutherans, whose regiments even included Lutheran chaplains. See John Laband, *Bringers of War: The Portuguese in Africa during the Age of Gunpowder and Sail from the Fifteenth to the Eighteenth Century* (London: Frontline, 2013), 16.

12. Maltby, *Reign of Charles V*, 44–45.

13. See Ibid., 45–47.

14. Hillerbrand, *Division of Christendom*, 190–191.

15. David Nicolle, *Granada 1492: The Twilight of Moorish Spain* (Westport, CT: Praeger, 2005), 7.

16. Motley, *Rise of the Dutch Republic*, 1:77.

17. Harald Kleinschmidt, *Charles V: The World Emperor* (Stroud, UK: Sutton, 2004), 144.

18. See Jacques Heers, *The Barbary Corsairs: Warfare in the Mediterranean, 1480–1580*, trans. Jonathan North (London: Greenhill, 2003), 77–78.

19. Gerhard Benecke, *Maximilian I (1459-1519): An Analytical Biography* (London: Routledge & Kegan Paul, 1982), 53.

20. Nicolle, *Granada 1492*, 12.

21. See, for example, Eltis, *Military Revolution*, 136–139. While many military scholars believe the changes in this one-hundred-year period were so rapid and so significant as to equate with a revolution in warfare, others have not been so sure regarding whether there was a true revolution in the sixteenth century, or in an earlier century, or in a later century, or within a number of centuries, or—if it was over several centuries—actually a "military evolution." See Col. Oliver Lyman Spaulding, Capt. Hoffman Nickerson, Col. John Womack Wright, *Warfare: A Study of Military Methods from the Earliest Times* (Washington, DC: Infantry Journal, 1937), 415 ("[T]he sixteenth century is transitional between the medieval and modern worlds."); John Childs, *Warfare in the Seventeenth Century* (London: Cassell, 2001), 17 ("These cautious and unspectacular changes [between 1450 and 1700 were] evolutionary, not revolutionary."); Niccolo Machiavelli, *The Art of War*, trans. and ed. Christopher Lynch (Chicago: University of Chicago Press, 2003), xxviii ("But no rapid change took place" militarily during the century.); Albert F. Calvert, *Spanish Arms and Armour, Being a Historical and Descriptive Account of the Royal Armoury of Madrid* (London: John Lane, the Bodley Head, 1907), 38 (With the introduction of firearms and other offensive weapons, "The fourteenth century witnessed a notable transformation in military equipment."); William L. Shea, *The Virginia Militia in the Seventeenth Century* (Baton Rouge: Louisiana State University Press, 1983), 2 (In the sixteenth century, Europe "experienced a 'military revolution'"); Sir Charles Oman, *The Sixteenth Century* (New York: E. P. Dutton, c. 1936), 211 (The end of the sixteenth century arrived "with cavalry still in the ascendant. . . . Infantry never came to its own till the invention of the [socket] bayonet put an end to the clumsy division of every unit into pikemen and musketeers—and enabled every musketeer to become his own pikeman."). See also James Raymond, *Henry VIII's Military Revolution: The Armies of Sixteenth-Century Britain and Europe* (London: Tauris Academic Studies, 2007), 1, 180–181. As an interesting contrast where the first half of the sixteenth century clearly did not show a revolution in military thought and practice (in a European nation still saddled with a backward reputation), see Alexander Filjushkin, *Ivan the Terrible: A Military History* (London: Frontline, 2008), 17.

22. John R. Hale, *The Art of War and Renaissance England* (Washington, DC: Folger Shakespeare Library, 1961), 1.

23. It has been said, "Gunpowder proper was used for the first time [in Europe] in the Spanish wars with the Moors in the twelfth century by both combatants." Charles Henry Ashdown, *British and Foreign Arms and Armour* (London and Edinburgh: T. C. and E. C. Jack, 1909), 361.

24. Robert Jones, *Knight: The Warrior and World of Chivalry* (Botley, UK: Osprey, 2011), 223.

25. F. L. Taylor, *The Art of War in Italy, 1494–1529* (London: Greenhill, 1993), 8.

26. See Taylor, *Art of War in Italy*, 8. Thus, in the first half of the sixteenth century, military distances often were expressed in terms of "a crossbow shot." The second half of the century saw the adoption of the "arquebus shot" or "musket shot" as a unit of distance.

27. Sir Charles Oman, *A History of the Art of War in the Sixteenth Century* (London: Methuen, 1937), 223–224.

28. Taylor, *Art of War in Italy*, 34, 37, 43.

29. See William H. Prescott, *History of the Reign of Ferdinand and Isabella the Catholic*, 3 vols., new and rev. ed. (Philadelphia: J. B. Lippincott, 1882), 3:150.

30. Hale, *Art of War*, 10; Prescott, *History of the Reign*, 2:280–281; Machiavelli, *Art of War*, 38–39.

31. See Taylor, *Art of War in Italy*, 58–59.

32. Ibid., 59.

33. Ian Roy, ed., *Blaise de Monluc: The Hapsburg-Valois Wars and the French Wars of Religion* (London: Longman Group, 1971), 41.

34. See Taylor, *Art of War in Italy*, 56.

35. Ibid., 61–63.

36. Ibid., 66–67.

37. Ibid., 65.

38. Ibid., 67. George Goodwin, *Fatal Rivalry: Henry VIII, James IV and the Battle for Renaissance Britain, Flodden 1513* (London: Weidenfeld & Nicolson, 2013), 189 (The armor of a dismounted man-at-arms "not only gave the wearer protection but could make him physically the hub of a fighting unit, rather like a Second World War tank with its supporting infantry exploiting the gaps it made in enemy defences."). However, unlike the English and the Spanish, the rest of Europe's men-at-arms were more reluctant to abandon their horses in attacking a fortified position. See Antonio Santosuosso, *Barbarians, Marauders, and Infidels: The Ways of Medieval Warfare* (Cambridge, MA: Westview, 2004), 283, 291; Christopher Hare, *Charles de Bourbon: High Constable of France, "The Great Condottiere"* (London: John Lane the Bodley Head, 1911), 77–78, 220, 271. The haughty French men-at-arms, in particular, who so often came to grief against the English because of hubris, were slow to accept their duty to lead the way dismounted. See Spaulding, Nickerson, and Wright, *Warfare*, 434–435.

39. Pierre de Bourdeille and C.-A. Saint-Beuve, *Illustrious Dames of the Court of the Valois Kings*, trans. Katharine Prescott Wormeley (New York: Lamb, 1912), 6–7.

40. Taylor, *Art of War in Italy*, 64–65.

41. See Ibid., 69–71.

42. Christopher Duffy, *Siege Warfare: The Fortress in the Early Modern World, 1494–1660* (New York: Barnes & Noble Books, 1996), 8–9.

43. See Funcken and Funcken, *Age of Chivalry, Part 3*, 99–100.

44. See Duffy, *Siege Warfare*, 9.

45. Roy, *Blaise de Monluc*, 107.

46. See Duffy, *Siege Warfare*, 8–9. In the early fifteenth century, England and Italy supposedly also led the way in some aspects of gunnery. See Funcken and Funcken, *Age of Chivalry, Part 3*, 90.

47. Nicolle, *Granada 1492*, 26.

48. See Duffy, *Siege Warfare*, 63–64.

49. See George Cameron Stone, *A Glossary of the Construction, Decoration and Use of Arms and Armor in All Countries and in all Times* (New York: Jack Brussel, 1961), 159–160.

50. Taylor, *Art of War in Italy*, 39.

51. Ibid.

52. Jack Coggins, *The Fighting Man: An Illustrated History of the World's Greatest Fighting Forces Through the Ages* (Garden City, NY: Doubleday, 1966), 153.

53. Andre Corvisier, *Armies and Societies in Europe, 1494–1789*, trans. Abigail T. Siddall (Bloomington: Indiana University Press, 1979), 12.

54. Contamine, *War in the Middle Ages*, 211.

55. Calvert, *Spanish Arms and Armour*, 60.

56. Cf. Hale, *Art of War*, 54.

57. See F. L. Taylor, *Art of War in Italy*, 158.

58. Machiavelli, *Art of War*, xi, xxvi. Much of this volume, while noting recent fighting, was a commentary on early Roman military methods.

59. For example, a new Latin language edition, translated by Theodore Gaza, of Aelian's military manual was published in Cologne in 1524. Christopher Matthew, trans. and ed., *The Tactics of Aelian, or, On the Military Arrangements of the Greeks: A New Translation of the Manual That Influenced Warfare for Fifteen Centuries* (Barnsley, UK: Pen & Sword Books, 2012), xv.

60. See Irving A. Leonard, *Books of the Brave: Being an Account of Books and of Men in the Spanish Conquest and Settlement of the Sixteenth-Century New World* (Cambridge, MA: Harvard University Press, 1949), 177, 202. Military biographies about such classical personages as Alexander the Great were used in the sixteenth century as helpful military books of instruction. See Sir John Smythe, *Certain Discourses Military*, ed. J. R. Hale (Ithaca, NY: Cornell University Press, 1964), 36n13. See also Contamine, *War in the Middle Ages*, 214.

## CHAPTER TWO: THE EARLY CONQUISTADOR ERA

1. Arthur Nelson, *The Tudor Navy: The Ships, Men and Organisation, 1485–1603* (Annapolis: Naval Institute Press, 2001), 31.

2. See, generally, Nicolle, *Granada 1492*.

3. Nelson, *Tudor Navy*, 31.

4. Ibid., 31–32. For a revisionist minority view rejecting this English (and Dutch and French) perspective that the pope presumed to divide the world, see Kleinschmidt, *Charles V*, 60–67.

5. See Hook, *Sack of Rome, 1527*, 20–26, 41, 148–150.

6. Peter Firstbrook, *The Voyage of the Matthew: John Cabot and the Discovery of North America* (London: BBC Books, 1997), 25. For a supportive contemporary Spanish Catholic opinion of decadent Rome, see Longhurst, *Alfonso De Valdes*, 50.

7. See Stephen R. Bown, *1494: How a Family Feud in Medieval Spain Divided the World in Half* (New York: Thomas Dunne/St. Martin's, 2012), 215.

8. See J. H. Elliott, *The Old World and the New, 1492–1650* (Cambridge: Cambridge University Press, 1978), 80–82.

9. See Kleinschmidt, *Charles V*, 50–51.

10. Firstbrook, *Voyage of the Matthew*, 148.

11. Maltby, *Reign of Charles V*, 87.

12. Hubert Howe Bancroft, *History of Mexico, Vol. 2, 1521–1600* (New York: Arno, 1967), 517.

13. See Weber, *Spanish Frontier*, 42, 55. See also Day, *Coronado's Quest*, 367n14. However, one respected scholar of Hapsburg Spain declared that "[b]y 1540 the greatest age of the *conquista* was over." J. H. Elliott, *Imperial Spain, 1469–1716* (New York: Mentor Books/New American Library, 1966), 61. While this assessment might be result oriented, based on the decreasing amount of mined, processed, and worked gold and silver revenue to be stolen from the natives, it ignores too many old-time expeditions—from Orellana on the Amazon River to Coronado's thrust beyond the northwest frontier of Mexico into terra incognita. It also would preclude consideration of the analogous Portuguese efforts to help reclaim Abyssinia from Muslim invaders, also occurring in the first years of the 1540s.

14. See T. Frederick Davis, "Ponce de Leon's First Voyage and Discovery of Florida," *Florida Historical Society Quarterly* 14, no. 1 (July 1935), 11–12. While an onerous rate, especially when no government services were provided, this royal 20 percent off the top also applied to those mining silver in Germany. See George H. Waring, "The Silver Miners of the Erzgebirge and the Peasant War of 1525 in the Light of Recent Research," *Sixteenth Century Journal* 18, no. 2 (Summer 1987), 231.

15. Herbert Eugene Bolton, *Spanish Explorations in the Southwest, 1542–1706* (New York: Charles Scribner's Sons, 1916), 3n1.

16. Oman, *Sixteenth Century*, 168.

17. See Harry Kelsey, *Juan Rodriguez Cabrillo* (San Marino, CA: Huntington Library, 1986), 28–43, 143–159. Cabrillo is one of those conquistadors claimed by both Portugal and by Spain. While Kelsey concludes that he was Spanish, that assessment is far from settled.

18. Indeed, some of Cortes's veteran conquistadors reportedly were present in the imperial army attacking Rome in 1527, and these were men who still lusted after gold, although it would be in the form of minted ducats and church chalices. See James H. McGregor, trans. and ed., *Luigi Guicciardini: The Sack of Rome* (New York: Italica, 1993), 81.

19. See Walter J. Karcheski Jr., *Arms and Armor of the Conquistador, 1492–1600* (Gainesville: Florida Museum of Natural History, 1990), [2]. This would be the type of warfare generally faced by De Soto in Florida.

20. Buckingham Smith, trans., *Relation of Alvar Nunez Cabeza de Vaca* (New York: Estate of Buckingham Smith, 1871), 39.

21. See Shea, *Virginia Militia*, 9. Shea was speaking only of the English.

22. William H. Prescott, *History of the Conquest of Mexico, with a Preliminary View of the Ancient Mexican Civilization and the Life of the Conqueror, Hernando Cortes*, new and rev. (Philadelphia: J. B. Lippincott, 1882), 1:280.

23. William H. Prescott, *History of the Conquest of Peru, with a Preliminary View of the Civilization of the Incas,* new and rev. (Philadelphia: J. B. Lippincott, 1883), 2:82–83.
24. David B. Ralston, *Importing the European Army: The Introduction of European Military Techniques and Institutions into the Extra-European World, 1600–1914* (Chicago: University of Chicago Press, 1990), 2.
25. Ralston, *Importing the European Army,* 11.
26. See Geoffrey Parker, ed., *The Cambridge Illustrated History of Warfare: The Triumph of the West* (Cambridge: Cambridge University Press, 1995), 2–3.
27. Anthony J. Bryant and Angus McBride, *Samurai, 1550–1600* (Botley, UK: Osprey, 1998), 50–51.
28. See Rene Chartand, *The Spanish Main: 1492–1800 (Fortress)* (Botley, UK: Osprey, 2006), 4.
29. Kleinschmidt, *Charles V,* 144.
30. Charles M. Robinson III, *The Spanish Invasion of Mexico, 1519–1521* (Botley, UK: Osprey, 2004), 22.
31. Patricia de Fuentes, ed. and trans., *The Conquistadors: First-Person Accounts of the Conquest of Mexico* (New York: Orion, 1963), 168.
32. Ibid., 168–169.
33. John Pohl and Charles M. Robinson III, *Aztecs and Conquistadors: The Spanish Invasion and the Collapse of the Aztec Empire* (Botley, UK: Osprey, 2005), 35–36.
34. See Smithsonian Institution and John R. Swanton, Chairman, *Final Report of the United States De Soto Expedition Commission* (Washington, DC: Government Printing Office, 1939), 293.
35. Roy, *Blaise de Monluc,* 50. Similarly, Otto von Bismarck observed that fools learned from their mistakes, but he learned from others' mistakes.
36. C. F. Beckingham and G. W. B. Huntingford, eds., *The Prester John of the Indies: A True Relation of the Lands of the Prester John, Being the Narrative of the Portuguese Embassy to Ethiopia in 1520 Written by Father Francisco Alvares,* 2 vols. (Cambridge: Published for the Hakluyt Society at the University Press, 1961), 2:516.
37. See David Mathew, *Ethiopia* (London: Eyre & Spottswoode, 1947), 36–37.
38. Charles R. Boxer, *The Portuguese Seaborne Empire: 1415–1825* (New York: Knopf, 1969), 73.

## CHAPTER THREE: PENETRATING WESTERN NORTH AMERICA

1. Just as the Aztec capital of Tenochtitlan (or Themistitan) ultimately became Mexico City, the province of Mexico, the land of the Aztecs, was rechristened New Spain by the conquerors. See Roger Schlesinger and Arthur P. Stabler, trans. and eds., *Andre Thevet's North America* (Kingston, ON, and Montreal: McGill University Press, 1986), 216–217. For convenience's sake, "Mexico" and "New Spain" will be used interchangeably hereafter.
2. See Andres Resendez, *A Land So Strange: The Epic Journey of Cabeza de Vaca* (New York: Basic Books, 2009), 26–36.
3. See William Cullen Bryant and Sidney Howard Gay, *A Popular History of the United States,* vol. I (New York: Charles Scribner's Sons, 1881), 151–152.
4. See ibid., 152–153.
5. See Resendez, *A Land So Strange,* 105–109.
6. See Bryant and Gay, *A Popular History,* 153–155.

7. See ibid., 156; Hodge, "Narrative by Castaneda," 288; Smith, *Relation of Alvar Nunez Cabeza de Vaca*, 41. Scholars are not unanimous that Esteban ethnically was a black African, rather than a Berber or other "fair-skinned" North African. See Douglas Preston, *Cities of Gold: A Journey across the American Southwest in Pursuit of Coronado* (New York: Simon & Schuster, 1992), 296. A quarter century ago, one eminent Coronado scholar was inclined to pronounce Esteban a Moroccan rather than a black African, although that scholar also erroneously substituted "Arab" for "Berber" for Esteban's nationality. See Cutter, *Journey of Coronado*, xxiii. There was one other known survivor of the Narvaez misadventure, Juan Ortiz, who was captured by the Indians, escaped death in the manner Captain John Smith later wrote of his salvation by Pocahontas, and ended up being rescued by the expedition of De Soto. While serving as an indispensible interpreter for De Soto, Ortiz died without ever seeing his home again. See Grace King, *De Soto and His Men in the Land of Florida* (New York: Macmillan, 1898), 20–30, 237.
8. See Donald E. Chipman and Harriett Denise Joseph, *Notable Men and Women of Spanish Texas* (Austin: University of Texas Press, 1999), 12–15, 18.
9. See Fuentes, *Conquistadors*, 197–198.
10. Hodge, "Narrative by Castaneda," 285–286.
11. See Fuentas, *Conquistadors*, 198.
12. Ibid., 199.
13. Arthur Scott Aiton, *Antonio de Mendoza: First Viceroy of New Spain* (Durham, NC: Duke University Press, 1927), 24. Guzman, during his endeavors, had four hundred Spaniards and supposedly "20,000 friendly Indians of New Spain" assisting him. Hodge, "Narrative by Castaneda," 286.
14. Fr. Angelico Chavez, O.F.M., *Coronado's Friars* (Washington, DC: Academy of American Franciscan History, 1968), 21–23. However, while the Franciscans had sympathy for the Indians, they also were subject to some of the biases of their times, for they were noted anti-Semites during the thirteenth century. Norman F. Cantor, *The Last Knight: The Twilight of the Middle Ages and the Birth of the Modern Era* (New York: Free Press, 2004), 37.
15. See Herbert Eugene Bolton, *Coronado: Knight of Pueblos and Plains* (New York and Albuquerque: Whittlesey House/University of New Mexico Press, 1949), 6.
16. See Fuentas, *Conquistadors*, 199–201.
17. Ibid., 203.
18. See ibid., 204.
19. Ibid., 204–205.
20. Ibid., 205.
21. Ibid., 206.
22. Ibid. See also Bolton, *Coronado*, 55.
23. Fuentas, *Conquistadors*, 207.
24. See Aiton, *Antonio de Mendoza*, 25.
25. Bolton, *Coronado*, 6–7.
26. Aiton, *Antonio de Mendoza*, 26.
27. To make matters worse for those who would attempt to salvage Guzman's reputation, he apparently was trained as a lawyer. Day, *Coronado's Quest*, 8.
28. Aiton, *Antonio de Mendoza*, 26. For one historian who saw Guzman as not as bad as all that, see Donald E. Chipman, *Nuno de Guzman and the Province of Panuco in New Spain, 1518–1533* (Glendale, CA: Arthur H. Clark Co., 1967).

29. See Aiton, *Antonio de Mendoza*, 34–40.

30. Bolton, *Coronado*, 10–11.

31. Ibid., 12; Smith, *Relation of Alvar Nunez Cabeza de Vaca*, 184–186.

32. Bolton, *Coronado*, 12; Smith, *Relation of Alvar Nunez Cabeza de Vaca*, 188, 190.

33. Bolton, *Coronado*, 12–13.

34. Ibid., 14–15.

35. See Smith, *Relation of Alvar Nunez Cabeza de Vaca*, ix–x.

36. Ibid., 144.

37. Ibid., 176–177.

38. Bolton, *Coronado*, 40–42.

39. See ibid., 44–45.

40. Leonard, *Books of the Brave*, 32–33.

41. *See* S. Baring-Gould, M.A., *Curious Myths of the Middle Ages* (Boston: Roberts Brothers, 1867), 30-53. As has been noted, Portuguese attempts to maintain contact with far-off Ethiopia—and to provide military support—will share other similarities with the Spanish dreams of finding—and subduing—notable potentates in the North American continent.

42. See Laband, *Bringers of War*, 61, 65.

43. Smith, *Relation of Alvar Nunez Cabeza de Vaca*, 132–136.

44. Ibid., 135.

45. See Ian Heath, *Armies of the Sixteenth Century: The Armies of the Aztecs and Inca Empires, Other Native Peoples of the Americas, and the Conquistadors, 1450–1608* (Guernsey, UK: Foundry Books, 1999), 165. Hereafter cited as Heath, *Armies of the Sixteenth Century [New World]*.

46. Smith, *Relation of Alvar Nunez Cabeza de Vaca*, 136.

47. Ibid., 39–40.

48. Ibid., 172. The presence of poisoned arrows in the sixteenth century might have been exaggerated both in Europe and in the Americas. For example, the French thought the arrows of the English longbowmen were poisoned because so many Frenchmen were killed on so many battlefields. Rust on the arrowheads (and this certainly also was an era in which excessive filth caused infections) was said by a sixteenth-century English defender of the use of the longbow to have been the real cause of festering arrow wounds. See Smythe, *Certain Discourses Military*, 75.

49. See Prescott, *History of the Reign*, 1:481. The Portuguese, in 1505, also fought Muslim bowmen on the east coast of Africa who were using poison-tipped arrows. See Laband, *Bringers of War*, 65.

50. See Carolly Erickson, *Bloody Mary: The Remarkable Life of Mary Tudor* (Garden City, NY: Doubleday, 1978), 202.

51. See Hugo Grotius. *The Law of War and Peace (De Jure Belli ac Pacis)*, trans. Louis R. Loomis (Roslyn, NY: Walter J. Black, 1949), 300.

52. Andres Resendez, "Cabeza de Vaca: A Desperate Trek across America," *American Heritage* 58, no. 5 (Fall 2008), 19.

53. See Bolton, *Coronado*, 18–19; Day, *Coronado's Quest*, 18–20. One historian, citing Bolton, incorrectly claims that "Mendoza freed Dorantes's slave, Esteban, and enlisted him to guide and aid Marcos." Stan Hoig, *Came Men on Horses: The Conquistador Expeditions of Francisco Vazquez de Coronado and Don Juan de Onate* (Boulder: University Press of Colorado, 2013), 28. Bolton said that Mendoza "acquired" Esteban. Bolton,

*Coronado*, 19. According to a sixteenth-century history, Dorantes, presumably out of some sense of friendship, refused to sell Esteban to the viceroy for five hundred pesos on a silver platter but acquiesced in lending his servant in the interest of the faith and the royal government. George P. Hammond and Agapito Rey, trans., *Obregon's History of 16th Century Explorations in Western America, Entitled Chronicle, Commentary, or Relation of the Ancient and Modern Discoveries in New Spain and New Mexico, Mexico, 1584* (Los Angeles: Wetzel, 1928), 8.

54. See George P. Hammond and Agapito Rey, *Narratives of the Coronado Expedition, 1540–1542* (Albuquerque: University of New Mexico Press, 1940), 59, "Instructions to Fray Marcos de Niza."

55. The Vatican, while still a secular military power, occasionally used its priests, traveling under presumed religious or diplomatic protection, to gain military intelligence on behalf of the Holy See. See Chamberlin, *Sack of Rome*, 84–85.

56. Hammond and Rey, *Narratives*, 59, "Instructions to Fray Marcos de Niza."

57. Ibid., 59-60, "Instructions to Fray Marcos de Niza."

58. Ibid., 60, "Instructions to Fray Marcos de Niza."

59. Ibid.

60. See Bolton, *Coronado*, 21. In ending the uprising, Coronado employed the assistance of Melchior Diaz. With the end of the rebellion, Coronado had its leader tried and executed by quartering. See Bolton, *Coronado*, 24. In addition, long after the rebellion was crushed, when an investigation was looking into his tenure as governor of New Galicia, Coronado blamed the outbreak on Diaz's having mistreated the natives. See Arthur S. Aiton, "Report on the Residencia of the Coronado Government in New Galicia," *Panhandle- Plains Historical Review* 13 (1940), 19.

61. See Hammond and Rey, *Narratives*, 63, "Report of Fray Marcos de Niza."

62. Hodge, "Narrative by Castaneda," 288.

63. Ibid., 288–289.

64. See Hammond and Rey, *Narratives*, 63, "Report of Fray Marcos de Niza." Marcos indicates Esteban was still with him when Onorato gave up.

65. Ibid., 66, "Report of Fray Marcos de Niza."

66. Ibid.

67. Ibid., 67–68, "Report of Fray Marcos de Niza."

68. Ibid., 71, "Report of Fray Marcos de Niza."

69. Ibid., 69, "Report of Fray Marcos de Niza."

70. Ibid., 71, "Report of Fray Marcos de Niza."

71. Hodge, "Narrative by Castaneda," 289.

72. Ibid., 289–290.

73. See Hammond and Rey, *Narratives*, 77, "Report of Fray Marcos de Niza."

74. Ibid., 75–76, "Report of Fray Marcos de Niza."

75. Ibid., 77, "Report of Fray Marcos de Niza."

76. Ibid., 76, "Report of Fray Marcos de Niza."

77. Ibid., 78–79, "Report of Fray Marcos de Niza."

78. Ibid., 79, "Report of Fray Marcos de Niza."

79. Ibid., 81, "Report of Fray Marcos de Niza."

80. Hsain Ilahiane, "Estevan—Moroccan Explorer of the American Southwest," *Archaeology Southwest* 19, no. 1 (Winter 2005), 11. However, a recent novel goes beyond even this, having at least two misstatements of fact in the title alone. See I. Mac Perry,

*Black Conquistador: The Story of the First Black Man in America* (Saint Petersburg, FL: Boca Bay Books, 1998).

81. Preston, *Cities of Gold,* 296.

82. With this initial episode of Indian warfare, it became more appropriate than ironic that three hundred years later, African Americans were in the United States Army, fighting alongside white soldiers to subjugate the region's natives.

83. Jesse Green, ed., *Zuni: Selected Writings of Frank Hamilton Cushing* (Lincoln: University of Nebraska Press/Bison Books, 1981), 173–174.

84. Ibid., 174.

85. Hammond and Rey, *Narratives,* 177–178, "Letter of Coronado to Mendoza, August 3, 1540." One writer has opined that because Esteban was said to be "not like the Christians," he might have been a pagan. See Preston, *Cities of Gold,* 297n. Unfortunately for this theory, the Spanish, to the detriment of other Christians who followed, always told the natives that they alone, not other Europeans (and certainly not Protestants), were Christians.

86. Winship, "Coronado Expedition," 366. For what it is worth, a writer twenty years later concluded that Niza did tell tall tales when he "was under the ministrations of the knight of the razor," commenting on the goldsmiths and silversmiths of Cibola. John Walker Harrington, "Cibola Revealed: Relics of Coronado's Seven Cities in a New York Museum," *Scientific American* 120, no. 2 (January 11, 1919), 24.

87. William K. Hartmann, "Pathfinder for Coronado: Reevaluating the Mysterious Journey of Marcos de Niza," in Richard Flint and Shirley Cushing Flint, eds., *The Coronado Expedition to Tierra Nueva: The 1540–1542 Route across the Southwest* (Niwot: University Press of Colorado, 1997), 100. Hartmann also notes that future historical and archaeological digging may yet vindicate much of the friar's tale.

88. Chavez, *Coronado's Friars,* 10.

89. Day, *Coronado's Quest,* 61.

90. See Winship, "Coronado Expedition," 367–369. It is true that de Niza, undoubtedly privy to the intelligence reported by Cabeza de Vaca, never gave credit to Vaca as a source of information. See Day, *Coronado's Quest,* 49.

91. Bolton, not one to step away from broad statements, said de Niza's report was "the story on which the Coronado Expedition was predicated." Bolton, *Coronado,* 38.

92. See Hodge, "Narrative by Castaneda," 87–88.

## CHAPTER FOUR: FINDING A GENERAL AND RECRUITING THE EXPEDITION

1. See Bolton, *Coronado,* 40–48. Proving that there was a two-way flow of European military knowledge in the sixteenth century, Cortes, by 1541, was providing advice to Charles V regarding an invasion of North Africa at Algiers. See Stephen Turnbull, *The Art of Renaissance Warfare: From the Fall of Constantinople to the Thirty Years War* (London: Greenhill, 2006), 98.

2. Cyrus Townsend Brady, *Colonial Fights and Fighters* (Garden City, NY: Doubleday, Page, 1913), 7.

3. Smythe and Hale, *Certain Discourses Military,* 18.

4. Kleinschmidt, *Charles V,* 145.

5. See Housley, *Documents on the Later Crusades,* 185–186.

6. Michael Wood, *Conquistadors* (Berkeley and Los Angeles: University of California Press, 2000), 108. Paid soldiery in Europe during this era actually was just part of military evolution, as the makeup of armies changed from feudal vassals to mercenaries. See Santosuosso, *Barbarians*, 278. Thus the establishment of entrepreneurial forces in the New World was also an evolutionary adaptation.

7. Flint and Cushing Flint, "Guido de Lavezariis," 2–3.

8. Bancroft, *History of Mexico*, 517. This was not unlike the situation in Italy, where some adventurer soldiers hoped to establish their own fiefdoms. See Santosuosso, *Barbarians*, 286.

9. Bancroft, *History of Mexico*, 517.

10. John, *Storms Brewed*, 14.

11. Bolton, *Coronado*, 71. But later, when defending certain brutalities as military necessity, Bolton reminded the reader, "The Indians of Arenal had killed horses belonging to the royal army." Bolton, *Coronado*, 213. For this relaxed style of pro-Spanish scholarship, Bolton early on received a Spanish knighthood. See Hurtado, *Herbert Eugene Bolton*, 155–156.

12. Stewart L. Udall, *To the Inland Empire: Coronado and Our Spanish Legacy* (Garden City, NY: Doubleday, 1987), 213.

13. See Ibid., 204–210. Since the present study is a military study, with some excitement but showing all the warts, there will be ammunition aplenty to argue either the Black Legend or the countervailing White Legend that washes Spain's deeds as white as snow. Cf. Weber, *Spanish Frontier*, 9.

14. Richard Flint, *No Settlement, No Conquest: A History of the Coronado Expedition* (Albuquerque: University of New Mexico Press, 2008), 57.

15. Also recently, in an effort to bolster the claims regarding the military efficacy of native warriors as allies, it has been asserted that "Spanish invaders in Mesoamerica were not soldiers in a formally structured army but armed members of companies of exploration, conquest, and—if successful—settlement." Oudijk and Restall, "Mesoamerican Conquistadors," 38. While this conclusion lacks much support—and would particularly surprise Spanish men-at-arms as well as footmen—it is particularly untrue here. Even if not regularly paid professionals or mercenaries, Coronado's force, as pointed out by Richard Flint, obviously conducted only a random exploration, which was "superficial and rudimentary" as it marched north (as befitting a military expedition with other specific aims). Flint, *No Settlement*, 78. And, other than attempting to establish a nascent presidio or two and attempting to embed priests with the native population, the expedition, unlike preliminary French and English attempts in the sixteenth century, obviously was not for settlement in the pioneering sense. Nonetheless, there is a recent statement that Coronado's endeavor was "a large group of 260 settlers and 60 soldiers in search of the fabled Seven Cities of Cibola." Henry Kamen, *Empire: How Spain Became a World Power, 1492–1763* (New York: HarperCollins, 2003), 245. This is a total misreading of the extant muster roll, as well as muddling the objectives of the expedition.

16. Of course, *conquistadors* as a general term was a later title. The sixteenth century Spaniards, at least those with Cortes, limited the term to those who served with Cortes in subduing Mexico. See Winship, "Coronado Expedition," 563n1. However, it was true that at the time of Coronado, *entradas* were considered conquests of new lands, a concept replaced by politically correct Spanish lawyers in 1573 with "pacification" of new lands. See Day, *Coronado's Quest*, 320, 369n13.

17. This is not to say that the Spanish did not create settlements. See Weber, *Spanish Frontier*, 7. However, Spain did not start off with the trading or colonizing companies of the British, Dutch, and Swedes. Neither did the Spanish perceive the Americas as a dumping ground for troublemakers, although Spain's competitors saw the potential of the new lands for relocating English and French dissenters or disenfranchised English Catholics. Nor did Spain have the somewhat laissez-faire attitude of the French in Canada when it came to "civilizing" the Indian natives.

18. Hodge, "Narrative by Castaneda," 291.

19. Hammond and Rey, *Obregon's History*, 13–14.

20. See James Lockhart and Enrique Otte, eds., *Letters and People of the Spanish Indies: Sixteenth Century* (Cambridge: Cambridge University Press, 2006), 3. Nonetheless, some apparently unfamiliar with the specifics of sixteenth-century European methods of recruitment and warfare have refused to designate Coronado's adventurers as soldiers. See, for example, Flint, "What They Never Told You," 206–207.

21. Aiton, *Antonio de Mendoza*, 36.

22. A. Grove Day, "Mota Padilla on the Coronado Expedition," *Hispanic American Historical Review* 20, no. 1 (February 1940), 91; Aiton, *Antonio de Mendoza*, 124.

23. See Marguerite Wood, *Flodden Papers: Diplomatic Correspondence between the Courts of France and Scotland, 1507–1517* (Edinburgh: T. and A. Constable, 1933), xv–xvi. In the early 1500s, King James IV of Scotland sought the position of captain general to lead a crusade against the Muslims.

24. Hammond and Rey, *Narratives*, 83–86, "Appointment of Coronado as Commander of the Expedition to Cibola, January 6, 1540."

25. See Bolton, *Coronado*, 19–21.

26. Ibid., 402. Probably supportive of having a fair complexion, Coronado reportedly was of noble French descent. Day, *Coronado's Quest*, 21.

27. Hammond and Rey, *Obregon's History*, 13.

28. George M. Addy, *The Enlightenment in the University of Salamanca* (Durham, NC: Duke University Press, 1966), xx–xxi.

29. There is no evidence that Coronado studied at the university. On the other hand, Cortes did study grammar for two years in Salamanca at the university. See Francisco Lopez de Gomara, *Cortes: The Life of the Conqueror by His Secretary*, ed. and trans. Lesley Byrd Simpson (Berkeley: University of California Press, 1964), 8; Pohl and Robinson, *Aztecs and Conquistadors*, 21.

30. See Maurice Keen, *Nobles, Knights and Men-at-Arms in the Middle Ages* (London: Hambledon, 1996), 189–191, 193–194, 210–211.

31. Richard M. Ketchum, ed., *The Horizon Book of the Renaissance* (New York: American Heritage, 1961), 78–79. For the life of the noted Giovanni delle Bande Nere, who led an adventurous life quite unlike that of Francisco Vasquez de Coronado, see Chamberlin, *Sack of Rome*, 81–83.

32. See Shirley Cushing Flint, "The *Sobresalientes* of the Coronado Expedition," in Richard Flint and Shirley Cushing Flint, eds., *The Latest Word from 1540: People, Places, and Portrayals of the Coronado Expedition* (Albuquerque: University of New Mexico Press, 2011), 13–32. Cushing Flint, while pointing out that there was only one true (genealogically valid) don in the force (Pedro de Tovar), argues that these upper-class volunteers constituted a governmental elite rather than mere dilettante adventurers. Portuguese gentlemen involved in this and other worldwide endeavors, the equivalent

of the hidalgos, were the *fidalgos*. See David Nicolle, *The Portuguese in the Age of Discovery, c. 1340–1665* (Botley, UK: Osprey, 2012), 13–14.

33. Hale, *Art of War*, 52.

34. See Richard Flint, *No Settlement*, 50–54.

35. See Marcelin Defourneaux, *Daily Life in Spain in the Golden Age*, trans. Newton Branch (New York: Praeger, 1971), 190–191.

36. See Arthur S. Aiton, *The Muster Roll and Equipment of the Expedition of Francisco Vazquez de Coronado* (Ann Arbor, MI: William L. Clements Library, 1939), 10, 20.

37. See Alexander Gallardo, *Spanish Economics in the Sixteenth Century: Theory, Policy, and Practice* (New York and Lincoln, NE: Writers Club Press, 2002), 25–26. At the same time, in the dual Kingdom of Aragon, the hidalgos made up a separate estate of nobles. Gallardo, *Spanish Economics*, 28. Presumably, this institutional difference would not shrink the number of hidalgos looking for employment.

38. The unwanted accumulation of the noninheriting sons of nobility and the gentry hardly was limited to the Spanish colonial experience and hardly limited to the sixteenth century. See, for example, John Milton Hutchins, *Diggers, Constables, and Bushrangers: The New Zealand Gold Rushes as a Frontier Experience, 1852–1876* (Lakewood, CO: Avrooman-Apfelwald Press, 2010), 273–274. In addition, throughout Europe, many third sons ended up in the military.

39. Day, "Mota Padilla," 91.

40. Flint, *No Settlement*, 54.

41. J. H. Elliott, *Imperial Spain, 1469–1716* (New York: Mentor Books/New American Library, 1966), 62. On the bright side, this resort to litigation probably was one reason the Spaniards, unlike much of the rest of Europe, were not known for killing each other through dueling. But some said (probably especially after the murder of the Prince of Orange in 1584) that the Spanish were committed instead to assassination rather than to dueling. See Barbara Holland, *Gentlemen's Blood: A History of Dueling from Swords to Pistols at Dawn* (New York: Bloomsbury, 2003), 23.

42. Elliott, *Imperial Spain*, 63.

43. See Ignacio Notario Lopez and Ivan Notario Lopez, *The Spanish Tercios, 1536–1704* (Botley, UK: Osprey, 2012), 14. The sixteenth century, with the Spanish and the French at the forefront, eventually saw the development of the important ranks of colonel and sergeant major at the regimental level. A Spanish or imperial camp master or army master was the equivalent of a senior captain or a colonel. See Tracy, *Emperor Charles V*, 31. The position would somewhat equate to the top of the pyramid in getting things done, as with a command sergeant major. See Eltis, *Military Revolution*, 54–59, 103, 125n52. See also Smythe, *Certain Discourses Military*, 35. The position would also include the duties of quartermaster, an office found in German Landsknecht armies. See John Richards, *Landsknecht Soldier, 1486–1560* (Botley, UK: Osprey, 2002), 15.

44. For these appointments, see generally, Hodge, "Narrative by Castaneda," 292–293.

45. Hodge, "Narrative by Castaneda," 310. Unfortunately, if Sotomayor ever wrote his chronicle, it never has surfaced.

46. Flint, *Great Cruelties*, 312, 315, "Alonso Alvarez, the Fourteenth de Oficio Witness."

47. See Notario Lopez and Notario Lopez, *Spanish Tercios*, 16.

48. See Hare, *Charles de Bourbon*, 296, 312.

49. Hammond and Rey, *Narratives*, 202, "Castaneda's History of the Expedition." This particular translation is more accurate than that of Hodge: "as part of their salaries . . . to those in the army who were in greatest need." Hodge, "Narrative by Castaneda," 293.

50. Smythe, *Certain Discourses Military*, 23.

51. Hammond and Rey, *Obregon's History*, 235. The many suggestions regarding proper crusading contained in this sixteenth-century history, produced subsequent to Coronado's Expedition, already might have been common military knowledge, but others might have been lessons learned specifically from the mistakes of Coronado's inland voyage.

52. See Aiton, *Muster Roll*, for the earliest English translation and printing of this important document.

53. Ibid., 26–27.

54. Ibid., 7–22. In more formal medieval times, a typical man-at-arms off to war might have six horses, one a warhorse of fourteen or fifteen hands (from Spain, Italy, or the Low Countries) and the others for various purposes, including a couple for packing. See Janet Barker, *Agincourt: Henry V and the Battle That Made England* (New York: Little, Brown, 2006), 116–117.

55. Aiton, *Muster Roll*, 26–27.

56. See Sadler and Walsh, *Flodden 1513*, 25. However, there is no hint of this particular problem with diminishing returns regarding the Coronado Expedition, at least until the endeavor was coming to an end.

57. Hodge, "Narrative by Castaneda," 291.

58. Richard Flint and Shirley Cushing Flint, eds. and trans., *Documents of the Coronado Expedition, 1539–1542: "They Were Not Familiar with His Majesty, nor Did They Wish to Be His Subjects"* (Dallas: Southern Methodist University Press, 2005), 136. In their reexamination of the original muster roll, Flint and Cushing Flint have shown it is much like a modern military table of organization and equipment. See Flint and Cushing Flint, *Documents*, 136–137.

59. Hodge, "Narrative by Castaneda," 292.

60. Ibid., 293. Regarding the brilliance of the individual Spaniard, while presumably most if not all of the gentlemen could read and write, this would not hold true for the lower ranks. As for Spain's army in Flanders, "there is no obvious way of measuring literacy in the Army. . . . One can only state the obvious and say that clearly a number of common soldiers *could* write their names and even compose a letter, but that a probably greater number could do neither." See Geoffrey Parker, *The Army of Flanders and the Spanish Road, 1567–1659: The Logistics of Spanish Victory and Defeat in the Low Countries' Wars* (Cambridge: Cambridge University Press, c. 1976), 172n1. Nonetheless, especially because of legal proceedings following Coronado's return, a sampling of the literate and illiterate soldiery is to be had.

61. Hodge, "Narrative by Castaneda," 293.

62. The more typical Spanish military officer of the period carried his home in his saddlebags, taking his entire estate of personal property and wealth on campaign. See Parker, *Army of Flanders*, 177.

63. Ian Heath, *Armies of the Sixteenth Century: The Armies of England, Scotland, Ireland, the United Provinces, and the Spanish Netherlands, 1487–1609* (Guernsey, UK: Foundry Books, 1997), 128. Hereafter cited as Heath, *Armies of the Sixteenth Century [European]*.

64. Nicolle, *Granada 1492*, 26.

65. Taylor, *Art of War in Italy*, 30n1.

66. Angus Konstam and Graham Turner, *Pavia 1525: The Climax of the Italian Wars* (Botley, UK: Osprey, 2001), 7, 17–18. Charles was emperor of the Spanish Empire in

1516 and inherited the Holy Roman Empire when his grandfather Maximilian I died.

67. Girolamo Benzoni, *History of the New World: Shewing His Travels in America, from A.D. 1541 to 1556, with Some Particulars of the Island of Canary,* trans. Admiral W. H. Smyth (London: Hakluyt Society, 1857), 117. One student of the conquistadors, who himself thought Italians "choleric," also believed Benzoni so hateful of Spaniards that he "lies his head off." George Millar, *A Crossbowman's Story of the First Exploration of the Amazon* (New York: Knopf, 1955), xi, xii.

68. Notario Lopez and Notario Lopez, *Spanish Tercios,* 21.

69. In 1574, the captain general in Flanders addressed some of his mutinous soldiers, saying, "[Y]ou are Spaniards, and . . . your King . . . is today the sole defender of the Catholic religion which . . . is persecuted and molested throughout most of the world, and you should esteem it highly that God has chosen you to be His instrument to remedy this situation." Parker, *Army of Flanders,* 178.

70. Bolton, *Coronado,* 71. Even the presence of the noncontinental European Scotsman was not that exceptional, for many Scots were mercenaries (or professional soldiers) during the sixteenth century, although, as at the Battle of Pavia in 1525, they were more likely to be with the French fighting Spaniards. See James Miller, *Swords for Hire: The Scottish Mercenary* (Edinburgh: Birlinn, 2007), 35.

71. See Defourneaux, *Daily Life in Spain,* 190.

72. See Richards, *Landsknecht Soldier,* 29.

73. Martin Luther, "Whether Soldiers, Too, Can be Saved (1526)," in Jacobs, *Works of Martin Luther,* vol. 5, 72. Luther, the German, was speaking here specifically of the mercenary Landsknechts. Nonetheless, as sometimes occurs with ordinary soldiery, the common fighting men of the century, including those among the often-bigoted Spanish, occasionally were more capable of showing mercy to their enemies than were their officers or chaplains.

74. Defourneaux, *Daily Life in Spain,* 190.

75. Even in the Middle Ages, *men-at-arms* was a term applied to all mounted fighting men who wore armor, and not just to those who would be considered knights. Terence Wise, *Medieval European Armies* (Botley, UK: Osprey, 2003), 14.

76. Hodge, "Narrative by Castaneda," 292, 322.

77. Heath, *Armies of the Sixteenth Century [European],* 59. Military surgeons, in an effort to avoid being shot at, wore colored baldrics—belts across the chest—as early as 1539, at least in England. Heath, *Armies of the Sixteenth Century [European],* 59.

78. Hammond and Rey, *Obregon's History,* 232.

79. See John Kirkup, ed., *The Surgeons Mate by John Woodall, Master in Chirurgery: A Complete Facsimile of the Book Published in 1617* (Bath, UK: Kingsmead, 1978), xvii.

80. Mills, *Renaissance and Reformation Times,* 193.

81. See Bax, *Peasants War,* 9–13.

82. See Parker, *Army of Flanders,* 171–172.

83. Ibid., 172.

84. See Chavez, *Coronado's Friars,* 7, 73. However, not all Franciscans were of one mind regarding their vows of humble poverty. See Cantor, *Last Knight,* 21.

85. Hodge, "Narrative by Castaneda," 372–373.

86. Ibid., 296, 372–373, 355n2. Friar Descalona, or De Escalona, also went by the name Luis deUbeda. Day, "Mota Padilla," 92n9; Hodge, "Narrative by Castaneda," 372n1; Chavez, *Coronado's Friars,* 29n3.

87. Day, "Mota Padilla," 92n9. Friar de la Cruz, not listed by Castaneda or Mota Padilla, broke his leg in Sonora and was left behind, as noted by Day. Hodge has him left behind in Cibola. Hodge, "Narrative by Castaneda," 373–374n1. Chavez attempted to straighten it all out. See Chavez, *Coronado's Friars*, 32–36.

88. Hodge, "Narrative by Castaneda," 307. This traditional biographic detail about Padilla has been disputed; one biographer, a fellow Franciscan, has contended that all that Castaneda meant was that Padilla had been "bellicose" since youth. Chavez, *Coronado's Friars*, 46–47. However, not only does the Latin-based *bellicose* mean warlike, it might be noted that Padilla's youth would have been during the Italian Wars. Also, Castaneda's point of insertion of the information would tend to answer why Padilla would volunteer for a mission with Tovar and his patrol. In addition, supposedly Padilla early on petitioned to go on the expedition as Coronado's chaplain. Chavez, *Coronado's Friars*, 26. Finally, as noted by Chavez, Padilla was in the habit of getting after soldiers for cursing and other misconduct, while other friars would correct such misbehavior in private. Chavez, *Coronado's Friars*, 21, 27. This direct approach is consistent with a chaplain who has been a real veteran, and soldiers more often will accept reprimands from such a nonplaster saint. As Erasmus observed in 1530, "the soldier more willingly obeys secular leaders than ecclesiastical ones." See Housley, *Documents on the Later Crusades*, 181.

89. Hodge, "Narrative by Castaneda," 373n1.

90. Chavez, *Coronado's Friars*, 7–8, 13.

91. Hammond and Rey, *Narratives*, 178, "Letter of Coronado to Mendoza, August 3, 1540."

92. See Hammond and Rey, *Narratives*, 156, "Letter of Coronado to Mendoza, August 3, 1540." Mendoza was speaking about personnel required to man a fort at Mexico City.

93. Hammond and Rey, *Obregon's History*, 233.

94. Ibid. However, it has been opined that perhaps each horseman in the expedition served as his own farrier, carrying his own nails, horseshoes, and tools. See Richard Flint and Shirley Cushing Flint, "A Death in Tiguex, 1542," *New Mexico Historical Review* 74, no. 3 (July 1999), 250–251. Nonetheless, whether one discusses gunsmiths, blacksmiths, or farriers, an anvil would be needed for each of these trades. See Charles Ffoulkes, *The Armourer and His Craft, from the XIth to the XVIth Century* (New York: Dover, 1988), 24.

95. Hammond and Rey, *Obregon's History*, 233.

96. Millar, *Crossbowman's Story*, xvi.

97. See Parker, *Army of Flanders*, 177.

98. Flint, *Great Cruelties*, 392, "A Translation of the Testimony Summary—Second de Parte Witness (Diego Lopez)."

99. Day, "Mota Padilla," 91.

100. Aiton, *Antonio de Mendoza*, 125. However, probably illustrative of the gulf that still divides the expeditions of Coronado and De Soto, a De Soto historian, not that long ago, credited Coronado with having but "an army of 230 soldiers, 800 Indian bearers, and livestock." Jerald T. Milanich, "The Hernando de Soto Expedition and Spain's Efforts to Colonize North America," in Gloria A. Young and Michael P. Hoffman, eds., *The Expedition of Hernando de Soto West of the Mississippi, 1541–1543: Proceedings of the De Soto Symposia, 1988 and 1990* (Fayetteville: University of Arkansas, 1993), 23.

101. See Flint and Cushing Flint, *Documents*, 136–137.

284 ᛞᛟᛞ *Notes to Pages 54–56*

CHAPTER FIVE: ARQUEBUSES, CROSSBOWS, FALCONETS, AND OTHER
IMPLEMENTS OF WAR

1. Hodge, "Narrative by Castaneda," 294.

2. Flint, *No Settlement*, 62. In other works, Flint cites himself (as previously published) as the authority regarding this 90 percent conclusion. See Flint, *Great Cruelties*, 533.

3. Flint and Cushing Flint, *Documents*, 138. This assumption that the weapons were like native ones actually is a repetition of the conclusion of an earlier noted scholar that weapons of the country meant "native weapons," including "*icha-huipiles* [quilted cotton vest], an ancient Aztec weapon, and other native arms." George P. Hammond, *Coronado's Seven Cities* (Albuquerque: United States Coronado Exposition Commission, 1940), 17, 19.

4. See Heath, *Armies of the Sixteenth Century [New World]*, 161. One member of the expedition, Don Lope de Gurrea, proudly proclaimed his "armor of Castile." Aiton, *Muster Roll*, 7.

5. See Heath, *Armies of the Sixteenth Century [New World]*, 161. Since Aragon, at some point, had a reputation as "a manufactory and storehouse" of arms and armor exceeding Castile, the term "of the country" likely also implicitly meant "not of Aragon." See Calvert, *Spanish Arms and Armour*, 5–6. Probably, however, other European armor, such as that produced in Germany or Italy, would be considered "not of the country" by the members of Coronado's Expedition. Of course, those weapons made locally, even if modeled on the Spanish imports, would not have been as good a quality. Castaneda, in extolling the accomplishments of himself and his fellows, noted "the few and poor weapons which they have in these parts." Hodge, "Narrative by Castaneda," 379.

6. See Notario Lopez and Notario Lopez, *Spanish Tercios*, 43.

7. See ibid., 12.

8. In the conquest of Mexico, according to Diaz, a Spanish pikeman got the allied Indians to make pikes "modeled after European forms" with native-made copper points. These were to arm the allies. Karcheski, *Arms and Armor*, [5]. However, the friendly Indians also reportedly made fresh crossbow bolts and pikes for the Spanish soldiery. See Gomara and Simpson, *Cortes*, 288. In addition, throughout the Americas, swords—"crude yet serviceable swords"—were some of the first weapons produced by local colonial blacksmiths. See, for example, George C. Neumann, *The History of Weapons of the American Revolution* (New York: Bonanza, c. 1967), 216. Because many of the male Spaniards in the New World were veterans of fighting in Europe, militia weaponry also might include various pieces brought home from the wars and pieces that, in official records, became "of the country." Finally, with Spain's growing insistence (starting in 1503) that its colonies trade only with properly licensed merchant exporters from the homeland, identifying items as either imported into New Spain from Spain or manufactured "in-country" meant such terminology became more than a trivial aside for the possessor of the item. Cf. James McDermott, *England and the Spanish Armada: The Necessary Quarrel* (London: Yale University Press, 2005), 64–66. Consequently, there also is a good chance that "of the country" occasionally was used as a label for smuggled goods from foreign ports.

9. See Heath, *Armies of the Sixteenth Century [New World]*, 161–162.

10. See, for example, Wise, *Medieval European Armies*, 35; Christopher Gravett, *Tudor Knight* (Botley, UK: Osprey, 2006), 25.

11. Calvert, *Spanish Arms and Armour*, 142.

12. See Lt. Col. Mike Snook, *Go Strong into the Desert: The Mahdist Uprising in Sudan, 1881–85* (Nottingham, UK: Perry Miniatures, 2010), 136, 169.

13. In addition, although the sixteenth century, as it proceeded, saw the gradual disappearance of many supplementary pieces of armor (such as gauntlets and greaves), headpieces, collar pieces, breastplates, and backplates still were considered of importance for European soldiery. See Smythe, *Certain Discourses Military*, 42.

14. Calvert, *Spanish Arms and Armour*, 3.

15. Not only did the Spanish of the New World know that obsidian, no matter how sharp, is broken easily when hit with metal, the Spaniards, who had been denied the right to possess iron or steel weapons under Moorish rule, were more jealous of their hard-earned privilege to possess such weaponry than were Englishmen, who had not lived under a similar foreign occupation. See Parker, *Cambridge Illustrated History of Warfare*, 135, 142 (chapter written by Dr. Patricia Seed).

16. See Day, *Coronado's Quest*, 335n12. The instructions directed Coronado to oppose intrusions by any other unauthorized expedition.

17. John Pohl, *The Conquistador, 1492–1550* (Botley, UK: Osprey, 2001), 62.

18. See Aiton, *Muster Roll*. The muster roll reads the opposite of the notorious hand receipts long in military usage ("You signed for it, you pay for it."). The list (given under oath) seems to specify personal items so that in case of death or other circumstance, the property would be part of a personal estate and not claimed by the viceroy or the government. Indeed, the traditional employment of a muster in the sixteenth century was to see if the enlistees possessed sufficient personal armament (not borrowed) to be accepted into the army—in addition to being fit for service. See Douglas Miller, *The Lanksknechts* (London: Osprey, 1976), 4; Richards, *Landsknecht Soldier*, 13. See also John Tincey, *The Armada Campaign, 1588* (London: Osprey, 1995), 47 (tendency to exaggerate readiness of English militia as to arms and armor listed in muster rolls during Elizabethan times). Even the fact that the Coronado muster document does not include the armor of the captain general does not argue against the roll being a list of personal property, for his armor likely was clearly marked with his heraldic devices and it would be well known to whom such quality equipment belonged. In any event, the roll does not specifically mention any issue items or arsenal property, some of which must have been present.

19. Even the muster roll notes that the "horsemen took their lances and swords in addition to the arms declared and other arms." As for the infantry, the roll noted that they had "said arms and additional arms of the country given to them." Aiton, *Muster Roll*, 26–27. This might include government arsenal items.

20. See Heath, *Armies of the Sixteenth Century [New World]*, 149.

21. See ibid., 149–150.

22. Arthur S. Aiton and Agapito Rey, "Coronado's Testimony in the Viceroy Mendoza Residencia," *New Mexico Historical Review* 12, no. 3 (July 1937), 315. This claim is supported both by Mendoza providing the six pieces of ordnance as well as by the lack of contemporary testimony complaining about a dearth of weaponry and military equipment (while noting the lack of winter clothing).

23. Aiton and Rey, "Coronado's Testimony," 304.

24. See Aiton, *Antonio de Mendoza*, 152n31.

25. See ibid., 39–40.

26. See Richards, *Landsknecht Soldier*, 51. Interpreting the headpiece data differently may explain why, for example, one archaeologist has stated that Aiton lists but thirty-eight helmets. See Matt Schmader, "Thundersticks and Coats of Iron," in Flint and Cushing Flint, *Latest Word from 1540*, 316.

27. Aiton, *Muster Roll*, 7–22.

28. Ibid., 22–26.

29. Juan Pizarro, the younger brother of Francisco, was killed by a rock in 1536 during the assault on an Inca fortress because he was unable to wear his helmet over his previously wounded jaw. H. W. Kaufmann and J. E. Kaufmann, *Fortifications of the Incas, 1200–1531* (Botley, UK: Osprey, 2006), 56.

30. Aiton, *Muster Roll*, 8. Codex from around 1550 of Cortes's army shows Spanish with close helmets with visors. Bradley Smith, *Mexico: A History in Art* (Garden City, NY: Doubleday, 1968), 162.

31. See Stone, *A Glossary of the Construction, Decoration and Use of Arms and Armor*, 173, 175, 158–159, 455, 457; Sadler and Walsh, *Flodden 1513*, 77 (kettle hat).

32. See Terence Wise, *The Conquistadores* (London: Osprey, 1996), 13; Notario Lopez and Notario Lopez, *Spanish Tercios*, 12. See also Coggins, *Fighting Man*, 152 (Spanish morion was combed); Robert Attard, *Collecting Military Headgear: A Guide to 5000 Years of Helmet History* (Atglen, PA: Schiffer, 2004), 45–47 (Spanish morion was peaked, not combed); Robert Woosnam-Savage and Anthony Hall, *Brassey's Book on Body Armor* (Washington, DC: Brassey's, 2001), 74 (Spanish morion was not combed).

33. Hammond and Rey, *Narratives*, 169, "Letter of Coronado to Mendoza, August 3, 1540," Sixteenth-century armor for the elite was fine art. "[O]ne of the most beautiful things that Man has ever produced," according to a curator of the Tower of London, "is a suit of 16th-century armor." John Fleischman, "Royal Armor Makes Great Escape from Tower of London: Shining Works of the Old-Time Armorers' Art Come to Cincinnati in First Exhibit Ever Sent Beyond the Walls of the British Fortress," *Smithsonian* 13, no. 7 (October 1982), 65.

34. See Stone, *Glossary*, 156–157. In addition to showing this glittering armor, illustrations portraying Coronado and his officers wearing starched and circular neck ruffles, *golas*, may not be out of place (especially when Mendoza reviewed the army), for the Spaniards stubbornly held onto these foppish affectations to the end of the sixteenth century. See Heath, *Armies of the Sixteenth Century [European]*, 139.

35. See Stone, *Glossary*, 165.

36. Karcheski, *Arms and Armor*, [1].

37. Ibid. [18]. Certainly others have believed that the morion helmet postdated the early conquistador era. See Pohl, *Conquistador*, 24; Woosnam-Savage and Hall, *Brassey's Book*, 74.

38. Funcken and Funcken, *Age of Chivalry*, 60.

39. Attard, *Collecting Military Headgear*, 49. Other students of the conquistadors have estimated that the comb on the morion became more prominent starting in 1530. Wise, *Conquistadores*, 36.

40. Philip Ainsworth Means, trans., *Relation of the Discovery and Conquest of the Kingdom of Peru by Pedro Pizarro* (New York: Cortes Society, 1921), 2:314. Of course, this assumes the translation was accurate—and, as noted, the term *morion* was sometimes applied to a wide variety of headgear.

41. See Attard, *Collecting Military Headgear*, 43, 61n12; Woosnam-Savage and Hall, *Brassey's Book*, 74.

42. See Woosnam-Savage and Hall, *Brassey's Book*, 10.
43. Wise, *Conquistadores*, 36. Even this rule is not inviolate. During the sixteenth century, some light cavalrymen did favor the morion. Liliane and Fred Funcken, *Arms and Uniforms, Part 1: Ancient Egypt to the 18th Century* (London: Ward Lock, 1977), 122. This likely refers to the light horsemen of the latter part of the century, who often were mounted arquebusiers or musketeers.
44. See, for example, Douglas Miller, *The Swiss at War, 1300–1500* (Botley, UK: Osprey, 1999), 11.
45. See Sadler and Walsh, *Flodden 1513*, 26. A relatively early historian of Coronado's expedition wrote that the mounted men wore "sallets with visors." Day, "Mota Padilla," 91.
46. Aiton, *Muster Roll*, 11, 12.
47. Perhaps—forgetting for the moment that many examples of European arms and armor in American museums were not found locally but were acquired from overseas—there are no known examples of falling beavors in Southwestern depositories because, absent an attached full suit of armor, such a fine and large piece of steel would have been easily recycled in the New World. It would seem that no better candidate for being beaten into a ploughshare would exist than a "chin piece."
48. Karcheski, *Arms and Armor*, [3].
49. See Stone, *Glossary*, 152–153; Ashdown, *British and Foreign*, 285 (volante piece). It is not unknown for such face guards to be called visors incorrectly, even though they are not fastened to the helmet and are impossible to raise. See Stone, *Glossary*, 445. In fact, when a helmet had a visor, the visor fell over the beavor when lowered. Calvert, *Spanish Arms and Armour*, 43.
50. In 1461, during the English Wars of the Roses, it was reported that Baron Clifford of Skipton was killed by an enemy archer when the nobleman removed his beavor during a skirmish to obtain a drink of water. Supposedly, the fatal shaft did not even have an arrowhead. John Sadler, *Towton: The Battle of Palm Sunday Field, 1461* (Barnsley, UK: Pen and Sword Military, 2011), 13, 90–91. While some historians believe the armor that Clifford removed was a gorget, this does not make as much sense. See David Santiuste, *Edward IV and the Wars of the Roses* (Barnsley, UK: Pen and Sword Military, 2010), 52, 161n25. In any event, later in the war, during the Battle of Bosworth, in 1485, the beavor of the Earl of Norfolk was knocked away by a sword blow and then an archer shot a death-dealing arrow into Norfolk's face. Peter Young and John Adair, *Hastings to Culloden: Battles of Britain* (Stroud, UK: Wrens Park, 1998), 104.
51. Beavors were often, but not invariably, worn with sallets. See Christopher Gravett, *English Medieval Knight 1400–1500* (Botley, UK: Osprey, 2001), 60.
52. See Stone, *Glossary*, 250–251; Ashdown, *British and Foreign*, 267; Woosnam-Savage and Hall, *Brassey's Book*, 132.
53. However, only on a couple of occasions does the Coronado muster roll note both front-plates and backplates.
54. See Stone, *Glossary*, 192–193, 195–196. Such breastplates of the Coronado era likely had braided or "rope" trim worked into the metal. See Wise, *Conquistadores*, 9.
55. Calvert, *Spanish Arms and Armour*, 9–10, 38.
56. The muster roll also includes some odd pieces of mail, such as sleeves or leggings, scattered among the horse and foot. Mail, which could not withstand the English longbow or the crossbow, would be more protective in the Americas. See Fleischman, "Royal Armor," 67.

57. See Eltis, *Military Revolution*, 12.

58. See Wise, *Conquistadores*, 13–14. As noted in Wise, in an effort to forestall rusting, armor (including mail) often was painted black. Supposedly, medium-mesh mail resisted rust better than fine-mesh mail and was a better defense against Indian arrows than fine or coarse mesh. Hammond and Rey, *Obregon's History*, 232. Even without rusting, little mail has survived the centuries, partly because it was cut up for scouring kitchen pots. Fleischman, "Royal Armor," 66.

59. See Gravett, *English Medieval Knight*, 55, 60. However, a mail gauntlet has been found at the Jimmy Owens archaeological site, a Texas Panhandle campsite of the Coronado Expedition. See Morris and Castaneda, *Narrative of the Coronado Expedition*, ciii.

60. See Aiton, *Muster Roll*, 23–26.

61. Wise, *Conquistadores*, 15. A jack-plate, a piece of metal sewn into such a protective jacket, has been found at a supposed Spanish camp near Bernalillo, New Mexico. Gayle Harrison Hartmann, "Finding Coronado's Route: Crossbow Points, Caret-Head Nails, and Other Oddments," *Old Pueblo Archaeology* 47 (December 2006), 3, 4.

62. See Wise, *Conquistadores*, 14. However, even this was a type of protection seen from the Far East to Europe. In the early sixteenth century, ordinary English and Scottish combatants "wore sleeveless jacks which were stuffed with tow—rough flax—and with layer upon layer of wool or linen material packed together. Goodwin, *Fatal Rivalry*, 189.

63. Heath, *Armies of the Sixteenth Century [New World]*, 162.

64. Ian K. Steele, *Warpaths: Invasions of North America* (New York: Oxford University Press, 1994), 11–12.

65. Calvert, *Spanish Arms and Armour*, 51.

66. See ibid., 67. Nonetheless, at least in the latter part of the fifteenth century, some European barding still was mail or brigandine style. See Nicholas Michael, *Armies of Medieval Burgundy, 1364–1477* (London: Reed International Books, 1996), 12. Charles V of the Holy Roman Empire would deduct from a man-at-arm's pay if his horse did not come equipped for action wearing a chamfrom (shaffron)—the equivalent of a helmet. Funcken and Funcken, *Arms and Uniforms, Part 1*, 116.

67. See Calvert, *Spanish Arms and Armour*, 79. This seventy pounds would be in addition to a similar weight for the outfit of a fully encumbered man-at-arms (not likely in the expedition), not counting the man's weight of about 150 pounds without armor.

68. See Nicolle, *Portuguese in the Age of Discovery*, 45.

69. R. B. Cunninghame Graham, *The Horses of the Conquest* (Norman: University of Oklahoma Press, 1949), 111. Likewise, the heavy bronze stirrups were Moorish in design. Wise, *Conquistadores*, 7. The horses would also have to withstand the steel spurs of their riders, which had long shanks and spiked rowels, sometimes chiseled and engraved, but nonetheless the ancestors of those cruel-looking "Mexican spurs" of later generations. See Aldo G. Cimarelli, *Arms and Armor in the Age of Chivalry* (Italy: Orbis, 1973), 18.

70. See Aiton, *Muster Roll*, 7.

71. Adolph F. Bandelier, "Francisco Vasquez de Coronado," in Charles G. Herbermann, ed., *The Catholic Encyclopedia*, vol. 4 (London: Universal Knowledge Foundation, 1913), 380.

72. Flint and Cushing Flint, *Documents*, 527 ("Juan Troyano's Proof of Service, 1560").

73. Phil Sharpe, "Guns and Gunners," *Street & Smith's Western Story* 185, no. 6 (October 5, 1940), 106. Sharpe, who gives no source for this assertion (written in commemoration of the Coronado quadricentennial), was a recognized firearms expert of his era, although he shows little sixteenth-century expertise in his brief article. He also commented that "[t]he brass [sic] cannons appealed to the Spaniard more than the heavy iron jobs appearing in that period and in later years." Actually, pound for pound, bronze was lighter and stronger than iron and resisted corrosion better. Regarding the safety of the gun crews, bronze barrels, unlike iron ones, would bulge before bursting (but they cost four times as much as iron guns). Nelson, *Tudor Navy*, 38–39. As for basic design of artillery pieces in the closing days of the fifteenth century, they, like the handguns, had touch holes on the side, and the resultant internal explosion propelled a lead ball. Taylor, *Art of War in Italy*, 40.

74. Heath, *Armies of the Sixteenth Century [European]*, 151. Another source—dealing with German and Swiss Landsknechts but perhaps unknowingly referring only to those enlisted in the Hapsburg armies of Maximilian I or Charles V—states that "the carriage was invariably painted black and the fittings red" but the "wheels were left in natural colours." Miller, *Lanksknechts*, 13.

75. Heath, *Armies of the Sixteenth Century [European]*, 151.

76. Actually, some of the best bronze guns were made in England after 1530 and were in great demand in the rest of Europe. Nelson, *Tudor Navy*, 37.

77. Prescott, *History of the Conquest of Mexico*, 3:241. These pieces fired stone cannonballs.

78. Prescott, *History of the Conquest of Peru*, 2:199–200.

79. See Flint and Cushing Flint, *Documents*, 689n589.

80. Peter Padfield, *Armada: A Celebration of the Four Hundredth Anniversary of the Defeat of the Spanish Armada, 1588–1988* (London: Victor Gollancz, 1988), 84–85.

81. Artillerists, not unlike sailors as to ships and aviators as to aircraft, have long been known to give nicknames to their pieces. See Adrian B. Caruana, *Grasshoppers and Butterflies: The Light 3 Pounders of Pattison and Townsend* (Bloomfield, ON: Museum Restoration Service, 1999), 13; Spaulding, Nickerson, and Wright, *Warfare*, 423.

82. See R. Roth, *The Visser Collection: Arms of the Netherlands in the Collection of H. L. Visser; Vol. 2, Ordnance: Cannon, Mortars, Swivel-Guns, Muzzle- and Breech-Loaders* (Zwolle, Netherlands: Waanders, 1996), 89–92.

83. Colin Martin, *Full Fathom Five: Wrecks of the Spanish Armada* (New York: Viking, 1975), 220–221. Ironically, these early breechloaders, which often employed several chambers—each of which could be preloaded and ready to replace the chamber that had just fired its round—tended to have a slower rate of fire (a shot every four or five minutes) than the muzzle-loading guns. See Neils M. Saxtorph, *Warriors and Weapons of Early Times* (London: Blandford, 1972), 203.

84. Apparently emulating the French, the Spanish also attempted to standardize their artillery at the end of the century, including adopting the "eighth cannon" or falconet. See Heath, *Armies of the Sixteenth Century [European]*, 136. In addition, even before this, sixteenth-century Spanish military men probably were familiar with the term *falconet;* although not yet standardized, falconets existed prior to the official French nomenclature. See Funcken and Funcken, *Age of Chivalry, Part 3*, 98–99 for a description and illustration of a 1505 example of a (twin) falconet mounted on a gun carriage. At least by 1578, the Spanish were using the French terms for artillery, calling, for

example, a culverin a *culebrina* and a falcon a *falcon*. *See* Karcheski, *Arms and Armor*, [18]. Since the Spanish faced effective French artillery in Italy, the French names could have been adopted by the time of the Coronado Expedition and be familiar terms to professional Spanish gunners.

85. See Charles Cruickshank, *Henry VIII and the Invasion of France* (Stroud, UK: Alan Sutton, 1990), 64; John Norris, *Artillery: A History* (Stroud, UK: Sutton, 2000), 62; Kaufmann, and Kaufmann, *Fortifications of the Incas*, 53.

86. See Heath, *Armies of the Sixteenth Century [New World]*, 163.

87. See Martin, *Full Fathom Five*, 104.

88. See Pohl, *Conquistador*, 29, for recent use of the more-generic term *falconet* rather than *swivel gun* or other Spanish name.

89. Raymond, *Henry VIII's Military Revolution*, 44.

90. Christopher Hare, *Bayard: The Good Knight Without Fear and Without Reproach* (London: J. M. Dent & Sons, 1911), 89.

91. Sir Ralph Payne-Gallwey, *The Crossbow: Mediaeval and Modern, Military and Sporting, Its Construction, History and Management* (London: Holland House, 1995), 41. Once again, the dates of the introduction of such technology are obscure; a type of matchlock might have been introduced in Spain by the French during the final stages of the Reconquista. See Nicolle, *Granada 1492*, 30.

92. Payne-Gallwey, *Crossbow*, 41–42. These dates, too, even by experts, are often only approximations. Primitive flintlocks, whether snaplocks or the more sophisticated snaphances, had been developed by 1530 in Holland but were not yet in general use. See Funcken and Funcken, *Age of Chivalry, Part 3*, 12. Apparently, flintlocks were not actually produced in Spain until the end of the sixteenth century. See Stone, *Glossary*, 233 (incorrectly claiming that the system was invented in Holland and Spain about the same time at the close of the century). In the event, the earliest flintlocks in Spanish service in New Spain had technical problems in that their works were more difficult to repair, and the powder in the flashpan got damp too easily. Hammond and Rey, *Obregon's History*, 232.

93. Helmut Nickel, Stuart W. Pyhrr, and Leonid Tarassuk, *The Art of Chivalry: European Arms and Armor from the Metropolitan Museum of Art* (New York: American Federation of Arts, 1982), 133.

94. See Karcheski, *Arms and Armor*, [7].

95. Millar, *Crossbowman's Story*, 72n.

96. Raymond, *Henry VIII's Military Revolution*, 43.

97. See Taylor, *Art of War in Italy*, 40.

98. See Funcken and Funcken, *Arms and Uniforms, Part 1*, 116. Normally, the round of an arquebus, reloaded every minute or so, had an effective range of fifty to sixty yards, about two-thirds the distance for a musket ball. See Angus Konstam, *Elizabethan Sea Dogs, 1560–1605* (Botley, UK: Osprey, 2000), 15.

99. In addition, since the early muskets were carried to battlefields by horses, they were classified as artillery. Taylor, *Art of War in Italy*, 47.

100. See ibid., 46–47. By the end of the sixteenth century, Spanish arquebuses fired a ball weighing a half ounce, while a musket fired a larger-caliber two-ounce ball. Martin, *Full Fathom Five*, 105.

101. See Taylor, *Art of War in Italy*, 47. In addition, as with other aspects regarding the sixteenth century, the pinning down of innovations is difficult. Another historian of

note has indicated that the musket only came into common use during the second half of the sixteenth century. See Oman, *History of the Art of War*, 224–225.

102. See Schmader, "Thundersticks," 316. Nonetheless, a relatively early historian of the expedition wrote that the "seventy infantrymen [were] both musketeers and har-quesbusiers." Day, "Mota Padilla," 91. Thus Mota Padilla entirely ignored the cross-bows.

103. Bernard and Fawn M. Brodie, *From Crossbow to the H-Bomb* (Bloomington: Indiana University Press, 1973), 56.

104. See Heath, *Armies of the Sixteenth Century [European]*, 139–140.

105. See Heath, *Armies of the Sixteenth Century [New World]*, 164.

106. See Heath, *Armies of the Sixteenth Century [European]*, 50.

107. See Notario Lopez and Notario Lopez, *Spanish Tercios*, 35, 44.

108. Heath, *Armies of the Sixteenth Century [New World]*, 164.

109. See Schmader, "Thundersticks," 316.

110. Nickel, Pyhrr, and Tarassuk, *Art of Chivalry*, 129.

111. Robert Furneaux, *Invasion 1066* (Englewood Cliffs, NJ: Prentice-Hall, 1966), 189.

112. Nickel, Pyhrr, and Tarassuk, *Art of Chivalry*, 129.

113. Payne-Gallwey, *Crossbow*, 20.

114. Ibid., 110.

115. Cf. Spaulding, Nickerson, and Wright, *Warfare*, 448.

116. See Payne-Gallwey, *Crossbow*, 73–89.

117. See Stone, *Glossary*, 11–12. However, the windlass may have been considered unfit for service in the field in the Americas, especially if relatively lightweight crossbows were carried. See Wise, *Conquistadores*, 3.

118. See Taylor, *Art of War in Italy*, 51.

119. Payne-Gallwey, *Crossbow*, 48–49. In Germany, where crossbow sport hunting became very popular (as with Swiss legend William Tell), local militias apparently retained the crossbow for the defense of walled towns for quite some time. See Nickel, Pyhrr, and Tarassuk, *Art of Chivalry*, 132. This supposition is supported by the fact that crossbows were extensively and effectively used by the Catholic peasant army of Nils Dacke when in rebellion against the Swedish Protestant crown forces in 1543. See Vilhelm Moberg, *A History of the Swedish People: From Renaissance to Revolution* (New York: Dorset, 1989), 249.

120. William H. Prescott, *History of the Reign of the Emperor Charles the Fifth*, 3 vols. (Philadelphia: J. B. Lippincott, 1882), 2:238.

121. See Wilfried Seipel, ed., *Der Kriegszug Kaiser Karls V Gegen Tunis: Kartons und Tapisserien* (Vienna: Kunsthistorisches Museum, 2000), 67–70, 76–79, 87–90, 94, 95, 116–118, 120 (contemporary illustrations of the conquest of Tunis). However, there apparently were at least some crossbows in the Turkish arsenal when it was captured. See Housley, *Documents on the Later Crusades*, 185.

122. Cf. Nicolle, *Portuguese in the Age of Discovery*, 39–41. In these far-off frontier fights, with such little armies, a few arquebusiers could make a big difference.

123. Payne-Gallwey, *Crossbow*, 49.

124. See ibid., 48.

125. See Paul E. Hoffman, ed. and trans., *The Juan Pardo Expeditions: Exploration of the Carolinas and Tennessee, 1566–1568* (Washington, DC: Smithsonian Institution Press, 1990), 341, 342.

126. See Raymond, *Henry VIII's Military Revolution*, 184–185.
127. Alfred W. Crosby, *Throwing Fire: Projectile Technology Through History* (New York: Cambridge University Press, 2002), 78–80.
128. See Doug Koenig, "Crossbow Myths and Misconceptions," *Petersen's Bowhunting: The Modern Bowhunting Authority* 23, issue 4 (July, 2012), 25.
129. However, matchlocks also usually were easy to repair. See Nickel, Pyhrr, and Tarassuk, *Art of Chivalry*, 133.
130. The unavailability of gunpowder supposedly extended the extensive use of crossbows in the New World into the 1570s. See Konstam, *Elizabethan Sea Dogs*, 60. Individual crossbowmen, like bow archers, usually carried on their person twenty-four missiles. Nickel, Pyhrr, and Tarassuk, *Art of Chivalry*, 129. In 1568, when crossbows were issued to an expedition under Juan Prado, the number of bolts supplied in the same issue were either forty-eight or sixty per bow. See Hoffman, *Juan Pardo Expeditions*, 341, 342. While additional bolts would have been carried in an army's baggage train, there is evidence, pointed out in a later chapter, that Coronado's army did manufacture extra bolts.
131. Crosby, *Throwing Fire*, 122.
132. Nickel, Pyhrr, and Tarassuk, *Art of Chivalry*, 129. Naturally, blinding battlefield smoke also would be absent.
133. See Crosby, *Throwing Fire*, 80.
134. See Koenig, "Crossbow Myths," 24.
135. See Taylor, *Art of War in Italy*, 31–33. Pikemen usually had swords and daggers as backup weapons. See ibid., 33.
136. While any pikemen with Coronado would not have been armored (the absence of armor being more in the Swiss style), even in Europe, Spanish pikemen, on the average, were less armored than their allies. See Heath, *Armies of the Sixteenth Century [European]*, 138.
137. See George Snook, M.D., *The Halberd and Other European Polearms, 1300–1650* (Alexandria Bay, NY, and Bloomfield, ON: Museum Restoration Service, 1998), 26.
138. See ibid., 26.
139. See Taylor, *Art of War in Italy*, 57–58. This climatic reliability was demonstrated in the Americas, as when Menendez captured Fort Caroline in rainy Florida in 1565. See Charles E. Bennett, *Laudonniere and Fort Caroline: History and Documents* (Tuscaloosa: University of Alabama Press, 2001), 37–38.
140. See Nugent Brasher, "The Red House Camp and the Captain General: The 2009 Report on the Coronado Expedition Campsite of Chichilticale," *New Mexico Historical Review* 84, no. 1 (Winter 2009), 14–16. The article, to prove its point, even has a modern illustration of an old-time Spanish infantryman, calling his hafted weapon both a spear and a lance—but not a pike. See ibid., 16. The ferrule conceivably could have been used on an arquebus rest.
141. See Heath, *Armies of the Sixteenth Century [New World]*, 149–150. See also Karcheski, *Arms and Armor*, [5]. A contemporary painting, apparently of Coronado's assault on the Zuni pueblo of Cibola, shows Spanish pikemen, mostly armored. See Bil Gilbert, *The Trailblazers* (New York: Time-Life Books, 1974), 22–23. The imaginative painting, by Flemish artist Jan Mostaert, is reminiscent of his biblical scenes. See Sander Pierron, *Les Mostaert: Jean Mostaert, Dit le Maitre d'Oultremont; Gilles et Francois Mostaert; Michel Mostaert* (Bruxelles/Paris: Librairie Nationale d'Art et d'Histoire, 1912), plates opposite 4, 8, 18, 24, 28.

142. Certainly, a Coronado expert of an earlier generation believed that the force displayed in its weapons "as great a variety" as in its dress. "Some of the soldiers carried swords and metal shields; some bore pikes, and others great two-handed swords; here and there a soldier was armed with a crossbow or harquebus." Hammond, *Coronado's Seven Cities*, 17.

143. Taylor, *Art of War in Italy*, 32, 37.

144. See Josef Berger, *Discoverers of the New World* (New York: American Heritage Publishing, 1960), 46, 49, 62, 75, 89. While the De Bry drawings might be considered merely European conventions, the native codex illustration is harder to dismiss. As for the halberds themselves, they may have been captured prizes from the numerous European victories of the Spaniards and, being considered second-rate weapons, shipped to the New World.

145. See Winston Graham, *The Spanish Armadas* (Garden City, NY: Doubleday, 1972), 80.

146. Bernardino de Sahagun, *Conquest of New Spain, 1585 Revision*, trans. Howard F. Cline (Salt Lake City: University of Utah Press, 1989), 83.

147. Rodney Hilton Brown, *American Polearms, 1526–1865* (New Milford, CT: N. Flayderman, 1967), 32. At least regarding Onate, Brown relied on Spanish documents. Ibid., 47n24. See also Pohl, *Conquistador*, 61, regarding the usefulness of the halberd in protecting crossbowmen and gunners when fighting the Aztecs.

148. See Snook, *Halberd*, 26. By the mid-sixteenth century, the halberd was seen as much as a badge of office as a weapon. See Nelson, *Tudor Navy*, 59.

149. This point, that swords (as well as lances) taken along were not declared by the men-of-arms in the muster roll, is supported by the estate summary of Juan Jimenez, who died at Tiguex. See Flint and Cushing Flint, "Death in Tiguex," 269n3. Of course, Jimenez also could have purchased his sword and lance point from the estate of a previous casualty.

150. Nicolle, *Granada 1492*, 30.

151. Prescott, *History of the Reign*, 2:342n13.

152. Nickel, Pyhrr, and Tarassuk, *Art of Chivalry*, 10, 85.

153. See Calvert, *Spanish Arms and Armour*, 6.

154. See Hammond, *Coronado's Seven Cities*, 17.

155. Calvert, *Spanish Arms and Armour*, 4. Nowhere mentioned in the Aiton muster roll are bucklers, targets, or shields (whether metal or wood reinforced with metal). However, in Hammond and Rey, *Narratives*, 101–103 ("Muster Roll of the Expedition, February 22, 1540"), several shields are listed as belonging to infantry swordsmen. A relatively early historian of the expedition wrote there were Spaniards armed "with swords and bucklers." Day, "Mota Padilla," 91. The omission in the Aiton muster roll might be an indication that, like many of the swords, they were just naturally considered standard weaponry and did not need to be itemized. Another plausible alternative is that a number were carried along as expedition, rather than individual, equipment, to be issued as needed. Codex illustrations from around 1540 show Spanish swordsmen with bucklers. Smith, *Mexico*, 166–167. Many of the shields or bucklers used by the Spanish in the New World were heart-shaped *adagas*, a style inherited from the Moors. Woosnam-Savage and Hall, *Brassey's Book*, 96.

156. Aiton, *Muster Roll*, 25 (sword possessed by Francisco Lopez).

157. See Stone, *Glossary*, 524–526.

294 %2% Notes to Pages 72–74

158. See Hodge, "Narrative by Castaneda," 302n2, regarding the supposed discovery of the sword blade of Juan Gallego in Kansas in the early twentieth century with such an inscription. (This supposed blade of Gallego's has since been discredited as an archaeological find related to Coronado.) Another Spanish inscription on a sword blade, undoubtedly not unique, proclaimed the weapon a "True friend." Calvert, *Spanish Arms and Armour*, 48. The many leather scabbards protecting Spanish swords undoubtedly would have had copper scabbard tips that would survive the centuries, and would be more likely than sword blades not to have been immediately picked up by the Spanish or the Indians. See Kathleen Deagan and Jose Maria Cruxent, *Columbus's Outpost among the Tainos: Spain and America at La Isabella, 1493–1498* (New Haven, CT: Yale University Press, 2002), 171, 172.

159. Calvert, *Spanish Arms and Armour*, 113.

160. See, for example, Hume, *Martin's Hundred*, 141–142. Hume, previously taught to think armor was quickly considered obsolete when it came to transporting it to the New World, was amazed by the amount of European armor found at this seventeenth-century site subject to Indian attack.

161. Taylor, *Art of War in Italy*, 39.

162. Ibid., 62.

163. See Graham, *Horses of the Conquest*, 124; Barker, *Agincourt*, 116. Archaeologists should note that according to Graham, the horseshoes of such war horses were larger than those of present western breeds. Graham, *Horses of the Conquest*, 123-124.

164. Miguel Leon-Portilla, ed., *The Broken Spears: The Aztec Account of the Conquest of Mexico* (Boston: Beacon, 1992), 30.

165. Benzoni, *History of the New World*, 134.

166. Ibid., 146–147. Sub-Saharan African tribesmen in the sixteenth century also were intimidated by mounted horsemen, as well as by arquebusiers and artillery pieces. Nicolle, *Portuguese in the Age of Discovery*, 40.

167. See Benzoni, *History of the New World*, 155–156. This was an exaggeration, of course. Horses (like armored vehicles) are limited by the terrain. In the swampy and brushy lands of western and northwestern Florida, the Narvaez Expedition came to grief, despite its war horses. See Steele, *Warpaths*, 12–13. Terrain also played a part when the Inca rose in rebellion between 1536 and 1544. A contingent of seventy Spanish horsemen was ambushed in a defile, and the Inca annihilated them by rolling boulders down on them. Wise, *Conquistadores*, 31.

168. Smith, *Relation of Alvar Nunez Cabeza de Vaca*, 135–136. See Calvert, *Spanish Arms and Armour*, 100–101.

169. Eltis, *Military Revolution*, 21. However, wheel locks did not make it to England until about 1540, the year Coronado set out. See Ashdown, *British and Foreign*, 368.

170. Turnbull, *Art of Renaissance Warfare*, 176.

171. See Heath, *Armies of the Sixteenth Century [New World]*, 20. The Germans were innovators in wheel-lock technology and subsequently became known for their pistol-packing *reiters*. See Spaulding, Nickerson, and Wright, *Warfare*, 449.

172. See Calvert, *Spanish Arms and Armour*, 100–101.

173. See Konstam, *Spanish Armada*, 56; Spaulding, Nickerson, Wright, *Warfare*, 450. Even with wheel-lock pistols, reloading on horseback remained almost impossible (as long as modern cartridges were only a dream). See Smythe and Hale, *Certain Discourses Military*, 115.

174. See Heath, *Armies of the Sixteenth Century [New World]*, 162–163.
175. Leon-Portilla, *Broken Spears*, 31.
176. See Marion Schwartz, *A History of Dogs in the Early Americas* (New Haven, CT: Yale University Press, 1997), 61.
177. See John Grier Varner and Jeannette Johnson Varner, *Dogs of the Conquest* (Norman: University of Oklahoma Press, 1983), 102.
178. See Payne-Gallwey, *Crossbow*, 33.
179. Hammond and Rey, *Obregon's History*, 13–14.
180. During the sixteenth century, when Spanish campaigners died off, their personal effects—especially their valuables such as clothing, arms, and armor—would be auctioned off to either sutlers or comrades for the benefit of the deceased members' estates. See Parker, *Army of Flanders*, 177. This European practice was carried on during the Coronado Expedition. See Flint and Cushing Flint, "Death in Tiguex," 247–270. In addition, other than some of the artillery pieces, there are no accounts of Coronado's men discarding their weaponry or their armor. The weapons, including crossbows with broken strings, apparently were repaired or set right whenever possible for continued use.
181. See Kaufmann, Kaufmann, and Hook, *Fortifications of the Incas*, 56, 58.
182. J. H. Parry, *The Audiencia of New Galicia in the Sixteenth Century: A Study in Spanish Colonial Government* (Westport, CT: Greenwood, 1985), 27.

## CHAPTER SIX: INDIAN WARRIOR ALLIES

1. See Nic Fields, *Roman Auxiliary Cavalryman, AD 14–193* (Botley, UK: Osprey, 2006), 4.
2. See Paul Cornish, *Henry VIII's Army* (London: Osprey, 1987), 17–18. The auxiliaries with Coronado had nothing over the Irish auxiliaries with the English army in 1544 France. These Irishmen, wearing cloaks and adorned with wild hairstyles, might go into battle shoeless, sometimes decapitated their fallen enemies (carrying the heads around) and were called "marvelously savage people" by their French opponents. Cornish, *Henry VIII's Army*, 17–18, 46–47, plate G3. On the continent, during the sixteenth century, armies had Albania irregular horsemen, or *stradiots*, as auxiliaries, who also were notorious headhunters. See Tracy, *Emperor Charles V*, 33; Roeder, *Man of the Renaissance*, 61.
3. See, for example, Edward J. Lowell, *The Hessians and the Other German Auxiliaries of Great Britain in the Revolutionary War* (New York: Harper and Brothers, 1884), 282, 291, in which the author, although labeling the Hessians "mercenaries" in the text, chose to call them (more gently—and more accurately) "auxiliaries" in the title.
4. Hodge, "Narrative by Castaneda," 291. Later, at page 298, Castaneda noted that the army had six hundred pack animals "besides the friendly Indians and the servants—more than a thousand persons."
5. Hammond, *Coronado's Seven Cities*, 18.
6. Aiton, *Antonio de Mendoza*, 124–125.
7. Duncan Robinson, "Coronado and His Army," *The Panhandle- Plains Historical Review* 13 (1940), 71.
8. Herbert E. Bolton, *Cross, Sword, and Gold Pan: A Group of Notable Full-Cover Paintings Depicting Outstanding Episodes in the Exploration and Settlement of the West* (Los Angeles: Primavera, 1936), interpretive historical essay opposite plate "Coronado Discovers Zuni" (unpaginated).

9. Arthur S. Aiton and Agapito Rey, "Coronado's Testimony in the Viceroy Mendoza Residencia," *New Mexico Historical Review* 12, no. 3 (July 1937), 314. Over history, many a commander, from the great Marlborough to many a lesser leader, has been said to exaggerate enlistments and desertions in order to fraudulently accumulate the pay and rations of those phantom soldiers. See Andre Corvisier and Siddall, *Armies and Societies in Europe*, 70–71. See also Hook, *Sack of Rome, 1527*, 133–134. In the sixteenth century, this embezzlement also occurred when casualties were not reported. See Smythe, *Certain Discourses Military*, 23–24. See also Roy, *Blaise de Monluc*, 229n1. This type of military corruption was also seen in China in the fifteenth century. See Christopher Peers and David Sque, *Medieval Chinese Armies, 1260–1520* (London: Osprey, 1992), 24.

10. Similarly, upon the discovery of the Jimmy Owens archaeological site, a Cox News Service story said there were "1,100 Mexican Indians who accompanied the expedition" without distinguishing between job descriptions. Jeff Nesmith, "Evidence of Coronado Camp Found," *Denver Post*, April 16, 1996, 13A.

11. Richard Flint, "Armas de la Tierra: The Mexican Indian Component of Coronado Expedition Material Culture," in Flint and Cushing Flint, *Coronado Expedition to Tierra Nueva*, 60.

12. Richard Flint, "What's Missing from This Picture? The *Alarde*, or Muster Roll, of the Coronado Expedition," in Richard Flint and Shirley Cushing Flint, eds., *The Coronado Expedition: From the Distance of 460 Years* (Albuquerque: University of New Mexico Press, 2003), 62.

13. Flint, *Great Cruelties*, 276.

14. Flint, "What's Missing?," 62.

15. Flint and Cushing Flint, *Documents*, 135, 164. Flint later dropped any hesitancy about the presumed appearance of these additional recruits, saying "another 500 or so were added as the force marched through what are now the Mexican states of Michoacan, Jalisco, Nayarit, and Sinaloa." Flint, *No Settlement*, 58.

16. Flint, *No Settlement*, 58. Regarding wild estimates of soldiers and fighters engaged in battles—a problem not limited to the sixteenth century—near-contemporary accounts of the Battle of Flodden in 1513 placed the English and Scottish combatants anywhere from one hundred thirty thousand to eighty-six thousand. Other modern historians, exercising the same appropriate caution as Flint regarding such hearsay inflation, think a total number of sixty-eight thousand about right. See Sadler and Walsh, *Flodden 1513*, 25, 27.

17. However, at one point, Flint and Cushing Flint claim that the Mexican Indians in the expedition joined "primarily as warriors." Flint and Cushing Flint, *Documents*, 135.

18. Maureen Ahern, "Mapping, Measuring, and Naming Cultural Spaces in Castaneda's *Relacion de la journada de Cibola*," in Flint and Cushing Flint, *Coronado Expedition: From the Distance of 460 Years*, 274.

19. Day, "Mota Padilla," 91–92. Of course, this intermingling of auxiliary warriors and camp followers has some logic affecting combat effectiveness for, based on the Aztec way of war, "[t]he Mexican women . . . stood by their husbands and fathers, . . . [and] nursed the sick, treated the wounded, made slings and missiles" and occasionally fought. Gomara, *Cortes*, 293.

20. See William Urban, *Bayonets for Hire: Mercenaries at War, 1550–1789* (London: Greenhill, 2007), 40. See also Spaulding, Nickerson, and Wright, *Warfare*, 422.

21. See Bolton, *Coronado*, 58, 98. This was not the first time that a Spanish expedition tried to get along without Indian porters (*tamemes*). In 1527, an invasion of the Mayan Yucatan attempted to manage without native ally tamemes carrying baggage. See John E. Chuchiak IV, "Forgotten Allies: Origins and Roles of Native Mesoamerican Auxiliaries and Indios Conquistadores in the Conquest of Yucatan, 1526–1550," in Matthew and Oudijk, *Indian Conquistadors*, 178–179.

22. See Aiton, *Antonio de Mendoza*, 91–92.

23. Frederick W. Hodge, ed., "The Narrative of the Expedition of Hernando de Soto, by the Gentleman of Elvas," in Jameson, *Original Narratives*, 160.

24. See Nicolle, *Granada 1492*, 71.

25. Heath, *Armies of the Sixteenth Century [New World]*, 152.

26. See Wise, *Conquistadores*, 9.

27. Gomara, *Cortes*, 250–251.

28. Hammond and Rey, *Obregon's History*, 238.

29. See Leon-Portilla, *Broken Spears*, 79. These traitors, when discovered, were killed by the resisting Aztecs.

30. See Heath, *Armies of the Sixteenth Century [New World]*, 152.

31. See Smith, *Mexico*, 182–185.

32. By the fifth century, the late Roman army excluded pagans from serving in its ranks. Contamine, *War in the Middle Ages*, 264. This exclusive attitude probably was shared by the Spanish once they had consolidated their control in the New World.

33. See Heath, *Armies of the Sixteenth Century [New World]*, 152.

34. See, for example, Oudijk and Restall, "Mesoamerican Conquistadors," 33.

35. Aiton and Rey, "Coronado's Testimony," 314.

36. The revolting peasants during the major war of 1525–1526 were armed with a motley collection of pitchforks, scythes, axes, spears, halberds, daggers, sickles, rusty swords, and the odd piece of old armor (in addition to some arquebuses and some pieces of artillery). Bax, *Peasants War*, 40, 141, 148, 197. Some also had crossbows. See Siegfried Hoyer, "Arms and Military Organisation in the German Peasant War," in Bob Scribner and Gerhard Benecke, eds., *The German Peasant War of 1525: New Viewpoints* (London: George Allen & Unwin, 1979), 101.

37. Heath, *Armies of the Sixteenth Century [New World]*, 167–168.

38. A codex picture of Guzman's Indian allies, in fact, does show them wearing the traditional outfits as when Cortes was leading them, but that was several years before the Coronado Expedition, and the interim period saw significant changes.

39. Francisco Lopez de Gomara, *The Pleasant Historie of the Conquest of the Weast India, Now Called New Spayn* (London: Henry Bynneman, 1578), 186–187.

40. A few obsidian pieces consistent both with a central Mexican source and with *macana* sword blades have been found at a presumed Spanish camp near Bernalillo, New Mexico. Hartmann, "Finding Coronado's Route," 4.

41. See John Pohl, *Aztec, Mixtec and Zapotec Armies* (Botley, UK: Osprey, 1996), 18.

42. Flint, "Armas de la Tierra," 60.

43. Bolton, *Coronado*, 69–70.

44. Pohl , *Aztec, Mixtec and Zapotec Armies*, 37–38.

45. Garcilasco de la Vega, *The Florida of the Inca: A History of the Adelantado, Hernandon de Soto, Governor and Captain General of the Kingdom of Florida, and of Other Heroic Spanish and Indian Cavaliers, Written by the Inca, Garcilasco de la Vega, an Officer of His*

*Majesty, and a Native of the Great City of Cuzco, Capital of the Realms and Provinces of Peru,* trans. and ed. John Grier Varner and Jeannette Johnson Varner (Austin: University of Texas Press, 1951), 16. De la Vega, however, added that the natives did "not understand and thus cannot use the arquebus and the crossbow."

46. See Heath, *Armies of the Sixteenth Century [New World],* 168.

47. Nigel Davies, *The Aztecs* (London: Folio Society, 2000), 218.

48. See C. R. Boxer, *The Dutch Seaborne Empire: 1600–1800* (New York: Knopf, 1965), 75–76; Kirkup, *Surgeons Mate,* 184–185. However, it might not have been until 1611 that this knowledge was put into a text. William H. McNeill, *Plagues and Peoples* (New York: History Book Club, 1993), 268. Corn also contains vitamin C.

49. See Charles Phillips, *Aztec & Maya: The Greatest Civilizations of Ancient Central America with 1000 Photographs, Paintings and Maps* (New York: Metro Books, 2012), 28.

50. Fuentes, *Conquistadors,* 172.

51. Ran Knishinsky, *Prickly Pear, Cactus Medicine: Treatments for Diabetes, Cholesterol, and the Immune System* (Rochester, VT: Healing Arts Press, 2004), 2.

52. Smith, *Relation of Alvar Nunez Cabeza de Vaca,* 92.

53. See Knishinsky, *Prickly Pear,* 2–3.

54. Mary Gunderson, *American Indian Cooking before 1500* (Mankato, MN: Blue Earth Books, 2001), 18.

55. Contrasted with the yucca, the South American yuca has edible roots. See Millar, *Crossbowman's Story,* 342.

56. Gunderson, *American Indian Cooking,* 18.

57. Ibid., 16, 18.

58. Kathleen Cain, *The Cottonwood Tree: An American Champion* (Boulder, CO: Johnson Books, 2007), 144. The Indians might have observed deer feeding off cottonwood in the winter. The secret of salicylic acid (often found in tree bark) was well known to the Egyptians and other ancient peoples.

59. Robinson, "Coronado and His Army," 78.

60. Heath, *Armies of the Sixteenth Century [New World],* 152.

61. Hoig, *Came Men on Horses,* 46.

62. Flint and Cushing Flint, *Documents,* 135.

63. Hammond and Rey, *Narratives,* 166, "Letter of Coronado to Mendoza, August 3, 1540."

64. Ibid., 164, "Letter of Coronado to Mendoza, August 3, 1540."

65. Hodge, "Narrative by Castaneda," 306.

66. Day, *Coronado's Quest,* 314.

CHAPTER SEVEN: A COLORFUL ACCOMPANIMENT OF WOMEN, SERVANTS, SLAVES, AND OTHER CAMP FOLLOWERS

1. Saxtorph, *Warriors and Weapons,* 216.

2. Ibid.

3. Parker, *Army of Flanders,* 176–177.

4. See Flint and Cushing Flint, "A Death in Tiguex, 1542," 251. Such supposition is not out of line when discussing the often-surprising off-duty activities of soldiers. However, when the Spanish marched in Europe, female camp followers also might act as sutlers. See Hook, *Sack of Rome, 1527,* 124.

5. Aiton, *Antonio de Mendoza*, 125.

6. Hammond and Rey, *Narratives*, 306, "Jaramillo's Narrative . . ."

7. Thus, even the protagonist Moor of Shakespeare's *Othello* is an apparent Christian convert in the service of Renaissance Venice, although this is an assumed fact for most literary scholars. See, for example, J. A. Bryant Jr., *Hippolyta's View: Some Christian Aspects of Shakespeare's Plays* (Lexington: University of Kentucky Press, 1961), 139–152.

8. Certainly this occurred on the Patriot side during the southern campaigns in the American War for Independence, even though the British often promised freedom—which was not always granted. See, generally, Alan Gilbert, *Black Patriots and Loyalists: Fighting for Emancipation in the War for Independence* (Chicago: University of Chicago Press, 2012).

9. Matthew Restall, *Seven Myths of the Spanish Conquest* (New York: Oxford University Press, 2003), 54–55.

10. See Heath, *Armies of the Sixteenth Century [New World]*, 169.

11. Restall, *Seven Myths*, 55.

12. Ibid., 55–56.

13. See ibid., 53–54.

14. See ibid., 59.

15. Ibid., 63.

16. Ibid., 59.

17. Heath, *Armies of the Sixteenth Century [New World]*, 169.

18. See Hodge, "Narrative by Castaneda," 333.

19. See Hammond and Rey, *Narratives*, 164, "Letter of Coronado to Mendoza, August 3, 1540."

20. Peter Wood, *The Spanish Main* (Chicago: Time-Life Books, 1979), 80.

21. Heath, *Armies of the Sixteenth Century [New World]*, 168–169.

22. Kamen, *Empire*, 356.

23. Saxtorph, *Warriors and Weapons*, 216.

24. Ibid.

25. Ibid., 217.

26. See Robinson, *Spanish Invasion of Mexico*, 71–73.

27. See Francis Augustus MacNutt, trans., *Fernando Cortes: His Five Letters of Relation to the Emperor Charles V* (Cleveland: Arthur H. Clark, 1908), 2:99n.

28. Bernal Diaz del Castillo, *The Discovery and Conquest of Mexico*, trans. A. P. Maudslay (New York: Farrar, Straus and Cudahy, 1956), 321.

29. Kamen, *Empire*, 243.

30. Bancroft, *History of Mexico*, 503.

31. Flint and Cushing Flint, *Documents*, 136.

32. Ibid., 137.

33. Ibid.

34. Flint, *No Settlement*, 57.

35. See David Nicolle, *The Venetian Empire, 1200–1670* (London: Osprey, 1989), 41.

36. See John Sadler and Rosie Serdiville, *The Battle of Flodden 1513* (Stroud, UK: History Press, 2013), 196.

37. Day, *Coronado's Quest*, 363n4; Flint, *No Settlement*, 57.

38. Flint and Cushing Flint, *Documents*, 137.

39. Michael Mallett, *Mercenaries and Their Masters: Warfare in Renaissance Italy*

(Barnsley, UK: Pen and Sword Books, 2009), 189–190. One British historian, however, recently suggested there might have been a few authorized prostitutes with the Tudor army. See Raymond, *Henry VIII's Military Revolution*, 69–70. As for the typical Swiss and German Landsknecht armies, all adult female camp followers, including wives, were called "whores," but these women were just seen as a fact of military life, not officially part of the force. See Miller, *Lanksknechts*, 9.

40. Mallett, *Mercenaries and Their Masters*, 190.

41. See Hook, *Sack of Rome, 1527*, 137.

42. George Ryley Scott, *The History of Prostitution* (London: Senate, 1996), 69. It apparently was no coincidence that the venereal disease of syphilis, perhaps introduced to Europe after recent discoveries and trade missions relating to the Caribbean and Africa, rapidly spread across the continent fueled by the soldiery of the Italian Wars. See Alan Haynes, *Sex in Elizabethan England* (Stroud, UK: Sutton, 1997), 147. Because of the Italian Wars, these rather unsocial social diseases early on gained the appellation of "the Italian diseases," only later to be renamed (at least by the English), "the French disease." See Chamberlin, *Sack of Rome*, 29.

43. Michael, *Armies of Medieval Burgundy*, 16.

44. Housley, *Documents on the Later Crusades*, 180.

45. Kamen, *Empire*, 178.

46. Parker, *Army of Flanders*, 175n5.

47. Motley, *Rise of the Dutch Republic*, 2:110.

48. During the sixteenth century Protestant Reformation, there was a backlash against widespread promiscuity. See Reay Tannahill, *Sex in History* (New York: Stein and Day, 1980), 327–328; Scott, *History of Prostitution*, 126–127. This, in turn, occasioned the Catholic Counter-Reformation, which attacked some of the long-standing and notorious abuses.

49. Parker, *Army of Flanders*, 175–176. For a line drawing of one of these ladies (unattractive, although stylishly dressed), see Heath, *Armies of the Sixteenth Century [European]*, 143.

50. Cf. Thomas P. Lowry, *The Story the Soldiers Wouldn't Tell: Sex in the Civil War* (Mechanicsburg, PA: Stackpole, 1994).

51. Flint, *Great Cruelties*, 391.

52. See Kamen, *Empire*, 242.

53. Hodge, "Narrative by Castaneda," 288. Of course, the Zuni also did not think much of Esteban's presumed conduct in asking for both women and turquoise—if such conduct occurred. See Hodge, "Narrative by Castaneda," 289–290.

54. Hammond and Rey, *Obregon's History*, 237.

55. See ibid., 236.

## Chapter Eight: The March North into Sonora

1. Hodge, "Narrative by Castaneda," 293.

2. Ibid., 294. Onate would be acting governor of New Galicia during the absence of Coronado.

3. Day, "Mota Padilla," 91.

4. See Hodge, "Narrative by Castaneda," 294.

5. Ibid. Regarding the doctrinal faithfulness—as opposed to saintliness—of the average Spanish soldiery, archaeologists should be encouraged that the typical Spanish fighting

men in the sixteenth century carried "religious effigies, crucifixes, *Agnus Dei* and other charms." See Parker, *Army of Flanders*, 179.

6. See Contamine, *War in the Middle Ages*, 277.

7. See Hammond and Rey, *Obregon's History*, 45. Probably, this standard had a representation of the Virgin Mary on it, as did Cortes's main banner. See Pohl and Robinson, *Aztecs and Conquistadors*, 96. However, such banners also were known to have a portrayal of Christ's crucifixion on one side, with Mary on the other. See Angus Konstam and Tony Bryan, *Lepanto 1571: The Greatest Naval Battle of the Renaissance* (Botley, UK: Osprey, 2003), 86.

8. Hodge, "Narrative by Castaneda," 294–295. Such a charge regarding loyalty was given in 1563 when a force left Mexico for Peru. See Hammond and Rey, *Obregon's History*, 45–46. Regarding Coronado's force, while Castaneda was not completely correct about the faithfulness of all the members of the expedition, the loyalty maintained would turn out to be more than many another conquistador endeavor.

9. Flint, *Great Cruelties*, 364, "Defense Offered by Vazquez de Coronado; First de Parte Witness (Lorenzo Alvarez)."

10. Hodge, "Narrative by Castaneda," 295. While the expedition, as noted, probably had a church flag, it also probably had a color representing the temporal authority of Charles V, perhaps the Hapsburg eagle (as was the case with the 1535 expedition against Tunis). See Housley, *Documents on the Later Crusades*, 184. Short-staffed colors, ensigns, or flags became standard with the Swiss or German Landsknechts—professional mercenaries—in the early sixteenth century, and they were early indicators of national allegiance, in addition to being used on the battlefield for signalling. See Saxtorph, *Warriors and Weapons*, 217–218. These military flags were adopted by the Spanish and the short, painted flagstaff allowed the ensign-bearer to hold the colors in one hand and wield a sword in the other. During the rule of Charles V, Spanish ensigns were most often decorated with some form of a red Saint Andrew's cross, or saltire. See Heath, *Armies of the Sixteenth Century [European]*, 144–145. The red-cross flags supposedly had been used since the end of the fifteenth century at least. See Hare, *Bayard*, 58. On the other hand, traditionalists are more likely to imagine Coronado's force carrying the romantic banner of Castile, quartered with two lions and two castles. See "First Flag over Arizona," *Arizona Highways* 60, no. 4 (April 1984), 46. Finally, it is known that at least some of the banners of the expedition, whatever they looked like, were of silk provided by a financier and investor of the endeavor. See Flint and Cushing Flint, "Guido de Lavezariis," 3.

11. Defourneaux, *Daily Life in Spain*, 190.

12. Heath, *Armies of the Sixteenth Century [European]*, 144. The Spanish probably adopted the regular employment of drummers and fifers from the Landsknechts. See Saxtorph, *Warriors and Weapons*, 218.

13. There is an early codex drawing of a piper and drummer with Cortes's army. See Varner and Varner, *Dogs of the Conquest*, 64. When Pedro de Menendez slaughtered virtually all of a group of Frenchmen he captured near Fort Caroline in Florida in 1565, he spared the musicians (a drummer, a fifer, and a trumpeter)—even though they were heretical Protestants—to incorporate into his own force. See John T. McGrath, *The French in Early Florida: In the Eye of the Hurricane* (Gainesville: University Press of Florida, 2000), 151. Even in Europe, foreign musicians were permitted to serve in otherwise all-Spanish outfits. Notario Lopez and Notario Lopez, *Spanish Tercios*, 12.

14. See Frazier and Robert Hunt, *I Fought with Custer: The Story of Sergeant Windolph* (New York: Charles Scribner's Sons, 1947), 52–54; Kenneth Hammer, *Biographies of the 7th Cavalry, June 25th 1876* (Fort Collins, CO: Old Army Press, 1972), 1.

15. Hodge, "Narrative by Castaneda," 295.

16. See Hodge, "Narrative by Castaneda," 336. Most of the musicians, drummers or fifers,  adding to the stepping off of Coronado's column probably belonged to Compostela or to the viceroy's retinue, whence they likely returned when the viceroy left.

17. See Parker, *Army of Flanders*, 95.

18. Matthew, *Tactics of Aelian*, 127.

19. See Hodge, "Narrative by Castaneda," 298.

20. See Parker, *Army of Flanders*, 95. Parker thought this "an astonishing total" for the number of soldiers. It is not.

21. Davies, *Aztecs*, 218.

22. John E. Rouse, *The Criollo: Spanish Cattle in the Americas* (Norman: University of Oklahoma Press, 1977), 20–21, 54, 79, 254. Rouse, a cowman by vocation, did not even attempt to estimate, the "large number of sheep and goats" with the column. Ibid., 79.

23. See Lisa Drew, "The Barnyard Restoration: About Half of Our Livestock Breeds Are in Peril of Disappearing Forever," *Newsweek*, May 29, 1989, 51.

24. Hodge, "Narrative by Castaneda," 382. Although amazing, this estimate (as well as Castaneda's count of five hundred head of cattle) has been accepted by some historians. *See* Robinson, "Coronado and His Army," 71.

25. Cantor, *Last Knight*, 43.

26. See Raymond, *Henry VIII's Military Revolution*, 72–73.

27. Richards, *Landsknecht Soldier*, 27.

28. See Boxer, *Dutch Seaborne Empire*, 76. Neither were the sixteenth-century Spanish known (at least according to the often snobbish Italians) for regular bathing. Chamberlin, *Sack of Rome*, 101.

29. See Parker, *Army of Flanders*, 95–96.

30. Ibid., 88–89, 92.

31. Ibid., 87.

32. See Hammond and Rey, *Obregon's History*, 232, 233.

33. In 1523, hostile natives of Guatemala attacked the baggage train of Pedro de Alvarado, taking "a good part of the baggage, with all the strings for the crossbows." Fuentes, *Conquistadors*, 192.

34. John D. Billings, *Hardtack and Coffee, or, The Unwritten Story of Army Life* (Boston: George M. Smith, 1887), 352.

35. See Hammond and Rey, *Obregon's History*, 233. However, the only archaeological evidence found so far related to the production of metal implements by the expedition hints at thin sheets of copper being cut, perhaps for additional crossbow bolts. See Frank R. Gagne Jr., "Spanish Crossbow Boltheads of Sixteenth-Century North America: A Comparative Analysis," in Flint and Cushing Flint, *Coronado Expedition: From the Distance of 460 Years*, 246; see also Diane Lee Rhodes, "Coronado Fought Here: Crossbow Boltheads as Possible Indicators of the 1540–1542 Expedition," in Flint and Cushing Flint, *Coronado Expedition to Tierra Nueva*, 50–51.

36. The Indians also captured from Alvarado in Guatemala "the horseshoes I carried for the war." Fuentes, *Conquistadors*, 192.

37. See Flint, *Great Cruelties*, 110, "Juan de Contreras, the Fifth de Oficio Witness."

38. Hodge, "Narrative by Castaneda," 295. In having to discard useless items, the Spanish force was similar to many green armies, including those at the beginning of America's Civil War. See Billings, *Hardtack and Coffee*, 355.

39. Paul A. Jones, *Quivira* (Wichita, KS: McCormick-Armstrong, 1929), 76–77. When figuring out distances, it only adds to the confusion that the Spaniards had two leagues— a linear league (about 3.5 miles) and a nonlinear league (about 2.6 miles)—and one is never sure which one is being referenced. See Charles Hudson, Chester B. DePratter, and Marvin T. Smith, "Appendix I: Reply to Henige," in Young and Hoffman, *Expedition of Hernando de Soto*, 265. Of course, the camp followers and herds of livestock would not be able to equal even the easiest pace of the soldiers and warriors.

40. Hodge, "Narrative by Castaneda," 295.

41. Neil Hanson, *The Confident Hope of a Miracle: The True History of the Spanish Armada* (New York: Knopf, 2005), 186.

42. Ibid.

43. Day, "Mota Padilla," 91–92.

44. Aiton, *Antonio de Mendoza*, 125. Of course, Aiton, in calling them light mountain guns, was making the weapons sound like the mountain howitzers that were packed on mules during the Civil War's New Mexico campaign of 1862. The weight of each falconet obviously would be excessive for all but the strongest mule.

45. See Funcken and Funcken, *Age of Chivalry, Part 3*, 100, for an illustration of a 1510 example of a cart hauling a heavy mortar and ammunition. The practice of carrying dismantled light artillery on pack animals, with the carriage on one mule, the wheels on another one or two, and the piece itself on a third—as with mountain or "pack" howitzers—was not unknown in the eighteenth century but did not become common until the nineteenth century.

46. Flint, *Great Cruelties*, 14.

47. Ibid. However, there is a contemporary hint that mere cast gun barrels were turned into actual artillery pieces by the process of building them carriages. Aiton and Rey, "Coronado's Testimony," 304. Indeed, in military parlance, artillery pieces implies guns on wheeled carriages. See, for example, Peers, *Medieval Chinese Armies*, 36.

48. Konstam, *Pavia 1525*, 24.

49. Funcken and Funcken, *Arms and Uniforms, Part 1*, 114.

50. Marjorie Quennell and C. H. B. Quennell, *A History of Everyday Things in England: The Rise of Industrialism, 1733–1851* (New York: Charles Scribner's Sons, 1934), 133–134.

51. See John Vince, *An Illustrated History of Carts and Wagons* (Bourne End, UK: Spurbooks, 1975), 16, 71.

52. See Parker, *Army of Flanders*, 95.

53. See ibid., 95–96.

54. See Taylor, *Art of War in Italy*, 45, speaking of the Battle of Ravenna.

55. Konstam, *Pavia 1525*, 8, 64, 66. At Pavia, the wagon train was attacked and the camp followers massacred.

56. Bolton, *Coronado*, 84.

57. See Chipman, *Nuno de Guzman*, 222.

58. During the Reconquista of their nation, Spanish pioneers did cut roads and move siege artillery over rugged country. See Nicolle, *Granada 1492*, 59.

59. See Hammond and Rey, *Obregon's History*, 232–233.

60. See ibid., 233.

61. See, for example, Hoig, *Came Men on Horses*, 45.

62. Richards, *Landsknecht Soldier*, 58.

63. Woosnam-Savage and Hall, *Brassey's Book*, 70. Even the cotton body armor of the Aztec, if worn incessantly day after day, had its drawbacks. Spaniards in humid Mexico complained that the native armor caused severe pains in the groin area. Ibid., 96.

64. See Fleischman, "Royal Armor," 71, referring to the soldiers of England's Elizabeth I.

65. See Heath, *Armies of the Sixteenth Century [European]*, 144. In addition, those artist depictions that show the Spaniards with puffed shoulders and pumpkin pants may not necessarily be anachronistic, although these styles may belong more to the late sixteenth century. See Wise, *Conquistadores*, 12. During the earlier period, Spanish soldiers dressed in a rather somber style and did not adopt the more extreme and colorful slashed style of clothing used by the Landsknechts. See Saxtorph, *Warriors and Weapons*, 228–230; Konstam and Turner, *Pavia 1525*, 19. However, even though the outlandish Landsknecht style was not generally seen in Spanish forces, uniformity in costume was long resisted by a Spain that felt uniforms impinged on individual pride. Tincey and Hook, *Armada Campaign*, 9, 51.

66. However, as in modern times, the steel helmets, both in Europe and in the Americas, often had fitted cloth covers, which would tend to reduce the temperature and slow the appearance of rust. See Wise and McBride, *Conquistadores*, 35.

67. See Jones, *Knight*, 107.

68. See Taylor, *Art of War in Italy*, 39, 47. See also Notario Lopez and Notario Lopez, *Spanish Tercios*, 43, excess armor with the baggage train. Even if the firearms were carried individually on the march, it is unlikely any would have burning matches and be ready to fire.

69. Pedro de Castaneda, in his roundabout sentence structure, seemingly supports the idea that at least some armament or armor was not individually carried at all times. When the expedition was pummeled by hail in the Texas Panhandle, "the negroes protected [two or three horses] . . . with the helmets and shields which all the rest wore." Hodge, "Narrative by Castaneda," 333. This and other translations imply that the armor normally was with the baggage train, even in camp. See also chapter 18, note 19, in this book.

70. See Peter Reid, *Medieval Warfare: Triumph and Domination in the Wars of the Middle Ages* (New York: Carroll and Graf, 2007), 413; Christopher Rothero, *The Armies of Crecy and Poitiers* (London: Osprey, 1989), 33.

71. See Notario Lopez and Notario Lopez, *Spanish Tercios*, 44. By about 1500, soldiers in northern Europe are known to have carried "wooden-barrel" canteens. See Richards, *Landsknecht Soldier*, 62. But those canteens tend to dry out in arid climes.

72. As previously mentioned, the Spanish were noted for engraving on their Toledo blades the motto, "Draw me not without reason and sheath me not without honor." See Hodge, "Narrative by Castaneda," 302n2. And when the forces of Cortes were expelled from Mexico City by the Aztec uprising of 1520, they lost all of their artillery and dropped most of their weapons (and most of their looted gold)—but they kept hold of their swords. Prescott, *History of the Conquest of Mexico*, 2:365–366.

73. See Nicolle, *Granada 1492*, 27.

74. Hodge, "Narrative by Castaneda," 295.
75. Day, "Mota Padilla," 92.
76. Ibid. See also Hodge, "Narrative by Castaneda," 295. Mota Padilla's statement that Samaniego was wearing a helmet, although no helmet specifically was attributed to the army master in the muster roll (see Aiton, *Muster Roll*, 7), is credible and would indicate that there was more metal armor present than indicated by the roll or that extra pieces were shared among the leadership or men-at-arms.
77. Hodge, "Narrative by Castaneda," 295. Reportedly, Captain Juan Jaramillo was in this group. Hammond and Rey, *Obregon's History*, 14.
78. Hodge, "Narrative by Castaneda," 295–296.
79. Ibid., 296.
80. Day, "Mota Padilla," 92.
81. Hammond and Rey, *Obregon's History*, 14.
82. Hammond and Rey, *Narratives*, 157, "Letter of Mendoza to the King, April 17, 1540."
83. See Bolton, *Coronado*, 88.
84. Ibid., 87. Bolton seemingly just relies on the usual course of vague army (or campus) gossip for assuming the ordinary soldiery heard.
85. Hodge, "Narrative by Castaneda," 296.
86. Hammond and Rey, *Narratives*, 158, "Letter of Mendoza to the King, April 17, 1540."
87. Hodge, "Narrative by Castaneda," 296.
88. This situation of low desertion was found to be true in medieval times with an army on the march. Jones, *Knight*, 107. It often still holds with modern armies.
89. See Hodge, "Narrative by Castaneda," 296–297.
90. See Day, "Mota Padilla," 92.
91. Hodge, "Narrative by Castaneda," 297.
92. Hoig, *Came Men on Horses*, 50.
93. See Flint, *No Settlement*, 76. The index calls the event a "ritual battle." Ibid., 350.
94. Raymond, *Henry VIII's Military Revolution*, 57.
95. Jones, *Knight*, 86.
96. Constance Brittain Bouchard, chief consultant, *Knights in History and Legend* (Buffalo, NY: Firefly, 2010), 100–112.
97. Nicolle, *Granada 1492*, 24.
98. Bouchard, *Knights*, 103, 106–107.
99. Jones, *Knight*, 223. However, another historian believes that in the England of the latter Middle Ages, unlike in the rest of Europe, the tournaments already had begun to evolve into royal exercises emphasizing training for active campaigning. See Keen, *Nobles, Knights*, 98–99.
100. Eltis, *Military Revolution*, 60.
101. See Taylor, *Art of War in Italy*, 136n6; 161.
102. See Hare, *Charles de Bourbon*, 88.
103. See Mallett, *Mercenaries and Their Masters*, 191.
104. Nicolle and Rothero, *Venetian Empire*, 18–19.
105. Heath, *Armies of the Sixteenth Century [New World]*, 149.
106. Apparently only one previous historian has recognized this benefit for the local militia. See Day, *Coronado's Quest*, 92.

107. Hare, *Charles de Bourbon*, 88.

108. Heath, *Armies of the Sixteenth Century [European]*, 151.

109. See Konstam, *Pavia 1525*, 24.

110. Hodge, "Narrative by Castaneda," 297. While training injuries and fatalities always are regrettable, one historian relegated this serious injury to a mere "good time" gone bad for no valid reason. Hoig, *Came Men on Horses*, 50. Historically, the known details of the injury to the artilleryman hint—but only hint—that the *versillos* were not breechloading swivel guns but were muzzle loaders. This tenuous assumption would indicate that calling the small cannon falconets gives more a sense of their physical appearance to students of military history.

111. Richard Flint and Shirley Cushing Flint, "Hernando de Alvarado," Office of the New Mexico State Historian, accessed January 24, 2014, newmexicohistory.org/people/hernando-de-alvarado. Munoz was a rather impecunious man-at-arms, for he possessed but one horse and arms of the country when mustered in. Aiton, *Muster Roll*, 8.

112. Hodge, "Narrative by Castaneda," 297–298.

113. Ibid., 297.

114. Ibid. Perhaps some of the soldiery did a little horse trading and got extra military equipment such as arms or armor from the locals in exchange. The expedition might even have enlisted a few new recruits from local impressionable youths—or disillusioned husbands fleeing their wives.

115. Hodge, "Narrative by Castaneda," 298.

116. Ibid.

117. Ibid.

118. See Robinson, "Coronado and His Army," 74.

119. Ironically, despite much sincere fanaticism among Catholics and Protestants during the sixteenth century, there were contradictory feelings (left over from medieval times) about the occult, as exemplified by some of Shakespeare's plays. One of Italy's sophisticated artists and bon vivants, Benvenuto Cellini, although a confidant of popes, dabbled in the black arts. See Benvenuto Cellini, *The Autobiography of Benvenuto Cellini, a Florentine Artist: Containing a Variety of Information Respecting the Arts and the History of the Sixteenth Century* (Reading, PA: Spencer, 1936), 116–120. Cellini apparently was not an isolated case. "While commonplace wizards and witches were being burned wholesale, a certain number of more distinguished practitioners of the same arts employed considerable court-influence." This despite the fact that witchcraft "was almost invariably malignant and destructive." Oman, *Sixteenth Century*, 213, 216. Although Trujillo apparently survived his story of having been tempted by the devil, much later in the expedition an Indian called Turk ultimately came to a bad end after having, among other offenses, reportedly been in communication with demonic forces.

## CHAPTER NINE: THE GARRISON LEFT AT SAN GERONIMO

1. Jones, *Knight*, 107.

2. Sir Roger Williams, *The Actions of the Low Countries*, ed. D. W. Davies (Ithaca, NY: Cornell University Press, 1964), 72.

3. Hodge, "Narrative by Castaneda," 298.

4. See Hammond and Rey, *Narratives*, 162, "Letter of Coronado to Mendoza, August 3, 1540."

5. Flint and Cushing Flint, *Documents*, 527, "Juan Troyano's Proof of Service, 1560."

6. Ibid.

7. For example, when Henry V marched from Harfleur to Calais in 1415, prior to the Battle of Agincourt, he left his wagons and heavy material behind and proceeded at a forced march with packhorses. Clive Bartlett, *English Longbowman, 1330–1515* (London: Osprey/Reed Consumer Books, 1997), 45.

8. See Hodge, "Narrative by Castaneda," 298. Castaneda said there were about eight hundred Indian allies and "most" of them went with the advance.

9. See Flint and Cushing Flint, *Documents,* 164. However, in defense of this seemingly illogical methodology, one military historian of the era (with real-world military experience) has argued that sometimes an eyewitness may make a more accurate estimation of percentages than of raw numbers. See Taylor, *Art of War in Italy,* 201, discussing an observer's guess at total casualties lying dead on the ground—tens of thousands—versus estimating there were three dead Spaniards and Vatican soldiers for each body of a Frenchman. Castaneda, however, only had to count in the hundreds, and those counts were of soldiers and warriors still standing on their feet and marching past.

10. Hammond and Rey, *Narratives,* 162, "Letter of Coronado to Mendoza, August 3, 1540."

11. Hodge, "Narrative by Castaneda," 298–299. One of the clerics, breaking his leg, soon left the advance guard and rejoined the main command to minister to the soldiers, "which was no slight consolation for all." Ibid., 299.

12. Hammond and Rey, *Narratives,* 164 ("Letter of Coronado to Mendoza, August 3, 1540").

13. Oman, *History of the Art of War,* 220.

14. Taylor , *Art of War in Italy,* 14.

15. Hodge, "Narrative by Castaneda," 301. This description probably inspired a well-known Frederic Remington illustration. When it left, the main army was only about two weeks behind Coronado, but at its slower pace and because it was ordered to establish the San Geronimo settlement and await orders, it would be many months before it rejoined the advance. Day, "Mota Padilla," 93n12.

16. Hodge, "Narrative by Castaneda," 301.

17. See Chartand and Spedaliere, *Spanish Main* (Botley, UK: Osprey, 2006), 14–17.

18. Hodge, "Narrative by Castaneda," 301–302.

19. See William K. Hartmann and Gayle Harrison Hartmann, "Locating the Lost Coronado Garrisons of San Geronimo I, II, and III," in Flint and Cushing Flint, *Latest Word from 1540,* 117.

20. Hodge, "Narrative by Castaneda," 302.

21. Ibid., 303.

22. Ibid.

23. Andrew C. Hess, *The Forgotten Frontier: A History of the Sixteenth-Century Ibero-African Frontier* (Chicago: University of Chicago Press, 2010), 42.

24. Max L. Moorhead, *The Presidio: Bastion of the Spanish Borderlands* (Norman: University of Oklahoma Press, 1991), 4.

25. Heath, *Armies of the Sixteenth Century [New World],* 150.

26. Moorhead, *Presidio,* 4.

27. Oman, *History of the Art of War,* 220.

28. Cf. Ibid.

29. Alfred Vincent Kidder, *An Introduction to the Study of Southwestern Archaeology, with*

*a Preliminary Account of the Excavations at Pecos* (New Haven, CT: Yale University Press, 1924), 39.

CHAPTER TEN: THE INVASION OF ZUNI

1. Hodge, "Narrative by Castaneda," 298.
2. Hammond and Rey, *Narratives*, 584, "Translation of the Narrative of Jaramillo."
3. Winship, "Coronado Expedition," 572, "Translation of the Relacion del Sucesco."
4. Flint and Cushing Flint, *Documents*, 497, "The Relacion del Sucesco (Anonymous Narrative), 1540s." Winship thought the text said "a small part of the artillery" was taken. Winship, "Coronado Expedition," 572, "Translation of the Relacion del Sucesco."
5. A painting of the era, by Flemish artist Jan Mostaert, shows an attack on an apparent pueblo supported by two falconets, mounted on wheeled carriages. See Gilbert, *The Trailblazers*, 22–23. Again, while complete documentary details about Coronado's artillery are lacking, it would appear that they were not packed on horses. "[T]he mounted gentlemen in my company and I carried a little food on our backs and on our horses, so that, after leaving this place, we carried no other necessary articles weighing more than a pound." Hammond and Rey, *Narratives*, 162–163, "Letter of Coronado to Mendoza, August 3, 1540." Mendoza, having contributed the guns, would have known that the heavier ordnance had wheeled carriages.
6. Hammond and Rey, *Narratives*, 162, "Letter of Coronado to Mendoza, August 3, 1540."
7. Ibid., 164, "Letter of Coronado to Mendoza, August 3, 1540."
8. Ibid.
9. Ibid.
10. See Flint, *Great Cruelties*, 145, "Seventh de Oficio Witness (Cristobal de Escobar)."
11. See Winship, "Coronado Expedition," 585, "Narrative of Jaramillo."
12. Hodge, "Narrative by Castaneda," 299.
13. Ibid.
14. Hammond and Rey, *Narratives*, 166, "Letter of Coronado to Mendoza, August 3, 1540."
15. See Frederick Webb Hodge, *History of Hawikuh, New Mexico: One of the So-Called Cities of Cibola* (Los Angeles: Southwest Museum ,1937), 56–57.
16. Hammond and Rey, *Narratives*, 586, "Translation of the Narrative of Jaramillo."
17. See Hodge, "Narrative by Castaneda," 299n2.
18. Ibid., 299.
19. R. Edgar Moore, "Trail of Conquest, 1540–1940," *Street & Smith's Western Story* 185, no. 6 (October 5, 1940), 38.
20. Hammond and Rey, *Narratives*, 344, "Testimony of Lopez de Cardenas. . . ." As long ago as Thermopylae, those who controlled a critical pass controlled movement. During the Peasants War of 1525–1526, the insurgents stole a march on the forces of the Archbishop of Salzburg by seizing an undefended pass. Bax, *Peasants War in Germany*, 197.
21. Hammond and Rey, *Narratives*, 167, "Letter of Coronado to Mendoza, August 3, 1540."
22. Ibid.
23. Hammond and Rey, *Narratives*, 322, "Coronado's Testimony Concerning the Expedition, . . . September 3, 1544."

24. Hodge, "Narrative by Castaneda," 299–300.
25. Hammond and Rey, *Narratives*, 344, "Testimony of Lopez de Cardenas. . . ."
26. Jonathan E. Damp, "The Summer of 1540: Archaeology of the Battle of Hawikku," *Archaeology Southwest* 19, no. 1 (Winter 2005), 4.
27. Hodge, "Narrative by Castaneda," 300.
28. Brenda L Shears and Rose Wyaco, "Hawikku: A Fabled City of Cibola," *Native Peoples* 3, no. 4 (Summer 1990), 24. This ancient Zuni village of Cibola (long since abandoned) is about a dozen miles from the present Zuni pueblo.
29. Hodge, "Narrative by Castaneda," 300.
30. Green, *Zuni*, 174.
31. Day, *Coronado's Quest*, 126–127.
32. Ibid., 127.
33. Green, *Zuni*, 174.
34. See Frank Hamilton Cushing, recorder and trans., *Zuni Folk Tales* (New York: G. P. Putnam's Sons/Knickerbocker Press, 1901), 336–337.
35. See Day, *Coronado's Quest*, 128–129.
36. Kidder, *Introduction to the Study of Southwestern Archaeology*, 40.
37. Hammond and Rey, *Narratives*, 168, "Letter of Coronado to Mendoza, August 3, 1540."

## CHAPTER ELEVEN: MODERN TACTICS VERSUS ANTIQUITY

1. However, as historian Angus Konstam wrote about the much bigger Battle of Pavia of 1525, because of the conflicting, vague, and self-serving contemporary accounts, "[A]ny attempt to reconstruct the events . . . is an interpretation that could differ from reconstructions posed by other historians." Konstam and Turner, *Pavia 1525*, 4. Also, as General William Sherman once observed more succinctly about the difficulty of reconstructing battlefield events, even by a major player, "[W]e all know that no three honest witnesses of [even] a simple brawl can agree on all the details."
2. Hodge, "Narrative by Castaneda," 300. Typical of Castaneda, it often is unclear to which noun a clause applies. Was the army drawn up in divisions or were the natives? According to how Castaneda described a later fight in the land of the Hopi, it probably was the Spanish. See Hodge, 307.
3. See Hammond and Rey, *Narratives*, 322, "Coronado's Testimony Concerning the Expedition."
4. Hope Gilbert, "He Found Six of the Fabled 'Seven Cities of Cibola,'" *Desert Magazine* 5, no. 6 (April 1942), 9.
5. Winship, "Coronado Expedition," 564–565, "Translation of the Translado de Las Nuevas."
6. Hammond and Rey, *Narratives*, 167–168, "Letter of Coronado to Mendoza, August 3, 1540." The notary would be a learned scribe and probably the legal adviser (like a judge advocate) in a military expedition.
7. See Isabelle Cazeaux, *French Music in the Fifteenth and Sixteenth Centuries* (New York: Praeger, 1975), 144.
8. Kamen, *Empire*, 97.
9. See Grotius and Loomis, *Law of War and Peace*, 356.
10. Hare, *Bayard*, 92.
11. Hammond and Rey, *Narratives*, 168, "Letter of Coronado to Mendoza, August 3, 1540."

12. Ibid.

13. Ibid., 323, "Coronado's Testimony Concerning the Expedition, . . . September 3, 1544."

14. Day, "Mota Padilla," 93. The fact that the Zuni marked a line in the sand was expanded by Day, using an acknowledgment by Mota Padilla that the adult male Cibolans on occasion used kivas "in diversion" and excluded women, to mean that this barrier line was "made with sacred corn meal and the custom still persists where Pueblo Indians wish to exclude strangers from some secret ceremony." Although this scenario is not mentioned in relatively early recorded Zuni oral tradition, modern Zuni have adopted this conclusion by Day to demonstrate that their people merely were exercising their annual religious beliefs and that the Spaniards simply misunderstood and became the aggressors. See Stewart L. Udall, "The Battle of Hawikuh [Hawikku]," *Native Peoples* 3, no. 4 (Summer 1990), 25. See also Edmund J. Ladd, "Zuni on the Day the Men in Metal Arrived," in Flint and Cushing Flint, *Coronado Expedition to Tierra Nueva*, 225–233. That the Zuni people would conduct such a ceremony (not even directed at the invaders) the day after the natives had staged a surprise attack at the "bad pass" ignores logic. However, assuming that this scenario is true—and drawing a line in the sand appears to be a universal warning in the sixteenth-century Southwest—the Spaniards, of course, would not have respected such cultural arguments, whether based on pagan beliefs or based on the men wanting to have a secret lodge meeting.

15. John Pohl, *Aztec Warrior AD 1325–1521* (Botley, UK: Osprey, 2001), 44. However, one also should note that the Aztecs formally schooled their citizens, high and low born, for warfare. Robinson, *Spanish Invasion of Mexico*, 22, 24. The Zuni were more amateurs-at-arms.

16. Winship, "Coronado Expedition," 565, "Translation of the Translado de Las Nuevas."

17. Hammond and Rey, *Narratives*, 344, "Testimony of Lopez de Cardenas . . ."

18. Ibid., 323, "Coronado's Testimony Concerning the Expedition, . . . September 3, 1544."

19. Ibid., 168, "Letter of Coronado to Mendoza, August 3, 1540."

20. Winship, "Coronado Expedition," 565, "Translation of the Translado de Las Nuevas." The complete battle cry was usually "Santiago! Y a ellos!" This is best translated as "Saint James and at them!" Pohl and Robinson, *Aztecs and Conquistadores*, 161. It would be employed with equal exuberance against heretical Europeans and pagan natives of the New World. The tradition of the cry went back to the Reconquista, when the body of the saint (the brother of Saint John, not the James who was the half-brother of Christ) supposedly was discovered in Spain. Thereafter, according to the Spaniards, Saint James occasionally would appear on the battlefield in time to inspire the Christians against the Muslim Moors. See Jonathan Brown, "Another Image of the World: Spanish Art, 1500–1920," in J. H. Elliott, ed., *The Spanish World: Civilization and Empire, Europe and the Americas, Past and Present* (New York: Harry N. Abrams, 1991), 168. Other European Christians, especially before the Reformation, also "were careful to invoke heavenly assistance" in their war cries, proclaiming the names of particular national or regional saints, such as Saint George for the English and Saint Denis for the French. See Contamine, *War in the Middle Ages*, 299–300.

21. See Samuel Johnson, Christopher Smart, and Oliver Goldsmith, eds., *The World Displayed; or a Curious Collection of Voyages and Travels*, vol. 2 (London: J. Newbery, 1761), 187–190.

22. See King, *De Soto and His Men*, 164–173.

23. See Nicolle, *Granada 1492*, 41. This risk of surprise, present in any era, certainly was a concern in the sixteenth century. During a battle between the Scots and English at Ancrum Moor or Lilliard's Edge in 1545, charging English horsemen pursuing withdrawing Scots ran into an ambush. Richard Brooks, *Cassell's Battlefields of Britain and Ireland* (London: Weidenfeld & Nicolson, 2005), 291–293.

24. See Wise, *Conquistadores*, 9–10.

25. Hammond and Rey, *Narratives*, 168, "Letter of Coronado to Mendoza, August 3, 1540."

26. Day, "Mota Padilla," 93.

27. Hammond and Rey, *Narratives*, 345, "Testimony of Lopez de Cardenas . . ."

28. Ibid., 170, "Letter of Coronado to Mendoza, August 3, 1540."

29. Winship, "Coronado Expedition," 565, "Translation of the Translado de Las Nuevas."

30. Hammond and Rey, *Narratives*, 170, "Letter of Coronado to Mendoza, August 3, 1540."

31. See Konstantin Nossov, *Ancient and Medieval Siege Weapons: A Fully Illustrated Guide to Siege Weapons and Tactics* (Staplehurst, UK: Spellmount, 2006), 253–254. Such an attempt worked in capturing a fort during the siege of Barcelona in 1705. See Capt. George Carleton, *Military Memoirs (1672–1713)* (London: Jonathan Cape, 1929), 102–110.

32. Flint and Cushing Flint, *Documents*, 497, "The Relacion del Sucesco (Anonymous Narrative), 1540s."

33. Hammond and Rey, *Narratives*, 168–169, "Letter of Coronado to Mendoza, August 3, 1540." Choosing to take a surrounded citadel by storm rather than waiting to starve out a city by a regular siege occurs throughout history, as when the famished Europeans during the First Crusade finally had no choice but to take Jerusalem by direct assault in 1099. See Bruce Allen Watson, *Sieges: A Comparative Study* (Westport, CT: Praeger, 1993), 143. Similarly, in 1527, the motley and starving army of Charles V, also lacking heavy guns, was forced by necessity to attack and capture Rome quickly. See Chamberlin, *Sack of Rome*, 9–10, 153, 157.

34. See Hook, *Sack of Rome, 1527*, 161–162; Chamberlin, *Sack of Rome*, 39; Hare, *Charles de Bourbon*, 234.

35. Hammond and Rey, *Narratives*, 345, "Testimony of Lopez de Cardenas . . ."

36. Coggins, *Fighting Man*, 153. In Europe at this time, taking a town by storm—without heavy artillery—was so difficult it was rarely considered. Hook, *Sack of Rome, 1527*, 157.

37. Only one actual veteran of the Italian Wars, Juan Troyano, has been identified as being among the army. See Flint and Cushing Flint, *Documents*, 525, "Juan Troyano's Proof of Service, 1560." Nonetheless, in addition to those who had been on ventures in the Americas, there must have been at least a few others with European experience, since such veterans did settle in the New World. See Heath, *Armies of the Sixteenth Century [New World]*, 149. Also, there would be those who had studied previous campaigns in Europe and the New World, if only by hearing war stories from authentic Spanish veterans.

38. Similarly, in 1541, during the Mixton War in New Galicia, when Pedro de Alvarado and Cristobal de Onate besieged and attacked the rebel stronghold of Nuchiztlan, the

"well provided [Spanish] army" employed "proper tactics." Hammond and Rey, *Obregon's History*, 32.

39. Flint, *Great Cruelties*, 162. By the sixteenth century, the general military expertise and technical skills of artillerymen—as contrasted with arquebusiers, who sometimes were seen as mere assassins—was recognized even by noble men-at-arms. See Miller, *Lanksknechts*, 14–15.

40. Flint and Cushing Flint, *Documents*, 527, "Juan Troyano's Proof of Service, 1560."

41. John L. Kessell, *Kiva, Cross, and Crown: The Pecos Indians and New Mexico, 1540–1840* (Albuquerque: University of New Mexico Press, 1987), 5.

42. Angus Konstam and Tony Bryan, *Spanish Galleon, 1530–1690* (Botley, UK: Osprey, 2004), 16–17. The English even had a piece slightly smaller than a falconet called the robinet. A. F. Scott, ed., *Every One a Witness—The Tudor Age: Commentaries of an Era* (New York: Thomas Y. Crowell, 1976), 244.

43. The earliest breechloading hailshot pieces, swivel guns that continued to be used for many years, sometimes were loaded with "a bag of small objects" to kill personnel. Roth, *Visser Collection*, 92.

44. See *Fine Antique Arms and Armour from the Henk L. Visser Collection* (London: Bonhams, 2007), 94–95.

45. See Konstam and Bryan, *Spanish Galleon*, 16.

46. See Flint, *No Settlement*, 111. See also Flint and Cushing Flint, "Hernando de Alvarado." A historian of the Italian Wars similarly described falconets as "breach-loading cannons, turning on a pivot," but he also had their individual shot weighing "thirty or forty pounds," clearly an error. Hare, *Charles de Bourbon*, 234. See Funcken and Funcken, *Age of Chivalry, Part 3*, 92–93, for a description and illustration of a 1505 example of a piece of very light artillery mounted on a tripod stand that was "ingeniously designed so that it can be dismantled into two parts." Another historian of the Spanish conquistadors, while he seemingly at one point endorses the use of an "ingenious makeshift timber structure" as an immobile gun mount of the conquistadors, later concedes that the artillery, once it was moved inland, may have been remounted on either "makeshift carriages or even timber scaffolds." Pohl, *Conquistador*, 21, 29.

47. See Nicolle, *Granada 1492*, 54, 65.

48. See Funcken and Funcken, *Age of Chivalry, Part 3*, 100–101, for a description and illustration of a 1510 example of a cart hauling a heavy mortar and ammunition. The practice of carrying dismantled light artillery on pack animals, with the carriage on one mule, the wheels on another one or two, and the piece itself on a third—as with mountain or pack howitzers—did not become common until the nineteenth century. But there is evidence the French used such a method as early as the late seventeenth century. See Childs, *Warfare in the Seventeenth Century*, 184. And there were, a hundred years later, the British 3-pounder "grasshopper" guns, which were intended to be light enough to accompany infantry columns. Although often pulled by a single horse, the grasshoppers, two of which were used at the Battle of Cowpens in 1781, could be disassembled and carried by pack animals when speed was of the essence. See Caruana, *Grasshoppers and Butterflies*, 6, 8, 16–17; John Buchanan, *The Road to Guilford Courthouse: The American Revolution in the Carolinas* (New York: John Wiley & Sons, 1997), 309, 321.

49. Dr. Ian Barnes, *Historical Atlas of Knights and Castles* (New York: Chartwell, 2010), 320. The Hussites used their wagons a number of times in this manner.

50. Charles Yriarte, *Venice: Its History, Art, Industries and Modern Life*, trans. F. J. Sitwell (Philadelphia: John C. Winston/International Press, c. 1900), 105–106. While these mobile, but primitive, artillery pieces were heavy harquebuses mounted on light carts (see Taylor, *Art of War in Italy*, 185–187), there is an earlier example of a Spanish breechloading bronze "cannon" on a wheeled carriage used at the "end of the fifteenth century." See Ashdown, *British and Foreign*, plate 37.

51. Peers, *Medieval Chinese Armies*, 36.

52. Deagan and Cruxent, *Columbus's Outpost*, 169.

53. Wise, *Conquistadores*, 15, 17. A circa 1560 tapestry commemorating the Portuguese conquest of Goa in India has small falconets being pulled in such a manner. See Nicolle, *Portuguese in the Age of Discovery*, 1, 16. Reportedly, in 1540, during one of the attempts to subdue the Yucatan, artillery was transported in some manner by native porters or slaves. See Chuchiak, "Forgotten Allies," 198.

54. Aiton, *Antonio de Mendoza*, 92.

55. See Gilbert, *Trailblazers*, 22–23.

56. See Wood, *Conquistadors*, 74, 87.

57. De Sahagun, *Conquest of New Spain*, 111. For an apparent codex illustration of this wheeled gun, see Pohl and Hook, *Conquistador*, 54.

58. See R. S. Whiteway, trans. and ed., *The Portuguese Expedition to Abyssinia in 1541–1543, as Narrated by Castanhoso, with Some Contemporary Letters, the Short Account of Bermudez, and Certain Extracts from Correa* (London: Hakluyt Society, 1902), 22, 24. Despite the original description by someone who was there, Whiteway opined that the guns might have been on sledges. This assumption does not make a lot of sense, even if one concedes the terrain was rough for carts. In general, humanity already had discovered that while "the sledge slid over the snow better than dragging poles, . . . in the summer, wheels would have made the sledge go better still." Quennell and Quennell, *History of Everyday Things in England*, 134. And, unlike the guns taken on sled from Ticonderoga to Boston in winter 1775, Coronado's artillery were small guns, capable of being manhandled. A recent illustration of one of the Portuguese guns in Abyssinia has it mounted on small wheels, but there is no accompanying discussion. See Nicolle, *Portuguese in the Age of Discovery*, 45–46.

59. Day, "Mota Padilla," 91.

60. See Theodore Irving, *The Conquest of Florida, Under Hernando De Soto* (London: Edward Churton, 1835), 2:145.

61. Nossov, *Ancient and Medieval Siege Weapons*, 75–76.

62. Hammond and Rey, *Narratives*, 169, "Letter of Coronado to Mendoza, August 3, 1540."

63. Ibid., 71, "Report of Fray Marcos de Niza."

64. Ibid., 158, "Letter of Mendoza to the King, April 17, 1540."

65. See Notario Lopez and Notario Lopez, *Spanish Tercios*, 33.

66. Of course, it is possible that the Spanish attackers piled baggage at the base of the pueblo, a methodology the Germans used to enter Rome in 896. See Christopher Gravett, *Medieval Siege Warfare* (London: Osprey, 1990), 31. However, it would seem that even Castaneda would have mentioned the occurrence of such a field solution as this—plus this advance party was traveling light, without much baggage.

67. Gravett, *Medieval Siege Warfare*, 30.

68. Nicolle, *Granada 1492*, 39. A contemporary wood carving of the exploit shows the elite *escaladores*, or "climbers," being supported by fire from harquebus, crossbow, and a small artillery piece. Nicolle, *Granada 1492*, 40.

69. See Prescott, *History of the Conquest of Peru*, 2:61–62.

70. See Gravett, *Medieval Siege Warfare*, 30.

71. When Henry VIII's army marched toward the French city of Therouanne in 1513, the English filled fifteen carts with scaling ladders. Cruickshank, *Henry VIII*, 76. But that was in Europe, not sixteenth-century New Mexico.

72. See Leonard C. Bruno, *The Tradition of Technology: Landmarks of Western Technology in the Collections of the Library of Congress* (Washington, DC: Library of Congress, 1995), 19. Even medieval military men were familiar with the writings of Flavius, although much of his theory would have been considered passé by the Renaissance. See Taylor, *Art of War in Italy*, 157.

73. When the Spanish-Italian-German army of imperialists approached Rome in 1527, they quickly built rickety ladders with whatever material they could find in the vineyards on the outskirts of the city. See Chamberlin, *Sack of Rome*, 10, 157; Hook, *Sack of Rome, 1527*, 162.

74. F. W. Hodge, "Recent Excavations at Hawikuh," *El Palacio* 12, no. 1 (January 1, 1922), 4. Juan Jaramillo of the expedition identified the trees around Hawikuh as savins—junipers. Hammond and Rey, *Narratives*, 299, "Jaramillo's Narrative."

75. Damp, "Summer of 1540," 4. Damp believes that when Hawikuh's walls were breached, "some of their horses lost the caret-head nails from their horseshoes." But the men-at-arms would not attack a fortification mounted. In addition, other archaeological evidence indicates that Coronado's force carried two types of nails: one type for horse shoeing and the other type larger and not appropriate for shoeing. See Donald J. Blakeslee and Jay C. Blaine, "The Jimmy Owens Site: New Perspectives on the Coronado Expedition," in Flint and Cushing Flint, *Coronado Expedition: From the Distance of 460 Years*, 212–213.

76. Hodge, "Recent Excavations at Hawikuh," 6. This was based on the single ladder found in excavating during 1920–1921.

77. Hammond and Rey, *Narratives*, 169, "Letter of Coronado to Mendoza, August 3, 1540."

78. Matthew, *Tactics of Aelian*, 49.

79. Cf. Pohl, *Aztec, Mixtec and Zapotec Armies*, 18.

80. See Wise, *Conquistadores*, 15.

81. Moore, "Trail of Conquest," 39.

82. See Green, *Zuni*, 174.

83. See Nicolle, *Granada 1492*, 32. While the Spanish retained stone-throwing slings as an offensive weapon almost into the fifteenth century, long after other European nations abandoned their use, they apparently replaced them thereafter with crossbows and firearms. See Calvert, *Spanish Arms and Armour*, 44–45.

84. Wise, *Conquistadores*, 27, 33.

85. See John Warry, *Alexander, 334–323 BC: Conquest of the Persian Empire* (Botley, UK: Osprey, 2004), 48; Julian Humphrys, *Enemies at the Gate: English Castles Under Siege from the 12th Century to the Civil War* (Swindon, UK: English Heritage, 2007), 149–150.

86. Taylor, *Art of War in Italy*, 144.

87. See Humphrys, *Enemies at the Gate*, 149–150.
88. See Taylor, *Art of War in Italy*, 56–58.
89. As previously noted, even proud men-at-arms usually would deign to dismount and fight as heavy infantry when the situation required, as demonstrated by the English at Crécy in 1346 and on other occasions. See Raymond, *Henry VIII's Military Revolution*, 15; C. W. C. Oman and John H. Beeler, *The Art of War in the Middle Ages, A.D. 378–1515* (Ithaca, NY: Great Seal, 1963), 149–150.
90. Matthew, *Tactics of Aelian*, 39.
91. Keen, *Nobles, Knights*, 8.
92. See Contamine, *War in the Middle Ages*, 254–255.
93. See Smythe, *Certain Discourses Military*, 43–44, 45–46.
94. Matthew, *Tactics of Aelian*, 39. See also Smythe, *Certain Discourses Military*, 46.
95. Thus, when the Spanish-Italian-German force assaulted Rome in 1527, it feinted at two points along the walls and hit a third location with its full force. See Hook, *Sack of Rome, 1527*, 162–163.
96. Means, *Relation of the Discovery*, 2:314–315. See also Prescott, *History of the Conquest of Peru*, 2:61–62.
97. Chuchiak, "Forgotten Allies," 209.
98. "Coronado's Letter to Mendoza, August 3, 1540," no. 20, in *Old South Leaflets*, vol. 1, nos. 1–25 (Boston: Directors of the Old South Work, Old South Meeting House, c. 1900), 7.
99. See Damp, "Summer of 1540," 5. As indicated elsewhere in this volume, while a number of boltheads were found at Hawikuh by F. W. Hodge, their historical importance was not then appreciated, and little is known of their site context. See Diane Lee Rhodes, "Coronado Fought Here," in Flint and Cushing Flint, *Coronado Expedition to Tierra Nueva*, 51.
100. Hammond and Rey, *Narratives*, 168, "Letter of Coronado to Mendoza, August 3, 1540."
101. Ibid., 169, "Letter of Coronado to Mendoza, August 3, 1540." Of course, Coronado was a commander who actually was in the hand-to-hand fighting, so his perspective naturally would be very personal and egocentric. See Keegan, *Face of Battle*, 47.
102. Damp, "Summer of 1540," 4–5.
103. Flint and Cushing Flint, *Documents*, 497, "The Relacion del Sucesco (Anonymous Narrative), 1540s."
104. Flint, *Great Cruelties*, 167, "Juan Troyano, the Eighth de Oficio Witness."
105. See Leon-Portilla, *Broken Spears*, 96–97, 112.
106. Flint and Cushing Flint, *Documents*, 497, "The Relacion del Sucesco (Anonymous Narrative), 1540s." If the guns were breechloaders, this would have meant the range and muzzle velocity, as well as potentially dangerous recoil, would be low. See Nelson, *Tudor Navy*, 40. These results also would occur with muzzle-loading guns if the gunpowder was inferior, a not-unlikely scenario. Finally, ordnance of the sixteenth century, because of overheating of the barrel, "could only be fired a limited number of times each day." Raymond, *Henry VIII's Military Revolution*, 35.
107. Mota Padilla wrote that Cibola's pueblos were "made of shale cemented by earthen mortar" while those found later at Tiguex were "made of pebbly earth [adobe], although very strong." Day, "Mota Padilla," 96. In either case, it would have been impossible for mere falconets to reduce Cibola.

108. See Turnbull, *Art of Renaissance Warfare*, 77.

109. Flint and Cushing Flint, *Documents*, 497, "The Relacion del Sucesco (Anonymous Narrative), 1540s."

110. "Coronado's Letter to Mendoza, August 3, 1540," 7. This translation appears to be that of Richard Hakluyt. Another translation says, "[T]he musketeers could do nothing, because they had arrived so weak and feeble that they could scarcely stand on their feet." Hammond and Rey, *Narratives*, 169, "Letter of Coronado to Mendoza, August 3, 1540." Harquebusiers, when going into action, would carry, in addition to the weapon and perhaps a forked rest, a length of match, lead balls, powder flask, ramrod and cleaning rod, powder measure, bullet mold, extra lead, and several other items. Millar, *Crossbowman's Story*, 72n.

111. See Smythe, *Certain Discourses Military*, 65–66.

112. Capt. E. Blake Knox, *Military Sanitation and Hygiene* (London: Bailliere, Tindall and Cox, 1911), 268.

113. McGregor, *Luigi Guicciardini*, 91.

114. Eltis, *Military Revolution*, 14. It might take only "seven or eight shots in haste" to cause this dangerous overheating. Smythe, *Certain Discourses Military*, 67.

115. Funcken and Funcken, *Arms and Uniforms, Part 1*, 116. Cervantes, in his satirical *Don Quixote*, gave an almost identical description of the "cowardly base hind" who was capable, by use of his harquebus, to end "the life of the bravest gentleman" with "a chance bullet." Calvert, *Spanish Arms and Armour*, 4–5. Also, modern readers should realize that in the sixteenth century, nearsightedness would be a more-or-less permanent condition for the masses, limiting the effectiveness of all missile weaponry when the marksmen, unbeknown to the command in those more primitive days, were so affected. Cf. Spaulding, Nickerson, and Wright, *Warfare*, 457. In this regard, the dusty climate of the American Southwest would not be helpful.

116. See Stehan Fussel, *Emperor Maximilian and the Media of his Day: The Theuerdank of 1517, A Cultural Introduction* (Cologne, Germany: Taschen, 2003), 63–67.

117. "Coronado's Letter to Mendoza, August 3, 1540," no. 20, in *Old South Leaflets*, 7. See also Hammond and Rey, *Narratives*, 169, "Letter of Coronado to Mendoza, August 3, 1540."

118. See Fussel, *Emperor Maximilian*, 64.

119. Sir Clements R. Markham, trans. and ed., *Civil Wars of Peru by Pedro de Cieza de Leon [Part 4, Book 2]: The War of Chupas* (London: Hakluyt Society, 1918), 17.

120. See H. C. Heaton, ed., and Bertram T. Lee, trans., *The Discovery of the Amazon, According to the Account of Friar Gaspar de Carvajal and Other Documents* (New York: American Geographical Society, 1934), 191. However, the crossbowmen of Orellana supposedly carried two extra bowstrings with them when going into action. See Millar, *Crossbowman's Story*, 47.

121. The Spaniards would have been well aware of particular New World climates affecting crossbow strings. See Wise, *Conquistadores*, 8. A preventative measure would have been to unstring the bows and keep the strings out of the weather. Cf. Charles Knightly, *Flodden: The Anglo-Scottish War of 1513* (London: Almark, 1975), 20, regarding protection of longbow strings. However, that measure would hinder quick use of the crossbows. As for proper regular maintenance, tallow or beeswax can be used to protect or maintain bowstrings. The presence of its cow herd would give the main column of the expedition a good source of tallow. It also should be noted that some crossbowmen

undoubtedly (as well as some arquebusiers) had covers to protect their weapons from the rain while on the march. See Michael, *Armies of Medieval Burgundy, 1364–1477*, 35.
122. Hammond and Rey, *Narratives*, 169, "Letter of Coronado to Mendoza, August 3, 1540."
123. Moore, "Trail of Conquest, 1540–1940," 40.
124. See Raymond, *Henry VIII's Military Revolution*, 27.
125. See Don de Villagutierre Soto-Mayor, *History of the Conquest of the Province of the Itza: Subjugation and Events of the Lacandon and Other Nations of Uncivilized Indians in the Lands from the Kingdom of Guatemala to the Provinces of Yucatan in North America*, ed. Frank E. Comparato, trans. Robert D. Wood, S.M. (Culver City, CA: Labyrinthos, 1983), 58.
126. See Cazeaux, *French Music*, 144.
127. Taylor, *Art of War in Italy*, 144.
128. Cf. Oman and Beeler, *Art of War in the Middle Ages*, 149.
129. Hammond and Rey, *Narratives*, 168–169, "Letter of Coronado to Mendoza, August 3, 1540."
130. One historian, ignoring the testimony of Coronado, recently claimed that the captain general was wounded when he attacked Cibola mounted on his steed. Hoig, *Came Men on Horses*, 60. As for Bolton, a good historian but no military historian, he called this assault by dismounted horsemen, including Coronado, "new tactics" born of necessity. Bolton, *Coronado*, 124. The tactics employed here were standard operating procedure. In the contemporaneous battle against the fortified Mayan town of Sihochac, on July 7, 1540, the commander of the main attacking column, Alonso Rosado, reportedly was the second Spaniard clambering over the wall, the first Spaniard having been killed by arrows. Behind Rosado followed a dozen Spaniards and dozens of Indian allies, and the Maya soon were in retreat. Chuchiak, "Forgotten Allies," 209.
131. Roy, *Blaise de Monluc*, 47.
132. See Hare, *Charles de Bourbon*, 326.
133. Hammond and Rey, *Narratives*, 169, "Letter of Coronado to Mendoza, August 3, 1540."
134. Winship, "Coronado Expedition, 1540–1542," 565, "Translation of the Translado de Las Nuevas."
135. Hodge, "Narrative by Castaneda," 300–301.
136. Hammond and Rey, *Narratives*, 169, "Letter of Coronado to Mendoza, August 3, 1540."
137. Hammond and Rey, *Narratives*, 323, "Coronado's Testimony Concerning the Expedition, . . . September 3, 1544."
138. Kirkup, *Surgeons Mate*, 134.
139. Flint, *Great Cruelties*, 366, "Defense Offered by Vazquez de Coronado; First de Parte Witness (Lorenzo Alvarez)."
140. See Hook, *Sack of Rome, 1527*, 164. At Rome, when the Duke of Bourbon toppled from an assault ladder—shot by an arquebus—his men first panicked and then turned the panic to a desire for revenge.
141. During his siege of Chaluz Castle in 1199, Richard the Lion-Hearted, while firing a crossbow at the castle, was wounded by a defending crossbowman, and the wound proved fatal due to an "unskilled surgeon." "Enraged at this wound, the King's men stormed the castle, carried it with sword and lance and hanged the defenders." The cap-

tured crossbowman, however, was flayed alive. Henry Dupray and William Maxwell, *British Battles* (London: Charles Letts, 1904), part 1, second plate. See also John Gillingham, *Richard the Lionheart* (New York: Time Books, 1978), 13–14; Frank McLynn, *Richard and John: Kings at War* (Cambridge, MA: Da Capo, 2007), 274–278.

142. See Saxtorph, *Warriors and Weapons*, 230.

143. Leon-Portilla, *Broken Spears*, 76.

144. One competent Coronado historian believed that "The hundreds of Indian allies were kept in the rear and took no part in the battle." Day, *Coronado's Quest*, 117. This conclusion, based on the silent record, lacks all military logic and would thoroughly demoralize the auxiliaries.

145. Cellini, *Autobiography of Benvenuto Cellini*, 62.

146. See, for example, Flint and Cushing Flint, *Documents*, 165; Flint, *No Settlement*, 112.

147. Indeed, a later estimate of total Indian casualties of the expedition, put forward by Coronado, indicated the Indians were neither treated as "cannon fodder" nor as first-wave storm troopers.

148. Hodge, "Narrative by Castaneda," 301.

149. Winship, "Coronado Expedition, 1540–1542," 565, "Translation of the Translado de Las Nuevas."

150. This scenario would be supported by the fact that a few nails, perhaps in this case from thrown horseshoes, have been found in lesser concentration around the site of the pueblo. See Damp, "Summer of 1540," 4–5.

151. Grotius and Loomis, *Law of War and Peace*, 356.

152. Gomara, *Cortes*, 270.

153. Pohl, *Aztec Warrior*, 45–46.

154. Hammond and Rey, *Narratives*, 345, "Testimony of Lopez de Cardenas . . ."

155. Bolton, *Coronado*, 125.

156. Flint and Cushing Flint, *Documents*, 135.

157. Dr. Patricia Seed, for example, has noted how the peoples of the New World, in their initial battles with European opponents, usually suffered disproportionate losses, since they had to learn the deadly nature of their advanced fighting abilities. Parker, *Cambridge Illustrated History of Warfare*, 141.

158. Hodge, "Narrative by Castaneda," 301.

159. Ibid., 300.

160. In addition, the victors in a premodern combat clash of arms usually, but not always, suffered fewer casualties than did the losers. See Contamine, *War in the Middle Ages*, 257–258.

161. Hammond and Rey, *Narratives*, 169, "Letter of Coronado to Mendoza, August 3, 1540."

162. See Reid, *Medieval Warfare*, 68–69.

163. Parker, *Army of Flanders*, 168.

164. Ibid. Although the American natives did not have deadly firearms during the conquistador era, the Spaniards often complained that their arrows were poisoned.

165. See Gravett, *Medieval Siege Warfare*, 17–18. This general lawfulness did not make such a slaughter of the defenders, including civilians, morally right, or even wise, for the destructiveness might destroy the usefulness of the conquered community as a base for the besiegers.

166. Hammond and Rey, *Narratives*, 169–170, "Letter of Coronado to Mendoza, August 3, 1540."
167. Roy, *Blaise de Monluc*, 47.
168. Hodge, "Narrative by Castaneda," 301.
169. Winship, "Coronado Expedition, 1540–1542," 565, "Translation of the Translado de Las Nuevas."
170. Day, "Mota Padilla," 94.
171. See Preston, *Cities of Gold*, 299.
172. See George Peter Hammond and Agapito Rey, trans., *Expedition into New Mexico Made by Antonio de Espejo, 1582–1583, as Revealed in the Journal of Diego Perez de Luxan, A Member of the Party* (Los Angeles: Quivira Society, 1929), 89–90.

CHAPTER TWELVE: MELCHIOR DIAZ SEEKS THE PACIFIC SUPPLY SHIPS
1. J. A. Doyle, *The English in America: Virginia, Maryland, and the Carolinas* (London: Longmans, Green, 1882), 42–43.
2. Nicolle, *Granada 1492*, 29.
3. See William K. Hartmann, "The Mystery of the 'Port of Chichilticale,'" in Flint and Cushing Flint, *Latest Word from 1540*, 210–211.
4. Hammond and Rey, *Narratives*, 124, "Report of Alarcon's Expedition." In one of the ironies of history, a portrait of Alarcon has survived from the sixteenth century, unlike the fate of any contemporary portrait of Coronado. Alarcon is pictured as balding, with a full mustache and a flowing gray or white beard, and he sat for his portrait in armor undoubtedly similar to that worn by Coronado on his expedition. See Don Jose March y Labores, *Historia de la Marina Real Espanola*, tomo (vol.) 2 (Madrid: Jose Maria Ducazcal, 1854), plate between 222 and 223.
5. Hammond and Rey, *Narratives*, 124, "Report of Alarcon's Expedition."
6. Ibid., 124–125.
7. Ibid., 125. Presumably, the extra supplies for the army, including the equipment sent to the ships from Coronado's column, reached the shore in carts.
8. Ibid.
9. Ibid.
10. Ibid., 126.
11. Ibid.
12. Somewhat ironically, Alarcon's definitive confirmation that Lower California was a peninsula and not an island caused Mendoza to forego further exploration north. See Bancroft, *History of Mexico*, 511. Of course, being kept in the dark about many details of Spanish discoveries, much of the rest of Europe long continued to believe that California was an island.
13. Hodge, "Narrative by Castaneda," 303.
14. See ibid., 304.
15. Ibid., 303.
16. Day, "Mota Padilla," 94.
17. Hodge, "Narrative by Castaneda," 303.
18. Ibid.
19. Ibid., 303–304.
20. Hammond and Rey, *Narratives*, 126, "Report of Alarcon's Expedition."
21. Henry R. Wagner, *California Voyages, 1539–1541* (San Francisco: John Howell, 1925), 84.

22. Hammond and Rey, *Narratives*, 127, "Report of Alarcon's Expedition."
23. Ibid., 145. One California historian doubted that any of the Indians "knew what he was talking about" regarding the inquiries Alarcon made about Cibola. Wagner, *California Voyages*, 82. But Alarcon was on the spot and had a strong incentive to establish communication and gain information in order to try to reach Cibola. Plus, his understanding of the situation regarding Coronado was borne out.
24. See Hammond and Rey, *Narratives*, 148, "Report of Alarcon's Expedition."
25. Ibid., 147.
26. Ibid., 149.
27. Ibid.
28. Ibid., 150.
29. Ibid., 153.
30. Day, "Mota Padilla," 95.
31. Hammond and Rey, *Narratives*, 154–155, "Report of Alarcon's Expedition."
32. Hodge, "Narrative by Castaneda," 324.
33. Ibid., 304.
34. See Miller, *Lanksknechts*, 9. Generally, early and medieval Christian thinkers rejected the lax ancient ideas about the morality and efficacy of torture, but the rise of the Inquisition seemed to relegitimize its use to many, whether Catholic or Protestant. See Malise Ruthven, *Torture: The Grand Conspiracy* (London: Weidenfeld and Nicolson, 1978), 43–52.
35. Hodge, "Narrative by Castaneda," 304.
36. Ibid.
37. Ibid., 304–305.
38. Ibid., 305.
39. Ibid., 325.
40. Day, "Mota Padilla," 95.
41. Hodge, "Narrative by Castaneda," 325. The historian Mota Padilla said the miscreant canine was "a little dog" but also said Diaz first attempted to warn the dog off. Day, "Mota Padilla," 95.
42. Hodge, "Narrative by Castaneda," 305.
43. Medieval Europeans, believing in due process as often as seeking justice, were known to put animals causing a human death on trial. It is doubtful that Diaz's companions would have gone to this trouble before dispatching the animal, but the dog's putative owner probably was present, so who can tell?
44. See Day, "Mota Padilla," 95–96.
45. Hodge, "Narrative by Castaneda," 325.
46. Ibid.
47. Ibid.
48. Day, "Mota Padilla," 95–96.
49. Ibid., 96.
50. Hodge, "Narrative by Castaneda," 325.
51. See Mallett, *Mercenaries and Their Masters*, 182.
52. Ronald L. Ives, "The Grave of Melchior Diaz: A Problem in Historical Sleuthing," *The Kiva: A Journal of the Arizona Archaeological and Historical Society* 25, no. 2 (December 1959), 32.
53. Ives, "Grave of Melchior Diaz," 39.

54. Hodge, "Narrative by Castaneda," 294.

55. Brevet Brigadier General J. H. Simpson, "Coronado's March in Search of the 'Seven Cities of Cibola' and Discussion of Their Probable Location," *Annual Report of the Board of Regents of the Smithsonian Institution . . . for the Year 1869* (Washington, DC: Government Printing Office, 1871), 316.

56. Hodge, "Narrative by Castaneda," 325–326.

57. Ibid., 326.

58. Ibid., 367–368.

59. Ibid., 370–371.

60. See Bolton, *Coronado,* 320–321.

61. Hodge, "Narrative by Castaneda," 371.

62. Flint, *Great Cruelties,* 210, "A Translation of the Testimony, Tenth de Oficio Witness (Melchior Perez)."

63. Hodge, "Narrative by Castaneda," 371.

64. Ibid., 372; Bolton, *Coronado,* 323.

65. Ives, "Grave of Melchior Diaz," 35–36.

66. Varner, and Johnson Varner, *Dogs of the Conquest,* 101. Obviously, the Varners, being dog lovers, also took umbrage at Diaz's trying to kill that canine.

67. See, for example, Flint, *Great Cruelties,* 235, "A Translation of the Testimony, Eleventh de Oficio Witness (Pedro de Ledesma)."

## CHAPTER THIRTEEN: RECONNAISSANCE WEST AND THE MARCH EAST INTO TIGUEX TERRITORY

1. Hodge, "Narrative by Castaneda," 306.

2. Flint, *Great Cruelties,* 94, "Fourth de Oficio Witness (Domingo Martin)."

3. Hammond and Rey, *Narratives,* 170, "Letter of Coronado to Mendoza, August 3, 1540."

4. Hodge, "Narrative by Castaneda," 302.

5. Douglas Miller, *Armies of the German Peasants' War, 1524–26* (Botley, UK: Osprey, 2003), 46.

6. See Day, "Mota Padilla," 94.

7. Oman, *History of the Art of War,* 220.

8. Hodge, "Narrative by Castaneda," 305.

9. Ibid.

10. Ernst Kern, *War Diary 1941–45: A Report* (New York: Vantage, 1993), 41–42.

11. Ibid., 48–49. Kern later found that the invading army of Alexander the Great had suffered a sweetly similar temporary incapacity two thousand years earlier.

12. Hodge, "Narrative by Castaneda," 305.

13. Hammond and Rey, *Narratives,* 84, "Appointment of Coronado as Commander of the Expedition to Cibola, January 6, 1540."

14. Hammond and Rey, *Narratives,* 176, "Letter of Coronado to Mendoza, August 3, 1540."

15. Ibid., 346, "Testimony of Lopez de Cardenas . . ."

16. See Chamberlin, *Sack of Rome,* 129.

17. See Robert Giddings, *Imperial Echoes: Eyewitness Accounts of Victoria's Little Wars* (London: Leo Cooper, 1996), 73.

18. Hodge, "Narrative by Castaneda," 306.

19. Ibid., 306–307.
20. Ironically, the Hopi and the Zuni each now claim descent from the same Puebloan "ancient ones." Chaz Evans, "Obtaining an Iconic Pueblo," *American Archaeology* 17, no. 2 (Summer 2013), 49.
21. Hodge, "Narrative by Castaneda," 307.
22. Ibid.
23. Ibid.
24. Ibid.
25. Ibid.
26. Ibid.
27. Ibid., 307–308. However, even during these very militant times for the Roman Catholic Church, while clerics or chaplains could advise engaging in battle (based upon pure motives regarding just warfare), the men of the cloth were prohibited strictly from engaging in individual combat, as much as they might want to (and as often as the rule might be broken). See Contamine, *War in the Middle Ages*, 265, 268–269, 287. This legal position regarding the status of chaplains is not unlike that taken in the modern Law of War.
28. Hodge, "Narrative by Castaneda," 308.
29. Ibid.
30. See Hammond and Rey, *Expedition into New Mexico*, 96.
31. See Day, *Coronado's Quest*, 344n8.
32. Hodge, "Narrative by Castaneda," 308.
33. Ibid., 309.
34. See Day, "Mota Padilla," 98–99.
35. Hodge, "Narrative by Castaneda," 308–309.
36. See Hammond and Rey, *Narratives*, 347, "Testimony of Lopez de Cardenas . . ."
37. Hodge, "Narrative by Castaneda," 308–309.
38. Ibid., 309.
39. Ibid.
40. Ibid., 309–310.
41. Hammond and Rey, *Narratives*, 287, "Relacion de Suceso: Relation of the Events on the Expedition That Francisco Vazquez Made to the Discovery of Cibola."
42. Hodge, "Narrative by Castaneda," 309.
43. Ibid.
44. Hammond and Rey, *Narratives*, 287, "Relacion de Suceso: Relation of the Events on the Expedition That Francisco Vazquez Made to the Discovery of Cibola."
45. Hodge, "Narrative by Castaneda," 310.
46. Bolton, *Coronado*, 141. Instead of a massive piece of statuary, the party ultimately got a miniature diorama in the Grand Canyon visitor's center. See "Visitor Center Diorama, Grand Canyon National Park," a postcard featuring Cardenas on the south rim (published by Grand Canyon Natural History Association). However, reflecting the changing attitudes of museum curators, the diorama reportedly has been removed and placed in storage.
47. See Day, "Mota Padilla," 98–99.
48. See Hammond and Rey, *Narratives*, 346, "Testimony of Lopez de Cardenas . . ."
49. Hodge, "Narrative by Castaneda," 310–311.
50. Ibid., 311.

51. Ibid.

52. Ibid., 311–312.

53. Ibid., 311.

54. Ibid., 311–312.

55. Hammond and Rey, *Narratives*, 288, "Relacion de Suceso: Relation of the Events on the Expedition That Francisco Vazquez Made to the Discovery of Cibola."

56. See Day, *Coronado's Quest*, 346n5.

57. Hodge, "Narrative by Castaneda," 312.

58. Ibid., 313.

59. Hammond and Rey, *Narratives*, 299, "Jaramillo's Narrative."

60. See Hammond and Rey, *Narratives*, 348, "Testimony of Lopez de Cardenas."

61. Hodge, "Narrative by Castaneda," 312.

62. See Alfred Vincent Kidder, "Pecos Excavations in 1924," *El Palacio* 18, nos. 10–11 (June 1, 1925), 217.

63. Day, *Coronado's Quest*, 348n15.

64. Hodge, "Narrative by Castaneda," 312.

65. See Flint, *Great Cruelties*, 169, "Juan Troyano, the Eighth de Oficio Witness." Getting involved in native wars on one side or the other was not uncommon in the European settlement of America. But, as Samuel de Champlain found out when he assisted the Algonquins against the Iroquois in 1609, it was a policy fraught with potential long-term disadvantages. See R. V. Coleman, *The First Frontier* (New York: Charles Scribner's Sons, 1948), 98–101.

66. See Hodge, "Narrative by Castaneda," 313.

67. Day, "Mota Padilla," 99.

68. See Hodge, "Narrative by Castaneda," 340–341. The present Taos reservation has a small stream with small bridges.

69. Ibid., 313.

70. Ibid., 314; Bolton, *Coronado*, 193.

71. Hodge, "Narrative by Castaneda," 314.

72. Ibid.

73. Ibid., 315.

74. Ibid.; see Hammond and Rey, *Narratives*, 350, "Testimony of Lopez de Cardenas."

75. Flint, *Great Cruelties*, 147, "Seventh de Oficio Witness (Cristobal de Escobar)."

76. Hodge, "Narrative by Castaneda," 315. See Hammond and Rey, *Narratives*, 350, "Testimony of Lopez de Cardenas."

77. See Hammond and Rey, *Narratives*, 350–351, 352, "Testimony of Lopez de Cardenas." While it was not considered exemplary behavior during the Italian Wars, victorious soldiers, especially Spaniards, were known to torture civilian captives in the hope of discovering hidden treasure or to encourage paying ransom. See Chamberlin, *Sack of Rome*, 177–178; Hook, *Sack of Rome, 1527*, 171–172, 175–176.

78. Lockhart and Otte, *Letters and People of the Spanish Indies*, 5, "Letter of Gaspar de Marquina, in Peru, to Marin de Garate, in Biscay, 1533."

79. Peter Russell, *Prince Henry "the Navigator": A Life* (New Haven, CT: Yale University Press, 2000), 154–155. Of course, this uncomfortable position of being limited to strategic strongholds has been a military dilemma in such modern locales as Vietnam and Afghanistan.

CHAPTER FOURTEEN: UNWELCOME OCCUPIERS AND THE TIGUEX WAR

1. Jochai Rosen, *Soldiers at Leisure: The Guardroom Scene in Dutch Genre Painting of the Golden Age* (Amsterdam: Amsterdam University Press, 2010), 15.

2. Ralph Roeder, *The Man of the Renaissance: Four Lawgivers: Savonarola, Machiavelli, Castiglione, Aretino* (New York: Viking, 1933), 188.

3. See Tracy, *Emperor Charles V*, 239.

4. Housley, *Documents on the Later Crusades*, 180.

5. See Smythe, *Certain Discourses Military*, 27–28.

6. See Flint, *Great Cruelties*, 110, 118, "Juan de Contreras, the Fifth de Oficio Witness." Flint translates *"dos y tres jornadas,"* the period of punishment, as "two or three days' travel," but it probably means "working days" (or even daily punishment walks or tours). See editorial staff, Bibliograf S. A., *Vox Modern College, Spanish and English Dictionary* (New York: Charles Scribner's Sons, 1972), 1136.

7. Flint, *Great Cruelties*, 391, "Diego Lopez, the Second de Parte Witness."

8. Hammond and Rey, *Obregon's History*, 234.

9. Notario Lopez and Notario Lopez, *Spanish Tercios*, 33.

10. Hammond and Rey, *Obregon's History*, 235. Although written after Coronado's Expedition, *Obregon's History*, at 236, used Coronado's San Geronimo settlement in Chiametla as an example (among several) of such an avoidable revolt.

11. Flint, *Great Cruelties*, 391, "Diego Lopez, the Second de Parte Witness."

12. Hammond and Rey, *Obregon's History*, 236.

13. Hammond and Rey, *Narratives*, 329, "Coronado's Testimony Concerning the Expedition."

14. Hodge, "Narrative by Castaneda," 317. Because of the name given him, Aleman, this Indian traditionally has been thought to look like a German to the Spanish. There was a Spanish secretary to Charles V in the 1520s who was named Juan Aleman. See Longhurst, *Alfonso De Valdes*, 11–13.

15. Hodge, "Narrative by Castaneda," 317–318.

16. Pohl, *Aztec Warrior*, 24.

17. Hodge, "Narrative by Castaneda," 318.

18. Terence D'altroy and Christine A. Hastorf, "The Architecture and Contents of Inka State Storehouses in the Xauxa Region of Peru," in Terry Y. Levine, ed., *Inka Storage Systems* (Norman: University of Oklahoma Press, 1992), 264–265.

19. Hodge, "Narrative by Castaneda," 353. This is an unbelievable agricultural claim and well exceeds the seven good years providing for the seven lean years in the ancient Egypt of Joseph and Pharaoh. See Gen. 41:47–57 (King James Version).

20. Day, "Mota Padilla," 97.

21. Flint, *Great Cruelties*, 171, "A Translation of the Testimony Summary, Eighth de Oficio Witness (Juan Troyano)."

22. Ibid.

23. See Hodge, "Narrative by Castaneda," 318, 319.

24. See Hammond and Rey, *Narratives*, 330n17, "Coronado's Testimony Concerning the Expedition."

25. Hodge, "Narrative by Castaneda," 318. Castaneda, in a rare specific omission, perhaps because Villegas still had powerful relations in Mexico, refused to name the miscreant, "out of regard for him."

26. Ibid.

27. See Hammond and Rey, *Narratives*, 349, "Testimony of Lopez de Cardenas." Indeed, one member of the expedition thought the incident was covered up so Coronado would not hear of it and hang Villegas. Flint, *Great Cruelties*, 214, "Melchior Perez, the Tenth de Oficio Witness." Supposedly, even in Europe, sexual assault, like murder, was an offense so serious that even members of the upper class could not escape punishment. Michael R. Weisser, *Crime and Punishment in Early Modern Europe* (Atlantic Highlands, NJ: Humanities Press, 1979), 40–41.

28. Hodge, "Narrative by Castaneda," 318.

29. Ibid., 318–319.

30. Stuart Stirling, *Pizarro: Conqueror of the Inca* (Stroud, UK: Sutton, 2005), 86. In a curious twist regarding this chauvinistic or protective attitude, in 1697, Spanish soldiers attempting to subjugate the last unconquered Indians of Yucatan supposedly resisted the temptations of Indian maidens sent by the Indian king to entice them, in a stratagem aimed at setting off a premature battle in which the Spaniards could be defeated. Philip Ainsworth Means, trans., *A Narrative of the Conquest of the Province of the Ytzas in New Spain,* part 1 (Paris: Les Editions Genet, 1930), 55.

31. Doyle, *English in America*, 35.

32. Nigel Davies, *The Aztecs: A History* (New York: G. P. Putnam's Sons, 1974), 246.

33. Michael McKernan, *All In!: Australia during the Second World War* (Melbourne: Thomas Nelson Australia, 1983), 197.

34. See Max Haines, *Multiple Murders* 2 (Toronto: Toronto Sun Publishing, 1995), 162–166.

35. Ivan Chapman, *Leonski: The Brownout Strangler* (Sydney: Hale & Iremonger, 1982), 238.

36. Hammond and Rey, *Narratives*, 177–178, "Letter of Coronado to Mendoza, August 3, 1540."

37. See Flint, *Great Cruelties*, 93, "Fourth de Oficio Witness (Domingo Martin)."

38. Hodge, "Narrative by Castaneda," 319.

39. See Hammond and Rey, *Narratives*, 348, "Testimony of Lopez de Cardenas."

40. Ibid., 331, "Coronado's Testimony Concerning the Expedition."

41. Flint, *Great Cruelties*, 238, "A Translation of the Testimony Summary, Eleventh de Officio Witness (Pedro de Ledesma)."

42. Nicolle, *Granada 1492*, 29. This saying, according to Nicolle, came from the early sixteenth century and gave resolve to the vaunted Spanish infantry facing enemy cavalry. This hard-nosed attitude contributed to the Spanish reputation for killing their opponent's horses.

43. Hodge, "Narrative by Castaneda," 319.

44. See Hammond and Rey, *Narratives*, 347–348, "Testimony of Lopez de Cardenas."

45. Hodge, "Narrative by Castaneda," 319.

46. See Smythe and Hale, *Certain Discourses Military,* 75–76.

47. As early as the late fifteenth century, the Spanish gained a negative reputation among Europeans for attacking their foes' horses. See Hare, *Bayard*, 34, 97. On the other hand, hard-pressed European farmers might be less ready to kill livestock, including war horses. When a force of north German peasants successfully fought off an army of Danish knights and mercenaries in 1500, the peasant-soldiers, in attacking the mounted men with polearms, cried out, "Spare the horse, kill the man." William Urban, *Medieval Mercenaries: The Business of War* (London: Greenhill, 2006), 266.

48. Hammond and Rey, *Narratives*, 331, "Coronado's Testimony Concerning the Expedition." Forty years later, the Tiguex Indians recalled that they had killed only ten horses. See Hammond and Rey, *Expedition into New Mexico*, 92.

49. Mallett, *Mercenaries and Their Masters*, 206.

50. See Flint, *Great Cruelties*, 439, "A Translation of the Testimony Summary." The Aztecs, when they killed horses, decapitated them and displayed the trophies in their temples alongside Spanish heads.

51. See Hammond and Rey, *Narratives*, 348, "Testimony of Lopez de Cardenas."

52. Hodge, "Narrative by Castaneda," 319.

53. Day, "Mota Padilla," 100.

54. See Hammond and Rey, *Narratives*, 352, "Testimony of Lopez de Cardenas."

55. Ibid., 333, "Coronado's Testimony Concerning the Expedition."

56. See ibid. This comment supports those who think Padilla was an ex-soldier, practical to the extreme, even when relying on hypertechnical legalities. His solution was like that reportedly recommended by some judge advocates during the Vietnam War: Since incendiary rounds may not be fired at enemy personnel but may be used to destroy equipment, such as tanks, infantrymen were advised to aim only at the canteens of the Viet Cong with incendiaries.

57. See Hammond and Rey, *Narratives*, 352, "Testimony of Lopez de Cardenas."

58. Hodge, "Narrative by Castaneda," 319.

59. Cf. Contamine, *War in the Middle Ages*, 298–299. When the force of Cortes approached that of Narvaez in the surprise night attack that would humble and half-blind Narvaez, the soldiers of Cortes, on their own accord, halted by a wayside cross and, kneeling, insisted that their accompanying priest hear their sins for absolution. Margaret Duncan Coxhead, *Mexico: Romance of History* (London: T. C. and E. C. Jack, 1909), 170.

60. Hodge, "Narrative by Castaneda," 319.

61. See Hammond and Rey, *Narratives*, 352–353, "Testimony of Lopez de Cardenas."

62. Ibid., 353, "Testimony of Lopez de Cardenas."

63. Hodge, "Narrative by Castaneda," 319.

64. In ancient times, besiegers would appear to threaten one side of a city and then overwhelmingly assault the opposite side. See Nossov, *Ancient and Medieval Siege Weapons*, 254.

65. See Hammond and Rey, *Narratives*, 353, "Testimony of Lopez de Cardenas."

66. Hodge, "Narrative by Castaneda," 319.

67. See Hammond and Rey, *Narratives*, 353, "Testimony of Lopez de Cardenas."

68. Hodge, "Narrative by Castaneda," 319.

69. Hubert Howe Bancroft, *History of Arizona and New Mexico, 1530–1888* (Albuquerque: Horn and Wallace, 1962), 56.

70. Day, "Mota Padilla," 100.

71. See Hammond and Rey, *Narratives*, 333, "Coronado's Testimony Concerning the Expedition."

72. Hodge, "Narrative by Castaneda," 319–320. Every historian seems to interpret this use of the cross at Arenal in his or her own way. Herbert H. Bancroft said the Spaniards made a sign by "crossing their arms." Bancroft, *History of Arizona*, 57. A. Grove Day believed that Captains Melgosa and Diego Lopez crossed their lances, "making the Indian gesture of peace." Day, *Coronado's Quest*, 200.

73. Hammond and Rey, *Narratives*, 353–354, "Testimony of Lopez de Cardenas."

74. Hodge, "Narrative by Castaneda," 320. Even in medieval times, there were those who believed that such moral responsibility, particularly when there was an ensuing massacre, was not a buck to be so lightly passed by subordinates. See Contamine, *War in the Middle Ages*, 268.

75. Flint, *Great Cruelties*, 174, "Juan Troyano, the Eighth de Oficio Witness."

76. Ibid., 174–175.

77. Hammond and Rey, *Narratives*, 353, "Testimony of Lopez de Cardenas."

78. Flint, *Great Cruelties*, 216, "Melchior Perez, the Tenth de Oficio Witness."

79. See ibid., 208.

80. Hodge, "Narrative by Castaneda," 320.

81. Flint, *Great Cruelties*, 113–114, "Fifth de Oficio Witness (Juan de Contreras)."

82. Ibid., 131, "Sixth de Oficio Witness (Rodrigo Ximon)."

83. See ibid., 172, "Juan Troyano, the Eighth de Oficio Witness."

84. Hammond and Rey, *Narratives*, 335, "Coronado's Testimony Concerning the Expedition."

85. As noted, many of the members of the expedition would recall that the captain general kept a tight rein on his command. See, for example, Flint, *Great Cruelties*, 132, "Sixth de Oficio Witness (Rodrigo Ximon)."

86. See Contamine, *War in the Middle Ages*, 265.

87. See Keegan, *Face of Battle*, 107–112.

88. See, for example, Parker, *Army of Flanders*, 169–170.

89. Corvisier and Siddall, *Armies and Societies in Europe*, 71.

90. See Miller and Embleton, *Lanksknechts*, 8–9; Richards and Embleton, *Landsknecht Soldier*, 60.

91. Hale, *Art of War*, 2. However, as the sixteenth century wound down into the seventeenth, times were changing. In early 1602, a Spanish commander was pleasantly surprised when he and his three thousand six hundred men (captured in Ireland) were treated humanely by the English and then repatriated to Spain, according to the terms granted by the English, "without ransoms, without massacre." See Graham, *Spanish Armadas*, 264–265. As for the Turks, their education and reformation would take considerably longer.

92. Gomara, *Cortes*, 177. Of course, while burning prisoners at the stake was a specialty of some North American woodland tribes, the Aztecs practiced other gruesome forms of execution.

93. Motley, *Rise of the Dutch Republic*, 1:80. As Motley noted, the edict was "rigidly enforced."

94. See Roeder, *Man of the Renaissance*, 129–130.

95. See Hillerbrand, *Division of Christendom*, 246–248; Jasper Ridley, *Bloody Mary's Martyrs: The Story of England's Terror* (New York: Carroll & Graf, 2001), 215–217.

96. As early as 1515, an Italian nobleman complained that the Swiss were noted for their brutality and the Spanish for their perfidy. Chamberlin, *Sack of Rome*, 40.

97. Prescott, *History of the Conquest of Peru*, 2:473n32.

98. For example, when the Swiss pikemen seemed invincible at the beginning of the sixteenth century, they gained a reputation for both avarice and treachery. Coggins, *Fighting Man*, 146.

99. See Matthew Carr, *Blood and Faith: The Purging of Muslim Spain* (New York: New Press, 2009), 52–72.

100. Prescott, *History of the Conquest of Peru*, 2:421–422, 471–474; Stirling, *Pizarro*, 42–43, 56.

101. For a cogent discussion of the scandalous details surrounding the death of Atahualpa, see John Hemming, *The Conquest of the Incas* (New York: Harcourt Brace Jovanovich, 1970), 78–85.

102. See McGrath, *French in Early Florida*, 149; George R. Fairbanks, *The History and Antiquities of the City of St. Augustine, Florida* (New York: Charles B. Norton, 1858), 97, dealing with the inducements and assurances made to get Protestant French interlopers in Florida to surrender.

103. See Konstam, *Spanish Armada*, 22–23; Peter Kemp, *The Campaigns of the Spanish Armada* (New York: Facts on File, 1988), 38, 40; Bryce Walker, *The Armada* (Chicago: Time-Life Books, 1982), McDermott, *England and the Spanish Armada*, 153, discussing the broken promise made to the English regarding a truce when their ships had put into a Mexican seaport for repairs and the breach of a trade agreement made with England when Spain enticed British grain ships to sail to Spain.

104. See Motley, *Rise of the Dutch Republic*, 2:160–179, 198–212, relating to the illegal execution of two Catholic Flemish noblemen who were entitled to safe-conduct protection when they met with Spanish representatives.

105. Turnbull, *Art of Renaissance Warfare*, 193. Rosen, *Soldiers at Leisure*, 20–21, regarding Dutch towns that were sacked—and whose populations were massacred—after surrendering under terms.

106. See Rosen, *Soldiers at Leisure*, 21.

CHAPTER FIFTEEN: MILITARY MISCALCULATION

1. See Warry, *Alexander*, 48. This essentially sound doctrine found support as recently as the Second World War, when the two atomic bombs were dropped on Japan, saving the lives of hundreds of thousands of Allied soldiers and sailors, as well as at least a million Japanese, including civilians.

2. Day, "Mota Padilla," 100.

3. See Flint, *Great Cruelties*, 440, "A Translation of the Testimony Summary."

4. See Hammond and Rey, *Narratives*, 331, "Coronado's Testimony Concerning the Expedition."

5. See Alfred Vincent Kidder, *The Artifacts of Pecos* (New Haven, CT: Yale University Press, 1932), 305, 307, apparent boltheads discovered.

6. See Day, "Mota Padilla," 101.

7. Hodge, "Narrative by Castaneda," 321.

8. Martin Hackett, *Lost Battlefields of Britain* (Stroud, UK: Sutton, 2005), 38–39, 42.

9. Hodge, "Narrative by Castaneda," 321.

10. Ibid.

11. See Contamine, *War in the Middle Ages*, 291–292.

12. Hodge, "Narrative by Castaneda," 321; Day, "Mota Padilla," 100.

13. Flint, *Great Cruelties*, 355, "Defense Offered by Vazquez de Coronado (Inquiry question)"; 363, "Defense Offered by Vazquez de Coronado; First de Parte Witness (Lorenzo Alvarez)."

14. Hodge, "Narrative by Castaneda," 321.

15. Day, "Mota Padilla," 100.

16. Ibid.

17. See Nicolle, *Granada 1492*, 64–65. The Moors gave the remains of their assassin tossed into the city a martyr's burial.

18. See Desmond Seward, *The Hundred Years War: The English in France, 1337–1453* (New York: Atheneum, 1978), 180; Michael, *Armies of Medieval Burgundy*, 3, 5.

19. "Safe passage [during a truce] must be afforded to a person to whom it has been promised." Grotius and Loomis, *Law of War and Peace*, 427.

20. See Chester L. Kieffer, *Maligned General: A Biography of Thomas S. Jesup* (San Rafael, CA: Presidio, 1979), 184–190. Kieffer defends Jesup's violation of the flag as a necessary part of an ugly war.

21. See Hammond and Rey, *Narratives*, 333, "Coronado's Testimony Concerning the Expedition."

22. Hodge, "Narrative by Castaneda," 321.

23. Day, "Mota Padilla," 100.

24. Hodge, "Narrative by Castaneda," 321–322.

25. Ibid., 322.

26. Ibid.

27. Cf. Watson, *Sieges*, 129.

28. Hodge, "Narrative by Castaneda," 322. By this time in the expedition, it likely would have been a worthless exercise for Coronado to address his weary veterans with a harangue before battle.

29. Cain, *Cottonwood Tree*, 149. There also may have been pines close enough to gather for ladder construction.

30. Generally, it might be said that in constructing temporary field structures (from towers to bridges), rope lashings are more secure for unsawn limbs, whereas nails are better for sawn wood. Proper bolts through drilled holes (with nuts), of course, would be best in either circumstance.

31. Hodge, "Narrative by Castaneda," 322.

32. See Hammond and Rey, *Expedition into New Mexico*, 92.

33. Day, "Mota Padilla," 101. The ancients had discovered the irony that sunbaked mud bricks (like adobe) resisted battering rams better than stone walls, which could shatter on repeated impacts. Duncan B. Campbell, *Greek and Roman Siege Machinery 399 BC–AD 363* (Botley, UK: Osprey, 2003), 40.

34. Day, "Mota Padilla," 100.

35. Hodge, "Narrative by Castaneda," 322.

36. See Gravett, *Tudor Knight*, 60. It was only about 1545 that French army physician and surgeon Ambroise Pares (a Huguenot) began to publicize that the ancient use of egg whites rather than cauterization was a better treatment to prevent infection of wounds. See Hale, *Art of War*, 30.

37. Day, "Mota Padilla," 101.

38. Winship, "Coronado Expedition," 576, "Translation of the Relacion de Suceso."

39. Hodge, "Narrative by Castaneda," 322.

40. Ibid.

41. See Day, "Mota Padilla," 101.

42. Hodge, "Narrative by Castaneda," 322.

43. Day, "Mota Padilla," 101.

44. Ibid.

45. Ibid.

46. Ibid.

47. Flint, *Great Cruelties*, 366, "Defense Offered by Vazquez de Coronado; First de Parte Witness (Lorenzo Alvarez)."

48. Hodge, "Narrative by Castaneda," 328.

49. See Day, "Mota Padilla," 101.

50. See Nossov, *Ancient and Medieval Siege Weapons*, 239.

51. Day, "Mota Padilla," 101.

52. Hodge, "Narrative by Castaneda," 322.

53. Day, "Mota Padilla," 101.

54. Hodge, "Narrative by Castaneda," 386.

55. Urban, *Medieval Mercenaries*, 263.

56. See Raymond, *Henry VIII's Military Revolution*, 26; Spaulding, Nickerson, and Wright, *Warfare*, 439.

57. Heath, *Armies of the Sixteenth Century [European]*, 151.

58. Taylor, *Art of War in Italy*, 185.

59. See ibid., 185–187. A rationale for contemporaries not mentioning the use of such carts by Coronado's force would be that this still was an age in which hiding behind artificers' obstacles was considered dishonorable. See Taylor, *Art of War in Italy*, 132.

60. Day, "Mota Padilla," 101.

61. Ibid., 101–102.

62. "Principles of Artillery: Weapons," *Technical Manual [TM] No. 9-3305-1* (Washington, DC: Department of the Army, November 14, 1956), 11.

63. See Peers, *Medieval Chinese Armies*, 37, 47, plate G2.

64. During medieval times, cloistered monks, translating ancient materials, often had no idea about the art of war and muddled their descriptions of Roman or Greek siege machines. Nossov, *Ancient and Medieval Siege Weapons*, 65.

65. The Chinese actually had explosive devices (similar to later Bangalore torpedoes) in the late fourteenth century, made out of lengths of bamboo, in which gunpowder was used to blow down gates or to kill people. See Peers, *Medieval Chinese Armies*, 37.

66. Christopher Duffy, *Fire and Stone: The Science of Fortress Warfare, 1660–1860* (North Vancouver, BC: Douglas David and Charles, 1975), 95–97. As noted by Duffy, the high point of the petard came after 1580, and it was a weapon especially used by the French. Another historian has concluded that in the great siege of Malta in 1565, the Turks unsuccessfully attempted to use a type of petard to breach a wall of the defenders' final citadel. Tim Pickles, *Malta 1565: Last Battle of the Crusades* (London: Osprey, 1998), 71.

67. Hodge, "Narrative by Castaneda," 386. For a description and visual representation of the likely classic Roman inspiration for such sling-throwing machines—onagers or scorpions—see Funcken and Funcken, *Arms and Uniforms, Part 1*, 66–67. However, since these Roman siege machines were heavy enough to be drawn by oxen, the Coronado versions obviously were tiny cousins. The same would be the case if the machines were miniatures of the medieval trebuchet, a sling catapult. See Crosby, *Throwing Fire*, 82–87.

68. Julian Smith, "Coronado's Deadly Siege: Hundreds of Metal Artifacts Pinpoint the Possible Site of a Bloody Battle between the Conquistadores and a Puebloan People," *Archaeology* 65, no. 2 (March/April 2012), 44.

69. See ibid., 43–44. Among the other items found is a link of chain mail.

70. Ibid., 44.

71. Ibid.

72. Day, "Mota Padilla," 101.

73. Smith, "Coronado's Deadly Siege," 44.

74. Ibid.

75. Ibid., 44–45. Supporting those who think Moho was atop a mesa and the occupants would have had to drill into rock, the Puebloans of Coronado's day actually were experienced excavators and miners. See Day, *Coronado's Quest*, 355n13. However, such a fortress foundation, in addition to the pueblo architecture, would discourage the Spaniards from attempting to mine under the pueblo to cause a collapse. See Watson, *Sieges*, 139.

76. See Smith, "Coronado's Deadly Siege," 43.

77. See Norris, *Artillery*, 57–58; Williams, *Actions of the Low Countries*, 83.

78. Smith, "Coronado's Deadly Siege," 44.

79. Hodge, "Narrative by Castaneda," 323.

80. Ibid., 322–323. Hodge has "sons" and "boys," but Hammond and Rey translate the intended meaning as "children," which makes more sense. See Hammond and Rey, *Narratives*, 229, "Castaneda's History of the Expedition."

81. See Nossov, *Ancient and Medieval Siege Weapons*, 255; Watson, *Sieges*, 132.

82. Hodge, "Narrative by Castaneda," 323.

83. Bolton, *Coronado*, 225.

84. "Again, a man who has a permit to come may come once, but not a second time." Grotius and Loomis, *Law of War and Peace*, 426.

85. Hodge, "Narrative by Castaneda," 354. Of course, part of this mortuary situation would be a natural benefit of a high desert climate.

86. Hammond and Rey, *Narratives*, 360, "Testimony of Lopez de Cardenas."

87. See E. A. Brininstool, *Troopers with Custer: Historic Incidents of the Battle of the Little Big Horn* (Harrisburg, PA: Stackpole, 1952), 258–259; Col. W. A. Graham, *The Custer Myth: A Source Book of Custeriana* (New York: Bonanza, [1953]), 376; Hunt and Hunt, *I Fought with Custer*, 110.

88. Flint, *Great Cruelties*, 96, "Fourth de Oficio Witness (Domingo Martin)."

89. Hodge, "Narrative by Castaneda," 323.

90. Day, "Mota Padilla," 102. According to Mota Padilla, the sleepy sentinel whose corpse was found—and whose mouth was smashed by the hoof of a Spanish cavalry mount being ridden over the body in the dark—was reputed to be "a recreant and a blasphemer."

91. Hodge, "Narrative by Castaneda," 323.

92. Ibid., 323–324.

93. Ibid., 324.

94. Ibid., 322.

95. See Hammond and Rey, *Narratives*, 333, "Coronado's Testimony Concerning the Expedition."

96. Flint, *Great Cruelties*, 95, "Fourth de Oficio Witness (Domingo Martin)."

97. Cf. Contamine , *War in the Middle Ages*, 300.

98. Williams, *Actions of the Low Countries*, 75.

99. See Watson, *Sieges*, 130.

100. Flint, *Great Cruelties*, 395, "Second de Parte Witness (Diego Lopez)."

101. Parker, *Army of Flanders*, 179.

102. Flint, *Great Cruelties*, 62, "Second de Oficio Witness (Alonso Sanchez)."

103. Ibid., 318, "Alonso Alvarez, the Fourteenth de Oficio Witness." Regarding the use of dogs against these pueblo Indians, there is scant evidence that such peoples dined on dogs regularly, as did the Aztecs. The Zuni raised long-haired dogs for weaving, while the Hopis and others may have resorted to such a dog diet only during starving times. See Schwartz, *History of Dogs*, 57, 86–87.

104. Flint, *Great Cruelties*, 96, "Fourth de Oficio Witness (Domingo Martin)."

105. See Gomara, *Cortes*, 106–107. Apparently in the case of the Indians captured by the forces of Coronado, each victim had one hand severed.

106. Villagutierre Soto-Mayor, *History of the Conquest*, 61n259.

107. Yet later, in 1489, when the Spanish captured Baza, they treated the city's population with leniency, perhaps to encourage the submission of other Muslim strongholds. See Nicolle, *Granada 1492*, 69. Such are the vagaries of war.

108. See ibid., 66. Even as late as the Irish Rebellion of 1798, some of the captured Irish combatants (those who avoided being mercilessly cut down in battle), being considered rebels, were hanged, while their allied Frenchmen—foreign invaders—were treated as honorable prisoners of war. See Thomas Pakenham, *The Year of Liberty: The Great Irish Rebellion of 1798* (London: Weidenfeld and Nicolson, 1997), 103–105.

109. Furneaux, *Invasion 1066*, 26.

110. See Fussel, *Emperor Maximilian*, 34.

111. See Hammond and Rey, *Narratives*, 333, "Coronado's Testimony Concerning the Expedition."

112. Kleinschmidt, *Charles V*, 144. While the sack of Rome—and the Vatican was a political player in the warfare in Italy and elsewhere—was against the specific intentions of Charles V, he set the stage for the natural consequences. See Longhurst, *Alfonso De Valdes*, 6–7.

113. See, for example, Flint, *Great Cruelties*, 391, "A Translation of the Testimony Summary—Second de Parte Witness (Diego Lopez)"; 361, "Defense Offered by Vazquez de Coronado—First de Parte Witness (Lorenzo Alvarez)."

114. See Hodge, "Narrative by Castaneda," 324.

115. See Richard Flint, *No Settlement*, 53.

116. Bolton, *Coronado*, 18, 28.

117. Indeed, one of the witnesses during the investigation of the expedition, Cristobal de Escobar, referred to this village, "hard pressed by the siege," as "the third pueblo." Flint, *Great Cruelties*, 149.

118. Ibid., 257, "Juan de Zaldivar, the Twelfth de Oficio Witness."

119. Ibid., 257–258, "Juan de Zaldivar, the Twelfth de Oficio Witness."

120. Hodge, "Narrative by Castaneda," 324.

121. See Taylor, *Art of War in Italy*, 15–16.

122. See Nossov, *Ancient and Medieval Siege Weapons*, 249.

123. See Hare, *Bayard*, 69–70.

124. Nicolle, *Granada 1492*, 61.

125. Hodge, "Narrative by Castaneda," 324.

126. Flint, *Great Cruelties*, 149, "Seventh de Oficio Witness (Cristobal de Escobar)."

127. Ibid., 80, "Third de Oficio Witness (Juan de Paradinas)."

128. See ibid., 96–97, "Fourth de Oficio Witness (Domingo Martin)."

129. See, for example, ibid., 113, "Fifth de Oficio Witness (Juan de Contreras)"; 131, "Sixth de Oficio Witness (Rodrigo Ximon)."

130. See, for example, Prescott, *History of the Reign*, 3:305.

131. Hodge, "Narrative by Castaneda," 328.

132. Simpson, "Coronado's March," 320.

133. Hammond and Rey, *Expedition into New Mexico*, 92. The Spaniards with explorer Antonio de Espejo to whom the Tiguexans related this history wisely did not admit that they knew anything about the Coronado Expedition.

## Chapter Sixteen: The Mixton War Rearranges Viceroy Mendoza's Military Priorities

1. Perhaps because the event did not noticeably affect Coronado until his return to Mexico, except for how it impacted the isolated post at San Geronimo, Bolton somewhat surprisingly notes the war only in passing. See Bolton, *Coronado*, 321.

2. See Day, *Coronado's Quest*, 363n1.

3. Parry, *Audiencia of New Galicia*, 27–28; Bancroft, *History of Mexico*, 491.

4. See Hammond and Rey, *Obregon's History*, 29–30. This scenario certainly was not unknown in the annals of the later Indian wars of North America.

5. Aiton, *Antonio de Mendoza*, 140.

6. Bancroft, *History of Mexico*, 491.

7. John M. Hutchins, *"The Scouts Have Always Been Loyal": Mutiny at Cibicu, Attack on Fort Apache, and Legal Retribution in 1881 Arizona Territory* (Lakewood, CO: published by author, 2011), 5.

8. See Major General William Harding Carter, *The Life of Lieutenant General Chaffee* (Chicago: University of Chicago Press, 1917), 91; John H. Monnett, "Prelude to the Battle of Cibicu," *Cochise Quarterly* 1, no. 1 (March 1971), 21–22.

9. See A. J. Smithers, *The Kaffir Wars, 1779–1877* (London: Leo Cooper, 1973), 263–265; Giddings, *Imperial Echoes*, 162.

10. See Giddings, *Imperial Echoes*, 84–85; Tim Ryan and Bill Parham, *The New Zealand Colonial Wars* (Wellington: Grantham House, 1986), 10, 109–110.

11. Carter, *Life of Lieutenant General Chaffee*, 91.

12. See Aiton, *Antonio de Mendoza*, 143.

13. Bancroft, *History of Mexico*, 491.

14. Aiton, *Antonio de Mendoza*, 142–144.

15. Ibid., 144–145.

16. Ibid., 145.

17. Ibid., 146–147.

18. Ibid., 148.

19. Ibid.

20. Ibid.

21. Ibid., 140–150.

22. Ibid., 150; Bancroft, *History of Mexico*, 499–500.

23. Aiton, *Antonio de Mendoza*, 150–151 (50,000); Bancroft, *History of Mexico*, 503 (50,000); Hammond and Rey, *Obregon's History*, 32 (15,000).

24. Bancroft, *History of Mexico*, 503–504.

25. Ibid., 504.

26. Ibid. It also was said, since the battle occurred on Saint Michael's Day, that Saint Michael likewise manifested himself and fought. Ibid.

27. For example, even as late as the First World War, there was an unsubstantiated legend (based on a fictional short story) that the British Expeditionary Force at Mons in Belgium was saved by the intervention of Saint George and the ghostly longbowmen of Henry V, while the Russians fighting the Germans on the eastern front also supposedly were assisted by divine intervention. See Arthur Machen, *The Angels of Mons: The Bowmen and Other Legends of the War* (London: Simpkin, Marshall, Hamilton, Kent, 1915), 5–27. Of course, unlike the case of the "more logical" visions of Constantine the Great at Milvian Bridge in AD 312, see Pat Southern, *The Roman Empire From Severus to Constantine* (London: Routledge, 2002), 175, and of the Spanish in the New World, the Great War largely was fought among Christians, not waged against pagans. More amazing—or disturbing—there still are historians who defend the presence of the angelic longbowmen of Mons in 1914, despite the complete absence of any contemporaneous eyewitness testimony. See David Clarke, *The Angel of Mons: Phantom Soldiers and Ghostly Guardians* (Chichester, UK, 2004), 229–231.

28. By 1584, the miraculous story had become passé, even among the devout Spanish, for Obregon's history discussing the Mixton War omits any reference to the appearance of the saint at the defense of Guadalajara and instead gives full credit to the defending soldiery, especially Onate's' men-at-arms. See Hammond and Rey, *Obregon's History*, 32–34.

29. Bancroft, *History of Mexico*, 505. Obregon estimated Mendoza's army to have six hundred Spaniards and sixty thousand allies. Hammond and Rey, *Obregon's History*, 34.

30. Heath, *Armies of the Sixteenth Century [New World]*, 152.

31. Bancroft, *History of Mexico*, 505.

32. Heath, *Armies of the Sixteenth Century [New World]*, 149.

33. Bancroft, *History of Mexico*, 506.

34. Ibid., 507.

35. See ibid., 507–508.

36. Ibid., 508–509.

37. Ibid., 509–510; Aiton, *Antonio de Mendoza*, 156.

38. See James Horn, *A Kingdom Strange: The Brief and Tragic History of the Lost Colony of Roanoke* (New York: Basic, 2010), 167–168.

39. See Day, *Coronado's Quest*, 352–353n18.

40. Winship, "Coronado Expedition," 578, "Relacion del Suceso." As will be seen, Coronado and his army only realized the full extent of the war—and their vulnerability—when they marched homeward in 1542.

41. See Hodge, "Narrative by Castaneda," 375, 379.

42. Ibid., 380.

43. See Bolton, *Coronado*, 324.

44. Hodge, "Narrative by Castaneda," 380.

45. See ibid.

46. See ibid., 380–381.

47. See ibid., 381.

48. Hodge, "Narrative by Castaneda," 381.

49. Bolton, *Spanish Explorations*, 5.

50. Ibid., 19. Other Indians likewise reported they had heard of the Europeans. See ibid., 24, 25, 26.

## CHAPTER SEVENTEEN: BUILDING THE FIRST BRIDGE ACROSS THE PECOS

1. Hodge, "Narrative by Castaneda," 327, 356–357, 357.
2. Day, *Coronado's Quest*, 220.
3. As Castaneda apparently knew, such handcrafted "artillery stones," in a variety of fairly standard sizes, were slung by catapults in ancient times. See Duncan B. Campbell, *Besieged: Siege Warfare in the Ancient World* (Botley, UK: Osprey, 2006), 118.
4. Hodge, "Narrative by Castaneda," 327.
5. See Nelson, *Tudor Navy*, 38–39.
6. See Konstam, *Spanish Armada*, 205–206.
7. Such collapses of rotten gun carriages did occur during frontier wars. One such system failure happened at the Battle of Cut Knife Creek, Canada, in 1885. See Charles Pelham Mulvaney, *The History of the North-West Rebellion of 1885* (Toronto: A. H. Hovey, 1885), 165.
8. Certainly, such happenstance discoveries have occurred. In 1862, on their retreat from the territory of New Mexico, Texas rebels buried four of the guns that had been captured from the federals at the Battle of Valverde. In the early twentieth century, the guns were dug up. See John H. Vaughan, *History and Government of New Mexico, 2nd ed.* (State College, NM: published by author, 1921), 175, photo of the guns.
9. Hodge, "Narrative by Castaneda," 328.
10. Ibid., 342.
11. Ibid., 328–329.
12. Ibid., 329.
13. Ibid.
14. Flint and Cushing Flint, *Documents*, 411, "Castaneda de Najera's Narrative, 1560s."
15. Hodge, "Narrative by Castaneda," 329.
16. Weber, *Spanish Frontier*, 52.
17. Indeed, so often have historians seen prior experts get burned by their learned conclusions about the route of Coronado that the modern trend, in the few maps that today try to portray the entire expedition, is to cut a broad, Sherman-like swath or to leave major portions blank. See, for example, Hartmann, "Finding Coronado's Route," 1, miles-wide trail.
18. See Weber, *Spanish Frontier*, 55–56.
19. See M. Robertson, *L'Historie de L'Amerique*, Tome 2 (Paris: Panckoucke, 1778), which has a map of the Mexico conquered by Cortes and, in place of what would be Texas, "Grande Espace de Terre inconnue," translated in the English edition as "Great Land of Unknown Spaces."
20. Hodge, "Narrative by Castaneda," 331.
21. See Simpson, "Coronado's March," 333–335. Simpson himself voted for the Pecos.
22. See Joseph P. Sanchez, "Old Heat and New Light Concerning the Search for Coronado's Bridge: A Historiography of the Pecos and Canadian Rivers Hypotheses," *New Mexico Historical Review* 67, no. 2 (April 1992), 106–107.
23. Albert H. Schroeder, "The Locale of Coronado's 'Bridge,'" *New Mexico Historical Review* 67, no. 2 (April 1992), 119.
24. Bolton, *Coronado*, 242–243.
25. Richard Flint and Shirley Cushing Flint, "The Coronado Expedition: Cicuye to the Rio de Cicuye Bridge," *New Mexico Historical Review* 67, no. 2 (April 1992), 136.

However, the location still is open to considerable debate. See Harry C. Myers, "The Mystery of Coronado's Route from the Pecos River to the Llano Estacado," in Flint and Cushing Flint, *Coronado Expedition: From the Distance of 460 Years*, 147.

26. Hodge, "Narrative by Castaneda," 329–330.

27. Sanchez, "Old Heat and New Light," 109.

28. Schroeder, "Locale of Coronado's 'Bridge,'" 115.

29. Flint and Cushing Flint, *Documents*, 525, 527, "Juan Troyano's Proof of Service, 1560."

30. Ibid., 528.

31. Lansing B. Bloom, "Early Bridges in New Mexico," *El Palacio* 18, no. 8 (April 15, 1925), 163–164.

32. Richard Flint, "Who Designed Coronado's Bridge across the Pecos River?," *Kiva: Quarterly Journal of the Arizona Archaeological and Historical Society* 57, no. 4 (1992), 331–342.

33. See Colonel Mertens, *Tactics and Technique of River Crossings*, trans. Major Walter Krueger (New York: D. Van Nostrand, 1918), 195.

34. See Gomara, *Cortes*, 351.

35. "Bridging. Stringer Bridges and the Use of Pile and Trestle Supports," *Training Regulations, No. 445-220* (Washington, DC: War Department, July 13, 1923), 5.

36. See Parker, *Army of Flanders*, 82.

37. Prescott, *History of the Reign*, 2:499–500.

38. Robinson, *Spanish Invasion of Mexico*, 53.

39. Graham, *Horses of the Conquest*, 31–33.

40. Gomara, *Cortes*, 351.

41. Edward Gaylord Bourne, ed., *Narratives of the Career of Hernando de Soto*, 2 vols. (New York: Allerton, 1922), 2:67.

42. Ibid., 2:71.

43. See US Army Corps of Engineers, Albuquerque District, *Environmental Assessment for the East Puerto de Luna Community Ditch Rehabilitation Project, Guadalupe County, New Mexico* (Albuquerque: US Army Corps of Engineers, Albuquerque, February 2010), 5, 6, photos. However, pueblo Indians were capable of carrying pine timbers for construction for miles, so the Spaniards could have done likewise. See Bloom, "Early Bridges in New Mexico," 165–166.

44. See Cain, *Cottonwood Tree*, 144.

45. Richard Flint and Shirley Cushing Flint, "The Location of Coronado's 1541 Bridge: A Critical Appraisal of Albert Schroeder's 1962 Hypothesis," *Plains Anthropologist* 36, no. 135 (1991), 175.

46. See "Bridging. Stringer Bridges," 12.

47. Ibid., 5, 15.

48. This discussion of the type of bridge that may have been constructed is based on Major General Sir Douglas Howard, *An Essay on the Principles and Construction of Military Bridges and the Passage of Rivers in Military Operations* (London: Thomas and William Boone, 1832), 351, 371, and 376.

49. See ibid., 371. Nonetheless, in Flanders, the Spanish had "special machines" to drive piles. Parker, *Army of Flanders*, 82.

50. Gomara, *Cortes*, 351. See Mertens, *Tactics and Technique of River Crossings*, 212–213, infantry would assist engineers.

51. See "Bridging. Stringer Bridges," 11.
52. See Howard, *Essay on the Principles and Construction of Military Bridges,* 376–378. A blacksmith with Coronado could provide some of the tools.
53. Hope of finding the location of the bridge today would be nothing "short of a far-fetched fantasy." Flint and Cushing Flint, "Coronado Expedition: Cicuye to the Rio de Cicuye Bridge," 137. Temporary military bridges tend to be very temporary. Regarding a pontoon bridge Cromwell threw across the River Teme of England before the Battle of Worcester in 1651 (and details regarding this engineering feat also have not survived), there is no credible information that archaeological remains survived to modern times. Burne, *Battlefields of England,* 464–467.
54. Cain, *Cottonwood Tree,* 149.
55. See Robert T. Lingle and Dee Linford, comps., *The Pecos River Commission of New Mexico and Texas: A Report of a Decade of Progress, 1950–1960* (Santa Fe: Rydal, 1961), 69.
56. In 1680, when the Spanish were withdrawing to El Paso del Norte because of the Pecos Pueblo Uprising, pack animals were able to ford a flooded Rio Grande when wagons were unable to do so. Bloom, "Early Bridges in New Mexico," 167–168. See also Hook, *Sack of Rome, 1527,* 154, imperial force fording an Italian river in spring flood.
57. Flint and Cushing Flint, "Coronado Expedition: Cicuye to the Rio de Cicuye Bridge," 124–125.
58. Bolton, *Coronado,* 243.
59. See Woosnam-Savage and Hall, *Brassey's Book,* 96.
60. Hodge, "Narrative by Castaneda," 362–363.
61. Cf. Gravett and Hook, *Medieval Siege Warfare,* 54.
62. When on active duty many years ago at a disfavored fort on the plains of central Texas, the author commented to the commander of a combat engineer battalion (the 8th Combat Engineers) how much trouble his troops got into on post. The lieutenant colonel replied that once his men got out into the field, busy building bridges, they were happy. Probably being exhausted had something to do with it as well.
63. While, under the right combat conditions, falconets could be more than useful, they often garnered little respect. During the Peasants War of 1525–1526, a town attempted to justify to Austrian authorities why it had provided four falconets to the rebels, saying the guns "had no great worth." Bax, *Peasants War in Germany,* 220.
64. Hodge, "Narrative by Castaneda," 386.
65. See Funcken and Funcken, *Age of Chivalry, Part 3,* 92.
66. The Ottoman Turks, in attempting to crush the Knights of Malta in 1565, built a massive siege tower, which the desperate Christian defenders were able to destroy by cannon fire. Pickles, *Malta 1565,* 69–71.
67. Alas, the catapult built for Cortes was designed by an incompetent amateur engineer, a supposed veteran of the Italian Wars. It launched its first (and last) projectile straight up into the air, and it was fortunate no one was killed by this friendly fire. See MacNutt, *Fernando Cortes,* 2:117–118; 117n1. It took expert knowledge to construct siege machines like trebuchets. See Crosby, *Throwing Fire,* 86–87. Another innovative engineering scheme by Cortes, when he was besieged in the Aztec capital, was having his men construct "battle wagons" built out of timbers, which probably were similar to such vehicles attempted in Europe. See Pohl and Hook, *Conquistador,* 30.

68. Gomara, *Cortes*, 363.

69. Indeed, concluding that the main motive in stopping to construct a bridge for four days was to reorganize and reinvigorate the expedition by working on a potentially important training project actually would answer those who argue that the Pecos was not the river bridged. "Coronado would not have found it necessary to build a bridge across the Pecos River to reach the east side, since the Indian trail [being followed] was on the east side of the river." Schroeder, "Locale of Coronado's 'Bridge,'" 122. A "make-work" project—especially if the expedition was split and marching down both sides of the Pecos—would answer this objection.

## CHAPTER EIGHTEEN: THE EXPEDITION ENTERS THE CAP ROCKS AND THE CANYONS OF THE LLANO ESTACADO

1. The discussion of the expedition's encounter with the Apaches is based on Hodge, "Narrative by Castaneda," 330.

2. Hammond and Rey, *Obregon's History*, 18.

3. See Hodge, "Narrative by Castaneda," 331.

4. See Hammond and Rey, *Obregon's History*, 18–19.

5. Hodge, "Narrative by Castaneda," 331.

6. Ibid.

7. See Bouchard, *Knights*, 56–57; Jones, *Knight*, 207–209. In the sixteenth century, bull-fighting with lances also enhanced this skill. See Roeder, *Man of the Renaissance*, 155. In Europe, such boar hunting was often done with dogs. Thus, when Melchior Diaz tried to kill that dog, he ironically also was showing European experience with hunting on horseback—although he did not long survive the demonstration.

8. Hodge, "Narrative by Castaneda," 363.

9. Ibid., 331.

10. Ibid. This was quite an endorsement for the Texas Panhandle, which later would become known as cattle country.

11. Ibid.

12. See ibid., 331–332. While much debate has occurred regarding the location of the various Texas Panhandle sites, the author suspects that this village was in Palo Duro Canyon, a traditional place for villages over the centuries. However, based on the directions and marches set out in Castaneda (if accurate), this supposition would seem to mean that it was the Canadian River that was bridged.

13. Ibid., 332.

14. Ibid.

15. Ibid. In mitigation of the Spanish soldiery, from medieval times there had been a custom regulating the division of war spoils and booty among armies, a formula probably not being observed by Coronado regarding these apparent gifts. See Contamine, *War in the Middle Ages*, 261. Even in Europe, when it was believed favoritism was involved regarding spoils, violence could erupt among the soldiery. See Hook, *Sack of Rome, 1527*, 213.

16. Hodge, "Narrative by Castaneda," 332.

17. Ibid., 333.

18. Dan Flores, *Caprock Canyonlands: Journeys into the Heart of the Southern Plains* (Austin: University of Texas Press, 1990), 53. The author, as a US Army officer in Texas, heard of (and occasionally saw) those storms called "blue northers" from their dark, cold

color as they sweep in with a suddenness that amazes, bringing hail or sleet that immediately becomes layered ice on hitting the ground, depending on the season.

19. Castaneda wrote, "the negroes protected [two or three horses] by holding large sea nets over them, with the helmets and shields which all the rest wore." Hodge, "Narrative by Castaneda," 333. While this Winship-Hodge version implies that the black servants protected the horses by holding over them netting that was used for packing and that was packed with helmets and shields—not an illogical effort, although requiring considerable strength on the part of the servants—other translations or editions of Castaneda indicate that the servants—or the horses—were wearing helmets and shields. See Hammond and Rey, *Narratives*, 238, "two or three [horses] which were held by negroes covered with helmets and shields"; Flint and Cushing Flint, *Documents*, 409, "two or three [horses] which Blacks went to hold, protected by helmets and round shields." Thus, Flint and Cushing Flint contend that the original Spanish talks about "shielded" animals, not nets, which still could indicate protection by canvas packing bags used for the armor. See also chapter 8, note 69.

20. Hodge, "Narrative by Castaneda," 333.

21. See, for example, Graham, *Spanish Armadas*, 143. Similarly, when a 1559 hurricane struck the Spanish ships landing a major expedition on the Florida coast, demons were seen flying in the air directing the carnage. See Herbert Ingram Priestly, *Tristan de Luna, Conquistador of the Old South: A Study of Spanish Imperial Strategy* (Glendale, CA: Arthur H. Clark, 1936), 108–109.

22. Hodge, "Narrative by Castaneda," 333.

23. See Deagan and Cruxent, *Columbus's Outpost*, 139–141; Colin Martin, *Full Fathom Five*, 105–106.

24. See Hammond and Rey, *Obregon's History*, 233. Obviously, drying powder with a campfire was something to be done carefully with small amounts at a time.

25. Hodge, "Narrative by Castaneda," 333n3.

26. Ibid., 333–334.

27. Ibid., 334.

28. Ibid.

29. See Blakeslee and Blaine, "The Jimmy Owens Site," 210–213; Donald J. Blakeslee, "Ysopete's Tantrum, or New Light on the Coronado Expedition's Route to the Jimmy Owens Site," in Flint and Cushing Flint, *Latest Word from 1540*, 419.

30. Bancroft, *History of Arizona and New Mexico*, 59–60.

31. Hodge, "Narrative by Castaneda," 334–335.

32. Ibid., 335.

33. See Winship, "Coronado Expedition," 571, "Relacion Postrera de Sivola."

34. Hodge, "Narrative by Castaneda," 335, 342.

35. Ibid., 335.

36. The discussion of Arellano's two weeks in the Panhandle is based on Hodge, "Narrative by Castaneda," 335–336.

37. Ibid., 339.

38. Ibid., 338. The record is silent as to whether the Pecos bridge had been left in place or dismantled. If the outward-bound expedition wanted to recover building materials such as nails or ropes for possible future use, it likely had been dismantled, a standard procedure for later military engineers. See Mertens, *Tactics and Technique of River Crossings*, 20. This would explain why the record also is silent regarding any attempt by the Spaniards to recross the Pecos on the bridge.

39. Hodge, "Narrative by Castaneda," 339.

40. See ibid.

41. Ibid.

42. See Hartmann, "Finding Coronado's Route," 4.

43. See Hodge, "Narrative by Castaneda," 339–341. At least one historian suspected that this really was the first visit of Coronado's men to Taos, the previous one by Alvarado's scouts not having occurred. Day, *Coronado's Quest*, 261–262.

## CHAPTER NINETEEN: CORONADO'S FLYING RECONNAISSANCE IN SEARCH OF QUIVIRA

1. Hammond and Rey, *Narratives*, 187, "Letter of Coronado to the King, . . . October 20, 1541."

2. Winship, "Coronado Expedition," 577, "Relacion del Suceso."

3. Hammond and Rey, *Narratives*, 187, "Letter of Coronado to the King, . . . October 20, 1541."

4. Ibid., 291, "Relacion de Suceso: Relation of the Events on the Expedition That Francisco Vazquez Made to the Discovery of Cibola."

5. Winship, "Coronado Expedition," 571, "Relacion Postrera de Sivola."

6. See Paul H. Carlson, *The Buffalo Soldier Tragedy of 1877* (College Station: Texas A&M University Press, 2003), 135–136.

7. The discussion of Coronado's time in buffalo country and his arrival in Quivira is based on Winship, "Coronado Expedition," 581–582, "Translation of a Letter from Coronado to the King, October 20, 1541."

8. Jones, *Coronado and Quivira*, 116–117.

9. Winship, "Coronado Expedition," 582–583, "Translation of a Letter from Coronado to the King, October 20, 1541."

10. Hoig, *Came Men on Horses*, 111. However, some Texans have insisted that Coronado never made it north of their Panhandle, denying even Oklahoma a portion of the historical excitement. See Pauline Durrett Robertson and R. L. Robertson, *Panhandle Pilgrimage: Illustrated Tales Tracing History in the Texas Panhandle, 2nd ed.* (Amarillo, TX: Paramount, 1978), 33. See also Cutter, *Journey of Coronado, 1540-1543*, xxii, reinterpretation of the itinerary indicates the expedition got no farther north than Texas.

11. One early Coronado historian (and a qualified military plainsman) thought the captain general got so far into Nebraska that he reached the Missouri River, almost to Omaha. See Simpson, "Coronado's March," 338. But Simpson's map accompanying his paper also had Coronado heading north from Tiguex and Pecos Pueblo into Colorado—not far from the later Santa Fe Trail.

12. Winship, "Coronado Expedition," 583, "Translation of a Letter from Coronado to the King, October 20, 1541."

13. The discussion of Coronado's decision to return to Tiguex and preparations for leaving Quivira is based on Winship, "Coronado Expedition," 590–591, "Translation of the Narrative of Jaramillo."

14. See Flint, *Great Cruelties*, 292–293, "Sworn Statement of the Governor, Francisco Vazquez de Coronado."

15. Ibid., 396, "Second de Parte Witness (Diego Lopez)."

16. Hoig, *Came Men on Horses*, 112.

17. See Day, *Coronado's Quest*, 360n14.

18. But there has always been the problem of determining whether such guides have been heroically patriotic, treacherous, or merely befuddled. In one case, a free black man hanged by Union Colonel Ulric Dahlgren during the abortive raid on Richmond in 1864 probably was just mistaken in his advice. See Edward Longacre, *Mounted Raids of the Civil War* (Lincoln: University of Nebraska Press, 1994), 247–248.

19. Although one must rely on Spanish sources, the proof of Turk's treachery seems logically convincing. Still, there is always room for debate. For a bit of sympathetic understanding and a skeptical discussion of the supposed conspiracies surrounding Turk, see Flint, *No Settlement*, 167–169.

20. Winship, "Coronado Expedition," 591–592, "Translation of the Narrative of Jaramillo."

21. Ibid., 578, "Relacion del Suceso."

22. Spanish borderlands historian Alfred Barnaby Thomas, writing for a Colorado audience, categorically concluded of Coronado, "At no time on this expedition did he pass through any of the territory of Colorado." But Thomas also accepted portions of the march that have since fallen out of historical and archaeological fashion. See Alfred Barnaby Thomas, "Spanish Expeditions into Colorado," *Colorado Magazine* 1, no. 7 (November 1924), 290.

23. Hodge, "Narrative by Castaneda," 341. One historian concluded that the shots sent into the pueblo and noted by Castaneda were from the expedition's falconets. See Kessell, *Kiva, Cross, and Crown*, 24. No one else has identified the transcription that way, and the volleys were just as likely from arquebuses.

24. See Kidder, *Artifacts of Pecos*, 305, 307. During the early twentieth century, archaeologists had little interest in Spanish artifacts, being primarily interested in pre-Columbian or precontact Indian relics. See, for example, Harrington, "Cibola Revealed," 24–25.

25. Hodge, "Narrative by Castaneda," 341–342.

26. See Flint, *Great Cruelties*, 80, "Third de Oficio Witness (Juan de Paradinas)." Because of this successful resistance, a later Spanish historian noted, "One must take along culverins to fight the Indians who are accustomed to fortify themselves in their houses as happened to Coronado at Cicuic [Pecos]." Hammond and Rey, *Obregon's History*, 232–233. This informed opinion regarding the necessity of heavier artillery would support—but not prove—the theory that falconets were used to shell Pecos. The successful armed deterrence occasioned by those defenders of Pecos Pueblo also undercut a broad statement by Herbert E. Bolton that "[i]n spite of his walled strongholds, the primitive red man armed with bows and arrows was no match for the white man armed with gun-powder." Bolton, *Cross, Sword, and Gold Pan*, interpretive historical essay opposite plate "Coronado Discovers Zuni" (unpaginated).

27. Hammond and Rey, *Narratives*, 188, "Letter of Coronado to the King, . . . October 20, 1541."

28. Hodge, "Narrative by Castaneda," 364–365. In addition to the African boy (a slave named Christopher) left behind to assist Padilla, two other blacks with the column remained in Quivira: a slave named Sebastian who belonged to Captain Juan Jaramillo and another male, apparently free, who had with him his wife and children. See Cutter, *Journey of Coronado*, 211–212, "Translation of the Narrative of Jaramillo."

29. Winship, "Coronado Expedition," 579, "Relacion del Suceso."

## CHAPTER TWENTY: HEADING FOR THE STABLE

1. Cf. Spaulding, Nickerson, and Wright, *Warfare*, 426, 433–434.

2. See Notario Lopez and Notario Lopez, *Spanish Tercios*, 19.

3. Winship, "Coronado Expedition," 579, "Relacion del Suceso." Not surprisingly, Kansans, during the Coronado quadricentennial celebrations of 1940–1942, quoted Coronado regarding what became the land of the Jayhawks, telling his liege that it was "a fair and productive land" worthy of colonization. From "Coronado Starts for Quivira," a postcard in the author's possession featuring the N. C. Wyeth painting, published by Curteich-Chicago.

4. Flint, *Great Cruelties*, 366, "First de Parte Witness (Lorenzo Alvarez)."

5. Hodge, "Narrative by Castaneda," 366–367.

6. See Winship, "Coronado Expedition," 578, "Relacion del Suceso."

7. Hodge, "Narrative by Castaneda," 367–368.

8. Ibid., 369.

9. Winship, "Coronado Expedition," 579, "Relacion del Suceso."

10. Hammond and Rey, *Narratives*, 306, "Jaramillo's Narrative: Narrative Given by Captain Juan Jaramillo . . ."

11. Hammond and Rey, *Narratives*, 293, "Relacion de Suceso: Relation of the Events on the Expedition That Francisco Vazquez Made to the Discovery of Cibola."

12. The discussion of Coronado's plotting to return home is based on Hodge, "Narrative by Castaneda," 369.

13. Hammond and Rey, *Narratives*, 306, "Jaramillo's Narrative: Narrative Given by Captain Juan Jaramillo . . ."

14. Hodge, "Narrative by Castaneda," 369–370.

15. Charles G. du Bois, *Kick the Dead Lion: A Casebook of the Custer Battle* (El Segundo, CA: Upton and Sons, 1987), 47–59. See also Robert Nightengale, *Little Big Horn* (Edina, MN: Far West, 1996), 172–173.

16. Hodge, "Narrative by Castaneda," 374.

17. There were known cases of Frenchmen and Portuguese going native (and naked). See Heath, *Armies of the Sixteenth Century [New World]*, 115, 116. Of course, those few survivors of the Narvaez Expedition had to go native to survive.

18. Hodge, "Narrative by Castaneda," 374.

19. Kessell, *Kiva, Cross, and Crown*, 5, 31.

20. Phil Sharpe, "Guns and Gunners," *Street & Smith's Western Story* 185, no. 6 (October 5, 1940), 106.

21. As noted, someday these guns may surface, as did the four Valverde guns from the Civil War.

22. See Hodge, "Narrative by Castaneda," 375.

23. See Hammond and Rey, *Expedition into New Mexico*, 89–90. More interesting, at least for any bibliophile, Coronado also left behind "a book," and "a small old trunk," both also seen forty years later. Ibid. Perhaps the trunk had contained the soldiers' petitions to return to Mexico.

24. Winship, "Coronado Expedition," 400–401.

25. See Day, *Coronado's Quest*, 343n21.

26. Rouse, *Criollo*, 54, 79.

27. Flint, *Great Cruelties*, 532.

28. Of course, this spread of disease by introduced pathogens was hardly limited to the natives of the New World (with the Europeans now often being considered morally culpable as biological aggressors). Even though Europeans were developing resistance to many diseases, this did not mean that epidemics from elsewhere did not remain a problem—one that would continue into the nineteenth and twentieth centuries and often was spread by both trade and warfare. In October 1532, Thomas Cranmer, soon to become archbishop of Canterbury, wrote to English King Henry VIII from Hapsburg Austria that there was "a great infection of the plague whereof many of the Emperor's household died, and among others Waldesius (Valdes) a Spaniard, the Emperor's Secretary, who enjoyed his singular favour." Mrs. [Susan] Hicks Beach, *A Cardinal of the Medici: Being the Memoirs of the Nameless Mother of the Cardinal Ippolitio de Medici* (New York: Macmillan, 1937), 403n26. Indeed, as previously indicated, although the evidence is not dispositive, there may be some truth to the belief that syphilis traveled from the New World to the Old World as a result of the post-Columbian conquests. See McNeill, *Plagues and Peoples*, 218–219.

29. Europeans, of course, were not morally above using biological warfare, but such conduct seemingly was limited to the Old World, as when medieval besiegers would lob human corpses or animal remains via catapult over castle walls to encourage the spread of disease. See Jones, *Knight*, 118; Humphrys, *Enemies at the Gate*, 29–30. During the Eighty Years' War, there was a fear—unfounded as it turned out—that the Calvinists of Geneva were prepared to spread the plague among the Spanish troops as they marched north to subdue the Dutch and Flemish in 1566–67. Parker, *Army of Flanders*, 66, 98–99.

30. For example, in 1521, during the Italian Wars, a mutinous Spanish force brutally pillaged the town of Como. Hook, *Sack of Rome, 1527*, 126. See also ibid., 136–137.

31. Oman, *History of the Art of War*, 62. See Hook, *Sack of Rome, 1527*, 136–137.

32. Hanson, *Confident Hope of a Miracle*, 376. Of course, old-time English armies drank weak beer on campaign because available water often was impure. See John Sadler, *Bannockburn: Battle for Liberty* (Barnsley, UK: Pen and Sword Military, 2008), 13.

33. Gomara and Simpson, *Cortes*, 89.

34. Brady, *Colonial Fights and Fighters*, 21.

35. See Fairbanks, *History and Antiquities*, 94–95.

36. Hodge, "Narrative by Castaneda," 375. Gallego, of course, was sort of an express rider for Coronado. It was with some excitement that a sword blade was found in Kansas in the 1890s that appeared to have the name Juan Gallego inscribed on it. Hodge, "Narrative by Castaneda," 302n2. It later was determined that the blade really said "Solingen," the name of a reputable sword manufactory in Germany, so the blade could not have dated to 1540. Hoig, *Came Men on Horses*, 316–317. However, proving nothing is easy in straightening out this expedition, it also is true that Solingen, like Toledo, was providing quality blades in the sixteenth century, a fact apparently unknown to Hoig. See Gravett, *Tudor Knight*, 22.

37. Hodge, "Narrative by Castaneda," 375.

38. Further discouraging any mutinous return north was the fact that there was no evidence that such a march would be profitable to any of the soldiery. Cf. Hook, *Sack of Rome, 1527*, 140.

39. Hodge, "Narrative by Castaneda," 375–376.

40. See Bancroft, *History of Mexico, Vol. 2*, 510.

41. Hodge, "Narrative by Castaneda," 376.
42. See ibid., 376–377.
43. Flint, *Great Cruelties*, 115, "Fifth de Oficio Witness (Juan de Contreras)."
44. Ibid., 81–82, "Third de Oficio Witness (Juan de Paradinas)."
45. See Hodge, "Narrative by Castaneda," 374 and 377.
46. Flint, *Great Cruelties*, 82, "Third de Oficio Witness (Juan de Paradinas)."
47. Hodge, "Narrative by Castaneda," 377.
48. See Sir Francis Drake, *The World Encompassed* (London: Nicholas Bourne, 1628), 29–33.
49. See Hodge, "Narrative by Castaneda," 377.
50. Ibid., 377–378.
51. See Day, *Coronado's Quest*, 382–383.
52. Hodge, "Narrative by Castaneda," 378.
53. Kleinschmidt, *Charles V*, 144.
54. Hodge, "Narrative by Castaneda," 378.
55. Winship, "Coronado Expedition," 402.
56. See Soto-Mayor, *History of the Conquest*, 59.

## Chapter Twenty-One: The Obligatory Spanish Inquiry into Conquistador Conduct

1. Hodge, "Narrative by Castaneda," 378.
2. Bolton, *Coronado*, 363–364, 367.
3. Millar, *Crossbowman's Story*, 223–224n.
4. See ibid. See also John Hutchins, "Book Review; *Great Cruelties Have Been Reported*," by Richard Flint, *Denver Westerners Roundup* 59, No. 2 (Mar-Apr 2003): 20-21.
5. This discussion of Bartolome de Las Casas and the New Laws is based on Bancroft, *History of Mexico, Vol. 2*, 516–521.
6. See Heath, *Armies of the Sixteenth Century [New World]*, 158.
7. Bolton, *Coronado*, 367–368, 376.
8. See, for example, Aiton, "Report on the Residencia," 12–20; Flint, *Great Cruelties*.
9. An eminent military historian (and instructor to active-duty soldiers) has written that the "propriety or impropriety" of battlefield atrocities—at least those involving the taking of prisoners in the heat of battle and the keeping of those prisoners on the battlefield—"does not . . . concern the military historian, at least at the professional level." Such a historian merely "is the judge of the significance of events, not of their morality or even strictly their utility." But this historian, the late John Keegan, noted that such questions are relevant at the lower levels of command, for they exemplify the soldiers' motivations. See Keegan, *Face of Battle*, 52–54. In addition (assuming Keegan's limitations are acceptable), such events may very well influence later military—and diplomatic—affairs of much importance.
10. Bolton, *Coronado*, 380, 392–393.
11. Most Reverend J. B. Salpointe, *Soldiers of the Cross: Notes on Ecclesiastical History of New-Mexico, Arizona and Colorado* (Banning, CA: Saint Boniface's Industrial School, 1898), 35.
12. Perhaps illustrating the fine line between being truthful and being inoffensive, the state of New Mexico in 1942 issued a pictorial tourist map that, while silent as to its meaning, had a small representation of a bound Indian being burned at the stake along

Coronado's route through the region. New Mexico State Tourist Bureau, *Battlefields of the Conquistadors in New Mexico* (Santa Fe: State Highway Department, 1942).

13. Flint, *Great Cruelties*, 537.

14. Hoig, *Came Men on Horses*, 134.

15. See Matthew Restall, *Maya Conquistador* (Boston: Beacon, 1998), 91–92, 121.

16. Hammond and Rey, *Narratives*, 85–86, "Appointment of Coronado as Commander of the Expedition to Cibola, January 6, 1540."

17. See Hanson, *Confident Hope of a Miracle*, 56.

18. Erasmus, a fellow Catholic who certainly was more open minded and tolerant than Las Casas, seemingly advocated, at least in theory, that the European Roman Catholic armies should not immediately prevent conquered pagan people from "openly . . . immolat[ing] their victims" in their temples, but impose restrictions in stages. Housley, *Documents on the Later Crusades*, 182.

19. As for Cortes, the strapped-for-cash Charles V "bestowed on him every honor" after his success in Mexico, and when Pizarro later asked permission to conquer Peru, "[w]ith no question about Pizarro's methods, Charles gave his hearty approval to proceed." James Reston Jr., *Defenders of the Faith: Charles V, Suleyman the Magnificent, and the Battle for Europe, 1520–1536* (New York: Penguin, 2009), 247.

20. Weber, *Spanish Frontier*, 9. Again, one must not forget the brutalities of the German ruling class against the Teutonic rebels of the Peasant Wars. See Bax, *Peasants War in Germany*, 265–266, 303, 313, 315–316, 353–354.

21. McGregor, *Luigi Guicciardini*, ix. Although the imperial army that captured and pillaged Rome contained Spaniards, Germans, and Italians (the vast majority of each group acting like animals), many Italian citizens believed that the Spanish were the worst when it came to butchery, pillage, and rape. See Chamberlin, *Sack of Rome*, 173–175, 184; McGregor, *Luigi Guicciardini*, 109–111.

22. Hanson, *Confident Hope of a Miracle*, 142–143. For more gruesome details of the sack of Antwerp, see Motley, *Rise of the Dutch Republic*, 3:108–120.

23. Hanson, *Confident Hope of a Miracle*, 143.

24. Ibid., 145. See also Motley, *Rise of the Dutch Republic*, 3:442–444, 594.

25. When it comes to a negative sixteenth-century reputation, Spain probably had less to complain about than the Russia of Ivan IV (the Terrible), whose military exploits also were pilloried at the time by the propaganda and public opinion of Western Europe. See Filjushkin, *Ivan the Terrible*, 243–257.

26. Bartolome de Las Casas, *In Defense of the Indians: The Defense of the Most Reverend Lord, Don Fray Bartolome de Las Casas, of the Order of Preachers, Late Bishop of Chiapa, against the Persecutors and Slanderers of the Peoples of the New World Discovered across the Seas*, trans. Stafford Poole, C.M. (De Kalb: Northern Illinois University Press, 1974), 306–307, 312.

27. Not surprisingly, Las Casas relegated Muslims—"African Moors or Turks"—to the same level of earthly hell offered Protestants. See Carr, *Blood and Faith*, 186. Therefore, it is going way too far to applaud Las Casas as part of "a group of contemporary Spaniards who led Europe in the first modern national debates on human rights." Flint, *Great Cruelties*, 540. This is an ethnocentric view of Spain seeking to protect human rights, for it was only attempting to protect the rights of Indians—those who were seen as pliable subjects within the Spanish sphere of influence. It also is relevant to note that the Dominicans, of which Las Casas was a member, were the dominant and enthusias-

tic members of the early tribunals of the Inquisition combating heresy. See Mills, *Renaissance and Reformation Times*, 282; Longhurst, *Alfonso De Valdes*, 13.

28. Although sometimes gallantry was seen in the battles between the Holy Roman Empire and its Muslim opponents, after the capture of Tunis in 1535 by the Spanish, Italian, and German troops of Charles V, thousands of inhabitants were massacred, and other thousands were reduced to slavery, "an atrocity that would stain Charles's reputation." Reston, *Defenders of the Faith*, 369. On the other hand, Erasmus wrote in 1530 that even considering the fighting with the Ottomans, "[W]hat Christians do to Christians is crueller [sic], even if they are repaid in kind." Housley, *Documents on the Later Crusades*, 179.

29. The Spanish soldiers of most of the sixteenth century were not unlike the German soldiers of most of the twentieth. While some might have seen them as the epitome of professional and successful soldiers, they could fight like hell and, fighting like hell, they often acted like devils.

30. Roy, *Blaise de Monluc*, 166.

## CONCLUSION

1. See Bolton, *Coronado*, 403–405.

2. See Weber, *Spanish Frontier*, 34; T. Frederick Davis, "Ponce de Leon's Second Voyage and Attempt to Colonize Florida," *Florida Historical Society Quarterly* 14, no. 1 (July 1935), 62.

3. Kim MacQuarrie, *The Last Days of the Incas* (New York: Simon and Schuster, 2007), 343, 352.

4. Alfred Barnaby Thomas, *After Coronado: Spanish Exploration Northeast of New Mexico, 1696–1727* (Norman: University of Oklahoma Press, 1935), 5.

5. See Hammond and Rey, *Obregon's History*, 17n49; 26n81.

6. Aiton, "Report on the Residencia," 12.

7. Smith, "Coronado's Deadly Siege," 42.

8. Hammond and Rey, *Narratives*, 83–86, "Appointment of Coronado as Commander of the Expedition to Cibola, January 6, 1540."

9. Flint, *No Settlement*, 197.

10. See Day, *Coronado's Quest*, 368n11.

11. Quoted in Buchanan, *Road to Guilford Courthouse*, 337.

12. Brady, *Colonial Fights and Fighters*, 30. But even De Soto's expedition could be considered a relative success compared with many other Spanish ventures, although it cost its namesake leader his life. "The survival of the force for more than three years indicates that it had overcome some of the problems of food and armor that had ruined the Narvaez expedition." Steele, *Warpaths*, 16.

13. Cf. Watson, *Sieges*, 141.

14. Especially in predemocratic times, there would be a tendency only to recall and count, at least in personal reminiscences, notable casualties, while a commander's report likely also would minimize losses. See Contamine, *War in the Middle Ages*, 257.

15. Flint and Cushing Flint, "Guido de Lavezariis," 4.

16. Certainly contributing to the high survival rate of the expedition's human members was the amazingly low attrition rate of the horses, at least until the very end. As Castaneda recalled, "The horses were in good condition for their work when they started, fat and sleek." When the mounts started dying off in significant numbers on the

return march, Castaneda noted that was "a thing that did not happen during all the rest of the journey." Hodge, "Narrative by Castaneda," 374. Why the horses suddenly showed evidence of being used up is not known. It might just have been, as American ranchers later would put it, that the West was good for men and cattle, but mighty hard on women and horses.

17. Aiton and Rey, "Coronado's Testimony," 316.

18. Those Indians killed in what became Old Mexico, because of the fighting around San Geronimo and especially when Juan Gallego was making his forced march north, must have numbered in the scores, if not a hundred or so.

19. Longacre, *Mounted Raids of the Civil War*, 12.

20. Ibid.

21. See Sadler, *Bannockburn*, 13.

22. John, *Storms Brewed*, 23.

23. See Weber, *Spanish Frontier*, 170–171.

24. On this expedition, see Priestly, *Tristan de Luna*.

25. Hodge, "Narrative by Castaneda," 284.

26. Kessell, *Kiva, Cross, and Crown*, 31. Perhaps not surprising for this Renaissance whistleblower, Troyano was petitioning from jail, where he had been put five years before for, in his words, "speaking the truth and remaining faithful [to Philip] . . . against those who exceed their authority." Ibid.

27. Hodge, "Narrative by Castaneda," 281–282.

28. Ibid., 379–380. The Twelve Peers of France were chivalrous heroes at the time of Charlemagne, including the noted Roland. See Rev. A. J. Church, *Stories of Charlemagne and the Twelve Peers of France from the Old Romances* (London: Seeley, 1902), 2. In literature, the twelve were not unlike the knights of the Round Table (and were an inspiration for Cervantes's *Don Quixote*). If nothing else, Castaneda's mention of them is proof that the conquistadors were inspired by the chivalric romances, as asserted by Irving Leonard in his *Books of the Brave*.

29. It was the opinion of one Coronado historian that Castaneda, in fact, so wanted to return to the northern lands that he accompanied Francisco de Ibarra's party in 1565 and was killed near Casa Grandes in northern Chihuahua when a startled horse kicked him. See Day, *Coronado's Quest*, 383. As for the expeditionaires not being ashamed of their overall conduct, this is a fact noted (somewhat incredulously) by Richard Flint. See Flint, *Great Cruelties*, 143, 164, 208, 252.

# Bibliography

PUBLISHED PRIMARY AND CONTEMPORARY SOURCES RELATING TO
CORONADO, THE CONQUISTADORS, OR THE SIXTEENTH CENTURY

Aiton, Arthur S. *The Muster Roll and Equipment of the Expedition of Francisco Vazquez de Coronado.* Ann Arbor, MI: William L. Clements Library, 1939.

———. "Report on the Residencia of the Coronado Government in New Galicia." *Panhandle- Plains Historical Review* 13 (1940): 12–20.

Aiton, Arthur S., and Agapito Rey. "Coronado's Testimony in the Viceroy Mendoza *Residencia.*" *New Mexico Historical Review* 12, no. 3 (July 1937).

Baylor, Michael G. *The German Reformation and the Peasants' War: A Brief History with Documents.* Boston: Bedford/St. Martin's, 2012.

Beckingham, C. F., and G. W. B. Huntingford, eds. *The Prester John of the Indies: A True Relation of the Lands of the Prester John, Being the Narrative of the Portuguese Embassy to Ethiopia in 1520 Written by Father Francisco Alvares.* 2 vols. Cambridge: Published for the Hakluyt Society at the University Press, 1961.

Benzoni, Girolamo. *History of the New World: Shewing His Travels in America, From A.D. 1541 to 1556, With Some Particulars of the Island of Canary.* Translated by Rear Admiral W. H. Smyth. London: Hakluyt Society, 1857.

Bourne, Edward Gaylord, ed. *Narratives of the Career of Hernando de Soto.* 2 vols. New York: Allerton, 1922.

Castaneda of Najera, Pedro de. *Narrative of the Coronado Expedition.* Edited by John Miller Morris. Chicago: R. R. Donnelly & Sons, 2002.

Cellini, Benvenuto. *The Autobiography of Benvenuto Cellini, a Florentine Artist: Containing a Variety of Information Respecting the Arts and the History of the Sixteenth Century.* Reading, PA: Spencer Press, 1936.

Cline, Howard F., trans. *Conquest of New Spain, 1585 Revision, by Bernardino de Sahagun.* Salt Lake City: University of Utah Press, 1989.

"Coronado's Letter to Mendoza, August 3, 1540," no. 20. *Old South Leaflets,* vol. 1, nos. 1–25. Boston: Directors of the Old South Work, Old South Meeting House, c. 1900.

Cushing, Frank Hamilton, recorder and trans. *Zuni Folk Tales.* New York: G. P. Putnam's Sons/Knickerbocker Press, 1901.

Cutter, Donald C., ed. *The Journey of Coronado, 1540–1543; Translated and Edited by George Parker Winship.* Golden, CO: Fulcrum, 1990.

Day, A. Grove. "Gomara on the Coronado Expedition," *Southwestern Historical Quarterly* 43, no. 3 (Jan. 1940): 348–355.

Diaz del Castillo, Bernal. *The Discovery and Conquest of Mexico.* Translated by A. P. Maudslay. New York: Farrar, Straus and Cudahy, 1956.

Flint, Richard, trans. and ed. *Great Cruelties Have Been Reported: The 1544 Investigation of the Coronado Expedition.* Dallas: Southern Methodist University Press, 2002.

Flint, Richard, and Shirley Cushing Flint, eds. and trans. *Documents of the Coronado Expedition, 1539–1542: "They Were Not Familiar with His Majesty, nor Did They Wish to Be His Subjects."* Dallas: Southern Methodist University Press, 2005.

Fuentes, Patricia de, ed. and trans. *The Conquistadors: First-Person Accounts of the Conquest of Mexico.* New York: Orion Press, 1963.

Gomara, Francisco Lopez de. *Cortes: The Life of the Conqueror by His Secretary.* Edited by Lesley Byrd Simpson. Berkeley: University of California Press, 1964.

———. *The Pleasant Historie of the Conquest of the Weast India, Now Called New Spayn.* London: Henry Bynneman, 1578. Readex reprint, 1966.

Hammond, George Peter, and Agapito Rey, trans. *Expedition into New Mexico Made by Antonio de Espejo, 1582–1583, as Revealed in the Journal of Diego Perez de Luxan, A Member of the Party.* Los Angeles: Quivira Society, 1929.

———. *Narratives of the Coronado Expedition, 1540–1542.* Albuquerque: University of New Mexico Press, 1940.

———, trans. *Obregon's History of 16th Century Explorations in Western America, Entitled Chronicle, Commentary, or Relation of the Ancient and Modern Discoveries in New Spain and New Mexico, Mexico, 1584.* Los Angeles: Wetzel, 1928.

Heaton, H. C., ed., and Bertram T. Lee, trans. *The Discovery of the Amazon, According to the Account of Friar Gaspar de Carvajal and Other Documents.* New York: American Geographical Society, 1934.

Hodge, Frederick W., ed. "The Narrative of the Expedition of Coronado, by Pedro De Castaneda." In *Original Narratives of Early American History: Spanish Explorers in the Southern United States, 1528–1543,* general editor J. Franklin Jameson, 273–387. New York: Charles Scribner's Sons, 1907.

———. "The Narrative of the Expedition of Hernando de Soto, by the Gentleman of Elvas." In *Original Narratives of Early American History: Spanish Explorers in the Southern United States, 1528–1543,* general editor J. Franklin Jameson, 127–272. New York: Charles Scribner's Sons, 1907.

Hoffman, Paul E., ed. and trans. *The Juan Pardo Expeditions: Exploration of the Carolinas and Tennessee, 1566–1568.* Washington, DC: Smithsonian Institution Press, 1990.

Housley, Norman, ed. and trans. *Documents on the Later Crusades, 1274–1580.* New York: St. Martin's Press, 1996.

Las Casas, Bartolome de. *In Defense of the Indians: The Defense of the Most Reverend Lord, Don Fray Bartolome de Las Casas, of the Order of Preachers, Late Bishop of Chiapa, against the Persecutors and Slanderers of the Peoples of the New World Discovered across the Seas.* Translated and edited by Stafford Poole, C. M. De Kalb: Northern Illinois University Press, 1974.

Leon-Portilla, Miguel, ed. *The Broken Spears: The Aztec Account of the Conquest of Mexico.* Boston: Beacon, 1992.

Lockhart, James, and Enrique Otte, eds. *Letters and People of the Spanish Indies: Sixteenth Century.* Cambridge: Cambridge University Press, 2006.

Longhurst, John E., trans. and ed. *Alfonso De Valdes and the Sack of Rome.* Albuquerque: University of New Mexico Press, 1952.

Machiavelli, Niccolo. *Art of War.* Translated and edited by Christopher Lynch. Chicago: University of Chicago Press, 2003.

MacNutt, Francis Augustus, trans. *Fernando Cortes: His Five Letters of Relation to the Emperor Charles V.* 2 vols. Cleveland: Arthur H. Clark, 1908.

Markham, Sir Clements R., trans. and ed. *Civil Wars of Peru by Pedro de Cieza de Leon [Part 4; Book 2]: The War of Chupas.* London: Hakluyt Society, 1918.

McGregor, James H., trans. and ed. *Luigi Guicciardini: The Sack of Rome.* New York: Italica Press, 1993.

Means, Philip Ainsworth, trans. *A Narrative of the Conquest of the Province of the Ytzas in New Spain.* Part 1. Paris: Les Editions Genet, 1930.

———. *Relation of the Discovery and Conquest of the Kingdom of Peru by Pedro Pizarro.* 2 vols. New York: Cortes Society, 1921.

Roy, Ian, ed. *Blaise de Monluc: The Hapsburg-Valois Wars and the French Wars of Religion.* London: Longman Group, 1971.

Smith, Buckingham, trans. *Relation of Alvar Nunez Cabeza de Vaca.* New York: Estate of Buckingham Smith, 1871. Readex reprint, 1966.

Smythe, Sir John. *Certain Discourses Military.* Edited by J. R. Hale. Ithaca, NY: Cornell University Press, 1964.

Varner, John Grier, and Jeannette Johnson Varner. *The Florida of the Inca: A History of the Adelantado, Hernandon de Soto, Governor and Captain General of the Kingdom of Florida, and of Other Heroic Spanish and Indian Cavaliers, Written by the Inca, Garcilasco de la Vega, an Officer of His Majesty, and a Native of the Great City of Cuzco, Capital of the Realms and Provinces of Peru.* Austin: University of Texas Press, 1951.

Villagutierre Soto-Mayor, Don de. *History of the Conquest of the Province of the Itza: Subjugation and Events of the Lacandon and Other Nations of Uncivilized Indians in the Lands from the Kingdom of Guatemala to the Provinces of Yucatan in North America.* Edited by Frank E. Comparato, translated by Robert D. Wood, S.M. Culver City, CA: Labyrinthos, 1983.

Whiteway, R. S., trans. and ed. *The Portuguese Expedition to Abyssinia in 1541–1543, as Narrated by Castanhoso, With Some Contemporary Letters, the Short Account of Bermudez, and Certain Extracts from Correa.* London: Hakluyt Society, 1902.

Williams, Sir Roger, and D. W. Davies, ed. *The Actions of the Low Countries.* Ithaca, NY: Cornell University Press, 1964.

Winship, George Parker. "The Coronado Expedition, 1540–1542." *Fourteenth Annual Report of the U.S. Bureau of American Ethnology, 1892–1893.* Part 1. Washington, DC: U.S. Bureau of American Ethnology, 1896, 329–613.

PUBLISHED NON-CONTEMPORARY OR SECONDARY SOURCES

Addy, George M. *The Enlightenment in the University of Salamanca.* Durham, NC: Duke University Press, 1966.

Ahern, Maureen. "Mapping, Measuring, and Naming Cultural Spaces in Castaneda's *Relacion de la journada de Cibola.*" In *The Coronado Expedition: From the Distance of 460 Years,* edited by Richard Flint and Shirley Cushing Flint, 265–289. Albuquerque: University of New Mexico Press, 2003.

Aiton, Arthur Scott. *Antonio de Mendoza: First Viceroy of New Spain.* Durham, NC: Duke University Press, 1927.

Ashdown, Charles Henry. *British and Foreign Arms & Armour.* London and Edinburgh: T. C. and E. C. Jack, 1909.

Attard, Robert. *Collecting Military Headgear: A Guide to 5000 Years of Helmet History.* Atglen, PA: Schiffer, 2004.

Bancroft, Hubert Howe. *History of Arizona and New Mexico, 1530–1888.* Albuquerque: Horn & Wallace, 1962.

———. *History of Mexico, Vol. 2, 1521–1600.* New York: Arno, 1967.

Bandelier, Adolph F. "Francisco Vasquez de Coronado." In *The Catholic Encyclopedia.* Vol. 4, edited by Charles G. Herbermann, 379–380. London: Universal Knowledge Foundation, 1913.

Bax, E. Belfort. *The Peasants War in Germany, 1525–1526.* New York: Augustus M. Kelley, 1968.

Benecke, Gerhard. *Maximilian I (1459–1519): An Analytical Biography.* London: Routledge & Kegan Paul, 1982.

Blakeslee, Donald J. "Ysopete's Tantrum, or New Light on the Coronado Expedition's Route to the Jimmy Owens Site." In *The Latest Word from 1540: People, Places, and Portrayals of the Coronado Expedition,* edited by Richard Flint and Shirley Cushing Flint, 398–422. Albuquerque: University of New Mexico Press, 2011.

Blakeslee, Donald J., and Jay C. Blaine. "The Jimmy Owens Site: New Perspectives on the Coronado Expedition." In *The Coronado Expedition: From the Distance of 460 Years,* edited by Richard Flint and Shirley Cushing Flint, 203–218. Albuquerque: University of New Mexico Press, 2003.

Bloom, Lansing B. "Early Bridges in New Mexico." *El Palacio* 18, no. 8 (Apr. 15, 1925): 163–182.

Bolton, Herbert Eugene. *Coronado: Knight of Pueblos and Plains.* New York and Albuquerque: Whittlesey House/University of New Mexico Press, 1949.

————. *Spanish Explorations in the Southwest, 1542–1706.* New York: Charles Scribner's Sons, 1916.

Bolton, Herbert E., John R. McCarthy, Carl Oscar Borg, and Millard Sheets. *Cross, Sword, & Gold Pan: A Group of Notable Full-Cover Paintings Depicting Outstanding Episodes in the Exploration and Settlement of the West.* Los Angeles: Primavera, 1936.

Boxer, C. R. *The Dutch Seaborne Empire: 1600–1800.* New York: Alfred A. Knopf, 1965.

Brady, Cyrus Townsend. *Colonial Fights and Fighters.* Garden City, NY: Doubleday, Page, 1913.

Brasher, Nugent. "The Chichilticale Camp of Francisco Vazquez de Coronado: The Search for the Red House." *New Mexico Historical Review* 82, no. 4 (Fall 2007): 433–468.

————. "The Red House Camp and the Captain General: The 2009 Report on the Coronado Expedition Campsite of Chichilticale." *New Mexico Historical Review* 84, no. 1 (Winter 2009): 1–64.

"Bridging. Stringer Bridges and the Use of Pile and Trestle Supports." *Training Regulations, No. 445-220.* Washington, DC: War Department, July 13, 1923.

Brown, Jonathan. "Another Image of the World: Spanish Art, 1500–1920." In *The Spanish World: Civilization and Empire, Europe and the Americas, Past and Present,* edited by J. H. Elliott, 149–184. New York: Harry N. Abrams, 1991.

Brown, Rodney Hilton. *American Polearms, 1526–1865.* New Milford, CT: N. Flayderman, 1967.

Bryant, William Cullen, and Sidney Howard Gay. *A Popular History of the United States.* Vol. 1. New York: Charles Scribner's Sons, 1881.

Burne, A. H. *The Battlefields of England.* London: Penguin, 1996.

Cain, Kathleen. *The Cottonwood Tree: An American Champion.* Boulder, CO: Johnson Books, 2007.

Calvert, Albert F. *Spanish Arms and Armour, Being a Historical and Descriptive Account of the Royal Armoury of Madrid.* London: John Lane, the Bodley Head, 1907.

Campbell, Duncan B. *Besieged: Siege Warfare in the Ancient World.* Botley, UK: Osprey, 2006.

Campbell, Duncan B., and Brian Delf. *Greek and Roman Siege Machinery 399 BC–AD 363.* Botley, UK: Osprey, 2003.

Carr, Matthew. *Blood and Faith: The Purging of Muslim Spain.* New York: New Press, 2009.

Cazeaux, Isabelle. *French Music in the Fifteenth and Sixteenth Centuries.* New York: Praeger, 1975.

Chamberlin, E. R. *The Sack of Rome.* New York: Dorset, 1985.

Chartand, Rene, and Donato Spedaliere. *The Spanish Main: 1492–1800.* Botley, UK: Osprey, 2006.

Chavez, Fr. Angelico, O.F.M. *Coronado's Friars.* Washington, DC: Academy of American Franciscan History, 1968.

Chipman, Donald E. *Nuno de Guzman and the Province of Panuco in New Spain, 1518–1533.* Glendale, CA: Arthur H. Clark, 1967.

Chipman, Donald E., and Harriett Denise Joseph. *Notable Men and Women of Spanish Texas.* Austin: University of Texas Press, 1999.

Chuchiak, John E., IV. "Forgotten Allies: Origins and Roles of Native Mesoamerican Auxiliaries and Indios Conquistadores in the Conquest of Yucatan, 1526–1550." In *Indian Conquistadors: Indian Allies in the Conquest of Mesoamerica,* edited by Laura E. Matthew and Michael R. Oudijk, 175–225. Norman: University of Oklahoma Press, 2007.

Coggins, Jack. *The Fighting Man: An Illustrated History of the World's Greatest Fighting Forces Through the Ages.* Garden City, NY: Doubleday, 1966.

Contamine, Philippe. *War in the Middle Ages.* Translated by Michael Jones. New York: Basil Blackwell, 1984.

Cornish, Paul. *Henry VIII's Army.* London: Osprey, 1987.

Cruickshank, Charles. *Henry VIII and the Invasion of France.* Stroud, UK: Alan Sutton, 1990.

Cutter, Donald. Review essay of *Great Cruelties Have Been Reported: The 1544 Investigation of the Coronado Expedition,* by Richard Flint, trans. and ed. *New Mexico Historical Review* 77, no. 3 (Summer 2002): 315–318.

D'altroy, Terence N., and Christine A. Hastorf. "The Architecture and Contents of Inka State Storehouses in the Xauxa Region of Peru." In *Inka Storage Systems,* edited by Terry Y. Levine, 259–286. Norman: University of Oklahoma Press, 1992.

Damp, Jonathan E. "The Summer of 1540: Archaeology of the Battle of Hawikku." *Archaeology Southwest* 19, no. 1 (Winter 2005): 4–5.

Davies, Nigel. *The Aztecs.* London: Folio Society, 2000.

———. *The Aztecs: A History.* New York: G. P. Putnam's Sons, 1974.

Davis, T. Frederick. "Ponce de Leon's First Voyage and Discovery of Florida." *Florida Historical Society Quarterly* 14, no. 1 (July 1935): 7–49.

———. "Ponce de Leon's Second Voyage and Attempt to Colonize Florida." *Florida Historical Society Quarterly* 14, no. 1 (July 1935): 51–66.

Day, A. Grove. *Coronado and the Discovery of the Southwest.* New York: Meredith Press, 1967.

———. *Coronado's Quest: The Discovery of the Southwestern States.* Berkeley: University of California Press, 1940.

———. "Mota Padilla on the Coronado Expedition." *Hispanic American Historical Review* 20, no. 1 (Feb. 1940): 88–110.

Deagan, Kathleen, and Jose Maria Cruxent. *Columbus's Outpost among the Tainos: Spain and America at La Isabella, 1493–1498.* New Haven, CT: Yale University Press, 2002.

Drew, Lisa. "The Barnyard Restoration: About Half of Our Livestock Breeds Are in Peril of Disappearing Forever." *Newsweek* (May 29, 1989): 50–51.

Duffy, Christopher. *Fire and Stone: The Science of Fortress Warfare, 1660–1860.* North Vancouver, BC: Douglas David & Charles, 1975.

———. *Siege Warfare: The Fortress in the Early Modern World, 1494–1660.* New York: Barnes & Noble, 1996.

Editorial staff, Biblograf S. A. *Vox Modern College, Spanish and English Dictionary.* New York: Charles Scribner's Sons, 1972.

Elliott, J. H. *Imperial Spain, 1469–1716.* New York: Mentor Books/New American Library, 1966.

———. *The Old World and the New, 1492–1650.* Cambridge: Cambridge University Press, 1978.

———, ed. *The Spanish World: Civilization and Empire, Europe and the Americas, Past and Present.* New York: Harry N. Abrams, 1991.

Eltis, David. *The Military Revolution in Sixteenth Century Europe.* London: Tauris Academic Studies, 1995.

Evans, Chaz. "Obtaining an Iconic Pueblo." *American Archaeology* 17, no. 2 (Summer 2013): 48–49.

Ffoulkes, Charles. *The Armourer and His Craft, from the XIth to the XVIth Century.* New York: Dover: 1988.

*Fine Antique Arms and Armour from the Henk L. Visser Collection.* London: Bonhams, 2007.

Firstbrook, Peter. *The Voyage of the Matthew: John Cabot and the Discovery of North America.* London: BBC Books, 1997.

"First Flag over Arizona." *Arizona Highways* 60, no. 4 (Apr. 1984): 46.

Fleischman, John. "Royal Armor Makes Great Escape from Tower of London: Shining Works of the Old-Time Armorers' Art Come to Cincinnati in First Exhibit Ever Sent Beyond the Walls of the British Fortress." *Smithsonian* 13, no. 7 (Oct. 1982): 65–73.

Flint, Richard. "Armas de la Tierra: The Mexican Indian Component of Coronado Expedition Material Culture." In *The Coronado Expedition to Tierra Nueva: The 1540–1542 Route across the Southwest,* edited by Richard Flint and Shirley Cushing Flint, 57–70. Niwot: University Press of Colorado, 1997.

———. *No Settlement, No Conquest: A History of the Coronado Expedition.* Albuquerque: University of New Mexico Press, 2008.

———. "Results and Repercussions of the Coronado Expedition to Tierra Nueva from Documentary and Archaeological Sources." *New Mexico Historical Review* 77, no. 3 (Summer 2002): 233–260.

———. "What's Missing from This Picture? The *Alarde,* or Muster Roll, of the Coronado Expedition." In *The Coronado Expedition: From the Distance of 460 Years,* edited by Richard Flint and Shirley Cushing Flint, 57–80. Albuquerque: University of New Mexico Press, 2003.

———. "What They Never Told You About the Coronado Expedition." *Kiva: The Journal of Southwestern Anthropology and History* 71, no. 2 (Winter 2005): 203–217.

———. "Who Designed Coronado's Bridge across the Pecos River?" *Kiva: Quarterly Journal of the Arizona Archaeological and Historical Society* 57, no. 4 (1992): 331–342.

———. "Without Them, Nothing Was Possible: The Coronado Expedition's Indian Allies." *New Mexico Historical Review* 84, no. 1 (Winter 2009): 65–118.

Flint, Richard, and Shirley Cushing Flint. "The Coronado Expedition: Cicuye to the Rio de Cicuye Bridge." *New Mexico Historical Review* 67, no. 2 (Apr. 1992): 123–138.

———. "A Death in Tiguex, 1542." *New Mexico Historical Review* 74, no. 3 (July 1999): 247–270.

———. "Guido de Lavezariis: The Life of a Financier of the Coronado and Villalobos Expeditions." *New Mexico Historical Review* 86, no. 1 (Winter 2011): 1–19.

———. "Hernando de Alvarado." Office of the New Mexico State Historian, *newmexicohistory.org/people/hernando-de-alvarado*. Accessed January 24, 2014.

———. "The Location of Coronado's 1541 Bridge: A Critical Appraisal of Albert Schroeder's 1962 Hypothesis." *Plains Anthropologist* 36, no. 135 (1991): 171–176.

———, eds. *The Coronado Expedition: From the Distance of 460 Years.* Albuquerque: University of New Mexico Press, 2003.

———, eds. *The Coronado Expedition to Tierra Nueva: The 1540–1542 Route across the Southwest.* Niwot: University Press of Colorado, 1997.

———, eds. *The Latest Word from 1540: People, Places, and Portrayals of the Coronado Expedition.* Albuquerque: University of New Mexico Press, 2011.

Flint, Shirley Cushing. "The *Sobresalientes* of the Coronado Expedition." In *The Latest Word from 1540: People, Places, and Portrayals of the Coronado Expedition,* edited by Richard Flint and Shirley Cushing Flint, 13–38. Albuquerque: University of New Mexico Press, 2011.

Flores, Dan. *Caprock Canyonlands: Journeys into the Heart of the Southern Plains.* Austin: University of Texas Press, 1990.

Funcken, Liliane and Fred. *The Age of Chivalry, Part 3: The Renaissance: Arms, Horses and Tournaments; Helmets and Armour; Tactics and Artillery.* London: Ward Lock, 1982.

———. *Arms and Uniforms, Part 1: Ancient Egypt to the 18th Century.* London: Ward Lock, 1977.

Fussel, Stephan. *Emperor Maximilian and the Media of his Day: The Theuerdank of 1517, a Cultural Introduction.* Cologne, Germany: Taschen, 2003.

Gagne, Frank R., Jr. "Spanish Crossbow Boltheads of Sixteenth-Century North America: A Comparative Analysis." In *The Coronado Expedition: From the Distance of 460 Years,* edited by Richard Flint and Shirley Cushing Flint, 240–252. Albuquerque: University of New Mexico Press, 2003.

Gallardo, Alexander. *Spanish Economics in the Sixteenth Century: Theory, Policy, and Practice.* New York and Lincoln, NE: Writers Club Press, 2002.

Gilbert, Bil. *The Trailblazers.* New York: Life Books, 1974.

Gilbert, Hope. "He Found Six of the Fabled 'Seven Cities of Cibola.'" *Desert Magazine* 5, no. 6 (Apr. 1942): 5–10.

Goodwin, George. *Fatal Rivalry: Henry VIII, James IV and the Battle for Renaissance Britain, Flodden 1513.* London: Weidenfeld & Nicolson, 2013.

Graham, R. B. Cunningham. *The Horses of the Conquest.* Norman: University of Oklahoma Press, 1949.

Graham, Winston. *The Spanish Armadas.* Garden City, NY: Doubleday, 1972.

Gravett, Christopher. *English Medieval Knight 1400–1500.* (Botley, UK: Osprey, 2001.

———. *Medieval Siege Warfare.* London: Osprey, 1990.

———. *Tudor Knight.* Botley, UK: Osprey, 2006.

Green, Jesse, ed. *Zuni: Selected Writings of Frank Hamilton Cushing.* Lincoln: University of Nebraska Press/Bison Books, 1981.

Grotius, Hugo. *The Law of War and Peace (De Jure Belli ac Pacis).* Translated by Louis R. Loomis. Roslyn, NY: Walter J. Black, 1949.

Gunderson, Mary. *American Indian Cooking before 1500.* Mankato, MN: Blue Earth Books, 2001.

Hale, John R. *The Art of War and Renaissance England.* Washington, DC: Folger Shakespeare Library, 1961.

Hammond, George P. *Coronado's Seven Cities.* Albuquerque: United States Coronado Exposition Commission, 1940.

Hanson, Neil. *The Confident Hope of a Miracle: The True History of the Spanish Armada.* New York: Alfred A. Knopf, 2005.

Hare, Christopher. *Bayard: The Good Knight Without Fear and Without Reproach.* London: J. M. Dent & Sons, 1911.

———. *Charles de Bourbon: High Constable of France, "The Great Condottiere."* London: John Lane the Bodley Head, 1911.

Harrington, John Walker. "Cibola Revealed: Relics of Coronado's Seven Cities in a New York Museum." *Scientific American* 120, no. 2 (January 11, 1919): 24–25.

Hartmann, Gayle Harrison. "Finding Coronado's Route: Crossbow Points, Caret-Head Nails, and Other Oddments." *Old Pueblo Archaeology* 47 (Dec. 2006): 1–6.

Hartmann, William K. "The Mystery of the 'Port of Chichilticale.'" In *The Latest Word from 1540: People, Places, and Portrayals of the Coronado Expedition,* edited by Richard Flint and Shirley Cushing Flint, 194–213. Albuquerque: University of New Mexico Press, 2011.

———. "Pathfinder for Coronado: Reevaluating the Mysterious Journey of Marcos de Niza." In *The Coronado Expedition to Tierra Nueva: The 1540–1542 Route across the Southwest,* edited by Richard Flint and Shirley Cushing Flint, 73–101. Niwot: University Press of Colorado, 1997.

Hartmann, William K., and Gayle Harrison Hartmann. "Locating the Lost Coronado Garrisons of San Geronimo I, II, and III." In *The Latest Word from 1540: People, Places, and Portrayals of the Coronado Expedition,* edited by Richard Flint and Shirley Cushing Flint, 117–153. Albuquerque: University of New Mexico Press, 2011.

Heath, Ian. *Armies of the Sixteenth Century: The Armies of England, Scotland, Ireland, the United Provinces, and the Spanish Netherlands, 1487–1609.* Guernsey, UK: Foundry Books, 1997.

Heath, Ian. *Armies of the Sixteenth Century: The Armies of the Aztecs and Inca Empires, Other Native Peoples of the Americas, and the Conquistadors, 1450–1608.* Guernsey, UK: Foundry Books, 1999.

Heers, Jacques, and Jonathan North, trans. *The Barbary Corsairs: Warfare in the Mediterranean, 1480–1580.* London: Greenhill, 2003.

Hemming, John. *The Conquest of the Incas.* New York: Harcourt Brace Jovanovich, 1970.

Herberman, Charles G., ed. *The Catholic Encyclopedia.* Vol. 4. London: Universal Knowledge Foundation, 1913.

Hess, Andrew C. *The Forgotten Frontier: A History of the Sixteenth-Century Ibero-African Frontier.* Chicago: University of Chicago Press, 2010.

Hillerbrand, Hans J. *The Division of Christendom: Christianity in the Sixteenth Century.* Louisville, KY: Westminster John Knox Press, 2007.

Hodge, F. W. "Recent Excavations at Hawikuh." *El Palacio* 12, no. 1 (January 1, 1922): 3–11.

Hodge, Frederick Webb. *History of Hawikuh, New Mexico: One of the So-Called Cities of Cibola.* Los Angeles: Southwest Museum Administrator of the Fund, 1937.

Hoig, Stan. *Came Men on Horses: The Conquistador Expeditions of Francisco Vazquez de Coronado and Don Juan de Onate.* Boulder: University Press of Colorado, 2013.

Hook, Judith. *The Sack of Rome, 1527.* London and Basingstoke: Macmillan London, 1972.

Howard, Major General Sir Douglas. *An Essay on the Principles and Construction of Military Bridges and the Passage of Rivers in Military Operations.* London: Thomas and William Boone, 1832.

Hudson, Charles, Chester B. DePratter, and Marvin T. Smith. "Appendix I: Reply to Henige." In *The Expedition of Hernando de Soto West of the Mississippi, 1541–1543: The Proceedings of the De Soto Symposia, 1988 and 1990,* edited by Gloria A. Young and Michael P. Hoffman, 255–269. Fayetteville: University of Arkansas, 1993.

Hume, Ivor Noel. *Martin's Hundred.* New York: Alfred A. Knopf, 1983.

Humphrys, Julian. *Enemies at the Gate: English Castles Under Siege from the 12th Century to the Civil War.* Swindon, UK: English Heritage, 2007.

Hurtado, Albert L. *Herbert Eugene Bolton: Historian of the American Borderlands.* Berkeley and Los Angeles: University of California Press, 2012.

Hutchins, John. "Book review of *Came Men on Horses: The Conquistador Expeditions of Francisco Vazquez de Coronado and Don Juan de Onate,*" by Stan Hoig. *Denver Westerners Roundup* 70, no. 5 (Sept.–Oct. 2013): 15–16.

Hutchins, John. "Book review of *Great Cruelties Have Been Reported: The 1544 Investigation of the Coronado Expedition,*" by Richard Flint. *Denver Westerners Roundup* 59, no. 2 (Mar.—Apr. 2003): 20–21.

Ilahiane, Hsain. "Estevan—Moroccan Explorer of the American Southwest." *Archaeology Southwest* 19, no. 1 (Winter 2005): 11.

Irving, Theodore. *The Conquest of Florida, Under Hernando De Soto.* 2 vols. London: Edward Churton, 1835. Island Press facsimile, 1973.

Ives, Ronald L. "The Grave of Melchior Diaz: A Problem in Historical Sleuthing." *Kiva: A Journal of the Arizona Archaeological and Historical Society* 25, no. 2 (Dec. 1959): 31–40.

John, Elizabeth A. H. *Storms Brewed in Other Men's Worlds: The Confrontation of Indians, Spanish, and French in the Southwest, 1540–1795* (College Station: Texas A&M University Press, 1975.

Jones, Paul A. *Coronado and Quivira.* Lyons, KS: Lyons Publishing, 1937.

———. *Quivira.* Wichita, KS: McCormick-Armstrong, 1929.

Jones, Robert. *Knight: The Warrior and World of Chivalry.* Botley, UK: Osprey, 2011.

Kamen, Henry. *Empire: How Spain Became a World Power, 1492–1763.* New York: HarperCollins, 2003.

Karcheski, Walter J., Jr. *Arms and Armor of the Conquistador, 1492–1600.* Gainesville: Florida Museum of Natural History, 1990.

Kaufmann, H. W., and J. E. Kaufmann. *Fortifications of the Incas, 1200–1531.* Botley, UK: Osprey, 2006.

Keegan, John. *The Face of Battle.* New York: Dorset, 1986.

Kelsey, Harry. *Juan Rodriguez Cabrillo.* San Marino, CA: Huntington Library, 1986.

Kemp, Peter. *The Campaigns of the Spanish Armada.* New York: Facts on File, 1988.

Kessell, John L. *Kiva, Cross, and Crown: The Pecos Indians and New Mexico, 1540–1840.* Albuquerque: University of New Mexico Press, 1987.

Ketchum, Richard M., ed. *The Horizon Book of the Renaissance.* New York: American Heritage, 1961.

Kidder, Alfred Vincent. *The Artifacts of Pecos.* New Haven, CT: Yale University Press, 1932.

———. *An Introduction to the Study of Southwestern Archaeology, With a Preliminary Account of the Excavations at Pecos.* New Haven, CT: Yale University Press, 1924.

———. "Pecos Excavations in 1924," *El Palacio* 18, nos. 10–11 (June 1, 1925): 217–223.

King, Grace. *De Soto and His Men in the Land of Florida.* New York: Macmillan, 1898.

Kirkup, John, ed. *The Surgeons Mate by John Woodall, Master in Chirurgery: A Complete Facsimile of the Book Published in 1617.* Bath, UK: Kingsmead, 1978.

Kleinschmidt, Harald. *Charles V: The World Emperor.* Stroud, UK: Sutton, 2004.

Knishinsky, Ran. *Prickly Pear, Cactus Medicine: Treatments for Diabetes, Cholesterol, and the Immune System.* Rochester, VT: Healing Arts, 2004.

Knox, Capt. E. Blake. *Military Sanitation and Hygiene.* London: Bailliere, Tindall and Cox, 1911.

Koenig, Doug. "Crossbow Myths & Misconceptions." *Petersen's Bowhunting: The Modern Bowhunting Authority* 23, issue 4 (July 2012): 24–25.

Konstam, Angus. *The Spanish Armada: The Great Enterprise Against England, 1588.* Botley, UK: Osprey, 2009.

Konstam, Angus, and Graham Turner. *Pavia 1525: The Climax of the Italian Wars.* Botley, UK: Osprey, 2001.

Konstam, Angus, and Tony Bryan. *Spanish Galleon, 1530–1690.* Botley, UK: Osprey, 2004.

Laband, John. *Bringers of War: The Portuguese in Africa during the Age of Gunpowder and Sail from the Fifteenth to the Eighteenth Century.* London: Frontline, 2013.

Ladd, Edmund J. "Zuni on the Day the Men in Metal Arrived." In *The Coronado Expedition to Tierra Nueva: The 1540–1542 Route across the Southwest,* edited by Richard Flint and Shirley Cushing Flint, 225–233. Niwot: University Press of Colorado, 1997.

Leonard, Irving A. *Books of the Brave: Being an Account of Books and of Men in the Spanish Conquest and Settlement of the Sixteenth-Century New World.* Cambridge, MA: Harvard University Press, 1949.

Levine, Terry Y., ed. *Inka Storage Systems.* Norman: University of Oklahoma Press, 1992.

Lingle, Robert T., and Dee Linford, comps. *The Pecos River Commission of New Mexico and Texas: A Report of a Decade of Progress, 1950–1960.* Santa Fe: Rydal, 1961.

Longacre, Edward G. *Mounted Raids of the Civil War.* Lincoln: University of Nebraska Press, 1994.

MacQuarrie, Kim. *The Last Days of the Incas.* New York: Simon & Schuster, 2007.

Mallett, Michael. *Mercenaries and Their Masters: Warfare in Renaissance Italy.* Barnsley, UK: Pen & Sword Books, 2009.

Maltby, William. *The Reign of Charles V.* Basingstoke, UK: Palgrave, 2002.

Martin, Colin. *Full Fathom Five: Wrecks of the Spanish Armada.* New York: Viking, 1975.

Matthew, Christopher, trans. and ed. *The Tactics of Aelian, or On the Military Arrangements of the Greeks: A New Translation of the Manual That Influenced Warfare for Fifteen Centuries.* Barnsley, UK: Pen & Sword Books, 2012.

Matthew, Laura E., and Michael R. Oudijk, eds. *Indian Conquistadors: Indian Allies in the Conquest of Mesoamerica.* Norman: University of Oklahoma Press, 2007.

McDermott, James. *England and the Spanish Armada: The Necessary Quarrel.* London: Yale University Press, 2005.

McNeill, William H. *Plagues and Peoples.* New York: History Book Club, 1993.

Mertens, Colonel, and Major Walter Krueger, trans. *Tactics and Technique of River Crossings.* New York: D. Van Nostrand, 1918.

Michael, Nicholas. *Armies of Medieval Burgundy, 1364–1477.* London: Reed International, 1996.

Milanich, Jerald T. "The Hernando de Soto Expedition and Spain's Efforts to Colonize North America." In *The Expedition of Hernando de Soto West of the Mississippi, 1541–1543: The Proceedings of the De Soto Symposia, 1988 and 1990*, edited by Gloria A. Young and Michael P. Hoffman, 11–28. Fayetteville: University of Arkansas, 1993.

Millar, George. *A Crossbowman's Story of the First Exploration of the Amazons.* New York: Alfred A. Knopf, 1955. Well-researched historical fiction.

Miller, Douglas. *The Lanksknechts.* London: Osprey, 1976.

———. *The Swiss at War, 1300–1500.* Botley, UK: Osprey, 1999.

Moore, R. Edgar. "Trail of Conquest, 1540–1940." *Street & Smith's Western Story* 185, no. 6 (October 5, 1940): 34–43.

Moorhead, Max L. *The Presidio: Bastion of the Spanish Borderlands.* Norman: University of Oklahoma Press, 1991.

Motley, John Lothrop. *The Rise of the Dutch Republic.* 3 vols. New York: Harper & Brothers, 1883.

Myers, Harry C. "The Mystery of Coronado's Route from the Pecos River to the Llano Estacado." In *The Coronado Expedition: From the Distance of 460 Years,* edited by Richard Flint and Shirley Cushing Flint, 140–150. Albuquerque: University of New Mexico Press, 2003.

Nelson, Arthur. *The Tudor Navy: The Ships, Men and Organisation, 1485–1603.* Annapolis: Naval Institute Press, 2001.

Nesmith, Jeff. "Evidence of Coronado Camp Found." *Denver Post,* April 16, 1996, 1A, 13A.

New Mexico State Tourist Bureau. *Battlefields of the Conquistadors in New Mexico.* Santa Fe: State Highway Department, 1942. Map.

Nicolle, David. *Granada 1492: The Twilight of Moorish Spain.* Westport, CT: Praeger, 2005.

———. *The Portuguese in the Age of Discovery, c. 1340–1665.* Botley, UK: Osprey, 2012.

Nicolle, David, and Christopher Rothero. *The Venetian Empire, 1200–1670.* London: Osprey, 1989.

Noble, David Grant, and Richard Woodbury. *Zuni and El Morro, Past & Present.* Santa Fe: Ancient City Press, 1993.

Nossov, Konstantin. *Ancient and Medieval Siege Weapons: A Fully Illustrated Guide to Siege Weapons and Tactics.* Staplehurst, UK: Spellmount, 2006.

Notario Lopez, Ignacio, and Ivan Notario Lopez. *The Spanish Tercios, 1536–1704.* Botley, UK: Osprey, 2012.

Oman, C. W. C., and John H. Beeler. *The Art of War in the Middle Ages, A.D. 378–1515.* Ithaca, NY: Great Seal Books, 1963.

Oman, Sir Charles. *A History of the Art of War in the Sixteenth Century.* London: Methuen, 1937.

———. *The Sixteenth Century.* New York: E. P. Dutton, c. 1936.

Oudijk, Michael R., and Matthew Restall. "Mesoamerican Conquistadors in the Sixteenth Century" In *Indian Conquistadors: Indian Allies in the Conquest of Mesoamerica,* edited by Laura E. Matthew and Michael R. Oudijk, 28–63. Norman: University of Oklahoma Press, 2007.

Padfield, Peter. *Armada: A Celebration of the Four Hundredth Anniversary of the Defeat of the Spanish Armada, 1588–1988.* London: Victor Gollancz, 1988.

Parker, Geoffrey. *The Army of Flanders and the Spanish Road, 1567–1659: The Logistics of Spanish Victory and Defeat in the Low Countries' Wars.* Cambridge: Cambridge University Press, c. 1976. Reprint of 1972 edition.

———, ed. *The Cambridge Illustrated History of Warfare: The Triumph of the West.* Cambridge: Cambridge University Press, 1995.

Parry, J. H. *The Audiencia of New Galicia in the Sixteenth Century: A Study in Spanish Colonial Government.* Westport, CT.: Greenwood, 1985. Reprint of 1948 edition.

Payne-Gallwey, Sir Ralph. *The Crossbow: Mediaeval and Modern, Military and Sporting, Its Construction, History & Management.* London: Holland House, 1995. Reprint of 1903 edition.

Perry, I. Mac. *Black Conquistador: The Story of the First Black Man in America.* St. Petersburg, FL: Boca Bay Books, 1998. Novel.

Phillips, Charles. *Aztec & Maya: The Greatest Civilizations of Ancient Central America With 1000 Photographs, Paintings and Maps.* New York: Metro Books, 2012.

Pierron, Sander. *Les Mostaert: Jean Mostaert, Dit le Maitre d'Oultremont; Gilles et Francois Mostaert; Michel Mostaert* (Bruxelles/Paris: Librairie Nationale d'Art et d'Histoire, 1912).

Pohl, John. *Aztec, Mixtec and Zapotec Armies.* Botley, UK: Osprey, 1996.

———. *Aztec Warrior AD 1325–1521.* Botley, UK: Osprey, 2001.

———. *The Conquistador, 1492–1550.* Botley, UK: Osprey, 2001.

Pohl, John, and Charles M. Robinson III. *Aztecs & Conquistadors: The Spanish Invasion & Collapse of the Aztec Empire.* Botley, UK: Osprey, 2005.

Prescott, William H. *History of the Conquest of Mexico, with a Preliminary View of the Ancient Mexican Civilization and the Life of the Conqueror, Hernando Cortes.* 3 vols. Philadelphia: J. B. Lippincott, 1882. New and revised edition.

———. *History of the Conquest of Peru, with a Preliminary View of the Civilization of the Incas.* 2 vols. Philadelphia: J. B. Lippincott, 1883. New and revised edition.

———. *History of the Reign of the Emperor Charles the Fifth.* 3 vols. Philadelphia: J. B. Lippincott, 1882. New edition.

———. *History of the Reign of Ferdinand and Isabella the Catholic*, 3 vols. Philadelphia: J. B. Lippincott, 1882. New and revised edition.

Preston, Douglas. *Cities of Gold: A Journey across the American Southwest in Pursuit of Coronado* (New York: Simon & Schuster, 1992.

Priestley, Herbert Ingram. *Tristan de Luna, Conquistador of the Old South: A Study of Spanish Imperial Strategy.* Glendale, CA: Arthur H. Clark, 1936.

Ralston, David B. *Importing the European Army: The Introduction of European Military Techniques and Institutions into the Extra-European World, 1600–1914.* Chicago: University of Chicago Press, 1990.

Raymond, James. *Henry VIII's Military Revolution: The Armies of Sixteenth-Century Britain and Europe.* London: Tauris Academic Studies, 2007.

Resendez, Andres. "Cabeza de Vaca: A Desperate Trek Across America." *American Heritage* 58, no. 5 (Fall 2008): 19–21.

———. *A Land So Strange: The Epic Journey of Cabeza de Vaca.* New York: Basic Books, 2009.

Restall, Matthew. *Maya Conquistador.* Boston: Beacon Press, 1998.

———. *Seven Myths of the Spanish Conquest.* New York: Oxford University Press, 2003.

Reston, James, Jr. *Defenders of the Faith: Charles V, Suleyman the Magnificent, and the Battle for Europe, 1520–1536.* New York: Penguin, 2009.

Rhodes, Diane Lee. "Coronado Fought Here: Crossbow Boltheads as Possible Indicators of the 1540–1542 Expedition." In *The Coronado Expedition to Tierra Nueva: The 1540–1542 Route across the Southwest,* edited by Richard Flint and Shirley Cushing Flint, 44–56. Niwot: University Press of Colorado, 1997.

Richards, John. *Landsknecht Soldier, 1486–1560.* Botley, UK: Osprey, 2002.

Robertson, Pauline Durrett, and R. L. Robertson. *Panhandle Pilgrimage: Illustrated Tales Tracing History in the Texas Panhandle.* Amarillo, TX: Paramount, 1978. Second edition.

Robinson, Charles M., III. *The Spanish Invasion of Mexico, 1519–1521.* Botley, UK: Osprey, 2004.

Robinson, Duncan. "Coronado and His Army." *Panhandle-Plains Historical Review* 13 (1940): 71–79.

Roeder, Ralph. *The Man of the Renaissance: Four Lawgivers: Savonarola, Machiavelli, Castiglione, Aretino.* New York: Viking, 1933.

Roth R. *The Visser Collection: Arms of the Netherlands in the Collection of H. L. Visser; Vol. 2, Ordnance: Cannon, Mortars, Swivel-Guns, Muzzle- and Breech-Loaders.* Zwolle, Netherlands: Waanders, 1996.

"The Roundup." *Street & Smith's Western Story* 185, no. 6 (October 5, 1940): 6.

Rouse, John E. *The Criollo: Spanish Cattle in the Americas.* Norman: University of Oklahoma Press, 1977.

Sadler, John. *Towton: The Battle of Palm Sunday Field, 1461.* Barnsley, UK: Pen & Sword Military, 2011.

Sadler, John, and Rosie Serdiville. *The Battle of Flodden 1513.* Stroud, UK: History Press, 2013.

Salpointe, Most Rev. J. B. *Soldiers of the Cross: Notes on Ecclesiastical History of New-Mexico, Arizona and Colorado.* Banning, CA: St. Boniface's Industrial School, 1898.

Sanchez, Israel Sanz. "Juan Jaramillo's 'Relacion': A Philological Reassessment of the Historical Approaches to a Document of the Coronado Expedition." *New Mexico Historical Review* 86, no. 1 (Winter 2011): 21–81.

Sanchez, Joseph P. "Old Heat and New Light Concerning the Search for Coronado's Bridge: A Historiography of the Pecos and Canadian Rivers Hypotheses." *New Mexico Historical Review* 67, no. 2 (Apr. 1992): 101–114.

Sauer, Carl. *The Road to Cibola.* Berkeley: University of California Press, 1932.

Saxtorph, Neils M. *Warriors and Weapons of Early Times.* London: Blandford, 1972.

Schmader, Matt. "Thundersticks and Coats of Iron." In *The Latest Word from 1540: People, Places, and Portrayals of the Coronado Expedition,* edited by Richard Flint and Shirley Cushing Flint, 308–347. Albuquerque: University of New Mexico Press, 2011.

Schroeder, Albert H. "The Locale of Coronado's 'Bridge.'" *New Mexico Historical Review* 67, no. 2 (Apr. 1992): 115–122.

Schwartz, Marion. *A History of Dogs in the Early Americas.* New Haven, CT: Yale University Press, 1997.

Seipel, Wilfried, ed. *Der Kriegszug Kaiser Karls V Gegen Tunis: Kartons und Tapisserien.* Vienna: Kunsthistorisches Museum, 2000.

Sharpe, Phil. "Guns and Gunners." *Street & Smith's Western Story* 185, no. 6 (Oct. 5, 1940): 105–106.

Shears, Brenda L., and Rose Wyaco. "Hawikku: A Fabled City of Cibola." *Native People* 3, no. 4 (Summer, 1990): 20–24, 26.

Simpson, Brevet Brigadier General J. H. "Coronado's March in Search of the 'Seven Cities of Cibola' and Discussion of Their Probable Location." *Annual Report of the Board of Regents of the Smithsonian Institution . . . for the Year 1869.* Washington, DC: Government Printing Office, 1871, 309–340.

Smith, Bradley. *Mexico: A History in Art.* Garden City, NY: Doubleday, 1968.

Smith, Julian. "Coronado's Deadly Siege: Hundreds of Metal Artifacts Pinpoint the Possible Site of a Bloody Battle between the Conquistadores and a Puebloan People." *Archaeology* 65, no. 2 (Mar./Apr. 2012): 41–45.

Smithsonian Institution and John R. Swanton, chairman. *Final Report of the United States De Soto Expedition Commission.* Washington, DC: Government Printing Office, 1939.

Snook, George, M.D. *The Halberd and Other European Polearms, 1300–1650.* Alexandria Bay, NY, and Bloomfield, ON: Museum Restoration Service, 1998.

Southern, Pat. *The Roman Empire from Severus to Constantine.* London: Routledge, 2002.

Spaulding, Col. Oliver Lyman, Capt. Hoffman Nickerson, and Col. John Womack Wright. *Warfare: A Study of Military Methods from the Earliest Times.* Washington, DC: Infantry Journal, 1937.

Spedaliere, Donato. *The Spanish Main: 1492–1800.* Botley, UK: Osprey, 2006.

Steele, Ian K. *Warpaths: Invasions of North America.* New York: Oxford University Press, 1994.

Stirling, Stuart. *Pizarro: Conqueror of the Inca.* Stroud, UK: Sutton, 2005.

Stone, George Cameron. *A Glossary of the Construction, Decoration and Use of Arms and Armor in All Countries and in all Times.* New York: Jack Brussel, 1961. Originally published in 1934.

Taylor, F. L. *The Art of War in Italy, 1494–1529*. London: Greenhill, 1993. Reprint of 1921 Cambridge University Press edition.

Thomas, Alfred Barnaby. *After Coronado: Spanish Exploration Northeast of New Mexico, 1696–1727*. Norman: University of Oklahoma Press, 1935.

———. "Spanish Expeditions into Colorado." *Colorado* Magazine 1, no. 7 (November 1924): 289–300.

Tincey, John, and Richard Hook. *The Armada Campaign, 1588*. London: Osprey, 1995.

Tracy, James D. *Emperor Charles V, Impresario of War: Campaign Strategy, International Finance, and Domestic Politics*. Cambridge: Cambridge University Press, 2002.

Turnbull, Stephen. *The Art of Renaissance Warfare: From the Fall of Constantinople to the Thirty Years War*. London: Greenhill, 2006.

Udall, Stewart L. "The Battle of Hawikuh [Hawikku]." *Native Peoples* 3, no. 4 (Summer 1990): 25.

———. *To the Inland Empire: Coronado and Our Spanish Legacy*. Garden City, NY: Doubleday, 1987.

Urban, William. *Bayonets for Hire: Mercenaries at War, 1550–1789*. London: Greenhill, 2007.

———. *Medieval Mercenaries: The Business of War*. London: Greenhill, 2006.

US Army Corps of Engineers, Albuquerque District. *Environmental Assessment for the East Puerto de Luna Community Ditch Rehabilitation Project, Guadalupe County, New Mexico*. Albuquerque: US Army Corps of Engineers, Albuquerque District, February, 2010.

Varner, John Grier, and Jeannette Johnson Varner. *Dogs of the Conquest*. Norman: University of Oklahoma Press, 1983.

Wagner, Henry R. *California Voyages, 1539–1541*. San Francisco: John Howell, 1925.

Walker, Bryce. *The Armada*. Chicago: Time-Life Books, 1982.

Watson, Bruce Allen. *Sieges: A Comparative Study*. Westport, CT: Praeger, 1993.

Weber, David. *The Spanish Frontier in North America*. New Haven, CT: Yale University Press, 1992.

Wise, Terence. *The Conquistadores*. London: Osprey, 1996.

———. *Medieval European Armies*. Botley, UK: Osprey, 2003.

Wood, Michael. *Conquistadors*. Berkeley and Los Angeles: University of California Press, 2000.

Wood, Peter. *The Spanish Main*. Chicago: Time-Life Books, 1979.

Woosnam-Savage, Robert, and Anthony Hall. *Brassey's Book on Body Armor*. Washington, DC: Brassey's, 2001.

Young, Gloria A., and Michael P. Hoffman, eds. *The Expedition of Hernando de Soto West of the Mississippi, 1541–1543: The Proceedings of the De Soto Symposia, 1988 and 1990*. Fayetteville: University of Arkansas, 1993.

Yriarte, Charles, and F. J. Sitwell, trans. *Venice: Its History, Art, Industries and Modern Life*. Philadelphia: John C. Winston/International Press, c. 1900.

# Acknowledgments

I would like to thank historian and author Robert W. Larson for his friendship and early support of this project by reading a draft of the manuscript and providing helpful suggestions; military historian and author Jack Stokes Ballard for his comradeship and support, and for reviewing a manuscript draft; historian and author LaVonne J. Perkins (of the Denver Westerners) for her friendship and suggestions; Robert "Bob" Terwilleger (of the Denver Westerners) for his moral support and suggestions on medieval weaponry; Greg McLeod for his consistent encouragement of my publications on Western American history; photographer John M. Sperry, for taking the jacket portrait photo; certified archivist Dennis Hagen of the Denver Public Library for his help in running down journal articles; retired US postal employee Jan L. Gersabeck, who delivered hundreds of Coronado reference books over a two-year period; my editor, Ron Silverman, for helping me significantly improve the manuscript (while insisting that I was not the most difficult author to deal with); Tracy Dugan, cartographer and historical researcher-in-his-own-right, for his wonderful map of obscure Spanish trails; publisher Bruce H. Franklin for his timely encouragement and for making this book a reality; and my patient wife, Dale Denise (Ockl) Hutchins, for her support and love. I also wish to acknowledge the support of the late Nancy Bathke (of the Pikes Peak Westerners of Colorado Springs) for allowing me, in 2012, to give an early presentation of the topics contained in the book, and the friendship of the late Army Captain John Bowman McLeod, who was with me when I discovered one of the scarcer sources cited in the notes. As for any shortcomings and errors in the book, they are—in addition to being honest mistakes—mine alone.

# Index